T0305493

"A fascinating and insightful book. It is sympathetic and informative on how the food system got where it is today, and is pragmatic, accessible and detailed on the future outlook. Essential reading for anyone interested in how we can reach net zero through the current food system."

Sarah Bridle, author of *Food and Climate Change: Without the Hot Air*

"Neil Ward has written a timely and compelling book about the challenges of net zero for the agri-food system. The book integrates social science research with the science of climate change, drawing on perspectives from the political economy of food and farming, science and technology studies, and research on sustainability transitions. This synthesising approach is essential if we are to rise to the challenge of climate change."

Kevin Morgan, author of *Worlds of Food: Place, Power and Provenance in the Food Chain*

"In this rich account of the food system and the challenge of delivering net zero, Neil Ward draws together social science and climate science while also providing sharp historical analysis. Clear and compelling, Ward makes a powerful case for applying historical lessons to implement urgent change in the contemporary agri-food sector. Indeed, while the scientific evidence amassed by Ward shows revolution must happen, the history he details proves, if the right forces align, it can. This is an essential read for anyone interested in food, the environment, agriculture and agricultural history."

Polly Russell, Food historian, The British Library

"In this book, Neil Ward discusses the potential and challenges of achieving a net zero agri-food system in the UK. He examines the problem through the lens of science, technology and politics, skilfully weaving together the evidence from the scientific literature with his deep knowledge of UK policy and politics. In addition to opportunities for emission reduction and for creating carbon sinks, he also discusses the role of demand-side measures, such as dietary change and reduction of food waste, in a net zero future. This comprehensive assessment of what is possible in the UK is a must read for anyone interested in how we produce our food and what we need to do to effectively tackle climate change."

Pete Smith FRS, Director of the Scottish Climate Change Centre of Expertise

NET ZERO, FOOD AND FARMING

This book examines the implications of the net zero transition for food and farming in the UK and how these can be managed to avoid catastrophic climate change in the crucial decades ahead.

For the UK to meet its international obligations for reducing greenhouse gas emissions, nothing short of a revolution is required in our use of land, our farming practices and our diet. Taking a historical approach, the book examines the evolution of agriculture and the food system in the UK over the last century and discusses the implications of tackling climate change for food, farming and land use, setting the UK situation in an international context. The chapters analyse the key challenges for this transition, including dietary change and food waste, afforestation and energy crops, and low-emission farming practices. This historical perspective helps develop an understanding of how our food farming and land use system has evolved to be the way that it is, and draws lessons for how the agri-food system could evolve further to support the transition to net zero and avoid catastrophic climate change.

Written in a clear and accessible style, this book will be essential reading to students and scholars of food, agriculture and the environment, as well as policymakers and professionals involved climate change policy and the agriculture and food industry.

Neil Ward is Professor of Rural and Regional Development at the University of East Anglia (UEA) in Norwich, UK. He was UEA's Deputy Vice Chancellor (2014–2021) and was formerly the Director of the Centre for Rural Economy at Newcastle University (2004–2008). He has worked on 50 funded research projects examining agriculture, environment, food and rural development, served as a Cabinet Office advisor on agriculture and rural affairs and has appeared before numerous parliamentary select committees.

EARTHSCAN FOOD AND AGRICULTURE

For more information about this series, please visit: www.routledge.com/books/series/ECEFA/

NET ZERO, FOOD AND FARMING

Climate Change and the UK Agri-Food System

Neil Ward

Routledge
Taylor & Francis Group

LONDON AND NEW YORK

Cover image: © Getty Images

First published 2023
by Routledge
4 Park Square, Milton Park, Abingdon, Oxon OX14 4RN

and by Routledge
605 Third Avenue, New York, NY 10158

Routledge is an imprint of the Taylor & Francis Group, an informa business

British Library Cataloguing-in-Publication Data
A catalogue record for this book is available from the British Library

Library of Congress Cataloging-in-Publication Data
Names: Ward, Neil, 1966– author.
Title: Net zero, food and farming: climate change and the UK agri-food system / Neil Ward
Other titles: Climate change and the UK agri-food system | Earthscan food and agriculture.
Description: First edition | New York, NY: Routledge, 2023 . |
Series: Earthscan food and agriculture | Includes bibliographical references and index.
Identifiers: LCCN 2022007785 (print) | LCCN 2022007786 (ebook) |
ISBN 9781032244266 (hardback) | ISBN 9781032235196 (paperback) |
ISBN 9781003278535 (ebook)
Subjects: LCSH: Crops and climate–Great Britain. |
Agriculture–Great Britain. | Agricultural ecology–Great Britain.
Classification: LCC S600.64. G7 W37 2023 (print) |
LCC S600.64.G7 (ebook) | DDC 338.1/40941–dc23/eng/20220225
LC record available at https://lccn.loc.gov/2022007785
LC ebook record available at https://lccn.loc.gov/2022007786

ISBN: 978-1-032-24426-6 (hbk)
ISBN: 978-1-032-23519-6 (pbk)
ISBN: 978-1-003-27853-5 (ebk)

DOI: 10.4324/9781003278535

Typeset in Bembo
by Newgen Publishing UK

In memory of Philip Lowe 1950–2020

CONTENTS

FIGURES

TABLES

PREFACE

Climate change is becoming all-consuming. During the 1980s and 1990s, like many of my colleagues, I experienced climate change principally as an academic issue. The emerging science on climate change was shocking. It had triggered Prime Minister Margaret Thatcher's green conversion and prompted her famous speeches to the Royal Society in 1988 and the United Nations in 1989. New international institutions were established, and arrangements were put in place for intergovernmental diplomacy and action. Climate change conferences and targets came and went. Research councils established research programmes, and a growing number of research projects and PhD theses on the subject commenced. I was a young social scientist working on agriculture, environmental policy and rural land use. Climate change in the 1990s mostly involved discussions about electricity generation and transport, and I was able to avoid getting too involved. Yet, at times, it felt like "global environmental change" was taking over everything in my academic world. After becoming a parent in 2000 climate change started to feel like not just an academic issue but more personal, visceral and existential. With TV images of melting ice crashing into the sea, heatwaves, flooding and Beasts from the East, what had been abstract became much less so. What once felt like a social, political and scientific phenomenon to be studied became something touching all our lives and likely to require radical action that will ultimately transform them.

My academic career began in 1988 at University College London (UCL), coinciding with a very particular moment in the history of environmentalism and climate change. In 1987, while I was an undergraduate student, the Brundtland Commission had set out its vision for sustainable development. After Brundtland, academic research on sustainable development and global environmental change took off. Graphs show dramatic increases in the number of scientific papers or newspaper mentions of "global warming" or "climate change" from 1988 onwards. Following my undergraduate degree, I began work as a researcher in

UCL's Department of Geography. UCL felt like an intellectual cauldron of ideas about environmental policy and social and economic change. David Pearce in the Department of Economics was producing his *Blueprint for a Green Economy* and a confidence around environmental economics pervaded government and think tanks. A central cleavage in debates at that time was whether the transition to sustainable development would simply be a technocractic exercise of getting the prices and incentives right, or something more profound that would require a more interventionist approach to the reorganisation of our whole economic system and way of life.

I worked on research projects examining the changing rural environment. I carefully measured farm landscape change, investigating the relationships between the social and economic characteristics of farms and rates of environmental change. Farming was coming under increasing pressure from environmental organisations as evidence mounted of extensive pollution of rivers and watercourses by livestock effluents and agricultural pesticides. I went on to study how livestock and arable farming had evolved in the ways they had, and how slurry, silage effluent and cereal herbicides had come to be such features of these systems and such problems for the environment. Central to this work were two aspects of change – understanding how we had got to the position we were in and understanding what might help and hinder practical solutions to these problems. A move to the Centre for Rural Economy (CRE) at Newcastle University in 1993 opened up my thinking. The CRE was located in a large Faculty of Agriculture and Biological Sciences, a vast source of expertise in crop and livestock systems, food and nutrition science and agricultural economics and food marketing. This placed my geographical thinking into the context of a large agricultural research institution. It also underlined the power and insight of the natural sciences. It was no use social scientists coming up with grand schemes and theories without a sound basic understanding of the bio-physical underpinnings of agriculture and the environment, and there was huge potential in social and natural scientists working more closely together on agriculture, food and environmental change.

Climate change became harder and harder to ignore. What once had seemed to be the preserve of the University of East Anglia (UEA) in Norwich, and one or two other institutions now seemed to be a strategic research priority for universities across the country. Schools and institutes of environmental science and global environmental change were seemingly being established everywhere. After the Foot and Mouth Disease crisis of 2001, the UK research councils developed a cross-council interdisciplinary research programme on Rural Economy and Land Use where natural and social scientists would have to work together if they were to access funding. I helped the councils design and plan the programme, then helped lead a project examining flood risk modelling, working closely with local communities affected by flooding. To work intimately over a couple of years with people whose homes had been flooded and who lived in fear of it happening again was humbling and eye-opening. What for me was a topic for just another research project was for them something that profoundly impacted upon their lives. An elderly couple were desperately worried about being stranded in their bungalow and unable to visit their disabled son because of flooding. They wanted to do their bit to help understand what was happening and what might be done to reduce flood-risk. They joined our flood group to work things through with a team of hydrological modellers. A running theme through this project and my other studies of agriculture and environmental management was how is change possible? What are the conditions that might make solutions work and spread?

In May 2021, after 13 years in university management at UEA, and with the first sabbatical of my career ahead of me, I decided to write this book. I had been immersed in Covid crisis management for almost 18 months. We had commenced crisis meetings at UEA in January 2020 as Covid was wending its way from Wuhan to Norwich. As Deputy Vice Chancellor and Pro Vice Chancellor for Academic Affairs, I was responsible for all the University's learning and teaching and the experience of over 15,000 students. It was a heavy burden of responsibilities as we went into lockdown but needed to be able to support students' learning and welfare. The Covid crisis underlined how radical change is possible. Locally, we flipped our teaching provision to online delivery, almost overnight, and turned our science teaching laboratories over to producing personal protective equipment and hand sanitiser for our neighbouring hospital. Nationally, what had been considered totally unworkable within Downing Street – a lockdown of the population and the closure of schools – took place. A furlough scheme was introduced to pay workers and keep the economy from collapse. Scientists developed viable vaccines in record time, and most of the adult population was fully vaccinated within six months. Covid meant crisis conditions, but it also showed that it is possible for a government and a population to achieve a radical change for the public good. Markets failed and fiscal rules had to be shelved. The challenge of addressing climate change will require planned, concerted action and human ingenuity on a Covid scale, and the experience of Covid helps us to look at the climate change challenge anew.

I had joined UEA in 2008 as a member of the University's Executive Team looking after its Faculty of Social Sciences. I was part of the University's leadership team when one Friday in November 2009 it became clear that our servers had been hacked and someone had been up to serious mischief with our e-mails. After this internet-age "smash-and-grab" raid on climate science, the University found itself in the eye of a global storm in the run up to the 2009 Copenhagen climate conference. I set about doing what I usually do when it feels like something significant and historic is happening – I started a clippings file. I was able to experience "Climategate" on the inside and the outside. What I found striking was the passion, energy and tenacity of the climate change sceptics. They were breathtaking. Their vehemence and determination to challenge and undermine climate science, coupled with febrile and sensationalist media coverage, produced a global furore. UEA's climate scientists had been dealing with climate change sceptics for years and had come to find it frustrating. Climategate highlighted how climate change had become so fiercely contested. With its emphasis on fakery, suspicion of elites and expertise, and the journalistic preoccupation with giving balanced airtime to both sides of an argument rather than seeking the truth, Climategate served as an environmental precursor to the political convulsions of Brexit and Trump that were to follow a few years later.

By 2021, mounting scientific evidence and people's direct experience of climate change had changed the political environment across much of the world. In August 2021, the IPCC published the headlines from its Sixth Assessment Report, flagging "code red for humanity". Compared with 2009, the reception and coverage of the report was noticeable for the lack of climate sceptic voices. The widespread experience of increasingly common extreme weather events seems to have killed off the idea that climate change is made up by climate scientists. The 13 years since Climategate have brought Brexit, the rise and fall of Trump and the "whoosh" of a global coronavirus pandemic, and those big lumps of ice keep falling into the sea and the weather gets weirder.

The 2021 COP26 meeting in Glasgow focussed attention on the goal of transitioning to net zero emissions and in the world of food and farming there have been innumerable reports, conferences and discussions about "Net Zero Agriculture". "Net Zero Agriculture" is an attempt to boil down all the complexities of sustainable development into one of those pithy slogans that political campaigners tell us are so successful these days – like "Make America Great Again", "Get Brexit Done", or "Stay Home, Protect the NHS, Save Lives". Behind a simple slogan can lie great complexity, but the experience of Covid shows us how transformational change to progress towards net zero need not be a pipedream. In the agri-food system, it is going to be a challenge for our farmers, our scientists, our policy-making institutions and ourselves. It will be a challenge for our thinking, our shopping, our farming and our eating. After more than 30 years of thinking about food, farming, land use and the environment, this is my contribution to understanding the dynamics of change. It is about those two aspects of the change equation – how and why did our food and farming systems evolve to become the way they are today, and how might they be reformed to help avoid catastrophic climate change.

ABBREVIATIONS

ADAS	Agricultural Development Advisory Service
AFRC	Agriculture and Food Research Council
ARC	Agricultural Research Council
BBSRC	Biotechnology and Biological Sciences Research Council
BECCS	Biomass energy with carbon capture and storage
BEIS	Department for Business, Energy and Industrial Strategy
BSE	Bovine Spongiform Encephalopathy
CAP	Common Agricultural Policy
CJD	Creutzfeldt-Jakob Disease
CO_2	Carbon dioxide
COP	Conference of the Parties
CRE	Centre for Rural Economy (University of Newcastle)
CRU	Climatic Research Unit (University of East Anglia)
CWAECs	County War Agricultural Executive Committees
Defra	Department for Environment, Food and Rural Affairs
ELMS	Environmental Land Management Scheme
ESRC	Economic and Social Research Council
FAO	Food and Agriculture Organisation
FMD	Food and Mouth Disease
FWAG	Farming and Wildlife Advisory Groups
GHG	Greenhouse gas/gases
$GtCO_2$	Gigatonnes of carbon dioxide
$GtCO_2e$	Gigatonnes of carbon dioxide equivalent
GVA	Gross Value Added
IPCC	Intergovernmental Panel on Climate Change
ISM	Individual, Social, Material model
JAEP	Joint Agriculture and Environment Programme

LEAF	Linking Environment and Farming
LULUC	Land Use and Land Use Change
MAFF	Ministry of Agriculture, Fisheries and Food
MCPA	2-methyl,4-chlorophenoxyacetic acid
Mha	Million hectares
$MtCO_2$	Million tonnes of carbon dioxide
$MtCO_2e$	Million tonnes of carbon dioxide equivalent
NAA	1-napthyl acetic acid
NAAS	National Agricultural Advisory Service
NDCs	Nationally Determined Contributions
NERC	Natural Environment Research Council
NFU	National Farmers' Union
OECD	Organisation for Economic Cooperation and Development
ppm	Parts per million
REDD+	Reducing emissions from deforestation and forest degradation
Relu	Rural Economy and Land Use Programme
UCL	University College London
UEA	University of East Anglia
WCED	World Commission on Environment and Development
WRAP	Waste and Resources Action Programme
WRO	Weed Research Organisation

1
FOOD, FARMING AND CLIMATE CHANGE

Food has shaped our bodies, habits, societies and environments since long before our ancestors were human. Its effects are so widespread and profound that most of us can't even see them, yet it is as familiar to us as our own face. Food is the great connector, the stuff of life and its readiest metaphor. It is this capacity to span worlds and ideas that gives food its unparalleled power. It is, you might say, the most potent tool for transforming our lives that we never knew we had. (Steel, 2021)[1]

Introduction

Climate change is going to transform agriculture and the food system across the world. Changing climatic conditions will affect land use and farming practices as agriculture is forced to adapt to warmer weather, changing growing seasons and more extreme weather events. And because agriculture and the food system are such significant contributors to greenhouse gas emissions, commitments to tackle climate change will mean change in land use and agricultural practices for most countries to reduce emissions. In the UK, as elsewhere, large tracts of current farmland are planned to be given over to forestry and energy crops in the next three decades and consumers will be encouraged to eat less of those foodstuffs that involve greater emissions. Farming practices will have to change to reduce the emissions from cultivating crops and rearing farm animals. The number of livestock will probably need to reduce, although this will be contested by the livestock industry, and sufficient food will have to be produced from less agricultural land. Food companies will pursue their own net zero strategies for their supply chains, publishing brochures filled with images of electric fleet vehicles and carbon-neutral supermarkets. The transition to net zero will require nothing less than a twenty-first-century revolution in land use, farming practice and the food system.

DOI: 10.4324/9781003278535-1

To talk in revolutionary terms might seem dramatic, but revolutions in food and farming have happened before. The first agricultural revolution saw humanity transition from hunter gatherers to farmers, keepers of domesticated farm animals and cultivators of land. This took thousands of years from around 10,000 BC. The second agricultural revolution, which took place in Britain just a few centuries ago, saw dramatic improvements in productivity through crop rotation, plant and animal breeding and improved farming techniques. Agricultural historians muse over precisely when this agricultural revolution took place – when it started and when it finished – but we can say this revolution took about a hundred years, from 1750 to 1850.[2] A third revolution, in the twentieth century, was forged in the United States but spread across much of the developed world and saw a dramatic uptake of chemical and mechanical technologies to increase agricultural productivity and reduce the need for farm labour. This third revolution has fundamentally shaped the agriculture we have today.[3] In the UK, it took place over just a few decades after the Second World War. A fourth revolution, for the twenty-first century, is required, and the urgency of climate change means this revolution will need to be swift and purposeful. It will need to embrace the techniques and technologies of farming practice for arable and livestock production, the pattern of land use for agriculture and other uses such as forestry and energy crops, and the way food is processed, distributed and sold. In the language of climate science, it will need to bring agriculture, land use and the food system within "safe operating limits" so that our food and land are helping keep humanity within the constraints of global atmospheric systems, rather than contributing to the risk of catastrophic, human-induced climate change.

Carolyn Steel writes about the profound significance of food to human society, culture and economy. She argues it is healthy and instructive to see the world *through food*. She uses the term *Sitopia* from the Greek *sitos*, meaning food, and *topos* meaning place. Food shapes our lives in so many ways yet so often we do not see it. It is too big to see. Its production has become separated from us, and we become complicit, not wanting to know about how what we eat is made. London needs food for around 30 million meals every day, but few stop to think about where this food came from, how it was produced, and with what implications for the planet and the people involved. Seeing the world through food opens up a world of flows, as food flows towards us from farmers, through processors, packagers, manufacturers and retailers, through our bodies, and back to the environment as waste, and as it flows it shapes our world for better or for worse.[4] These flows are managed and so as individuals and societies we have choices about how we engage with food and the food system and how these flows might be managed in future. *Sitopia* is Steel's food-centred version of utopia, where we use food as a medium for seeing the world and as a way of connecting people with the food system and with each other. Eating food is a political act, a social act and an economic act, and we do it every day. Steel argues that food can become a powerful force shaping our world. By thinking about how and what we eat, we can change the world.[5]

Our world, and our food system, is going to have to change if we are to successfully navigate away from the risk of catastrophic climate change. How this change is thought about and influenced will need to draw upon different systems of knowledge-production and different disciplines. Work on agriculture, food and climate change spans a range of disciplines across the natural and social sciences. Among the former, atmospheric physicists, oceanographers and earth systems scientists measure and model what is happening to the Earth's atmosphere and how the atmosphere interacts with the land and seas. Paleoecologists help us understand how the Earth's environment has evolved over thousands of years. Crop and animal scientists work on plants and animals to understand how production systems can be improved. Among the social sciences, research investigates farmer and consumer behaviour and decision-making, the role of institutions in the food system, and changing social and cultural values around food, diet and environment. With its focus on food, farming and the net zero challenge, this book spans two main bodies of academic work. The first is social science research into the agri-food system by, among others, geographers, sociologists, economists and political scientists. This work takes as its focus agriculture and the food industry and looks at producers, consumers institutions and places. The second is research into climate change and climate policy, which addresses the governance of climate policy globally, nationally and sub-nationally, and the relationships between the science and politics of climate change. It deals with integrated models of recent and future trends in biological, physical and economic systems. Broadly speaking, recent academic research in the social sciences on contemporary agri-food issues has paid insufficient attention to the question of mitigating climate change. At the same time, climate change research often suffers from a lack of social science analysis of the context of agriculture, food and rural land use. This book attempts to bring these worlds together to yield new insights for both audiences.

The Climate Challenge and Net Zero Emissions

It was once thought that climate was fixed and stable. There could be no such thing as "climate change". By the end of the twentieth century, it had become well established not only that the climate can change but that human activities are an important influence on climate change. Anthropogenic greenhouse gas emissions influence the carbon cycle and contribute to the warming of the atmosphere. Until industrial times, atmospheric carbon dioxide concentrations remained fairly static, remaining within 10 parts per million (ppm) of an average of 280 ppm that had been stable for at least 2000 years before 1850. However, since the industrial revolution, carbon dioxide concentrations have increased by almost 50 per cent from 280 ppm in 1850 to 410 ppm in 2019.[6] According to the Intergovernmental Panel on Climate Change's (IPCC) most recent assessment, the longest and most extensive dataset suggests that between the periods 1850–1900 and 2001–2020 the Earth's mean surface temperature increased by 0.99°C, while the mean land surface air temperature has increased by 1.59°C.[7] The IPCC concludes, with a high level of confidence, that anthropogenic warming has resulted in shifts of climate zones. Ongoing warming is projected to result in new, hotter climates in tropical regions and to shift climate zones poleward in the mid- to high latitudes and upward in regions of higher elevation. In August 2021, the National Atmospheric and Oceanographic Administration in the United States reported that July 2021 was the Earth's hottest month on record.[8] The same month the IPCC published its strongest statement yet on climate change, with the United Nations Secretary General declaring "code red for humanity".

In the UK, according to the Met Office, the climate is getting warmer and wetter. The most recent decade (2011–2020) has been on average 0.5°C warmer than the 1981–2010 average and 1.1°C warmer than 1961–1990. In a data series from 1884, all the top ten warmest years for the UK have occurred since 2002. UK winters have been 4 per cent wetter over the most recent decade compared to 1981–2010 and 9 per cent wetter than 1961–1990, and summers have been 15 and 17 per cent wetter, respectively.[9] Forecasts suggest winters will be warmer and wetter and summers will be hotter and drier, with more frequent and more severe extreme weather events. If greenhouse gas emissions are not reduced, average temperatures are forecast to be 0.7–4.2°C warmer in winter and 0.9–5.4°C in summer with increases in rainfall of 11 to 35 per cent in winter and decreases of up to 47 per cent in summer.[10] In summer 2021, the catastrophic effects of extreme weather events dominated the news. In July 2021, hundreds of people were killed by flooding as a result of heavy rainfall in Germany, Belgium and the Netherlands. The highest ever temperature in Europe, 48.8°C, was recorded in Italy on 11th August and forest fires raged in Greece, which suffered over 580 fires in a month.

The 1980s and 1990s saw significant advances in the science of climate change and in international efforts to co-ordinate responses to seek to stabilise and then bring down greenhouse gas emissions. The IPCC was established in 1988. In the three decades since, successive international climate conferences have taken place, with the annual rhythm of the "Conference of the Parties" (COP) meetings in between. First came the Rio Summit in 1992, hailed as the largest intergovernmental conference ever convened, and resulting in a new international climate framework and a commitment by national governments to measure, monitor and try to address greenhouse gas emissions. At Kyoto in 1997, governments agreed to set fixed targets for reductions in emissions, based on 1990 baseline levels, in the form of the Kyoto Protocol. Then came the Paris Agreement in December 2015 where, in the face of evidence of the worsening scale, pace and impact of climate change, targets were strengthened and tightened, and governments committed to bring emissions down to within a fixed measure of global warming – well below 2°C above pre-industrial levels – and to strive to limit the temperature increase to 1.5°C above pre-industrial levels. The Paris Agreement committed signatory countries to achieve a balance between anthropogenic emissions by sources and removals by sinks of greenhouse gases in the second half of this century. Countries develop their own plans for reducing emissions and increasing carbon capture through Nationally Determined Contributions (NDCs). The Glasgow COP26 meeting in November 2021 was the first opportunity to take stock of the NDCs. It was estimated that if all the commitments in them were honoured, the world would still be facing warming in the order of 2.5–2.7°C and so the Glasgow Pact required countries to revisit and revise their NDCs and bring more ambitious reduction targets back in 2022.

The UK committed to reducing its emissions to 80 per cent below 1990 levels by 2050 after the Kyoto Protocol and enacted by the Climate Change Act 2008. In June 2019, the UK became the first of the world's major economies to commit legally to ending its net contribution to greenhouse gas emissions and to global warming by 2050. The 80 per cent target in the Climate Change Act was amended to 100 per cent, a commitment to net zero. The 2008 Act established the UK Government's statutory advisor on climate change policy, the Climate Change Committee, to advise on how the UK can meet its international obligations on climate change including how to transition to net zero by 2050. The Committee produces carbon budgets that help inform the UK Government's overall approach to reducing emissions. The UK has reduced its greenhouse gas emissions by almost a half since 1990 and much of this reduction has come from changes in electricity generation and the switch from coal-fired power stations towards lower emission sources including renewable energy. The UK Government set out its new Net Zero Strategy in October 2021.[11] The goal is to fully decarbonise the power system by 2035, develop four carbon capture and storage industrial clusters by 2030 to remove and store carbon, move towards low-carbon heat sources for homes and workplaces by 2035 and end the sale of new petrol and diesel cars by 2030. The Strategy also aims to treble woodland creation rates in England to contribute to the UK's overall target of planting 30,000 hectares per year by the end of the current Parliament.[12]

In the UK, emissions from agriculture did fall from 1990 to 2009 but have not fallen any further over the last decade (Figure 1.1). Other parts of the food system display different trends over the past three decades (see Figures 1.2–1.5). The Climate Change Committee published a major report on land use and the path to net zero in January 2020 to set out measures where the agri-food and land-use system can contribute to the UK's overall transition.[13] The first set of changes, on the demand side, involves dietary change among the population to reduce their consumption of meat and dairy products. The Committee estimates approximately a 20 per cent reduction is necessary although other bodies suggest a target of 30 per cent[14] or even 50 per cent.[15] Reduced demand for meat and dairy would mean less land is needed for livestock farming. A further demand-side measure is to reduce waste in the food chain, from farms and at all points in the processing and manufacture of food and in households, by 20 per cent by 2050. In addition, land-use changes include a significant increase in the area of land under forestry, increasing the total proportion of forested land from 13 per cent today to around 18–19 per cent by 2050, and an increase in bioenergy crops that can be harvested and processed to produce energy, but with the emissions captured and safely stored. Also included among land-use changes is the restoration of peatland to better store carbon, with at least 50 per cent of upland peatland and 25 per cent of lowland peat having to be restored. Finally, a range of low-carbon farming practices must be adopted to ensure that agriculture is still productive enough to produce sufficient food, but in ways that minimise the emission of greenhouse gases. Overall, the Climate Change Committee anticipates that around 9 per cent of agricultural land will be needed for actions to reduce climate change emissions and sequester carbon by 2035 and 21 per cent will be needed by 2050. When land needed for population and settlement growth is included, these proportions increase to 11 per cent by 2035 and 23 per cent by 2050.[16] In this vision of the future, the UK's domestically produced food will have to come from almost a quarter less land by 2050.

According to the Climate Change Committee, these strategies for UK agriculture and land use together need to reduce emissions by almost two-thirds by 2050. Of this reduction, the largest proportion (almost a half) comes from the afforestation of agricultural land, including the savings that accrue from the harvesting of forest products. Agro-forestry, which involves planting trees among crops on agricultural land, together with the growing of energy crops, accounts for another third of intended savings. Dietary change to reduce consumption of meat and dairy products, along with reducing food waste, accounts for a further 12 per cent of the total. The remainder of emissions savings is made up of restoring peatlands (8 per cent) and the adoption of low-carbon practices on farms (17 per cent) (see Figure 1.6).[17]

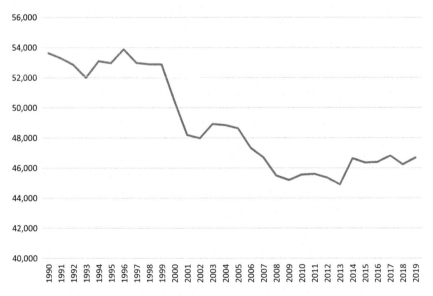

FIGURE 1.1 UK Greenhouse Gas Emissions from the Agricultural Sector, 1990–2019 ($ktCO_2e$)

Source: Graph derived from the UK's official emissions accounts (Department for Business, Energy & Industrial Strategy).[18]

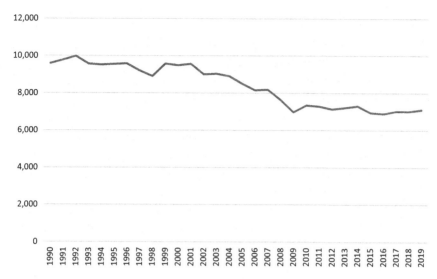

FIGURE 1.2 UK Greenhouse Gas Emissions from Food and Drink Manufacturing and Processing, 1990–2019 (ktCO$_2$e)

Source: Graph derived from the UK's official emissions accounts (Department for Business, Energy & Industrial Strategy. Standard Industrial Classification Groups 10.1–11.07).

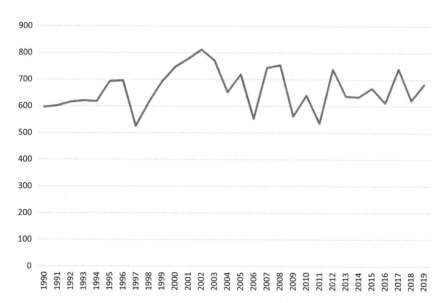

FIGURE 1.3 UK Greenhouse Gas Emissions from Fertiliser Manufacture, 1990–2019 (ktCO$_2$e)

Source: Standard Industrial Classification Groups 20.15/1.

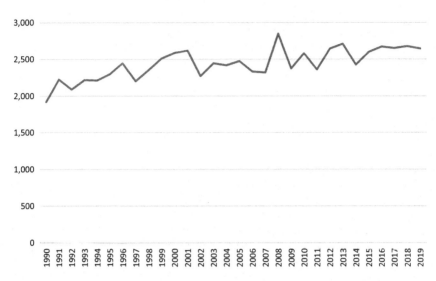

FIGURE 1.4 UK Greenhouse Gas Emissions from Food and Beverage Serving Services, 1990–2019 (ktCO$_2$e)

Source: Standard Industrial Classification Group 56.

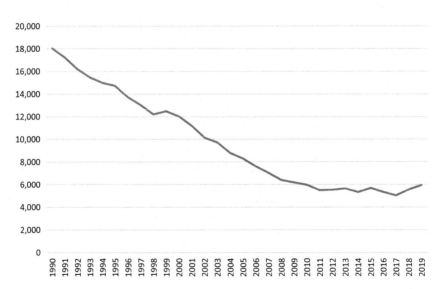

FIGURE 1.5 UK Greenhouse Gas Emissions from Land Use, Land-Use Change and Forestry, 1990–2019 (ktCO$_2$e)

Source: Standard Industrial Classification Groups 20.15/1.

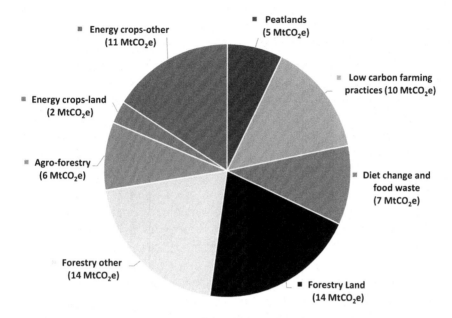

FIGURE 1.6 Greenhouse Gas Savings from Measures to Reduce UK Agriculture and Land-Use Emissions, 2050

Notes: Savings are compared with business-as-usual emission in 2050. "Energy crops – other" and " Forestry – other" refer to the greenhouse gas savings from the use of harvested products in other sectors of the economy. Savings from diet change and food waste are from direct agricultural emissions reduction only. Reproduced by permission of the Climate Change Committee.

Source: Climate Change Committee (2020a), p. 9.

Food, Farming and Land Use

The agri-food system includes agriculture, food manufacturing and processing, distribution and retail. Globally, it accounts for more greenhouse gas emissions than any other sector except energy, a third of the total or some 18 GtCO$_2$e per year (Table 1.1), a proportion that far outstrips the 3.5 per cent of emissions caused by air travel.[19] Of this, just over a quarter (27 per cent) comes from industrialised countries and just under three quarters (73 per cent) come from developing countries (including China). Of the emissions from the global food system, in 2015, 71 per cent came from the land-based sector, defined as agriculture and associated land use and land use change activities (LULUC), although the significance of these primary sector emissions varied between industrialised and developing countries. In industrialised countries, downstream sectors such as food processing, distribution and retailing contributed more than half (53 per cent) of total emissions from the food system, while in developing countries almost three quarters (73 per cent) came from agriculture and LULUC. The food system's share of total emissions has been relatively stable among industrialised countries at around a quarter but has fallen

TABLE 1.1 Share of Greenhouse Gas Emissions (GHG) from the Food System Globally and from Regions

	Total GHG emissions (from food systems) GtCO₂e, 1990	Total GHG emissions (from food systems) GtCO₂e, 2015	GHG shares from food system (%), 1990	GHG shares from food system (%), 2015	Share of global emissions (%), 1990	Share of global emissions (%), 2015	Per capita GHG emissions from food system (tCO₂e cap⁻¹ yr⁻¹), 1990	Per capita GHG emissions from food system (tCO₂e cap⁻¹ yr⁻¹), 2015
World	36.5 (16.1)	52 (18)	43	34	100	100	3.0	2.4
By continent								
Africa	3.8 (2.7)	4.7 (3.1)	69	67	16	17	4.6	2.8
Asia	9.8 (5.7)	24.0 (7.1)	58	29	35	39	1.9	1.8
Europe	5.6 (1.4)	4.2 (1.3)	26	30	8.8	7.1	2.8	2.4
Latin America	3.8 (3.2)	4.5 (3.0)	84	66	20	17	7.1	4.7
North America	6.5 (1.5)	7.3 (1.9)	23	25	9.1	10	5.3	5.2
Oceania	0.5 (0.2)	0.7 (0.3)	47	38	1.5	1.4	11	8.2
Russia	6.5 (1.4)	6.6 (1.3)	22	20	8.9	7.4	3.1	2.2

Notes: Each region's share of global GHG emissions is reported in brackets. Total GHG emissions, including methane, nitrous oxide and fluorinated gases, are expressed as carbon dioxide equivalents using the method and values used in the IPCC's Fifth Assessment. Latin America includes central and South America. Data for Russia also includes Ukraine, Central Asia, the Middle East and Turkey.

Source: Crippa et al. (2021a), p. 204. Reproduced by permission of Monica Crippa.[1]

[1] Crippa, M. et al. (2021a); see also Crippa, M., et al. (2021b) *GHG Emissions of All World Countries – 2021* Luxembourg: Publications Office of the European Union.

TABLE 1.2 Average Annual Total Greenhouse Gas Emissions from the UK Food System by Sub-sector, 1990–2018 (ktCO$_2$e^{-y})

	1990–1999	%	2000–2009	%	2010–2018	%	% change, 1990–2018
Production	66,943.7	42.6	58,118.5	42.8	54,880.3	48.3	−21.6
Retail	6,810.6	4.3	10,880.2	8.0	12,460.8	11.0	87.2
Transport	14,134.2	9.0	14,337.8	10.6	13,417.9	11.8	−1.4
End of life	34,368.1	21.9	20,529.9	15.1	7,882.5	6.9	−78.3
Processing	12,247.1	7.8	9,872.7	7.3	7,298.9	6.4	−50.7
Packaging	9,402.3	6.0	9,089.4	6.7	6,428.3	5.7	−56.9
Consumption	6,110.9	3.9	6,123.6	4.5	4,448.8	3.9	−51.8
LULUC	6,947.6	4.4	6,863.1	5.1	6,847.7	6.0	−1.7
Total	156,964.4	100.0	135,815.3	100.0	133,665.2	100.0	−27.4

Source: Derived from supplementary data published with Crippa *et al.* (2021a), drawn from the Emissions Database of Global Atmospheric Research – Food Database (see also Crippa *et al.*, 2021b). Produced by permission of Monica Crippa.

in developing countries from 68 per cent in 1990 to 39 per cent in 2015 as other sources of emissions have grown.[20] Per capita emissions from the food system are falling globally although falls are most modest in North America and Asia. Across the different parts of the food system, the production stages up to the farm gate contributed 39 per cent of all food system emissions globally, while other LULUC contributed 32 per cent and distribution, processing and consumption contributed 29 per cent. In the UK, the food system accounts for 23 per cent of all greenhouse gas emissions, a proportion that has remained relatively stable since 1990. However, the contributions of the different parts of the food system have changed over time, with production becoming a more significant contributor to total emissions from the system (Table 1.2).[21]

As agriculture has expanded globally over the past century, so forest lands have been cleared. In the UK, most forests were cleared many centuries ago, and by the end of the Second World War, only 6 per cent of the land was forested. Agricultural expansion has also resulted in the destruction of peat bogs that are important carbon sinks and as peat dries out it releases its stored carbon as carbon dioxide into the atmosphere. UK farming's twentieth-century agricultural revolution has replaced the former system of mixed farming with more specialised systems of production. Specialised arable systems rely heavily on pesticides, especially herbicides, manufactured fertilisers and large and powerful machinery. Any fertiliser that is not taken up by crops either gets washed into watercourses or converted into nitrous oxide, which is almost 300 times more potent as a greenhouse gas than carbon dioxide. Methane and manure, bemoaned as "the food system's two biggest climate sins",[22] pose the most significant problem. Globally, agriculture accounts for about half of all methane emissions and much of this comes from ruminant livestock, especially cattle and sheep. Ruminants' digestive systems mean animals emit methane almost continually and their manure or slurry emits methane and nitrous oxide. Ruminant emissions and manure account for 58 per cent of UK farming's emissions and there are additional emissions from soil associated with growing ruminant feed.[23] Globally, as diets change and demand for meat grows, more ruminant animals are being reared for food than ever before, which means meat is a central issue in avoiding catastrophic human-induced climate change. Agriculture, food and land use stand out as one of the most difficult and challenging sectors to address in the transition to net zero. In the UK, like in many OECD countries, it is recognised that progress with reducing emissions from agriculture has lagged behind other sectors such as electricity generation and road transport.[24] As decarbonisation in these other sectors progresses, then the agri-food system is likely to become an even more prominent challenge for climate change mitigation and responsible for an even greater proportion of total emissions.

Agriculture is part of an increasingly integrated food system. Its inputs are purchased from agricultural supply industries producing machinery, agrochemical pesticides and fertilisers, and animal feeds. Each of these sectors is highly concentrated with a small number of very large companies holding large shares of the market.[25] Farmers sell to food processors, manufacturers and retailers and these sectors too are characterised by very large, often multinational, companies who hold large market shares and compete intensely with each other for customers. Hemmed between the upstream and downstream sectors are the farmers who manage the land and produce crops and animals for the market. They also take most of the risk in food production and for an ever-diminishing share of the value added in the food chain. Agriculture accounts for approximately half the greenhouse gas emissions from the UK food system, but what happens on farms cannot be seen simply as the sole responsibility of the farmer. Rather, our system of producing crops and animals has been shaped by several decades of highly interventionist agricultural policy, the increasing influence of the companies producing inputs and processing and retailing its outputs and, of course, by the demands we collectively make of the agri-food system as consumers. Mindful of Carolyn Steel's suggestion that we see the world through food and trace the flows, our food system has to be seen as a complex one where agricultural production, food processing and retail are shaped by networks and relationships that have evolved over the last century. The relationships extend across the globe, with food and agricultural inputs imported from all parts of the world. British food, farming and land use is essentially a product of a national system of consumer preferences, regulation and innovation operating in an international context where trade and intellectual property rights are managed according to international rules.[26]

UK food consumption patterns make us distinctive compared to our neighbours. Our food retailing sector is particularly concentrated among a small number of large supermarket chains. We cook less and have more food cooked for us (as takeaways, for example) and spend a smaller proportion of our income on meals at home than any other European country. Our culinary culture is coming to resemble that of the United States, as is our obesity problem. We eat more ready meals and spend more on pre-prepared foods than our European neighbours and have embraced home delivery apps for food. We eat too much processed food, too much salt, sugar, red meat and saturated fat and, on average, we only eat about a quarter of the recommended daily intake of fruit and vegetables.[27] We also waste a lot of food. Globally, over a billion tonnes of food is wasted every year.[28] In the UK, around 13 million tonnes of food are wasted, of which just over a quarter is on farm with the rest wasted after leaving the farm gate.[29] Our diet is causing us significant health problems as a population in the UK. According to the World Health Organisation's "disability-adjusted life years" measure, which quantifies the burden of disease including early death, ill-health and disability, 300,000 years of good health were lost to diet-related illness or disability in the UK in 2017, and if early deaths are included, then total years lost to the UK population that year was 1.6 million.[30]

The climate change problem brings together food, farming and land use. Addressing the problem goes to the heart of questions of what we eat, how and where it is grown, and how we balance our different demands on rural land – in producing our food, as home to valued biodiversity, as a space of recreation and living, and as a place of carbon sequestration. The changes required to our food and diet, land use and farming practices are marked, but they also bring wider benefits beyond climate change mitigation. They could contribute to a healthier diet and healthier population and should also bring other environmental benefits from a different way of managing rural land. Habitats and biodiversity ought to improve, there should be more opportunities for recreational uses of the countryside and changing land use can be managed in ways that also help reduce the risk of flooding. The sorts of changes required mean we need a more sophisticated approach to understand behaviour change among individuals as consumers or land managers, among households and small family businesses, and among large corporations and public institutions. Traditionally, when it comes to change in the agri-food system, this has not warranted enough thought and research. There is a tendency among policymakers to see agri-food issues in technological terms. This is not helped by the structure of research funding, in which engineering, biotechnological and biological sciences and the natural sciences have traditionally dominated spending. We risk a situation where we know more about, and pour ever more research funding into better understanding, the belches and burps of cattle, yet still struggle to understand the dynamics of decision-making among the land managers in whose hands a large portion of the UK's climate change mitigation depends. This book is a social science contribution to the question of how, as individuals, households, small firms and big companies, we might approach the transition to a net zero world. It is also a call for more consideration of system change and the role of individual and institutional behaviour change within it.

So, what does "net zero" mean as a national target? Net zero emissions does mean *zero emissions*. It means that emissions are brought into balance with the capacity to capture and sequester greenhouse gases so that, on balance, the *net* emissions amount to zero. The Climate Change Committee's carbon budgets set out the pathways for emissions reductions and break down targets across sectors, one of which covers agriculture and land use, land-use change and forestry.[31] For many sectors of the economy, the trajectory of emissions reduction is similar. However, for agriculture and land use, the scenarios are most varied and the kinds of policy choices still to be made have the greatest bearing on the UK's overall ability to reach net zero. Under one scenario (termed "balanced pathway"), emissions from the agricultural sector fall from 54.6 $MtCO_2e$ in 2018 to 35 $MtCO_2e$ in 2050.[32] The land-use sector under this pathway moves from 12.8 $MtCO_2e$ emitted in 2018 to a net sink of 19 $MtCO_2e$ in 2050.[33] An alternative scenario (named "wide-spread engagement") assumes greater benefits from dietary change and food waste reduction and higher rates of new woodland planting and a "tailwinds" scenario assumes even faster progress on behaviour change and technological improvements. By 2050, land use and land-use change and forestry could be delivering between 12 and 30 $MtCO_2e$ of net sink, compared to 12.8 $MtCO_2e$ of emissions today. For accounting purposes, different greenhouse gases are standardised into "carbon dioxide equivalents" to produce a simple target. With the agri-food sector, this concerns industry interests as methane and nitrous oxide are significant greenhouse gases yet persist in the atmosphere for much shorter lengths of time compared to carbon dioxide. Nevertheless, they become incorporated into an overall green-house gas emissions target expressed as carbon dioxide equivalents. Views differ as to whether food, farming and rural land use together should be contributing more to the UK's emissions reductions. Forestry and growing energy crops may be able to deliver net sequestration, but some argue that the whole of the agriculture industry could contribute more to net emissions reductions. The current thinking within the Government is that there will continue to be net emissions from food production. The term "net zero food and farming" is, therefore, best understood to mean "food and farming in the net zero age", and not strictly food and farming that yields net zero emissions.

Governing Change in Agriculture and the Food System

The transition to a net zero UK means that people, households, small businesses and large corporations will have to change their ways. Never in the history of the agri-food system has there been a need for such extensive system transformation and behaviour change, instigated by the Government. Over the course of the next three decades, the net zero transition will require changes to diet, shopping choices, land use and farming practices. Currently, this transition takes the form of scenarios and pathways, coupled with interesting looking graphs that show, for example, declining consumption of red meat or increasing area under forest cover projected through the 2030s and 2040s to the goal of net zero by 2050.[34] Together, these representations may give some reassurance and comfort. They give a sense of there being a plan. However, when it comes to precisely who is going to do precisely what, all sorts of questions and complications unsettle things. In 2020, the Climate Change Committee complained that "there are no national or UK-wide policies that directly target the reduction of greenhouse gas emissions in the agriculture sector beyond the provision of advice and information".[35] The transition to net zero will be a huge experiment, and we shall have to learn as we go along, while always mindful of the 2050 net zero goal and the pace of emissions reductions necessary to get us there. There are no clear models of behaviour change that we can be confident about. Social science is not like the natural and physical sciences. As individuals, groups and organisations, people can be much less predictable than machines or even cows. What we do have is some experience of the state-sponsored active management of change in the agri-food system over the last century or so, both in modernising and expanding production but also in addressing the unanticipated environmental and public health consequences of that modernisation. There are insights that can be derived from this experience. So, what are the "big shift" changes in the agri-food system of the last century that we can learn from?

First is the revolution in agricultural productivity that began during the Second World War.[36] This period saw change in farming practices and land use on a scale comparable with the changes now required to curb climate change. The surge in agricultural productivity was not a spontaneous initiative born of the agricultural community. It was the result of a new and assertive approach to agricultural support and modernisation, forged in direct contrast to the laissez-faire approach that had prevailed through much of the preceding decades since the 1850s. It saw new institutions and governance arrangements established in order to lead and manage change both at the national level, through the concept of the productivity of "the national farm", and also at the level of the myriad of individual farm businesses up and down the land.[37] For these farmers, day-to-day farming practices had to be encouraged, incentivised and cajoled along particular pathways of development. The construction and maintenance of what we will call the productivist model of agricultural development was led by the state which played a central and active role in orchestrating changing farming practice and land use. Given its goal of raising the productivity of British agriculture, this can be thought of, and learned from, as a highly successful transformational change project on its own terms.

Second is the gradual and highly contested evolution of an alternative model of more environmentally benign "sustainable agriculture", the origins of which we can date to the 1981 Wildlife and Countryside Act. Controversies accumulated around the environmentally damaging consequences of agricultural productivism, and the mounting pressure on government came from the growing environmental movement. In response, a new approach to "greening" British agriculture had to be sought. This began with the development of voluntary schemes to pay farmers not to continue with agricultural improvements such as land drainage, hedgerow and woodland removal. This approach to "agri-environment" schemes became formalised within the Common Agricultural Policy, and by the late 1980s, there were agri-environment payments being made to farmers in 19 different "Environmentally Sensitive Areas". Farmers were free to choose to enter these schemes if they wished and, if so, became subject to management agreements to modify farming practices to deliver environmental benefits. By the mid-1990s, similar schemes were opened up to many more farmers, not just those in designated areas. This voluntary approach to delivering environmental benefits was coupled with a tightening of the regulatory baseline in some key aspects of farming practice. Pollution, animal disease and public health problems prompted efforts to "clean" as well as "green" British agriculture. A straw-burning ban was introduced, tighter farm pollution regulations had to be adhered to, and farm animal health became subject to tighter restrictions as a result of the BSE and Foot and Mouth Disease crises. This second example of the "post-productivist" cleaning and greening of farming has brought mixed results but does provide lessons from both voluntary and regulatory approaches where farmers are incentivised and subsidised, or legally compelled, to act differently. While efforts to clean and green British farming over the past 40 years cannot be characterised overall as a success, there are nevertheless valuable lessons for the transition to net zero.

A *third* example is the transformation in the economic structure and logistics for food retailing since the 1970s. The self-service model, where effectively the consumer replaces shopworkers, was first developed in the United States in the early twentieth century and started to be adopted in the UK after the Second World War. British food retailing had been epitomised by the independent shopkeeper but underwent a profound structural change from the 1960s and the development of an oligopoly of a small number of very large supermarket chains.[38] After the 1964 Resale Price Act prevented the use of resale price agreements, which were seen to prohibit price competition between food retailers, the share of total grocery sales by the multiple chains (with 10 or more stores) increased from 27 per cent in 1961 to 44 per cent in 1971 at the expense of Co-Ops, independent stores and smaller chains (with fewer than 10 stores), whose share fell from 73 to 56 per cent over the same period.[39] Among the multiples, centralised head offices were responsible for purchasing, capital raising and distribution, and large-scale, high-productivity supermarkets were built across the country in most urban centres. As a result, the British food retailing market has become highly concentrated. By 2016, of the 87,141 retail outlets selling groceries in the UK, 57 per cent of sales were concentrated in the 7 per cent (5,952) of largest stores.[40] The supermarket retailers have revolutionised food shopping and continue to innovate in internet shopping and home delivery of groceries. In terms of power and influence in the food system, the retailers have become dominant, displacing the power of processors and manufacturers. In 2018, food and drink wholesaling and retailing together accounted for £33 billion of gross value added compared to just £10 billion for agriculture.[41] Large supermarket multiples have made a huge impact on the functioning of towns and cities with the development of edge of town retail parks and shape the functioning of the food system through their contracting arrangements with farmers and growers. They have driven a food retailing revolution and will be centrally important in any transition to net zero. Crucially, it was a UK policy decision in the regulation of retail competition that established the competitive environment in which supermarket multiples were able to thrive.

These three "big shifts" in the agri-food system over the past century contain lessons for the transition to net zero. Sometimes such structural changes are characterised, glibly, as the result of "market forces". Closer examination usually shows that it is a policy or regulatory change that establishes new market conditions that then help drive change. Markets, whether well-functioning or otherwise, are always the outcome of sets of governing arrangements and technologies.[42] Even free markets are based on rules, and Adam Smith's "invisible hand of the market" is always connected to "the strong arm of the law".[43] With the development of agricultural productivism, it was a combination of guaranteed prices for farm products, coupled with public investment in research and development and in agricultural advice and education, which helped oil the wheels of a technological transformation in land use and farming practice. With the rise of the supermarkets, it was a change in competition regulation that opened up the opportunity for large supermarket multiples to take on such a dominant role in food retailing. And in the attempt since the 1980s to clean and green agriculture and reduce damage to biodiversity and valued landscapes, cause less pollution of watercourses and generate fewer risks to animal and public health, we see a smörgåsbord of market mechanisms, public subsidies and restrictive regulation, alongside advice, persuasion and appeals to farmers' better nature.

The British tradition of liberal government has come to imply a reluctance to interfere in markets and consumer choice. Within this tradition, farmers are sometimes cast as free entrepreneurial spirits (no matter how dependent on subsidies they may be), ideally unhampered by rules, regulations and the petty bureaucracy of environment, health and animal welfare.[44] However, the central role of the agri-food system within UK emissions reduction and the urgency of the climate challenge mean that a further four decades of experimentation with voluntarism in agri-environmental measures does not look a viable strategy. Food and farming policy in the second decade of the twenty-first century has been a mix of "nudge and fudge". Given the scale of the challenge, current policy levers look at best desperately under-developed. At worst, what may be required seems the very antithesis of what prevailing political opinion sees as the role of the state in its relationship with individual producers and individual consumers. A historical perspective can be useful in understanding the capacity for governmental action, the potential and limits of market approaches, and the role of advice, moral suasion and regulation. The environmental governance of the agri-food system requires that governments not only shape the context within which individual actors make decisions, but also the ways in which actors make sense of and respond to this context through their capacity for self-calculation and self-regulation. Responsible environmental behaviour will need to become "hardwired" into the routine and regular practices of farmers and land managers, shoppers and households, and food manufacturers and retailers.

The Structure of the Book

This book considers the prospects for the transition to a net zero UK from a historical perspective which seeks to understand how we have arrived at the current juncture. Chapter 2 discusses the conceptual approach adopted for the rest of the book. It outlines the relative roles of social and natural sciences in understanding climate change and agriculture's environmental challenges and introduces the concepts of sociotechnical systems and technological momentum from science and technology studies. It briefly outlines the key tenets of neoliberalism when it comes to economic policy, regulation and consumerism, and introduces cosmopolitanism as a contrary political philosophy associated with moderating individual behaviour for the sake of concerns about others. It discusses recent thinking in public policy to promote behaviour change and the limits to a focus on individual behaviour.

Chapter 3 traces the twentieth-century history of British agricultural policy and the food system. It explains how the UK, like other western countries, came to adopt a particular model of agricultural policy centred on supporting production through the promotion of particular technological systems that have given rise to the farming and the food system that we have today. The chapter draws on historical research on the founding of this productivist model and maps out the stunning improvements in agricultural productivity from the 1940s to the 1980s. It traces the power relations around productivism before explaining how the model entered a period of crisis and flux from the 1980s and became subjected to a cycle of incremental reforms.

Chapter 4 places British agriculture's current climate change challenge in the context of an ecological critique of intensive farming that has evolved since the 1960s. It traces the history of concerns about the environmental and public health consequences of an intensive farming and cheap food policy that began with controversies about the losses of valued landscape features, habitats and wildlife in the British countryside and developed through a string of scandals in the 1980s and 1990s around farming's contribution to water pollution and public health scares. It maps out the protracted development of environmental sustainability objectives for agri-food and rural land-use policy from the 1990s before the gradual realisation that combating climate change would require significant changes to the functioning of the agri-food system. Chapter 5 then provides a parallel account of how climate change emerged as a problem in the realm of science before becoming a pre-eminent issue for international governance. It tells the story of how we gradually came to be worried about climate change between the 1850s and the 1980s, and how growing scientific understanding of the physical processes of the Earth's atmosphere interacted with the political world. It traces the history of international climate policy since the 1980s, the struggles between climate science and activism, on the one hand, and climate change denial, on the other, and explains the international climate commitments that now provide the context for the UK's approach to its food, farming and land-use system.

Chapter 6 explains how despite international efforts to address climate change and curb emissions dating back to the late 1980s and early 1990s it is only recently that the challenge of reducing emissions from agriculture and land use, and the development of tangible prescriptions for action, have come into sharper focus. The chapter explains the work of the IPCC in assessing climate change and land, before examining the UK Climate Change Committee's suggested approach to agriculture and land use. Other organisations, including the National Farmers' Union, have also set out plans to achieve net zero. These other pathways are assessed and compared before the chapter concludes by explaining the main tensions to be reconciled if the quest for a transition to net zero is to be successful.

Accounting for a third of emissions, the food system plays an important part in anthropogenic emissions and so is crucial in bringing emissions within safe limits. Chapter 7 looks at the challenge of changing food consumption patterns to help deliver a safer world and address human-induced catastrophic climate change over the coming decades. It first examines the global evolution of humanity's unsustainable diet before turning to look at the UK case in more detail. It considers how behaviour change might be managed in relation to diet and then sets out the key strategies that have been advocated for what has been called the "great food transformation".

Chapter 8 examines the land-use changes likely to be prompted by the UK's commitment to net zero emissions. Expanding forestry so that its coverage of our land mass rises from 13 per cent to 18 to 19 per cent is itself a significant change, requiring that at least 30,000 hectares and possibly up to 50,000 hectares of new forest be planted each year until 2050. In addition, the switch to energy crops and any reduction in the number of farm livestock will also change the way our land is used. The chapter explores the debates about how best this part of the UK's shift can be managed, with a twin emphasis on the science and politics of land-use change.

Chapter 9 examines in more detail the changes to farming practice that will be required to contribute to the UK's net zero objective. Given the anticipated shift from farmland to forestry and energy crops, current levels of food production may be required to be delivered from significantly less land. This challenge is leading to a bifurcated debate about so-called sustainable intensification, on the one hand, which sees the solution in the adoption of ever-more sophisticated technology and precision farming techniques, and agro-ecology or high-nature-value farming, on the other, which is a more ecological approach rooted in the appreciation of environmental processes and constraints. This debate reproduces ideas that have featured in the struggles between farming and environmental interests for the past half-century including between land-sparing and land-sharing approaches to conservation. The chapter maps out the main arguments and the institutions and networks that seek to advance them.

Chapter 10 draws together some of the insights from Chapters 6 to 8 with a particular emphasis on the dynamics of the transition and the factors likely to advance and facilitate it and those more likely to pose obstacles to progress. The chapter maps the forces influencing the key sets of actors, farmers, consumers, companies and government. Finally, Chapter 11 draws together the conclusions of the book. It returns to the question of the lessons to be learned from the UK's twentieth-century experience of transformational change from the 1940s and the subsequent efforts to "clean and green" food and farming from the 1980s onwards. The chapter considers the implicit and sometimes naïve models of behaviour change at play in debates about the climate change challenge and concludes by reflecting on the prospects for the UK's transition to net zero and the successful transformation of the food, farming and land-use system.

Notes

1 Steel, C. (2021) *Sitopia: How Food Can Save the World*. London: Penguin, p. 2.
2 Overton, M. (1996) *Agricultural Revolution in England: The Transformation of the Agrarian Economy 1500–1850*. Cambridge University Press.
3 Brassley, P. *et al.* (2021) *The Real Agricultural Revolution: The Transformation of English Farming 1939–1985*. Woodbridge: Boydell Press.
4 Morgan, K. *et al.* (2006) *Worlds of Food: Place, Power, and Provenance in the Food Chain*. Oxford University Press.
5 Steel (2021); Bridle, S. (2020) *Food and Climate Change: Without the Hot Air*. Cambridge: UIT Cambridge.
6 Royal Academy of Engineering & Royal Society (2018) *Greenhouse Gas Removal*. London: Royal Society and Royal Academy of Engineering, p. 19; Intergovernmental Panel on Climate Change [IPCC] (2021) Summary for policymakers, in V. Masson-Delmotte *et al.* (eds.) *Climate Change 2021: The Physical Science Basis. Contribution of Working Group I to the Sixth Assessment Report of the Intergovernmental Panel on Climate Change*. Cambridge University Press, p. 5.
7 IPCC (2021).
8 National Atmospheric and Oceanographic Administration (2021) It's official: July was the Earth's hottest month on record. *News Release*, 13th August. US Department of Commerce, National Atmospheric and Oceanographic Administration.
9 Kenton, M. *et al.* (2021) State of the UK climate 2020. *International Journal of Climatology* 41, 1–76, p. 3.
10 Met Office (2019) *UKCP18 Science Overview Executive Summary*. Exeter: Met Office; Ortiz, M. *et al.* (2021) *Towards Net Zero in UK Agriculture: Key Information, Perspectives and Practical Guidance*. London: University College London Institute for Sustainable Resources.
11 UK Government (2021) *Net Zero Strategy: Build Back Greener*. London: Stationary Office.
12 UK Government (2021), p. 167.
13 Climate Change Committee (2020a) *Land Use: Policies for a Net Zero UK*. London: Climate Change Committee.
14 National Food Strategy (2021) *National Food Strategy – Independent Review: The Plan*. London: National Food Strategy.
15 EAT-Lancet (2019) Food in the Anthropocene: the EAT-Lancet Commission on healthy diets from sustainable food systems. *The Lancet* 393, 447–92.
16 Climate Change Committee (2020b) *The Sixth Carbon Budget: The UK's Path to Net Zero*. London: Climate Change Committee, p. 163.
17 Climate Change Committee (2020a), p. 9.
18 Department for Business, Energy and Industrial Strategy (2021) *Provisional UK Greenhouse Gas Emissions National Statistics*. London: BEIS.
19 National Food Strategy (2021), p. 73; Food and Agriculture Organisation (2021) *The Share of Agri-food Systems in Total Greenhouse Gas Emissions—Global, Regional and Country*

Trends 1990–2019. Rome: FAO; Crippa, M. *et al.* (2021a) Food systems are responsible for a third of global anthropogenic GHG emissions. *Nature Food* 2, 198–209.

20 Crippa *et al.* (2021a).

21 These data come from the supplementary data tables published with Crippa *et al.* (2021a).

22 National Food Strategy (2021), p. 76.

23 Climate Change Committee (2019) *Land Use: Reducing Emissions and Preparing for Climate Change.* London: Climate Change Committee, p. 31.

24 OECD (2019) *Enhancing Climate Change Mitigation Through Agriculture.* Paris: OECD.

25 Tansey, G. and Worsley, T. (1995) *The Food System: A Guide.* London: Earthscan; Howard, P. (2021) *Concentration and Power in the Food System: Who Controls What We Eat?* Revised Edition. London: Bloomsbury Academic.

26 Tansey, G. (2008) Food, farming and global rules, pp. 3–4 in G. Tansey and T. Rajotte (eds.) *The Future Control of Food: A Guide to International Negotiations and Rules on Intellectual Property, Biodiversity and Food Security.* London: Earthscan.

27 National Food Strategy (2020) *National Food Strategy – Part One.* London: National Food Strategy, p. 35.

28 Reynolds, C. (2021). *Food waste, sustainable diets and climate change: coherent solutions in the long view.* Paper presented at the Food Values Research Group, The University of Adelaide, June 2021 seminar.

29 Climate Change Committee (2020a), p. 119; WRAP (2021) *Food Surplus and Waste in the UK – Key Facts.* Estimates of food wastage are notoriously difficult and likely to be underestimates.

30 National Food Strategy (2020), p. 31.

31 Climate Change Committee (2020b).

32 Climate Change Committee (2020b), p. 164.

33 Climate Change Committee (2020b), p. 167.

34 See, for example, Climate Change Committee (2020b), p. 14.

35 Climate Change Committee (2020a), p. 77.

36 Brassley *et al.* (2021).

37 Murdoch, J. and Ward, N. (1997) Governmentality and territoriality: the statistical manufacture of Britain's 'national farm'. *Political Geography* 16, 307–24; Short, B. *et al.* (2000) *The National Farm Survey 1941–1943: State Surveillance and the Countryside in England and Wales in the Second World War.* Wallingford: CAB International

38 Alexander, A. and Phillips, S. (2006) 'Fair play for the small man': perspectives on the contribution of the independent shopkeeper 1930–c.1945. *Business History* 48 (1), 69–89; Morelli, C. (1998) Constructing a balance between price and non-price competition in British multiple food retailing 1954–64. *Business History* 40 (2), 45–61.

39 Morelli (1998).

40 Lang, T. (2020) *Feeding Britain: Our Food Problems and How to Fix Them.* London: Pelican, p. 358.

41 Defra figures quoted in Lang (2020), p. 362.

42 Callon, M. *et al.* (eds.) (2007) *Market Devices.* Oxford: Blackwell.

43 Harvey, D. R. (1996) The role of markets in the rural economy. pp. 19–39 in P. Allanson and M. Whitby (eds.) *The Rural Economy and the British Countryside.* London: Earthscan.

44 North, R. (2001) *The Death of British Agriculture: The Wanton Destruction of a Key Industry.* London: Duckworth.

2

SCIENCE, TECHNOLOGY AND POLITICS: THE CONCEPTUAL APPROACH

Introduction

Agriculture and the food system are impacted by climate change and at the same time generate climate emissions themselves. The principal focus of this book is the second of these two processes and the challenge that addressing climate change poses for agriculture and the food system. Climate change directly affects land management practices through, for example, changing weather patterns and growing seasons. Yet, in the coming years, it will be the measures to reduce greenhouse gas emissions that will have significant implications for the agri-food system, as changes to land use, farming practices and food products are introduced in efforts to bring greenhouse gas emissions within safe limits. What will the agriculture and food system need to look like in a net zero world, and how might the transition to this desired state of affairs be managed?

Traditionally, understandings of climate change and its mitigation have been produced by climate scientists, such as those involved in the work of the IPCC, who focus on processes of atmospheric and oceanic systems and warming.[1] A second group that focuses more on the human dimensions of these questions are economists.[2] The domination of climate change analyses by the natural and physical sciences and economics has tended to mean the adoption of reductionist understandings of people's patterns of living and working using economic calculations that have implicit models of rational and optimising behaviour. This is not enough on its own and wider social science perspectives are necessary. Economic institutions are important in the governance of economic sectors and economic life, but society matters too. People's everyday social practices are deeply implicated in the causes of climate change and will play a key part in the solutions to global warming. The social sciences beyond economics have a valuable role to play in helping to understand how and why high-emission systems and societies

DOI: 10.4324/9781003278535-2

function as they do, and what may need to happen to help them transition to a net zero world.[3]

From this starting point, this chapter sets out the conceptual basis and analytical rationale for the rest of the book. It first discusses the roles of social and natural sciences in understanding climate change and agriculture's environmental challenges and introduces the concepts of sociotechnical systems and technological momentum from Science and Technology Studies as a way of understanding technological change. It briefly outlines the key concepts of neoliberalism in governing economy and society, and cosmopolitanism as a counter political philosophy associated with moderating individual behaviour for the sake of concerns about others. It then discusses power and governance and the conceptual underpinnings of recent thinking in promoting behaviour change. The chapter is intended to provide a social science context for the analysis that follows. It is written with every effort to avoid obscure jargon. This is in the hope that the ideas and concepts, drawn principally from the sociology of science and technology, human geography and environmental social science, will be of some interest to a readership beyond social science scholars.

Science and Society

Through much of the twentieth century, the worlds of science on the one hand and of the social sciences and humanities on the other were treated as separate and distinct, with different approaches to producing new knowledge. Over recent decades, there have been calls for better understanding between the two communities and efforts to orchestrate stronger interdisciplinary collaboration. A range of natural and physical sciences are preoccupied with agriculture, land use and the food system. Agricultural production draws on natural and physical sciences, including plant and animal sciences, soil chemistry and engineering. Food science includes biologists, chemists, nutrition scientists and public health specialists. Understanding agriculture's environmental relationships involves biologists and ecologists, water chemists and, more recently, atmospheric scientists. In the UK, there has been a strong tradition of nature conservation and environmental scientists working on the ecology of the farmed environment and the wider countryside in public research institutions as well as universities. From time to time, particularly around questions of policy reform, natural and social scientists would come together to deliberate. However, when producing research, it has been unusual to involve teams that spanned social and natural sciences until recent years.

Although research funding for work on agriculture and food has been dominated by the natural and physical sciences, a range of social science disciplines have investigated agriculture, rural land management and the food system. These include economics, sociology, geography, anthropology and planning. In food and consumer studies, sociologists and economists have been joined by psychologists and social scientists interested in marketing, operations and supply chain management.[4] Political scientists and other policy studies specialists have also worked on the evolution of policies for food, farming and land use. As food and farming systems became subject to stronger critique and challenge during the 1980s, so more social scientists became involved in applied research that sought to develop prescriptions for how food and farming might be managed differently. And from the 1990s, climate change became an increasingly significant issue in the mix of problems those social and natural scientists working in food and farming were preoccupied with.

Like all environmental and public health controversies, climate change and its solutions are a site of struggle between different world views. How problems are framed can also affect the science and the social science that is produced. Three broad perspectives on climate change can be characterised.[5] A *sceptical* view has tended to challenge the claims and insights generated by climate science and see a self-interested global environmental movement in alliance with what are sometimes seen as self-interested scientists.[6] A *gradualist* view accepts the fact of climate change and the necessity for mitigating action, but adopts a relatively pragmatic perspective on behaviour change, innovation and technological change, a form of "ecomodernism"[7] dependent upon the more technocratic arts of modelling, futures analysis, risk management and adaptation. A third perspective is *catastrophism*, which emphasises the significance of uncertainty, the limits of scientific knowledge, and the unanticipated risks and tipping points that cast the global climate as complex and highly fragile. These different perspectives have shaped the arguments about what should be done about climate change. The sceptics are relatively doubtful about the whole enterprise of mitigating climate change. Their emphasis has tended to be on the potential costs and harms caused by a state-driven transformation of energy, transport and economic systems. They were able to exploit debates between climate scientists about the scale of change, along with media organisations' preoccupations with hearing both sides of an argument, to gain disproportionate airtime and influence for a period, but the influence and coverage of climate change scepticism have waned. The gradualists tend to focus on how existing socio-economic systems can be comfortably reformed. Different forms of gradualism call for different levels of urgency and different scales of action.[8] Among catastrophists are those more likely to see the climate crisis as a fundamental indictment of our social and economic systems and urge more radical change, often involving a retreat from modernism and capitalism into simpler and more traditional forms of living.

These different perspectives also pervade debates about the knowledge base underpinning our understanding of what has been happening, and what will happen under different future scenarios.[9] Climate science and climate policy are therefore riddled with "knowledge controversies" that mix science and society – "those events in which the knowledge claims and technologies of environmental science, and the regulatory and policy practices of government agencies that they inform, become subject to public interrogation and dispute".[10] Climate change has generated particularly intense levels of dispute and controversy. Very powerful interests are involved and are threatened, not least those of the global carbon economy, including fossil fuel producing industries and states.[11] The science of understanding the causes and consequences of climate change and the dynamics of mitigation is complex and involves many different scientific specialisms each themselves institutionalised and operating in what is sometimes a very competitive scientific world. The creation of the IPCC is in part an attempt to coordinate and synthesise scientific insights across this wide range of activities. In addition, climate science has had to evolve and develop in a complex, messy and sometimes heated social and political world under heightened public scrutiny.

A central argument of this book is that in order to transition to net zero in the coming decades, we must consider how we got to where we are. In the case of agriculture and the food system, any vision of a net zero world and prescriptions about the emissions reduction pathways to that world must be informed by a sound understanding of the evolution of the agriculture and food system we have today. And because this agri-food system involves a mix of physical, biological and social artefacts and processes, this conceptual perspective needs to embrace the natural and the social, the non-human and the human.[12] However, the institutions of science and knowledge production have been highly siloed. Separate funding bodies have tended to fund different people to pursue separate research programmes and who disseminate their findings through different conferences and journals. From time to time, there have been efforts to overcome this separateness and bring natural and social sciences together. Results have been mixed. One relatively early example in the field of agriculture's environmental problems was the Joint Agriculture and Environment (JAEP) Programme that ran from 1989 to 1994. This was at a time of heightened public and political concern about agriculture's environmental problems and in the midst of controversies about BSE, water pollution and loss of biodiversity. The Programme involved three research councils collaborating – the Agricultural and Food Research Council (AFRC, the forerunner to the Biotechnology and Biological Sciences Research Council or BBSRC), the Economic and Social Research Council (ESRC) and the Natural Environment Research Council (NERC). The JAEP Programme began in 1989, with £5.4 million of funding to support a programme of research.[13] Research activities were organised in three areas – ecology of farmland (led by NERC); plant/herbivore interactions and vegetation dynamics (led by AFRC); and changing farm economies and their environmental relationships (led by ESRC). There was little overlap or interaction between them. Thirty-six individual projects were funded, eight of which were predominantly social science projects. Although a joint management board oversaw the programme, the researchers across the three communities prepared their proposals that were assessed by peers largely within their own fields and then went about prosecuting their research, relatively oblivious to what the researchers working to the other two research councils were doing.

JAEP failed to achieve its interdisciplinary aspirations with little dialogue between the three scientific communities. The research unfolded within disciplinary frontiers rather than across them. An end of programme conference in Westminster in February 1994 to showcase findings merely served to highlight the lack of integration between these three strands of research activity. Presentations covered the nibbling practices of sheep, the ecology of the wood mouse and the social science of pesticide use in front of a perplexed audience. Several of the social science projects focused on farm household "pluriactivity", or multiple income-earning, and whether part-time farming was less of a problem for the environment. The research rather limply found that whether a farm household was pluriactive was not in itself a sufficient explanatory factor in accounting for environmental relationships. For long after it finished, JAEP's reputation among research council officials was as a lesson in how not to arrange interdisciplinary research programmes. Some years later, in the aftermath of the 2001 Food and Mouth Disease crisis, the research councils again put together a joint programme of research. This time the Treasury allocated £25 million for the Rural Economy and Land Use (Relu) Programme, which adopted a markedly different approach. Compared to JAEP, where different Councils administered separate funds under the Programme, Relu used its funding as a "single pot". From the outset, the Programme would only fund research projects that in each case involved social scientists working in teams with natural scientists specialising in land and environmental management or biosciences. Relu research was much more likely to be at the edge of, or beyond, comfort zones.

Relu ran from 2003 until 2013 directed by Philip Lowe and his team at Newcastle University. The Programme focused on new questions about rural economy and land use including the potential for new uses of rural land to mitigate climate change and the promotion of food quality and supply chain innovation. It also sought to dissolve the sharp distinctions between the producers and users of knowledge and between the scientific process and application of research results. It helped demonstrate the need and scope for change in the institutional structures and practices that reinforce expert and disciplinary divides and hinder the ability of research to address complex sustainability problems.[14] It illustrated to the research councils the value of interdisciplinary research, equipping them with insight into the techniques for enabling this approach. Relu went on to influence the design of several major new research programmes, as well as processes of interdisciplinary research commissioning, assessment and decision making. Academic research projects into the environmental challenges around food, farming and land use are now more likely to routinely involve collaboration across academic disciplines. This is particularly useful when it comes to understanding the relationship between technologies, social and economic processes, and impacts on the biosphere.

The UK research councils are currently funding the "Transforming UK Food Systems for Health and Environment" Programme led by BBSRC, but also involving the ESRC, NERC and others. This £47.5 million research programme is unfolding over three phases, and while research projects can be led by any discipline, following Relu's example they must integrate both social and natural sciences. Two phases of funding by the Science and Technology Facilities Council have funded a "Network Plus" to bring together researchers from different disciplines with industry in the agri-food sector to provide a stimulus for collaboration and innovation.[15] In autumn 2021, a call was issued for a further "Network Plus" initiative to develop a research network to focus specifically on net zero and the sustainability of the UK agri-food system. Again, an explicit objective is to synthesise insights and perspectives across the natural and social sciences and engineering. A central concern is the development and exploration of new technologies to either enhance productivity or reduce detrimental environmental impacts within the agri-food system.[16]

Socio-technical Systems and Technological Change

Today's high-emissions agri-food system is a socio-technical system that has evolved in profound ways over the past century. The technologies of agricultural production and food manufacturing and distribution have played a vital and transformational role in this evolution and will play an important role in the emissions reduction pathway to net zero. Technologies here means both the technical artefacts, but also the practices, knowledges and organisational forms that go with them, the hardware and the software. The technologies of the agri-food system have not developed on their own or separate from the social world of institutions and politics. The geographer David Harvey writes of what he calls the "fetish of technology", rooted in the tendency to endow technologies with powers they do not have, causative powers such as the ability to solve social or environmental problems, generate economic growth, improve the quality of life.[17] The fetish of technology leads to technological determinism and a misplaced confidence that it is essentially in the technological realm that environmental issues like climate change will be "solved". Technological determinism assumes that technical forces determine social and cultural change. It assumes we have a problem with greenhouse gas emissions from the food and farming system simply because of the technologies that have come to be used in food production and manufacturing. As a counterpoint to technological determinism, the social constructionist perspective starts from the view that social and cultural forces determine technological change and social interests define and give meaning to technical artefacts. It assumes we have the technologies in farming and the food system today simply because of social processes that have fostered and stimulated their production and adoption. An intermediate, but more complex, perspective is that the social world shapes and is shaped by technologies. The social world is never wholly social but is influenced by the technologies in use and likewise, the technological world is never wholly technical but bears the imprint of social, economic and institutional values and preoccupations. As Bruno Latour has put it, technology is society made durable.[18]

Work in the history and sociology of science and technology has traced the evolution of technological systems, which include physical artefacts, but also institutions, practices and knowledge. Because systems include the physical and the social or organisational, they are often called socio-technical systems.[19] Components of socio-technical systems interreact and their characteristics derive from the system. That is to say, the organisation and management structures within technological systems often reflect the character of functioning hardware. Conceptualising the modern agri-food system as a socio-technical system opens a way of thinking about how this system came into being and evolved, and what were the key socio-technical processes that shaped this system over time. This provides a richer starting point for considering the key challenges in changing diet and food consumption, changing land uses between food production and carbon sequestration, and changing production practices to reduce emissions. This conceptual approach to technological systems is inspired by the work of Thomas Hughes,[20] an American historian of technology who produced influential studies of the development of electric power networks in the United States and Europe in the late nineteenth and early twentieth century.[21] He argued that the history of technology should be understood as the history of interconnecting socio-technical systems within which technological change comes to evolve along particular technological trajectories.

Hughes highlights how the interaction between technological systems and society varies over time. Systems build up acquired skills and knowledge, special-purpose techniques and artefacts, expensive physical infrastructures and organisational bureaucracies. Technological development is often patterned in the form of a *technological regime* or a *technological paradigm*, similar to Thomas Kuhn's notion of scientific paradigms.[22] A regime or paradigm forms an "entire constellation of beliefs, values, techniques and so on shared by the members of a given [scientific] community".[23] A technological regime contains a dominant definition of the relevant problem that must be tackled, the tasks to be fulfilled, a pattern of inquiry, the material technology to be used, and types of basic artefacts to be developed and improved. Technological regimes or paradigms help structure or channel innovation and so give rise to *technological trajectories*. This means that existing technologies provide an important set of preconditions for new technologies, although existing technology does not necessarily determine innovation.[24] As technological systems become larger, more complex and more established, so they seem to gather momentum. The system becomes less shaped by and more shaping of society.[25] As Hughes puts it:

> Technological systems, even after prolonged growth and consolidation, do not become autonomous; they acquire momentum. They have a mass of technical and organisational components; they possess direction, or goals; and they display a rate of growth suggesting velocity. A high level of momentum often causes observers to assume that a technological system has become autonomous.[26]

Brian Arthur, who trained as an electrical engineer before shifting to work on economic history and technological change, argues that, in essence, "technology is a programming of nature".[27] He writes of structural deepening of technological systems and technological "lock in" where it becomes increasingly difficult to shift from one technological paradigm to another. (Economists talk of "increasing returns to adoption" as a similar phenomenon.) Crucial for our analysis of the agri-food system is to understand how technologies, technological systems and paradigms evolve, how they become obdurate and constraining, and how these constraints might be overcome by new rounds of innovation and technological development.

John Urry explores the key socio-technical systems of the twentieth century that underpin what he calls "high carbon lives" that include systems of electric power generation, the growth in production and use of the "steel-and-petroleum car", suburban housing and transport systems, electricity-based information and communication technology systems, and the growth of "beyond the neighbourhood" leisure and retail. His particular focus is on "how people have become habituated to social practices which presuppose high carbon forms of producing … goods and services".[28] Understanding the system effects and prevailing ideologies within socio-technical systems is a vital precursor to advancing change. Over the last decade, literature has developed on sustainability transitions – the condition and dynamics of socio-technical systems transitioning to a more sustainable basis.[29] Regimes endure because key actors remain committed to them and they are stabilised by various lock-in mechanisms. Shared mindsets and taken-for-granted beliefs and regulatory institutions also contribute to inertia.[30] Accelerating socio-technical transitions are seen to involve three mutually reinforcing processes: increasing momentum of niche innovations; weakening of existing systems; and the strength of external pressures. Transitions can also be accelerated by actively phasing out existing technologies and systems that lock-in emissions.

In addressing climate change, it has often seemed that efforts at socio-technical transformation have faced an overwhelmingly uphill struggle against the forces of neoliberalism that shape and often dominate debates about how just about every issue should be dealt with. Brian Arthur, writing over a decade before Covid, expresses caution about the potential for systems revolutions. "A revolution does not arrive until we reorganise our activities … around its technologies, and until those technologies adapt themselves to us. For this to happen, the new domain must gather adherents and prestige. It must find purposes and uses … This time is likely to be decades, not years, and during this time the old technology lives on".[31] Nevertheless, shocks to systems do come along and bring "malleable moments",[32] when more profound change and radical futures can be imagined and advanced. Milton Friedman, for example, wrote, "Only a crisis – actual or perceived – produces real change" going on to add that when a crisis does occur, the real change that follows is often heavily shaped by what sorts of ideas are "lying around", like solutions waiting for a problem.[33] It is an open question whether the global Covid pandemic that unfolded in 2020 or the crisis triggered by war in Ukraine in 2022 will bring such a malleable moment. Covid did bring profound change in governmental action on an unprecedented scale. As Adam Tooze puts it, some "very middle-of-the-road politicians ended up doing very radical things", including Joe Biden's $1.9 trillion economic stimulus package in the United States.[34] As a result, more people are exploring the ways that Covid unsettled some core underpinning assumptions about the relationship between the state, the individual and our previously taken-for-granted ways of everyday life.[35]

Optimistic visions of transformational socio-technical innovation can be found among writers who point to the capacity and potential of the state to orchestrate and stimulate purposeful innovation and technological change. For example,

Mariana Mazzucato draws on the experience of the US space missions of the 1960s that put a man on the moon to highlight how the careful coordination of public and private sector efforts can generate spectacular technological innovation. Her argument, based on an analysis of policies to support innovation, is that there is a need to rethink the capacities and role of government to help tackle the biggest social and economic problems of our time such as climate change. She argues that the Covid crisis provided a litmus test of the capacity of states and public agencies to innovate and invest in social goods and services such as developing vaccines and rapidly expanding production of personal protective equipment and switching to online learning in schools, colleges and universities. Forty years of neoliberal government had promoted the idea that governments should take a back seat and only act to fix problems when they arise, and this had led to weakened capabilities and loss of institutional memory. To address the climate challenge requires "a massive rethink of what government is for and the types of capabilities and capacity it needs".[36] She argues:

> Far from retrenching to the role of being at best fixers of market failures and at worst outsourcers, governments should invest in building their muscle in critical areas such as productive capacity, procurement capabilities, public-private collaborations that genuinely serve the public interest, and digital and data expertise.[37]

Debates about the transition to net zero inevitably involve competing visions of the future and prescriptions for how best to evolve socio-technical systems to reduce the risk of catastrophic climate change. The future is placed at the very centre of attention although perspectives on how far governments can actively intervene to direct matters vary widely.[38] The climate crisis has generated renewed interest in modelling future scenarios, a central technique in the age of climate change. In turn, a critical social science of futures analysis has developed building on a tradition in sociology that dates back at least 50 years[39] Many organisations involved in climate science and policy have developed sets of future scenarios to help frame and structure thinking about responding to climate change and reducing emissions. These exercises find it notoriously difficult to identify disruptive technological changes and events (such as global pandemics, for example). They nevertheless provide rich sources of material for social scientists in understanding contrasting visions of the role of individuals vis-à-vis states, markets and institutions, along with ideas of the possible and plausible social, political and technological changes. They also reveal changes in the "ownership of the future" and the ethics of who acts and for whom when it comes to portraying future options and capacity for change.[40] One difficulty in futures analysis is to be able to identify current prevailing social and political norms that can often become so deep-rooted and taken for granted that they can lack visibility. Included among these is neoliberalism as a way of understanding the relationship between the state, markets and individuals. It is to the concept of neoliberalism and countervailing ideas of cosmopolitanism that we now turn.

Neoliberalism and Cosmopolitanism

Neoliberalism is best understood as "a theory of political economic practices that proposes that human well-being can be best advanced by liberating individual entrepreneurial freedoms and skills within an institutional framework characterised by strong private property rights, free markets and free trade".[41] It has become a doctrine that market exchange is an ethic in itself and is capable of acting as a guide for all human action. From a neoliberal perspective, the role of the state is to create and preserve an institutional framework suitable for facilitating enterprise and entrepreneurship with market arrangements favoured as much as politically practicable. Where markets do not exist, neoliberal orthodoxy is to seek to establish them. Beyond this, state intervention in markets should be kept to a bare minimum. This is because, according to the theory, states will always struggle to have sufficient information to second guess market signals such as prices and because powerful interest groups will seek to lobby the state and distort state actions and markets to serve their own purposes. Neoliberalism is built on a fundamental faith in individuals and businesses as rational, welfare-maximising actors and a profound and fatalistic suspicion of the world of politics and public administration to determine the best outcomes for people and places. There has been "an emphatic turn" towards neoliberalism in political-economic practices across much of the world since the 1970s.[42] The 1980s economic reforms of Ronald Reagan and Margaret Thatcher were pivotal in this shift. Neoliberal reforms brought economic deregulation, privatisation and the withdrawal of the state from areas of social provision. In agriculture and food, neoliberalism has meant pressures to reduce public subsidies to the farming industry, the withdrawal of the state from funding much near-market agricultural and food research and the privatisation of formerly public sector advisory services. It has also meant the paring back and hollowing out of many of the public agencies responsible for the monitoring and regulation of the environmental and health aspects of food and farming. Neoliberal ideology is pervasive because its advocates hold senior and influential positions across governments and the public sector, including in think tanks, the media, universities, key state institutions and international organisations such as the World Bank and World Trade Organisation. Part of its power derives from the fact that its central tenets have become so established and "common sense" that they become taken for granted and no longer appear ideological by its exponents.

A key feature of neoliberalism has been its universalising mode of discourse that has provided a foundation for public policies across the world. The establishment of neoliberalism as a seemingly hegemonic worldview has coincided with the revolution in information technology and increasing global interconnectedness. A neoliberal approach to economic and political practices, coupled with the ability to move money and information around the world in an instant, has created a sense of a "flat world", with a freer and almost frictionless ability to do business just about anywhere.[43] Identities, cultures and economic prospects of people all around the world have the appearance of becoming increasingly interconnected. What Manuel

Castells calls the network society has played its part in helping portray globalisation and neoliberalism as an inevitability.[44] Famously, Tony Blair in 2005 claimed that to argue about globalisation made as much sense as arguing whether autumn should follow summer.[45] Likewise, numerous scholarly papers and blogs have posed the question, "are we all neoliberals now?"

Of course, neoliberalism has its critics, but they are far less likely to be in powerful positions than its exponents. The inequalities generated between winners and losers across most advanced economies have become increasingly marked and visible and bring with them political pressures in some parts of the world.[46] Limited and highly unequal improvements in health, wellbeing and living standards among large proportions of populations raise questions about the success of neoliberalism even on its own terms.[47] The ability to move manufacturing jobs around the world has caused significant social disruption and dislocation and it has become clear that the world has only become "flatter" for money, corporate finance, and the wealthy. From his interest in the power dynamics of spatial relationships, Harvey writes "all universalising projects, be they liberal, neoliberal, conservative, religious, socialist, cosmopolitan, rights-based or communist, run into serious problems as they encounter the specific circumstances of their application".[48]

A purist neoliberal view that the state's only significant role, apart from providing security, should be in creating markets and maintaining competition implies that the response to climate change ought to be to establish a price for carbon and create carbon markets. However, we are some distance from this purist view, and it is widely recognised that states will need to do much more than this. Nevertheless, making the case for reform to our everyday high-carbon forms of living for the sake of the global climate can be difficult because climate change turns the prevailing politics of much of the last century on its head. It is a politics directed at lower consumption of goods and services for one's own social group for the sake of others now and in the future. It is then a form of what has been called cosmopolitan politics or cosmopolitanism that has developed over the last two decades as a counterbalance to, and critique of, neoliberalism.[49] Sociologist Ulrich Beck developed a cosmopolitan vision. He argued that "the human condition has itself become cosmopolitan"[50] through the globalisation of politics, economic relations, communications and environmental risks.

> Cosmopolitanism has ceased to be merely a controversial rational idea … it has left the realm of philosophical castles in the air and has entered reality. Indeed, it has become the defining feature of a new era, the era of reflexive modernity, in which national borders and differences are dissolving and must be renegotiated.[51]

Beck argues that the interrelatedness of people and populations across the globe, "a global sense of boundarylessness", requires a cosmopolitan perspective and cosmopolitan politics.[52] Cosmopolitanism implies an empathy and connection between people, places and societies, often between distant others. Its philosophical roots lay in the writings of Immanuel Kant. "By what set of institutional arrangements might all the inhabitants of planet earth hope to negotiate, preferably in a peaceful manner, their common occupancy of a finite globe?"[53] This is the question at the heart of the cosmopolitan quest.

Cosmopolitanism became widely debated in the first decade of the twenty-first century among social scientists and political theorists.[54] Beck identified the underpinnings of the cosmopolitan outlook, including the rising awareness of the experience of crisis in world society and the interconnectedness of experience through the globalisation of risks such as climate risk. At the same time, there has been increasing recognition of, and curiosity about, differences in culture and in social identities. Associated with these two trends is the principle of cosmopolitan empathy and perspective-taking. Nevertheless, because of the implausibility of living in a single world society without borders, there remains a compulsion to redraw old boundaries and rebuild old walls, but local, national, ethnic and religious cultures penetrate and intermingle with cosmopolitan cultures. "Cosmopolitanism without provincialism is empty, provincialism without cosmopolitanism is blind", Beck argued.[55]

The EU was widely pointed to as a cosmopolitan construction, designed to prevent military conflict among previously warring nations through economic integration and Beck was almost evangelistic about the European tradition of cosmopolitan openness to otherness and tolerance of difference.[56] Harvey, however, points out that the EU can equally be seen as a neoliberal construct. He criticises the new cosmopolitans for their ambiguous position on the role of the nation-state and for their lack of consideration of geographical differences but is less antithetical to a form of cosmopolitanism rooted in the thinking and practices of social movements opposed to neoliberalism, a form of "globalisation from below".[57] Cosmopolitanism has, of course, been challenged by politicians from the political Right, especially since the rise of the nativist populism around Brexit and Trump. Former UK Prime Minister Theresa May has been widely quoted as saying at her party's 2016 conference "if you believe you are a citizen of the world you are a citizen of nowhere".[58]

Cosmopolitanism has been deployed by social scientists considering the social and political implications of climate change.[59] Increasingly global media and scientific institutions help generate the sense of climate change as a common global issue. By its very nature, climate change means causes in some places have consequences in others. Cosmopolitanism as a political philosophy and social force is therefore seen by some to go hand in hand with the increasing global understanding and experience of climate change. Mike Hulme argues that climate change "effortlessly transcends boundaries and categories and is making cosmopolitans of us all".[60] In transcending and dissolving boundaries, climate change is "doing significant work in extending and deepening the cosmopolitan perspective".[61]

Isabelle Stengers, a philosopher of science, writes of the need for a "cosmological space" where continuous dialogue between every possible worldview can take place. Concerned that scientific practice requires that scientists act as if their approaches are the only inherently rational and objective method, she advocates for *Cosmopolitics* where conventional scientific practice is worked through with other experiential ways of knowing.[62] The implications of Stengers' *Cosmopolitics* are that the place of scientific knowledge and practice must be continually opened up and reconceptualised. In her manifesto, *Another Science is Possible*, she implores scientists to accept that their concern for the "facts" must also embrace the ways these facts come to matter to others.[63] Her cosmopolitical notion of "slow science" goes far beyond conventional models of public engagement with science to recognise the distributed nature of expertise. She suggests science cannot race ahead of social interests but should, more modestly, engage openly and honestly with an intelligent public. A form of cosmopolitanism can therefore be found at the heart of recent critiques of the scientific method and philosophy.

Cosmopolitanism, defined as the overriding loyalty to and concern with the welfare of humanity as a whole, has evolved into a whole host of cosmopolitanisms across academic disciplines and various times and places.[64] While the concern for and empathy with others remains at the heart of the idea, the proliferation of cosmopolitanisms has done little to help the coherence of the idea as an alternative to neoliberal orthodoxies. Indeed, when it comes to the question of how, specifically, to address climate change, the neoliberal narrative remains a dominant one. The Covid crisis may have unleashed a cosmopolitan impulse as economies locked down and people stayed at home for the sake of each other but, in the UK and elsewhere, since the pandemic's first wave, the emphasis has been on striving to return economic activity to as near to pre-pandemic normal as possible, with the return of international tensions around the distribution of vaccines, trade disputes and defence and security matters.[65] Climate change and the transition to net zero is still going to require that individuals, businesses and governments change the way they do things. The extent to which this is to be achieved within a neoliberal context that is a continuation of the pre-Covid world or is one infused with a stronger cosmopolitan ethic remains to be seen. Much depends upon the extent to which Covid and the climate crisis are shifting prevailing notions of the legitimate scope of state power and how governments govern the conduct of their citizens. It is the question of how conduct might be managed and governed that we now turn.

Governing Populations: Nudging and Behaviour Change

It is national governments that signed the Paris Agreement and Glasgow Pact and committed to reducing greenhouse gas emissions and it is governments that will be responsible for the transition to net zero. How populations are governed is the focus of a body of thought inspired by Michel Foucault's writings on "governmentality", by which he meant both the rationalities and the art of government, or the conduct of conduct.[66] The fundamental question concerns how the state thinks about and reflects upon the legitimate scope of government in regulating or governing the conduct of others.[67] Governmentality refers to the way the state problematises life within its borders and acts in response to these problematisations. Foucault characterises the state as an assemblage of governing rationalities. In order to govern, the state has to employ forms of calculation and representation that help render problems visible and establish goals. What might seem mundane and ubiquitous techniques of collection and computation of statistics, for example, become much more central to understanding state power and influence. Foucauldian scholars of governmentality identify a shift from the liberalism of the nineteenth century to what they call the advanced liberalism of the mid-twentieth century onwards. Where under liberalism, states sought to govern *through* society, that is governing from a social point of view, under advanced liberal rule the state employs rationalities of competition, accountability and consumer demand.[68] "It does not seek to govern through 'society', but through the regulated choices of individual citizens, now construed as subjects of choices and aspirations to self-actualisation and self-fulfilment".[69] In other words, under advanced liberalism, states seek to govern through instrumentalising the self-governing properties of individuals and institutions.

Human behaviour is important in the response to climate change, whether this be around travel, shopping or diet. Conventionally, the knowledge base supporting government thinking on the behaviour of citizens and consumers is informed by economic models that assume perfect information and rational decision-making. However, as Urry points out, "most of the time, most people do not behave as individually rational separate economic consumers maximising their individual utility from the basket of goods and services they purchase ... People are rather creatures of social routine and habit, but also of fashion and fad".[70] An economistic conception of "individual behaviour" has underpinned a whole industry of academic social scientists and think tanks dedicated to better understanding "behaviour change",[71] and Prime Minister David Cameron famously established a "Nudge Unit" dedicated to harnessing behavioural science within policymaking.[72]

The influence of behavioural science upon public policy can be traced to the emergence of the new behavioural economics in the 1970s and a set of dialogues between economists and psychologists around the rationality of human decision-making.[73] The publication in 2008 of a book by two economists, Richard Thaler and Cass Sunstein, titled *Nudge,* helped popularise the new behavioural economics. The philosophy of the approach is one of libertarian (or "soft") paternalism. It embraces the insights of marketing psychology which show that it is possible to influence people to make desirable choices without having to coerce them, while at the same time recognising that there are barriers to rational decision making that suggest the need for some paternalist intervention by government. In the language of "nudge", the approach requires policy interventions to alter the "choice environments" (or "choice architectures") within which individuals make decisions. Crucially, choice environments are not neutral or accidental outcomes of the evolution of society. Rather, they have been designed by commercial or other interests "in ways that make it very difficult to make choices that serve our long-term interests".[74] For Thaler and Sunstein, a nudge is:

> [a]ny aspect of the choice architecture that alters people's behaviour in a pre-
> dictable way without forbidding options or significantly changing their eco-
> nomic incentives. To count as a mere nudge, the intervention must be easy or
> cheap to avoid. Nudges are not mandates. Putting the fruit at eye level counts
> as a nudge. Banning junk food does not.[75]

New insights from behavioural science began to be picked up by think tanks during the 1990s and by the New Labour government, particularly through the work of the Cabinet Office Strategy Unit and key figures such as Geoff Mulgan and David Halpern.[76] At that time, economics was a much more significant influence upon national policymaking than psychology. Conventional (neoclassical) economic perspectives on understanding human behaviour pervaded government and were formalised through the role of economic analysis and expertise within the civil service. These new approaches to behaviour change reflect a deep sense of caution about public policy to change behaviour. For example, when the Cabinet Office published its first review of the literature on changing behaviour, Halpern described how Number 10 "freaked out" about it.[77] There were acute sensitivities around the question of disincentivising the consumption of unhealthy foods, for example, and it was common for the right-wing media to whip up controversy about the government even considering intervention in such matters. Prime Minister Tony Blair was, according to Halpern, "very wary" of being accused of " nanny statism".[78] Influential in the media in whipping up controversy about the "nanny state" was a young journalist on *The Daily Telegraph* and then *The Spectator*, Boris Johnson.[79] Despite Prime Ministerial queasiness, senior civil servants across government were increasingly interested in new approaches to behaviour change, especially in the spheres of health and environment. A cross-Whitehall group was established by the Department for Environment, Food and Rural Affairs and research and reviews were produced across Whitehall and among think tanks. The first comprehensive guide to influencing behaviour was commissioned in 2009 and published in 2010.[80] With the change of government in 2010, behaviour change became a more prominent and formalised part of government under the Conservative-led Coalition Government of 2010–2015 and the Behavioural Insights Team (or "Nudge Unit") was established.[81]

The "Nudge Unit" seems an archetypical example of Foucault's governmentality under advanced liberalism. Instead of the direct exercise of state power through the law, the governmental power of "nudge" is realised through the re-engineering of choice architectures, leaving citizens to exercise their "free will". The approach has been adopted by both left and right and its adoption is less a shift from one political ideology to another and more a shift in knowledge about decision-making that enabled this social science knowledge to be brought into policymaking. Behaviour change policies are essentially an expression of neoliberalism, although the relationship between behaviour changes and neoliberalism is an ambiguous one. "Paternalism" is essentially seen as a bad thing with neoliberal governments keen to avoid being seen as telling citizens what to do. Nevertheless, there is the desire to "govern temptation" to do things that cause an individual or collective harm. Thus, behaviour change offers a more subtle, or timid, approach. New Labour politicians were reportedly more comfortable being more paternalistic (or regulatory) when it came to smoking compared to food. This is perhaps because smoking poses health risks not only to the smoker but also to those around them. A House of Lords inquiry into behaviour change concluded that a weakness of the approach was its focus on individuals when often what is required is change among whole populations.[82] A further set of criticisms came from sociologist Elizabeth Shove who points out that the behaviour change approach – what she calls the "ABC" of attitude, behaviour, choice – does not address the broader socio-technical systems within which people's everyday lives are embedded. She argues that

> understanding social change is in essence a process of characterising and analysing the emergent qualities and characteristics of different types of sociotechnical configurations. In the present context the crucial point is that history matters, generating pockets of stability and pathways of innovation and effectively shaping behaviour in ways that figure not at all, or not at all explicitly, in the ABC.[83]

Conclusions

This brief tour through science and technology studies, neoliberalism, cosmopolitanism, governmentality and nudging brings us to the question of how to make sense of the challenge for government, business and scholars posed by the commitment to reduce greenhouse gas emissions including from the seemingly problematic food and farming sectors. This review highlights four key issues for the conceptual and analytical approach to the study. *First*, the problem of greenhouse gas emissions from food and farming is manifest in physical and environmental processes resulting from farming practices, food manufacture, distribution and consumption. While the social and political framing of problems can have a significant bearing on how they are analysed and addressed, understanding the nature of the climate change problem for the agri-food system requires knowledge and insight into matters of natural science and social science. Furthermore, social science needs to be broader than just the economics that has until very recently tended to dominate thinking and policy debates about societal change to reduce emissions.

Second, reducing greenhouse gas emissions involves adaptations in a complex socio-technical system, the agri-food system, that has evolved over the decades. The contemporary agri-food system can be understood in terms of its technological paradigms and trajectories, including the ways that socio-economic forces have shaped their development over time. Technological momentum can be a key feature of large, sophisticated and well-established socio-technical systems and the processes underpinning this momentum, whether they be social, technical or ideological, requires some understanding. In short, to change direction and bring a marked reduction in emissions requires a clear understanding of how the contemporary agri-food system has evolved into its current form and, ideally, a conceptual model of system transformation.

Third, the state has a vital role in leading and facilitating the transition to a net zero world, but our conception of the legitimate scope of state action has been heavily shaped by several decades of neoliberal ideology that has at times struggled to accommodate the need for collective action and regulation to combat climate change. While a cosmopolitan ethic can be identified as a counterpoint to neo-liberalism, this does not have the cogency and coherence required to offer a pro-grammatic vision for collective climate action. Post-Covid, we still live in a world where neoliberal models of the legitimate scope for state action prevail, and any analysis of the options and potentials for change has to deal explicitly with taken-for-granted assumptions about economic and environmental behaviour among individuals and firms.

Fourth, how governments conceive of the range of options open to them in tackling climate change is contingent, can vary over time and space and is itself a useful subject of analysis. The seeming "rolling back" of the state has had the effect of simply introducing new forms of governing conduct. Neoliberalism does not mean less government but brings new and particular forms of gov-ernment that serve neoliberal interests. The Covid crisis brought radical shifts in the scope of state action to control populations and manage the conduct of conduct. Thus far, however, other approaches to individual behaviour change have been dominated by a timid approach to "nudging" behaviour, rooted in a neoliberal conception of rational economic decision-making. An approach to behaviour change is required that embraces much more than the individual, and incorporates families, farms, businesses large and small and government, indeed whole socio-technical systems.

Notes

1 Steffen, W. *et al.* (2020) The emergence and evolution of Earth System Science. *Nature Reviews Earth and Environment* 1, 54–63.
2 Stern, N. (2007) *The Economics of Climate Change: The Stern Review*. Cambridge University Press; see also Stern, N. (2009) *A Blueprint for a Safer Planet: How to Manage Climate Change and Create a New Era of Progress and Prosperity*. London: Bodley Head.
3 Urry, J. (2011) *Climate Change and Society*. Cambridge: Polity Press.
4 See Murcott, A. (ed.) (1998) *The Nation's Diet: The Social Science of Food Choice*. London: Longman.
5 Urry (2011); Urry, J. (2016) *What Is the Future?* Cambridge: Polity Press.
6 See Hulme, M. (2009) *Why We Disagree About Climate Change: Understanding Controversy, Inaction and Opportunity*. Cambridge University Press; Giddens, A. (2009) *The Politics of Climate Change*. Cambridge: Polity.
7 Symons, J. (2019) *Ecomodernism: Technology, Politics and the Climate Crisis*. Cambridge: Polity Press.
8 See Symons (2019).
9 Hulme (2009).

10 Whatmore, S. (2009) Mapping knowledge controversies: science, democracy and the redistribution of expertise. *Progress in Human Geography* 33, 587–98, p. 588; see also Lane, S. *et al.* (2011) Doing flood risk science differently: an experiment in radical scientific method. *Transactions of the Institute of British Geographers* 36, 15–36.

11 Mann, M. (2021) *The New Climate War: The Fight to Take Back Our Planet.* London: Scribe.

12 Whatmore, S. (2002) *Hybrid Geographies: Natures, Cultures, Spaces.* London: Sage; Murdoch, J. (2001) Ecologising sociology: actor-network theory, co-construction and the problem of human exemptionalism. *Sociology* 35, 111–33; Murdoch, J. (2006) *Post-structuralist Geography.* London: Sage.

13 Agricultural and Food Research Council, Economic and Social Research Council and Natural Environment Research Council (1994) *Joint Agriculture and Environment Programme: The JAEP Report.* Swindon: The Research Councils.

14 Lowe, P. and Phillipson, J. (2009) Barriers to research collaboration across disciplines: scientific paradigms and institutional practices. *Environment and Planning A* 41, 1171–84.

15 www.stfcfoodnetwork.org/.

16 www.ukri.org/opportunity/build-a-network-to-research-sustainable-agri-food-for-net-zero/.

17 Harvey, D. (2003) The fetish of technology: causes and consequences. *Macalester International* 13, Article 7, pp. 2–30.

18 Latour, B. (1991) Technology is society made durable, pp. 103–31 in J. Law (ed.) *A Sociology of Monsters: Essays on Power, Technology and Domination.* London: Routledge.

19 Bijker, W. *et al.* (eds.) (1987) *The Social Construction of Technological Systems: New Directions in the Sociology and History of Technology.* Cambridge, MA: MIT Press.

20 Hughes, T. (1983) *Networks of Power: Electrification in Western Society, 1880–1930.* Baltimore: John Hopkins University Press; Hughes, T. (1987) The evolution of large technological systems, pp. 51–82 in W. Bijker *et al.* (eds.) (1987) *The Social Construction of Technological Systems: New Directions in the Sociology and History of Technology.* London: MIT Press; Hughes, T. (1994) Technological momentum, pp. 101–14 in M. Roe Smith and L. Marx (eds.) *Does Technology Drive History? The Dilemma of Technological Determinism.* Cambridge, MA: MIT Press.

21 Hughes (1983, 1987).

22 Nelson, R. and Winter, S. (1982) *An Evolutionary Theory of Economic Change.* Cambridge, Mass: Harvard University Press; Dosi, G. (1982) Technological paradigms and technological trajectories: a suggested interpretation of the determinants and directions of technical change. *Research Policy* 11, 147–62; Kuhn, T. (1962) *The Structure of Scientific Revolutions.* University of Chicago Press.

23 Kuhn (1962), p. 175 (also in 1996, p. 175 – 3rd edition).

24 Arthur, W. B. (2009) *The Nature of Technology: What it is and How it Evolves.* London: Penguin.

25 Hughes (1994), p. 108.

26 Hughes (1987), p. 76.

27 Arthur (2009), p. 203.

28 Urry (2011), p. 55; see also Urry (2016).

29 Geels, F. *et al.* (2017) Sociotechnical transitions for deep carbonization. *Science* 357(6357), 1242–44; Köhler, J. *et al.* (2019) An agenda for sustainability transitions research: state of the art and future directions. *Environmental Innovation and Societal Transitions* 31, 1–32.

30 Turnheim, B. and Geels, F. (2013) The destabilisation of existing regimes: confronting a multi-dimensional framework with a case study of the British coal industry (1913–1967). *Research Policy* 42, 1749–67.

31 Arthur (2009), p. 157.

32 Klein, N. (2007) *The Shock Doctrine*. London: Penguin Allen Lane, p. 21.

33 Friedman, M. (1982) *Capitalism and Freedom*. Chicago, IL: University of Chicago Press, p. viii.

34 Tooze, A. (2021) *Shutdown: How Covid Shook the World's Economy*. London: Allen Lane, p. 12.

35 See, for example, Farrar, J. (2021) *Spike: The Virus vs the People*. London: Profile Books; Mazzucato, M. (2021) *Mission Economy: A Moonshot Guide to Changing Capitalism*. London: Allen Lane; Latour, B. (2021) *After Lockdown: A Metamorphosis*. Cambridge: Polity Press; Lord, T. (2021) *Covid-19 and Climate Change: How to Apply the Lessons of the Pandemic to the Climate Emergency*. London: Tony Blair Institute for Global Change, 7 April.

36 Mazzucato (2021), p. xxiv.

37 Mazzucato (2021), p. xxiii.

38 Urry (2016), p. 156.

39 Bell and Wau (1971) *The Sociology of the Future*. New York: Russell Sage; Adam, B. and Groves, C. (2007) *Future Matters: Action, Knowledge, Ethics*. Leiden: Brill, p. 186; Urry (2016).

40 Adam and Groves (2007); Booth, R. (2021) Pathways, targets and temporalities: analysing English agriculture's net zero futures. *Environment and Planning E: Nature and Space* (Online first).

41 Harvey, D. (2005) *A Brief History of Neoliberalism*. Oxford University Press, p. 2.

42 Harvey (2005), p. 2.

43 Harvey, D. (2009) *Cosmopolitanism and the Geographies of Freedom*. New York: Columbia University Press.

44 Castells, M. (1996) *The Rise of the Network Society*. Oxford: Blackwell.

45 Tony Blair's Labour Party Conference speech, 2005, *Guardian* 27 September, quoted in Tooze (2021), p. 3.

46 Piketty, T. (2014) *Capital in the Twenty-First Century*. Cambridge, MA: Harvard University Press.

47 Savage, M. (2021) *The Return of Inequality: Social Change and the Weight of the Past*. Cambridge, MA: Harvard University Press.

48 Harvey (2009), p. 8.

49 Beck, U. (2000) The cosmopolitan perspective: sociology of the second age of modernity. *British Journal of Sociology* 51, 79–105; Szerszynski, B. and Urry, J. (2002) Cultures of cosmopolitanism. *The Sociological Review* 50, 461–81; Beck, U. (2006) *Cosmopolitan Vision*. Cambridge: Policy Press; Norris, P. and Inglehart, R. (2009) *Cosmopolitan Communications: Cultural Diversity in a Globalized World*. New York: Cambridge University Press; Robbins, B. and Horta, P. L. (2017) *Cosmopolitanisms*. New York University Press.

50 Beck (2006), p. 2.

51 Beck (2006), p. 2.

52 Beck (2006), p. 3.

53 Harvey (2009), p. 77.

54 Beck (2006); Harvey (2009).

55 Beck (2006), p. 7.

56 Beck, U. and Grande, E. (2007) *Cosmopolitan Europe*. Cambridge: Polity; Latour, B. (2018) *Down to Earth: Politics in the New Climate Regime*. Cambridge: Polity Press.

57 Harvey (2009).

58 Her Chief of Staff later reported her frustration that the phrase had been taken out of context and misunderstood – see Barwell, G. (2021) *Chief of Staff: Notes from Downing Street.* London: Atlantic, pp. 21–2.

59 Hulme, M. (2010) Cosmopolitan climates: hybridity, foresight and meaning. *Theory, Culture and Society* 27, 267–76; Urry (2011).

60 Hulme (2010), p. 268.

61 Hulme (2010), p. 268; see also Morgan, K. (2010) Local and green, global and fair: the ethical foodscape and the politics of care. *Environment and Planning A* 42, 1852–67.

62 Stengers, I. (2010) *Cosmopolitics I.* Minneapolis: University of Minnesota Press; Stengers, I. (2011) *Cosmopolitics II.* Minneapolis: University of Minnesota Press.

63 Stengers, I. (2017) *Another Science is Possible: A Manifesto for Slow Science.* Cambridge: Polity.

64 Robbins and Horta (2017).

65 Farrar (2021); Tooze (2021).

66 Foucault, M. (1991) Governmentality, pp. 87–104 in G. Burchell *et al.* (eds.) *The Foucault Effect.* London: Harvester Wheatsheaf.

67 See Rose, N. (1993) Government, authority and expertise in advanced liberalism. *Economy and Society* 22, 283–99.

68 Miller, P. and Rose, N. (2008) *Governing the Present.* Cambridge: Polity Press.

69 Rose, N. (1996) Governing 'advanced' liberal democracies, pp. 37–64 in A. Barry *et al.* (eds.) *Foucault and Political Reason: Liberalism, Neo-liberalism and Rationalities of Government.* London: UCL Press, p. 41.

70 Urry (2011), p. 3.

71 Jones, R. *et al.* (2013) *Changing Behaviours: On the Rise of the Psychological State.* Cheltenham: Edward Elgar.

72 Halpern, D. (2015) *Inside the Nudge Unit: How Small Changes Can Make a Difference.* London: Penguin.

73 Kahnerman, D. *et al.* (eds.) (1982) *Judgement Under Uncertainty: Heuristics and Biases.* Cambridge: Cambridge University Press; Cialdini, R. (1984) *Influence: The Psychology of Persuasion.* New York: Harper Collins.

74 Jones *et al.* (2013), p. 18.

75 Thaler, R. and Sunstein, R. (2008) *Nudge: Improving Decisions about Health, Wealth and Happiness.* London: Yale University Press, p. 6.

76 See Halpern, D. *et al.* (2004) *Personal Responsibility and Changing Behaviour: The State of Knowledge and Its Implications for Public Policy.* London: Cabinet Office Strategy Unit; Jones *et al.* (2013).

77 Quoted in Jones *et al.* (2013), p. 31.

78 Halpern, quoted in Jones *et al.* (2013), p. 32; see also Halpern (2015), pp. 301–2.

79 Purnell, S. (2012) *Just Boris: A Tale of Blond Ambition.* London: Aurum Press, pp. 111–41; see also Johnson, B. (2003) *Lend Me Your Ears: The Essential Boris Johnson.* London: Harper Collins.

80 Dolan, P. *et al.* (2010) *MINDSPACE: Influencing Behaviour through Public Policy.* London: Institute for Government and Cabinet Office.

81 Halpern (2015).

82 House of Lords Science and Technology Committee (2011) *Behaviour Change.* Session 2010–12. London: Stationary Office.

83 Shove, E. (2010) Beyond the ABC: climate change policy and theories of social change. *Environment and Planning A* 42, p. 1278.

3

FOOD AND FARMING IN TWENTIETH-CENTURY BRITAIN

Productivism and Its Aftermath

Introduction

Climate change and its mitigation pose significant challenges for agriculture and food systems across the world. The need to progress towards net zero emissions by 2050 will require a revolution in how food is produced and how land is used. The British agri-food system has been through revolutions before and there are lessons to be learned about how these unfolded and how change was promoted and managed. Between the mid-eighteenth and mid-nineteenth century, British agriculture saw dramatic improvements in output, land productivity and labour productivity. These improvements were associated with significant changes in husbandry including technical change, but also with a more commercial approach to farming as a capitalist business.[1] The repeal of the Corn Laws in the mid-nineteenth century ushered in a laissez faire approach to farming by the Government which left prices and farmers' economic fortunes to the world market. This approach lasted almost a century, despite a long farming depression in Britain from the 1870s to the 1930s. The state gradually began to intervene in agricultural markets and production during the 1930s and at the outbreak of the Second World War the state engaged much more strongly to expand domestic food production. After the war, a very strong and effective model of state-sponsored agricultural modernisation was established that brought about a technological revolution in farming and radically improved productivity. By the 1980s, wheat yields were three times those of the 1930s and cows produced twice as much milk. These far greater yields in the 1980s were delivered by only a fifth of the agricultural workforce of the 1930s, but with much higher greenhouse gas emissions.[2] Agriculture effectively became a ward of the state, and farming practices were not just strongly encouraged but compelled along a particular path. This model, which we will call agricultural productivism, lasted for several decades until it began to be reformed from the 1980s, although

DOI: 10.4324/9781003278535-3

the ideologies associated with it have lasted much longer. Central to Britain's twentieth-century agricultural revolution was the successful promotion of technological change – the adoption of new products, processes and practices.

Technological change in agriculture is not an autonomous process operating outside of social processes and born simply of objective scientific endeavour. As we saw in Chapter 2, technological determinism is a widespread idea, but the development of socio-technical systems always involves social and regulatory choices. The twentieth-century farming revolution did not "just happen". Rather, British agricultural development and technological change in the decades after the 1930s resulted from very particular public policy decisions. The structure of agriculture and changes in farming techniques were actively shaped by a successful alignment of interests between the state, developers of new technologies and farmers. This chapter examines how agricultural productivism was brought into being, how a particular trajectory of technological change was established and promoted and how the adoption of new farming approaches was encouraged and with what implications.

British Agriculture 1900–1939: Productivism's Pre-history

For the first four decades of the twentieth century, the British approach to agriculture and food supply was to import cheap food from across the world. This laissez-faire approach had prevailed for much of the second half of the nineteenth century and was part of a broader model of imperial economic management in which Britain acted as a major market for imported food and primary products, while British industry exported manufactured goods.[3] The First World War brought some limited intervention in domestic food production, but after the war there was a swift return to laissez-faire. The radically different model of agricultural support and development established during and after the Second World War must be seen in the context of this prolonged period of agricultural depression and imperial food preference from the 1850s to the 1930s.

The laissez-faire approach to British food and farming lasted for seven decades following the repeal of the Corn Laws in 1846. It meant that British farmers were paid for the output they produced based on prices determined by the market and were open to competition from produce imported from overseas. This was a highly distinctive model which served British consumers well and existed nowhere else in the world. Cheap food helped keep industrial wage claims down. The commitment to this approach was so strong that even when grain and meat prices fell sharply over the last quarter of the nineteenth century and British farming was plunged into a deep recession, the introduction of tariffs to protect farmers from overseas competition was never seriously considered. The expansion of efficient agricultural production in the New World meant the import of cheap grains into Britain from North America and refrigerated meat and dairy products from Argentina and Australasia. This spelt disaster for British farming which could not compete. Its political influence was in decline too. Far fewer members of Parliament had farming interests in 1900 compared to the 1860s, and as industry and commerce became more politically powerful, British trade policy evolved to operate more in their interests. Farming was simply left to flounder. "What British farmers did with their land and resources, and whether they sank or swam, mattered to few save themselves".[4]

Prior to the great agricultural depression, the incomes of farmers and farmworkers had been broadly comparable with urban workers but then dropped dramatically. The ratio of agricultural to non-agricultural incomes fell to 63 per cent in 1900 and to 61 per cent in 1930. Understandably, farmers and farmworkers left the land in large numbers. The proportion of the national workforce working in agriculture fell from 19.1 per cent in 1871 to just 6.8 per cent in 1931 and agriculture's share of national income fell from 20 to just 4 per cent over the same period.[5] The exodus from the land was helpful as workers were required in the growing towns and cities and cheap overseas food supplies kept the nation fed.

The outbreak of the First World War did not initially have much impact on the pattern of British agriculture and food supply, although a system of County War Agricultural Committees was established comprising local landowners, farmers and farmworkers to co-ordinate central guidance. However, two years of rising prices and the threat to food supply ships from German submarines prompted the Government to step in and subsidise production. The Corn Production Act 1917 provided guaranteed prices to farmers for wheat and oats for the harvests of 1917 and 1918 and for three further years. The guaranteed prices were to ensure that farmers were adequately compensated over a normal crop rotation for the costs of ploughing their grassland and investing in the implements required. Between January 1917 and June 1918, some 1.5 million acres (approximately 600,000 hectares) of permanent grass and 0.5 million acres (approximately 200,000 hectares) of temporary grass were ploughed and planted for arable production.[6] A Royal Commission was established in 1919 to enquire into the economic prospects of the agricultural industry. As a consequence, the Agriculture Act 1920 committed the Government to continue with the system of guaranteed prices for wheat and oats for a further four years to protect farmers against the risk of losses if market prices fell. As grain production expanded after the war market prices dropped and the anticipated spiralling costs of guaranteeing minimum prices became a concern to the British Government. In June 1921, it suddenly repealed the 1920 Act and ceased supporting prices in what became known in twentieth-century farming lore as "the Great Betrayal".[7] Farmers were left to fend on the open market once more and the Government reverted to its pre-war laissez-faire approach. This short-lived bout of interventionism from 1917 to 1921 soon came to feel like an aberration, with Lord Ernle writing in 1925 "nothing seems to me to be more certain in politics than that British agriculture will be neither subsidised nor protected".[8]

With the exception of the introduction of some limited subsidies for sugar beet, the state's role remained limited throughout the 1920s. However, after the economic slump of 1929–32, agricultural policy began a gradual drift into interventionism.[9] Agriculture was seen alongside coal, steel and cotton textiles as an industry in particular difficulty because of the depression and a more general mood of public intervention in economic affairs began to take hold in Britain, echoing the huge interventions in the United States under the New Deal.[10] The methods of intervention to support production in the 1930s were quite different from those that were to follow after the Second World War. The approach centred on the establishment of producer-elected marketing boards for milk, potatoes and hops which began regulating supplies and markets to stabilise prices. Import quotas were imposed for bacon, ham, mutton and beef, and there were experiments with international agreements to regulate supplies of wheat, beef and sugar. Modest price subsidies were gradually introduced for a range of agricultural products, including sugar beet, wheat, barley, oats and fat cattle. Four-fifths of the subsidies paid to farmers in the inter-war years were focussed on sugar beet and wheat and so largely benefited the arable farmers of eastern England, but even with these pre-war intervention measures British farming as a whole remained in a very depressed state.

The first four decades of the twentieth century also saw the early and gradual development of public infrastructure to support agricultural research and development, in part in response to the agricultural depression and a general perception of a rural malaise, and partly reflecting trends elsewhere. In the United States, for example, the Hatch Act of 1888 had set up State Agricultural Experimental Stations and Land Grant Colleges in each state. In Britain, new institutions of agricultural training began to be established.[11] For example, Durham University's College of Science in Newcastle appointed its first chair in agriculture and forestry in 1891 and Harper Adams Agricultural College was established in Shropshire in 1901. In 1908, the University of Oxford established a School of Rural Economy and a Chair to head it. In 1909, a new Development Commission was established to promote rural modernisation and reform. It developed a plan for a system of research centres concentrating scientific research in agriculture across specialist areas which included Rothamsted Experimental Station, Cambridge University, Wye College and the John Innes Institute.[12] A national centre for research in dairying was established based at Reading in 1912, as was the Plant Breeding Institute at Cambridge and a centre for animal nutrition in Aberdeen. A Provincial Advisory System was also established in 1912 with the number of advisors rising from 16 in 1914 to 68 in 1928.[13] The service was intended to promote the findings of scientific research to farmers, but its impact was initially limited, not least because of the continuing financial hardship facing much of the sector left most farmers unable to invest to modernise. In 1930, the Agricultural Research Council (ARC) was established to fund and co-ordinate pure research in agricultural science and it began setting up its own research institutes.[14] Government encouragement for agricultural research prompted American and European chemical companies to become more research-orientated, and during the 1930s, the systematic search for new pesticides began to gather momentum.[15]

Compared with what was to follow, the 1920s and 1930s saw only incremental changes in the public sector shaping of British agricultural science, the development of new technologies and the promotion of innovation and new farming practices. This was coupled with a gradually more interventionist approach to agricultural markets in the 1930s in response to the Great Depression, which reflected trends in state intervention elsewhere, such as the US New Deal. The impact of these preliminary moves and new institutions was modest, however. British agriculture remained largely in the doldrums, there was little capital for investment and technological change was slow.[16] Although tractors had been available for some time and their use was growing rapidly in the United States, there were still almost 700,000 horses being used on British farms in 1940 and only 168,000 tractors as late as 1944.[17]

The Second World War and the Birth of Productivism

The Second World War was pivotal in the development of agricultural productivism in Britain and the bold new framework that actively stimulated farming's twentieth-century revolution. Practices were introduced that became "institutionalised and habitualised" and endured after the war was over.[18] In particular, the war years helped establish an assertively state-led approach to agricultural production, but also regular and routine consultation and close partnership working between the Ministry of Agriculture and the National Farmers' Union.

In 1938, the UK was importing 70 per cent of its food needs, which left the UK population vulnerable to food shortages if imports were disrupted by the German navy. After the outbreak of war, the Government took a lead in directing agriculture, assuming far-reaching control of production and purchasing farm products at fixed prices, so providing farmers with a guaranteed market and prices for their principal products. Food rationing was introduced, and a "dig for victory" campaign launched, with grants paid to encourage farmers to plough up permanent pasture for cropping. The Government's approach was to maintain the calorific value of the national diet and optimise the use of Britain's agricultural resources. This meant prioritising arable crops for direct human consumption such as wheat and potatoes which was around ten times more efficient at producing calories than growing feedstuffs to feed to farm animals for meat.[19]

The First World War system of County War Agricultural Executive Committees (CWAECs) was resurrected to direct farm production and supervise a major expansion of arable cropping. In 1939, only a third of farmland had been ploughed with two-thirds under permanent grass. By 1945, staggeringly, these proportions were reversed. Cropping and livestock programmes throughout the war were reviewed and amended in light of the situation with shipped imports. As imports were increasingly disrupted, so more land was put under the plough to grow food crops for human consumption. Pre-war food imports of 22.9 million tonnes fell to 20.8 million tonnes in the first year of the war and 14.7 million tonnes in the second, reaching a low point of just over 6.1 million tonnes. The pre-war target for ploughing grassland had been 1.3 million acres (526,000 hectares) in the first year, but this was increased to 2 million (809,000 hectares) and then to 2.2 million (890,000 hectares). By the end of the war, the total area of crops and grass had increased by 5.75 million acres (2.3 Mha) compared to 1939, an increase of two-thirds and a breath-taking transformation in agricultural land use.[20]

Grants and guaranteed prices provided the carrot, but the CWAECs could also weald a stick. Committees were empowered to give directions over the cultivation, management or use of agricultural land and, with the consent of the Minister, to take possession of land or terminate tenancies. In 1942, the Committees were given further powers to control livestock production. The powers were formidable, but it was the implied threat from their mere existence that was most effective. They became the "primary instrument of the state" in managing agriculture.[21] The Minister of Agriculture repeatedly emphasised that he wished the Committees to use their powers in full. Compliance with the Direction Orders issued by the Committees was generally high and the system delivered spectacular results in transforming production. The Committees could requisition land or terminate tenancies and between 1940 and 1945 almost 3,000 tenancies were terminated covering almost 250,000 acres (100,000 hectares). In total, the amount of land taken into possession amounted to almost 400,000 acres (157,000 hectares). About half of the requisitioned land was farmed by the Committees themselves, with the remainder let to new tenants.[22] CWAECs were effective because they embodied a sense of patriotic effort during wartime. They included leading and authoritative agriculturalists among their members which gave them a sense of legitimacy and authority. They were able to harness the knowledge of modern science at the time and promoted key new technologies such as milking machines, combine harvesters, pick up balers and grain driers, and effectively ensured that the doctrines of the agricultural modernisation triumphed.[23] In the official history of British agriculture during the Second World War, Keith Murray wrote of:

> an almost crusading enthusiasm to bring about a renaissance in British farming; this applied not merely to landlords and farmers but also to educationalists, research workers and administrators connected with agriculture. Whereas in many other industries the war often entailed the sacrifice of peace-time plans and ambitions, in agriculture it offered an opportunity such as it could never have been given in peace-time to apply new knowledge and to revive the productivity of the land.[24]

The war experience was a formative one for all involved in agriculture. Farming prospered under the stability and security provided by the new system and war conditions reinforced a new unity of purpose. The experience of the depression and the war economy fundamentally altered public and political attitudes towards the relationship between state, economy and society, and led to a new conception of the active role of government in managing the economy including agriculture. By 1944, the Government and farming unions were looking to post-war options and a broad consensus emerged for continuing to protect and support agriculture. This was reinforced in the immediate post-war years when a serious threat of world food shortages left Britain particularly exposed. At the same time, financial difficulties arose with the United States in what became known as the "dollar crisis".[25] Britain found itself facing a shortage of both food and dollars and was unable to buy all its food requirements on the world's markets. To save dollars and help address the massive balance of payments deficit, extra monies were provided to encourage a further wave of domestic agricultural expansion.[26] The experience of the dollar crisis contributed to a whole new perception of British agriculture and the establishment of values of partnership, protection, expansion and modernisation.

> Practices previously seen as "visionary" were now acceptable because the whole understanding of what agricultural policy should be had changed. Gone was the belief that British agriculture should be fairly small, livestock based and dependent on imports of feedingstuffs. It was now accepted that the aim of policy must be to expand agriculture to its limits, regardless of the assumptions of traditional economists. The policy had become unquestionable.[27]

The war also stimulated research into agrochemicals to increase domestic self-sufficiency in food production. Imperial Chemical Industries (ICI) developed 1-napthyl acetic acid (NAA) for its selective weed control properties and its derivative, 2-methyl,4-chlorophenoxyacetic acid (MCPA), was launched in the UK in 1945 as the first scientifically produced selective herbicide.[28] In the United States, NAA's chemical relative 2,4-D was patented in 1944 by AmChem and marketed as "Weedone". The availability of MCPA and 2,4-D in the immediate post-war period helped revolutionise weed control in British cereal cropping and led to significant improvements in yields. Yet, for the chemical revolution to take off, it was not just the development of new chemicals that was required. Farmers also had to be actively encouraged to adopt these new practices, and this required a new policy framework.

Three key pillars of productivism ensured its success in revolutionising farming. These pillars – technological, economic and ideological – underpinned the productivist model and endured from the 1940s to the early 1980s. *First* was the production and active promotion of new agricultural technologies. This required the state-sponsored development of public institutions of agricultural science and close collaboration between the public sector and commercial developers of technologies. In addition, the expansion of the public advisory system was important in providing advice to farmers in the field, but also, crucially, in keeping farm advisors abreast of new technical developments that evolved at pace during the 1950s and 1960s. A *second* pillar was pricing and protection – the economic regulation of the agricultural sector. The 1947 Agriculture Act set the legislative framework for a continued system of guaranteed prices which provided farmers with the financial security to invest in technological change to boost yields, save labour and strengthen profitability. This economic system was supported by the political management of agricultural policy, through a close partnership between government and farming representatives, particularly the National Farmers' Union (NFU), which came to be seen as the archetypal form of corporatism. The *third* pillar of productivism was ideological. It centred on the prevailing perception of what constituted "good farming", an idea that proved potent and became deeply ingrained. This established a moral cause to farm as productively as possible, for the national good, to stave off the balance of payments crisis and to feed the country during the post-war reconstruction – a radical turnaround from the prevailing ideology around farming during the 70 years prior to the war. The ideology pervaded beyond the agricultural policy community. Alongside the 1947 Agriculture Act, the Town and Country Planning Act of the same year provided strong protection for agricultural land, enshrined farmers property rights and placed the Ministry of Agriculture in a key position to protect the land resource for production purposes.[29]

The establishment of the productivist framework after the war must be seen in the context of the experiences of the 1920s and 1930s and as a rejection of the long period of laissez-faire that had prevailed since the 1850s. Farming interests were anxious not to see a repeat of the post-First World War "Great Betrayal" and emphasised the need for confidence and security if farmers were to be asked to invest to modernise. State-supported expansion of agriculture was part of a general international trend in the immediate post-war years, and the experience of food shortages and threat of starvation across much of Europe was one of the reasons for the Marshall Plan to support economic reconstruction.[30] In Britain, the war-time Government had drawn up details of possible legislation for post-war agriculture, and so the incoming 1945 Labour Government was able to adopt a ready-made policy. Farm prices would be set in the light of changing farm incomes compared to other sectors, and the war-time system of guaranteed prices would be continued. Crucially, the Act required that the Government consult farming industry representatives on setting farm prices through an Annual Review process. This meant that it was only the Ministry and NFU's views that really mattered in guiding subsidy levels.[31]

The Government accepted that nothing short of guaranteed markets and prices for all that they could produce would ensure the necessary stability in agriculture to enable farmers to plan and invest in modernisation. However, the *quid pro quo* was that farmers would be expected to strive to maximise efficiency, so that the state would get value for public money. The 1947 Act formalised the requirement that farmers abide by "rules of good husbandry", which were to be enforced through the continuation of the County Agricultural Executive Committees. If farmers were not sufficiently compliant with the modernisation and expansionist approach, they would continue to be liable to supervision orders and, if they failed to improve, notices to quit. This extension of the wartime system of direction and supervision by the state served as a self-disciplining mechanism to encourage (or exhort) farmers to farm in particular ways. The powers tended to only need to be used for "occasional intractable individuals", but their very existence proved potent in shaping behaviour.[32] The powers to issue supervision orders and dispossess farmers remained in place until 1958 and the Committees continued to operate until the early 1970s.

Under this regime of supervision and direction, each farm was visited by two district committee members, accompanied by one or more officials. Assessments were made of crop rotation plans, efficiency of grassland management, use of fertilisers, adequacy of machinery, labour force, yields and output. Farms were graded "A" (good), "B" (fair) and "C" (poor), and efforts were made to persuade those responsible for poor farms improve in particular ways. There were follow-up visits and farmers were urged to avail themselves of the assistance of advisory officers. Farmers were notified in advance if supervision orders were being considered, and supervision orders, once issued, were reviewed annually. Even after the war, the system was applied with some vigour. Between 1947 and 1952, 5,000 farmers were placed under supervision orders and 400 were dispossessed.[33] Indeed, the new Conservative administration in 1952 exhorted the committees to take an even stronger line with supervision orders and dispossessions. The Parliamentary Secretary, Lord Carrington, wrote in the Manchester Guardian, "there is no room for the inefficient farmer, and the county agricultural executive committees will have to take stern action in future to keep up a high standard of husbandry".[34]

The multi-faceted state intervention in agriculture was unprecedented in British history. The emphasis on stimulating production and the adoption of new farming practices set in motion a treadmill of technological change.[35] The Act even set out principles of weed and pest control that were becoming integral to notions of good husbandry. It included a section on "Pest and Weed Control" that contained provisions "for securing the destruction of injurious weeds". In effect, the fight against all types of pest on farmland, including weeds, became embodied in policy, and if farmers did not fulfil their duties to ensure "clean" fields, they risked being placed under supervision orders and dispossessed.

New technologies of government were developed to support the productivist framework. Statistics became crucial in providing a picture of the pattern and pace of modernisation and productivity improvements. During the war, a National Farm Survey had been conducted to help provide a comprehensive picture of the diversity of the farming sector and, through statistical aggregation, to help bring into being the concept of the "national farm".

> The state assumed responsibility for the agricultural industry and sought to guide its development through the use of both sanctions and incentives. This entailed the development of institutions capable of such intervention and the use of government rationalities and mechanisms that would allow the state to develop its own vision of how the industry should look and how it should be governed. This 'look', and the type of governance that it entailed, depended to a large degree upon a representation of the sector derived from statistics.[36]

Considerable new investment was made in agricultural research and education. There was little public expenditure on research before the war, but this rose during the war with the ARC's spending reaching almost £4 million at current prices in 1956/1957, almost £15 million by 1969/1970 and over £80 million by the early

1980s.[37] The number of agricultural scientists employed by the ARC grew significantly from 294 in 1949 to 366 in 1953 and 438 in 1955.[38] And the number of PhDs awarded in agriculture rose rapidly. For example, at the University of Reading, the annual average of PhDs awarded in agriculture rose from 1.4 in the 1930s to 2.8 in the 1940s, 8.9 in the 1950s and 9.6 between 1960 and 1966.[39] There was a significant expansion in the numbers of students studying agriculture in further and higher education. During the war, it had been estimated that around 50 graduates a year had been entering agriculture. By 1957, 2,600 students entered the industry from agricultural education in universities, colleges and farm institutes.[40]

A new National Agricultural Advisory Service (NAAS) was formed in 1946 to encourage the adoption of new practices through the provision of free advice. The NAAS were strongly linked into a network of experimental husbandry farms, ten of which had been acquired by the ARC by the early 1950s covering some 9,000 acres (3,600 hectares).[41] There was a strong sense of the public sector orchestrating the flow of technologies from publicly funded scientific institutes through the advisory system and onto farms. NAAS advisors enthusiastically pursued the latest developments in agricultural science and promoted them widely to farmers.[42] A highly unified approach to technological change, modernisation and raising productivity prevailed, such that "it was very difficult for farmers to farm in any other way even if they wanted to".[43]

New pesticides were an important part of the transformation of arable production and chemical herbicides became seen as the "common sense" route for crop protection. The ARC's herbicide team was reorganised in 1950 into the Unit of Experimental Agronomy and eventually evolved into the Weed Research Organisation (WRO). The WRO grew to enjoy a staff complement of 70 by 1964 and 170 by 1980 (ARC, 1965). The WRO liaised closely with the NAAS, with two senior NAAS officers permanently stationed there to help keep up the flow of up-to-date techniques onto farms via local NAAS advisors.[44] A close relationship thrived between commercial pesticide research and development and the public sector, and there was much interchanging of senior staff.[45] The network of research, development and advice promoting new chemical methods was extremely effective in encouraging adoption.[46] The switch to chemicals was made across much of the western world. Internationally, the agrochemical industry grew dramatically, with the world market for crop protection chemicals increasing from around $700 million in 1945 to around $2,500 million by the early 1960s, $4,500 million in the early 1970s and $10,000 million by 1980 (all at 1979 prices).[47]

British Farming's Twentieth-Century Technological Revolution

In 1951, a Conservative Government replaced Labour and started to strengthen the promotion of efficiency in agriculture. After 1951, additions to price guarantees through the Annual Price Review were usually kept below the increase in the costs of production and were sometimes (in 1954, 1958 and 1960, for example) negative. If farmers were to improve their incomes, they would have to increase efficiency.

Through this "cost-price squeeze" the take up of new technologies which either boosted yields or saved labour became more strongly incentivised.[48] This overall direction of British agricultural policy was pursued through the 1950s and 1960s by Conservative and Labour governments. Policy trends in the 1950s and 1960s, particularly the drift into tariffs on agricultural imports, prepared British agriculture for entry into the European Common Agricultural Policy (CAP) from the early 1970s. National intervention agencies, acting as agents of the European Community, would buy any excess produce at a minimum price and put this surplus into store until it could be released. For the formulators of British agricultural policy, entry into the CAP was, therefore, more a process of continuity rather than one of change and provided an opportunity to compete effectively within a much larger "domestic" market. The Labour Government published a broad policy statement in 1975 entitled *Food from Our Own Resources*, which stated that

> the Government take the view that a continuing expansion of food production in Britain will be in the national interest. It is mainly the cost in sterling terms of alternative supplies from abroad which determines whether expansion of home production is economically worthwhile ... but the objective of Government policy will be to provide farmers with a prospect of stability in their returns at levels encouraging the greater home production which would give the country an insurance against periods of shortage and higher prices.[49]

The transition period for Britain's entry into the European Community ended in 1978. Even then, the policy of agricultural expansion was re-emphasised with the publication in 1979 of *Farming and the Nation*, a White Paper which outlined further expansion over a five-year period, despite evidence of looming European surpluses for most major commodities.[50]

The implications of agricultural productivism for levels of production, farming practices and the structure of the industry were revolutionary. The policy framework also ensured that agriculture became a significant source of greenhouse gas emissions. The total value of British agricultural output increased 40-fold between 1939 and 1989. In real terms, the value of output rose steeply from 1938 to 1955, but then generally flattened off, other than a brief boom in 1973–1974. After the mid-1970s, the prices of farm products fell behind the general rate of inflation, which only served to intensify the quest for saving labour, boosting yields and generally improving productivity.[51] Although the economic context had changed, the industry had by then become locked into a particular technological path.

The average size of farms grew as larger farms expanded and smaller farms were more likely to go out of business. The agricultural workforce almost halved, from around 1.1 million in 1951 to 0.6 million in 1984, largely as a result of mechanisation. The number of horses used on farms declined rapidly after the war and by the mid-1960s they were no longer recorded in the agricultural census. Tractor numbers grew rapidly in the 15 years after the war to over half a million by the early 1960s (Table 3.1) deepening the industry's dependence upon fossil fuels. The

TABLE 3.1 Estimated Number of Agricultural Machines (000)

	1944	1952	1961	1966	1970	1977	1980	1986
Tractors	168	387	512	517	511	519	530	532
Corn drills	94	100	135	124	132			101
Tractor ploughs		99	359	323	308	246	287	258
Combine harvesters	2	17	55	67	66	58	57	55

Source: Marks and Britton (1989), p. 19. Reproduced by permission of the Royal Agricultural Society of England.

use of other agricultural inputs changed radically over the period too. The rapid increase in the use of ammonium sulphate in the 1940s and 1950s had a significant impact on agricultural output. Fertilisers were subsidised up until the mid-1970s and expenditure on them rose from £8 million in 1937–1938 to £51 million in 1950, £325 million in 1975 and £954 million in 1984.[52] The total quantity of nitrogen used on UK farms rose more than five-fold from less than two hundred thousand tons in the late 1940s to over a million tons by the late 1970s.[53] This growth will have also contributed markedly to UK agriculture's growing green-house gas emissions. Likewise, more fossil fuels were needed for farm production as mechanisation continued apace during the late 1960s and 1970s. At current prices, agricultural expenditure on fuel and oil rose ten-fold between 1960 and 1985.[54]

Pesticide use increased exponentially. Between 1942 and 1946, the number of ground crop sprayers in use in England and Wales more than doubled from 1,600 to 3,455. Change accelerated in the 1950s, with a more than five-fold increase in the number of sprayers from 9,330 to 49,075 by 1959. By the late 1970s, the number of sprayers had almost doubled again to 90,000, while over the same period their size and scale had also increased.[55] By the 1960s, herbicides had become the most important of the crop protection chemicals. Their use signalled a turning point in arable cropping in general and especially cereal production. Before the development of herbicides, weeds were managed through crop rotations and cultivations, so that no weed species developed an advantage. When they were first adopted, herbicides were simply incorporated into existing husbandry systems saving the need for manual or mechanical weeding. However, during the 1960s, herbicides began to become a far more integral part of the production process, enabling successive cereal crops to be grown.[56] The move from rotations to more continuous cereal cropping was an important change in arable farming. Herbicides helped transform cereals from a "fouling" crop to a "cleaning" crop. By the late 1960s, "rotation was considered an old-fashioned word" with many believing that "farmers could have an almost complete freedom of cropping so far as weed control was concerned".[57]

The area of cereals grew considerably from 2.3 Mha in 1930 to 3.3 Mha in 1950, and to 4.0 Mha by 1986.[58] More and more cereals were fed to farm animals. As else-where in the European Community, there was a concentration and specialisation of production in the UK which saw an increasing focus on cereals in eastern England

and livestock elsewhere.[59] Indeed, the number of holdings growing cereals almost halved between 1969 and 1989.[60] Although cereal yields per hectare had changed little between 1880 and the Second World War, they improved spectacularly after the war. Average wheat yields grew from 2.81 tonnes per hectare in 1950–1954 to over 6.7 tonnes in 1983–1987. The total wheat harvest grew from 2.6 million tonnes in 1950 to 14.9 million tonnes in 1984, an almost six-fold increase.[61] There were other marked increases in arable crop yields. For example, potato yields averaged 17 tonnes per hectare in 1939, but this had more than doubled by the 1980s.[62] Sugar beet yields improved from around 20 tonnes per hectare in 1939 to almost 50 tonnes by the mid-1980s and the UK's total production of the crop more than doubled over the same period.[63] The UK's annual production of carrots increased more than three-fold from 157,000 tonnes pre-war to over 500,000 tonnes by the 1980s.[64]

Livestock farming saw spectacular improvements in productivity too. Beef and veal production ranged between 600,000 and 700,000 tonnes per annum prior to the Second World War but grew after the war reaching 944,000 tonnes in 1963 and 1,216,000 tonnes by 1975.[65] A key development was the shift from feeding cattle hay to silage and the development of more intensive grazing systems. Silage production is less dependent upon the weather, has major nutritional advantages and involves lower labour costs. Production almost doubled from 4.3 million tonnes in 1962 to 8.3 million tonnes in 1969. It then expanded rapidly during the 1970s and 1980s, reaching over 45 million tonnes by the late 1980s.[66]

Sheepmeat is a major livestock product from British agriculture and the UK is Europe's largest producer. Because of the emphasis on cereals during the war, there was a reduction in sheepmeat production, but by 1966 the sheep population had recovered. The total number of sheep and lambs increased from around 20 million in 1950 to over 35 million by the mid-1980s. Numbers grew with the development of the CAP's Sheepmeat Regime, especially during the 1980s. National production of sheepmeat doubled from around 150,000 tonnes in 1950 to over 300,000 tonnes by the mid-1980s.[67] The productivist period also saw a significant growth in the national pig herd. In 1943, there were only 1.8 million pigs on farms in the UK, but after the war numbers grew to over 3 million by 1951 and trebled to 9 million by 1973.[68] Over time, pig production became more concentrated on a smaller number of specialist farms. In 1969, there were 78,400 holdings with breeding pigs in the UK, but by 1987 this number had dramatically fallen by three-quarters to just 15,700 holdings.[69] Another sector to experience marked concentration and specialisation was poultry production. At the time of the Second World War, chickens were primarily kept for egg production and poultry meat was regarded as an expensive luxury. However, after the introduction of broiler shed systems in the 1950s, an idea imported from the United States, production expanded rapidly and by 1987 amounted to over 1 million tonnes per annum, although production was concentrated on just 2,000 holdings.[70]

Dairying also saw significant structural and technological changes during the productivist period. From 1960 to 1983, the number of dairy cows remained relatively stable at 3.2 million, although production became concentrated into fewer larger herds. The number of holdings on which dairy cows were kept fell by nearly two-thirds in two decades from 132,000 in 1967 to just 50,000 in 1987, and average herd size trebled from 21 cows in 1961 to 61 cows by 1987.[71] Herd management, nutrition and disease control all improved over that period. This meant that milk production improved markedly, more than doubling from around 8,000 million litres before the war to 16,590 million litres in 1983. The output per cow rose from 3,412 litres in 1955–1959 to 4,913 litres in 1985–1987.[72] Dairy cows were increasingly housed inside farm buildings and slurry-based systems replaced farmyard manure systems. As we shall see in Chapter 4, these technological changes led to serious water pollution problems as well as greater greenhouse gas emissions. During the productivist period, capital grants were made available to farmers to help stimulate investment in the modernisation of farm buildings, machinery and land (Table 3.2). Rates were highest for field drainage, and by the 1970s, around 100,000 hectares were being drained each year. Capital grants were particularly helpful in supporting the technical transformation of intensive livestock production and the switch to slurry and silage-based systems of housing and feeding.[73]

The 40 years from 1940 to 1980 saw a revolution in British agriculture, with output increasing sharply and especially in the 20 years from 1945 to 1965.[74] The volume of output did not increase much during the Second World War because the emphasis was on building up national self-sufficiency and switching from livestock towards arable cropping. There were dramatic changes in land use, but essentially increases in arable output were balanced by restrictions in livestock output which were needed to minimise the purchase of animal feed. Once the wartime restrictions were relaxed, British agriculture took a great leap forward. From the late 1940s to the early 1960s, favourable prices and technological change helped raise the volume of output "more rapidly than ever before or since".[75] Using the language of Hughes, a technological system was brought into being bringing with

TABLE 3.2 Capital Grants Available to UK Farmers

Grant scheme	Period of operation	Most common rate of grant
Field drainage	1940–1970	50%
Farm water supply	1941–1970	50%
Silo subsidy	1956–1966	50%
Farm Improvement Scheme	1957–1970	One-third
Small Farmer Scheme	1959–1965	Maximum £1,000
Farm Capital Grant Scheme	1971–1980	30% (50% for drainage)
Farm and Horticulture Development Scheme	1974–1980	25% (60% for drainage)
Agriculture and Horticulture Development Scheme	From 1980	32.5% (50% for drainage)

Source: Brassley *et al.* (2021), p. 180. The rates shown are those most commonly applied. Reproduced by permission of Paul Brassley and Boydell Press.

Such changes often left farmers feeling that their position was being undermined by the new people moving into the countryside.[83] Farm diversification and the conversion of farm buildings meant that many farmers now had new neighbours with quite different perceptions of the function of the countryside. This sometimes led to direct pressure to change their farming practices. More generally, farmers felt that local social change was diminishing their autonomy. Middle-class newcomers often brought with them new values by which farming was increasingly judged by society at large. A sense of alienation and growing frustration developed among a farming community that had seen the goalposts of public policy moved dramatically. The certainties of the productivist era were replaced by the ambiguities of rural and agricultural policies which sought to contain the costs of support, promote farm diversification and strengthen the protection of the rural environment.

Conclusions

The changes in British land-use and agricultural practices in the three decades after the war were profound and probably more significant in scale and scope than those now required to address the challenge of climate change. Agriculture's productivity, resource use and technological character were transformed in this period. However, British agriculture's twentieth-century revolution was not the result of the simple operation of market forces, nor a natural progression along some linear path of progress. Rather, enhanced productivity and efficiency were explicit objectives of public policy and what now might be called a mission-oriented approach to the technological development of a sector.[84] The state played a key and catalytic role in the development of new technologies and in the promotion of the adoption of the latest approaches. Through public financial support for research and development, and via grants, subsidies and advice, farmers were actively encouraged along a very particular path with huge success in terms of productivity growth. Indeed, for almost two decades up until 1958, they could be actively compelled and directed to change their ways and maximise productivity through official edict and legal sanction.

Of course, the technological path along which British agriculture developed has accentuated its contribution to greenhouse gas emissions and climate change. However, this did not begin to come into focus until the 1990s.[85] Before then, a host of other environmental and public health concerns emerged around intensive farming, and the sector became the focal point for an increasingly vociferous critique by environmental pressure groups and campaigners from the 1960s onwards. The various incremental responses to farming's environmental and public health problems contained a range of measures to influence farmers' practices in their fields and farmyards for the sake of the environment, animal health and public health. They have never amounted to a rounded environmental policy for farming of the kind now called for to ensure agriculture and the food system plays its part in the transition to net zero. They do, however, provide a set of lessons about what has worked effectively and what has been less effective in redirecting farming and land-use practices. It is this environmental critique and the vision for a cleaner and greener agriculture that we turn to in the next chapter.

Notes

1 Overton, M. (1996) *Agricultural Revolution in England: The Transformation of the Agrarian Economy 1500–1850*. Cambridge University Press.
2 Brassley, P. *et al.* (2021) *The Real Agricultural Revolution: The Transformation of English Farming 1939–1985*. Woodbridge: Boydell Press, p. 2.
3 Collins, E. (ed.) (2000) *The Agrarian History of England and Wales Volume VII 1850–1914*. Cambridge University Press.
4 Self, P. and Storing, H. (1962) *The State and the Farmer*. London: George Allen & Unwin, p. 17.
5 Self and Storing (1962), p. 17.
6 Whetham, E. (1974) The Agriculture Act 1920 and its repeal—the 'Great Betrayal'. *Agriculture History Review* 22, 36–49.
7 Whetham (1974) reports of interviewing farmers in the early 1970s and finding older men who, unprompted, would go back to the repeal in 1921 of the Corn Production Acts as the cause of great difficulties for themselves or their fathers in the years after the First World War.
8 Quoted in Self and Storing (1962), p. 18.
9 Whetham, E. (1978) *The Agrarian History of England and Wales Volume VIII 1914–1939*. Cambridge University Press.
10 Hamby, A. (2004) *For the Survival of Democracy: Franklin Roosevelt and the World Crisis of the 1930s*. New York: Free Press.
11 Brassley, P. (2000a) Agricultural science and education, pp. 594–649 in E. Collins (ed.) *The Agrarian History of England and Wales Volume VII 1850–1914*. Cambridge University Press.
12 Rogers, A. (1999) *The Most Revolutionary Measure: A History of the Rural Development Commission 1909–1999*. Salisbury: Rural Development Commission, p. 17.
13 Holmes, C. (1988) Science and the farmer: the development of the Agricultural Advisory Service in England and Wales, 1900–1939. *Agricultural History Review* 36, 77–86, p. 77.
14 deJager, T. (1993) The origins of the Agricultural Research Council, 1930–37. *Minerva* 31, 129–50.
15 Achilladelis, B. *et al.* (1987) A study of innovation in the pesticide industry: analysis of the innovation record of an industrial sector. *Research Policy* 16, 175–212; Ward, N. (1995) Technological change and the regulation of pollution from agricultural pesticides. *Geoforum* 26, 19–33.
16 Whetham (1978).
17 Marks, H. and Britton, D. (1989) *A Hundred Years of British Food and Farming – A Statistical Survey*. London: Taylor and Francis, pp. 18–19.
18 Smith, M. (1990) *The Politics of Agricultural Support in Britain*. Aldershot: Dartmouth, p. 88.
19 Murray, K. (1955) *Agriculture – History of the Second World War Series*. London: HMSO, pp. 40–3; see also Collingham, L. (2011) *The Taste of War: World War Two and the Battle for Food*. London: Allen Lane.
20 Murray (1955), pp. 229–31.
21 Short, B. (2014) *The Battle of the Fields: Rural Community and Authority in Britain During the Second World War*. Woodbridge: Boydell Press, p. 56.
22 Murray (1955), pp. 302–3; see also Short (2014), pp. 162–7.
23 Short (2014), p. 152.

24 Murray (1955), p. 339.
25 The United States sought more liberal trading conditions and Britain's trading arrangements became the main target for reform. This was achieved during negotiations over post-war commercial and monetary policy and over the terms of Britain's dollar loan to fund the Labour Government's welfare reforms. The loan, agreed in December 1945, was smaller than had been hoped for in Britain. It was also interest bearing and was dependent on sterling convertibility, sterling balances, import policy and the ratification of the Bretton Woods agreement (see Smith, 1990, pp. 101–03).
26 A Treasury official wrote to the Ministry of Agriculture observing that: "the prospect of a dollar shortage has created the greatest opportunity for British agriculture that has occurred in a time of peace for a hundred years … [W]e are now in the position where agriculture will be under fire for not expanding enough … In these circumstances the time may come when certain advances which have hitherto been regarded as visionary may become practical politics" (quoted in Smith, 1990, p. 108).
27 Smith (1990), p. 108.
28 Achilladelis *et al.* (1987).
29 Marsden, T. *et al.* (1993) *Constructing the Countryside*. London: University College London Press.
30 Brandt, K. (1945) *The Reconstruction of World Agriculture*. New York: Norton; Tracy, M. (1989) *Government and Agriculture in Western Europe, 1880–1988*. Hemel Hempstead: Harvester Wheatsheaf; Steil, B. (2018) *The Marshall Plan: Dawn of the Cold War*. Oxford University Press, pp. 99–100.
31 Smith (1990), p. 109.
32 Self and Storing (1962), p. 112.
33 Self and Storing (1962), p. 238.
34 Quoted Self and Storing (1962), p. 116.
35 Cochrane, W. (1979) *The Development of Industrial Agriculture: A Historical Analysis*. Minneapolis: University of Minnesota Press.
36 Murdoch, J. and Ward, N. (1997) Governmentality and territoriality: the statistical manufacture of Britain's 'national farm'. *Political Geography* 16, 317; see also Short, B. *et al.* (2000) *The National Farm Survey 1941–1943: State Surveillance and the Countryside in England and Wales in the Second World War*. Wallingford: CAB International.
37 Brassley *et al.* (2021), p. 44.
38 Brassley *et al.* (2021), p. 33.
39 Brassley *et al.* (2021), p. 35.
40 Brassley *et al.* (2021), pp. 54–8.
41 Brassley *et al.* (2021), p. 50.
42 McCann, N. (1989) *The Story of the National Agricultural Advisory Service: A Mainspring of Agricultural Revival, 1946-1971*. Ely: Providence Press; Dancey, R. (1993) The evolution of agricultural extension in England and Wales. *Journal of Agricultural Economics* 44, 375–93.
43 Smith (1990), p. 142.
44 Agricultural Research Council (1982) *Weed Research Organisation, Ninth Report, 1980–1981*. Oxford: Agricultural Research Council; McCann, 1989, p. 55.
45 Brassley *et al.* (2021), p. 42.
46 McCann (1989); Dancey (1993).
47 Braunholtz, J.T. (1982) Crop protection: the evolution of a chemical industry, in D. Sharp and T. West (eds.) *The Chemical Industry*. Chichester: Ellis Horwood.
48 Bowers, J. (1985) British agricultural policy since the Second World War. *Agricultural History Review* 33, 66–77.

49 Ministry of Agriculture, Fisheries and Food (MAFF) (1975) *Food from Our Own Resources*, Cmnd. 6020. London: HMSO, Para. 4.

50 MAFF (1979) *Farming and the Nation*, Cmnd. 7458. London: HMSO.

51 Marks and Britton (1989), p. 23.

52 Marks and Britton (1989), p. 103.

53 Royal Commission on Environmental Pollution (1979) *Agriculture and Pollution*, Seventh Report. London: HMSO, quoted in Brassley *et al.* (2021), p. 127.

54 Marks and Britton (1989), p. 106.

55 Ward (1995); Southcombe, E. (1980) Developments in herbicide application, pp. 232–333 in R. Hurd *et al.* (eds.) *Opportunities for Increasing Crop Yields*. London: Pitman.

56 Robinson, D. (1980) The impact of herbicides on crop production, pp. 297–312 in R. Hurd, P. Biscoe and C. Dennis (eds.) *Opportunities for Increasing Crop Yields*. London: Pitman, p. 299.

57 Elliott, J. (1980) Weed control: past, present and future – a historical perspective, pp. 285–95 in R. Hurd *et al.* (eds.) *Opportunities for Increasing Crop Yields*. London: Pitman, p. 288.

58 Marks and Britton (1989), p. 36.

59 Bowler, I. (1986) *Intensification, concentration* and specialization in agriculture — the case of the European Community. *Geography* 71, 14–24.

60 Marks and Britton (1989), p. 36.

61 Marks and Britton (1989), p. 37.

62 Marks and Britton (1989), p. 45.

63 Marks and Britton (1989), p. 48.

64 Marks and Britton (1989), p. 190.

65 Marks and Britton (1989), p. 63.

66 Brassley, P. (1996) Silage in Britain, 1880–1990: the delayed adoption of an innovation. *Agricultural History Review* 44, 63–87.

67 Marks and Britton (1989), p. 69.

68 Marks and Britton (1989), p. 73; see also Woods, A. (2012) Rethinking the history of modern agriculture: British pig production, c. 1910–65. *Twentieth Century British History* 23, 165–91.

69 Marks and Britton (1989), p. 73.

70 Marks and Britton (1989), p. 80; see also Jackson, P. *et al.* (2010) Manufacturing meaning along the chicken supply chain, pp. 163–87 in D. Goodman *et al.* (eds.) *Consuming Space: Placing Consumption in Perspective*. Aldershot: Ashgate.

71 Marks and Britton (1989), p. 84; see also Lowe, P. *et al.* (1997) *Moralising the Environment: Countryside Change, Farming and Pollution*. London: Routledge.

72 Marks and Britton (1989), p. 85.

73 Brassley *et al.* (2021), pp. 179–81.

74 Brassley, P. (2000b) Output and technical change in twentieth century British agriculture. *Agricultural History Review* 48, 60–84.

75 Brassley (2000b), p. 77.

76 Hughes, T. (1983) *Networks of Power: Electrification in Western Society, 1880–1930*. Baltimore: John Hopkins University Press; Hughes, T. (1987) The evolution of large technological systems, pp. 51–82 in W. Bijker *et al.* (eds.) *The Social Construction of Technological Systems: New Directions in the Sociology and History of Technology*. London: MIT Press.

77 Jackson, P. *et al.* (2018) *Reframing Convenience Food*. Cham: Springer & Palgrave Macmillan, p. 23.

78 Tracy (1989).

79 Tubiana, L. (1989) World trade in agricultural products: from global regulation to market fragmentation, pp. 23–45 in D. Goodman and M. Redclift (eds.) *The International Farm Crisis*. Basingstoke: MacMillan, p. 25.

80 Winter, M. (1996) *Rural Politics: Policies for Agriculture, Forestry and the Environment*. London: Routledge, p. 130.

81 For example, Body, R. (1982) *Agriculture: The Triumph and the Shame*. London: Temple Smith; Body, R. (1984) *Farming in the Clouds*. London: Temple Smith; Body, R. (1991) *Our Food, Our Land: Why Contemporary Farming Practices Must Change*. London: Random.

82 Marsden *et al.* (1993).

83 Ward, N. *et al.* (1995) Rural restructuring and the regulation of farm pollution. *Environment and Planning A* 27, 1193–1211.

84 Mazzucato, M. (2021) *Mission Economy: A Moonshot Guide to Changing Capitalism*. London: Allen Lane.

85 Adger, N. and Brown, K. (1994) *Land Use and the Causes of Global Warming*. Chichester: Wiley.

4
CLEANING AND GREENING FOOD AND FARMING

Introduction

Climate change is not the British agri-food system's first environmental challenge but is one of a succession of environmental and public health problems to trouble the sector. An ecological critique of productivist agriculture evolved from the 1960s through cumulative waves of public concern about the impacts of changing farming practices on the natural environment and public health risks around food. Each controversy involved scientific debate and political struggle and brought efforts to change farming practices, sometimes through voluntary measures and sometimes through regulatory controls. Prior to the climate change challenge, agriculture's environmental and health problems were principally associated with landscape change, biodiversity loss, water pollution, animal welfare and disease risks from pathogens. In addition, there was considerable debate about the social and economic implications of changes in the agriculture and food system, and the distributional consequences for smaller farms and smaller businesses in food manufacturing and retailing. This chapter traces the evolution of these environmental and health concerns and the responses to them over the past few decades. Since the 1990s, the crisis of productivism has been cast as the need to move towards a more "sustainable agriculture", although what constitutes sustainable agriculture has been far from clear. Greenhouse gas emissions have gradually become a more important component of what a sustainable agriculture might look like but, when compared to other sectors such as energy and transport, climate policy has not impinged upon agriculture until recently. The chapter considers the responses to agriculture's controversies and any lessons that might apply to the quest to reduce greenhouse gas emissions.

We saw in Chapter 3 how the period from the Second World War brought a revolution in farming practices, actively shaped by national priorities around expanding food production. This was initially to strengthen domestic self-sufficiency and to

DOI: 10.4324/9781003278535-4

reduce the balance of payments pressures during the dollar crisis and its aftermath in the late 1940s. New farming technologies led to significant increases in agricultural productivity across all farm commodities, the like of which had never been seen before. The technological changes included mechanisation, the growth in the use of agrochemicals and the development of intensive broiler and pig production and dairying, with ideas and technologies often imported from the United States.[1] It was also from the United States that the first signs of disquiet emerged about the environmental implications of this technological revolution in farming. Rachel Carson was a marine biologist at the US Government's Fish and Wildlife Service who became concerned about the impacts of agricultural pesticides on wildlife during the 1950s. She helped develop a network of scientists across the United States who established that pesticides were bioaccumulating in food chains. She became a popular science writer and campaigner publishing widely read articles on ecology in *The New Yorker* and *Reader's Digest*. Her seminal work, *Silent Spring*, helped develop an ecological sensibility among the public around the world and raised concerns about modern agriculture's technological path and its associated ideologies.[2] *Silent Spring* played a catalytic role in the birth of modern environmentalism. It sold more than half a million copies and was on the bestseller lists for more than 30 weeks.[3] The argument and evidence presented in Carson's work were picked up in the UK and fuelled emerging disquiet about modern farming's impact on the ecology of the countryside. The environmental challenge to UK agriculture's productivist model that unfolded in the aftermath of *Silent Spring* can be traced through three broad sets of concerns, around farming's impacts on wildlife, biodiversity and landscape, on water quality, and on public health and animal welfare. This chapter traces these three phases of twentieth-century controversy and the types of measures developed to reorient production practices to accommodate environmental and health concerns. It then turns to the politics of sustainable food and farming reform since 2000.

Farming, Landscape Change and Biodiversity

As in many other countries, *Silent Spring* prompted worries about the possible impact of pesticides on British wildlife. In an introduction to its British edition in 1963, Lord Shackleton noted that the national statutory body for nature conservation, the Nature Conservancy Council, was becoming concerned about reports of wildlife poisonings. The anxiety was that this indicated a systemic problem. He quoted the Duke of Edinburgh who had said: "Miners use canaries to warn them of deadly gases. It might not be a bad idea if we took the same warning from the dead birds in our countryside".[4] By the early 1970s, concerns had broadened to the loss of wildlife habitats caused by farm landscape rationalisation as well as pesticides. Fears were originally expressed in terms of the threat to wildlife, but environmental groups also began to call for the protection of attractive rural landscapes for their aesthetic appeal too.

Since the 1940s, farming practices had put pressure on wildlife habitats and altered the rural landscape. Most damaging were hedgerow removal, ploughing up uncultivated field margins, reclaiming scrub and woodlands, reducing rotations and fallows, replacing permanent pasture with leys and arable cropping, land drainage and the elimination of standing water and farm ponds, as well as the treatment of grassland and arable land with herbicides and insecticides. Landscape changes were obvious and visible for all to see but the production of data helped politicise the issue. The 1968 Countryside Act established a new national agency to protect rural landscapes, the Countryside Commission, which began to compile evidence and produce reports on rates of landscape change.[5] Systematic studies used air photography to measure change and revealed how large tracts of countryside were being radically altered.[6] This evidence allowed countryside and environmental pressure groups to bring the issue to wider public attention and ask fundamental questions about farming's environmental impacts. Popular and influential books began to highlight the threat that modern farming posed to the countryside, including Marion Shoard's *The Theft of the Countryside*.[7]

Shoard examined the impact of agricultural intensification on the seven most acutely affected and habitat-rich landscape features – hedgerows, hedgerow trees, woods, roughlands, downs, moors and wetlands. She highlighted how a quarter of the hedgerows in England and Wales had been removed in the 27 years between 1946 and 1974, about 120,000 miles in all, at a rate of almost 4,500 miles a year.[8] In some areas, the loss was much higher than the national average. In Norfolk, for example, 45 per cent of hedgerows (some 8,000 miles) were removed in the 24-year period between 1946 and 1970.[9] Hedgerows often became redundant following the shift from mixed farming to specialised arable production. They lost their purpose as livestock barriers and the use of larger farm machinery required larger, more regular-shaped fields. The annual rate of hedgerow removal in England and Wales was calculated to have slowed during the 1970s but then accelerated again to 4,000 miles a year between 1980 and 1985. Again, national figures masked the level of impact in some local areas. Over the 15 years from 1970 to 1985, there was a 30 per cent reduction in hedgerows in Bedfordshire and 35 per cent in Dorset.[10]

Field boundaries provide important wildlife habitats for at least 20 species of mammals, 37 species of birds and 17 species of butterflies, and so the combined impact of the removal of hedgerows with other aspects of the intensification of agricultural production was the loss of, or damage to, many habitats and the increasing threat to the survival of some plant and animal species. Evidence mounted of declines in farmland and other birds, for example. Shoard reported how the stone curlew, a bird of the chalk downlands, and the woodlark, which depended on sandy heathlands, had virtually disappeared.[11] Numbers of wetland birds such as redshank, lapwing and snipe fell dramatically and the population of one popular and distinctive bird, the corncrake, collapsed. A 1978 survey by the Royal Society for the Protection of Birds found corncrakes in fewer than a quarter of the 10 km squares in which they had been recorded breeding in 1968–1972.[12] They later disappeared completely from England. The "grim chronicle" of loss between the 1940s and the 1980s was summed up by the Nature Conservancy Council as follows: "Over the past 35 years, the nation has lost 95 per cent of lowland herb-rich grasslands, 80 per cent of chalk and limestone grasslands, 45 per cent of limestone pavements, 50 per cent of ancient woodlands, 50 per cent of lowland fens and marshes, over 60 per cent of lowland raised bogs, and a third of all upland grasslands, heaths and mires".[13] The Council reported that 30 lowland and 6 upland bird species had shown an appreciable long-term decline since the late 1940s. Among mammals, the otter had become extremely rare and four of Britain's 12 reptiles and amphibians had become endangered. Agriculture's role in wildlife loss soon became a major public and political controversy and Britain's already well-established conservation movement grew in size and influence as a result. The Royal Society for the Protection of Birds saw its membership multiply nearly seven-fold during the 1970s[14] and was able to build up a significant team of its own scientific specialists, employing over 350 staff by the mid-1980s.[15] This large and increasingly professionalised environmental movement was coupled with a strong tradition of field natural sciences in universities, research institutes and societies for amateur naturalists.[16] Ecological and environmental sciences grew in the 1970s and 1980s and scientific efforts to understand the processes of environmental damage in the countryside became a counterweight to that focused on supporting agricultural productivity.

The farming industry's first response to the growing evidence of landscape change and loss of habitat and species was to blame bad or "maverick" farmers, preferring to draw attention to the good stewardship of most farmers and the efficiency of the industry as a whole.[17] However, as the rate and scale of change became clearer, this explanation increasingly appeared inadequate. Studies of farmers' attitudes to conservation revealed many who regretted the environmental changes they felt forced to make in order to stay in business.[18] This evidence shifted attention from individual behaviour to structural factors and agricultural policy was increasingly blamed for the environmental change. It had provided farmers with access to guaranteed markets, fixed prices, capital grants and an advisory service, conditions that created confidence, encouraged the specialisation and concentration of production, increased output and led to a more intensive use of farmland.[19] However, farm businesses were not all responding to the policy framework in exactly the same ways. Clive Potter suggested that those farmers who made systematic and programmed investments in land improvement, as part of an active strategy of farm development, were the harbingers of greatest change.[20] Other research demonstrated how landscape rationalisation was most likely to take place when farmland changed hands.[21]

The policy responses to threats posed to valued landscapes and habitats were largely mild and voluntaristic. Incentive schemes were gradually introduced which farmers could choose to join if they so wished. Even within National Parks, those localities with highest levels of landscape protection, there was little that could be done to prevent farmers from improving farmland and removing landscape features if they chose to. Instead, farmers gradually began to be paid incentives to farm in economically sub-optimal ways for the sake of wildlife and conservation. This approach was made possible by the 1981 Wildlife and Countryside Act which permitted management agreements to be negotiated with farmers for conservation purposes. It was expanded after 1985 through the introduction of Environmentally Sensitive Areas, which became permitted under Common Agricultural Policy (CAP) rules and eventually became more widespread through the Countryside Stewardship Scheme and the further greening of the CAP in the 1990s.[22] There were calls in the 1980s for the reintroduction of County Agriculture Committees similar to those of the 1940s and 1950s, but charged with strengthening the conservation and environmental management role of agriculture.[23] The farming industry itself developed Farming and Wildlife Advisory Groups (FWAGs) during the late 1970s and early 1980s as a response to the increasing popular interest in wildlife and conservation. FWAGs represented "the prime expression of the voluntary principle in conservation".[24] These initiatives, coupled with the growth of voluntary agri-environment schemes, attracted a lot of attention. However, they were nowhere near sufficient to undo the damage that had been done by 40 years of productivism, the legacy of which was a more rationalised and intensively farmed rural landscape and a collapse in many wildlife species.

Over time, the scientific understanding of biodiversity loss became more sophisticated, implicating not just the removal of habitats but also crop husbandry practices.[25] These included the growth in silage production and autumn-sown cereals, greater dependence upon pesticides and especially pre-emergent cereal herbicides that lessened the need for crop rotations.[26] Agri-environment schemes were largely about preventing further rationalisation and environmental damage rather than large-scale efforts at restoration, and they tended initially to be confined to tightly designated geographical zones that left large swathes of rural Britain still relatively unprotected. New incentive schemes encouraged particular farming practices to support biodiversity. These included the provision of over-wintered stubble and planted wild bird crop covers to provide winter seeds, leaving uncropped field margins and sensitive hedgerow management. However, these voluntary schemes have not been enough to turn the tide. Although the rate of decline slowed compared to the 1970s and 1980s, the general trend in farmland birds has continued downwards over the past two decades.[27]

Water Pollution from Farm Livestock Effluents and Agricultural Pesticides

During the 1980s, water pollution from agriculture became a major environmental controversy and a further indictment of the productivist model. In England and Wales, the number of reported farm pollution incidents more than doubled during the 1980s, with the most frequent pollutants being cattle slurry and silage effluent.[28] Livestock effluents usually entered watercourses because of inadequate storage facilities or poor management. This arose primarily because of the concentration and specialisation of intensive livestock production, especially in dairying, where a smaller number of farms were carrying much larger herds, making safe disposal of slurry and effluents more difficult. The problem was exacerbated by the switch from straw-based to slurry-based livestock housing systems and the concreting of farmyards, along with the expansion of silage production since the 1960s.[29] Pollution incidents from livestock effluents were causing large-scale fish kills, but more insidious leakage of effluents over time also led to chronic deoxygenation and nutrient enrichment damaging river ecology. By the mid-1980s, agricultural pollution had become the most significant problem for river water quality in the UK. It was also identified as one of the reasons for the UK's poor compliance with the environmental quality standards in the European Bathing Waters Directive as rivers carried farm effluents into coastal waters.

Farming interests initially questioned the severity of the problem and again pointed the finger at "bad farmers". It was only after strongly contested debates that the production systems themselves began to be regarded as potentially unsound. Water quality regulation prior to the 1980s had concentrated on urban and industrial sources, with pollution control oriented towards point source problems. This meant that the lack of control over farming became more and more apparent as industrial point source problems were gradually cleaned up, leaving diffuse pollution a much more intractable regulatory problem. In addition, the growing recognition that agricultural policy was actively stimulating intensification led to a realisation that, unlike most other environmental problems, government policies were implicated alongside market forces. There was a sense that agricultural productivism was leading to the separation of farming activities from the natural resource base upon which they traditionally depended. The move away from mixed farming, along with the specialisation and concentration of production, was producing a serious pollution problem that called into question the environmental sustainability of whole production systems.[30]

Pollution from farm livestock effluents became such a serious issue by the late 1980s that it could not be left to the voluntarism that had hitherto been the Government's preferred approach. The mid-1980s saw the first recorded decline in river water quality nationally, and this prompted a 1987 House of Commons Environment Committee to examine the water pollution problem.[31] The Committee concluded that the growing farm pollution problem was an important contributory factor to the decline in river quality.[32] This also came at a time when several environmental groups were becoming more involved in campaigning about water pollution and saw environmental protection as a weak point in Thatcherite free-market deregulation.[33] The Parliamentary debates around the privatisation of the water industry gave a high profile to questions of how water quality should be regulated.[34]

This time a "carrot and stick" approach was developed. Grants were made available to help support investment in improved pollution control facilities, in part funded by farm modernisation measures within the CAP. These were initially set at 50 per cent of the costs of installing pollution control facilities. Farmers were also provided with free initial advice on pollution problems. Concerted information campaigns were pursued nationally and in particularly problematic parts of the country such as South West England in order to raise awareness among farmers of pollution risks and the kinds of support available. Then there were the sticks. The 1989 Water Act that privatised the water industry also brought with it a much tougher regime for regulating agricultural pollution. It established the National Rivers Authority, which in 1996 became the Environment Agency, as a strong national regulatory body with powers to compel farmers to upgrade their storage facilities, and set statutory technical standards for the storage of manure, slurry, dirty water such as yard-washings and silage effluent. Although there were all sorts of ways in which some farmers pleaded hardship and resisted investing what sometimes amount to several tens of thousands of pounds in pollution control equipment, gradually the regulatory authorities were able to cajole the livestock industry into improving slurry storage and effluent management. The Act also significantly increased the levels of fines that farmers could be subject to if found guilty of causing pollution from £2,000 to £20,000 and increasing numbers were prosecuted. The number of convictions for farm pollution rose from 34 in 1980 to 221 in 1990.[35] Prosecution was always treated as a last resort by the regulators, but high-profile court cases and significant fines for farmers caught polluting helped establish a new moral framework around the acceptability or otherwise of allowing polluting farm effluents to get into rivers. What had once been largely tolerated as merely an unfortunate technical side effect of efficient livestock production became more morally charged as a form of "environmental crime" and it was this social stigmatisation of farm pollution that helped effect a shift in slurry and effluent management across the sector.[36]

Water pollution by agricultural pesticides gradually began to materialise as a problem later in the 1980s. The Royal Commission on Environmental Pollution, in its major study of agriculture and pollution in 1979, devoted over a quarter of its report to looking at pesticides but water pollution was not specifically dealt with. Instead, the main concerns were risks to human health from pesticide residues in food, risks to farmworkers from contact with sprays and risks to wildlife from the cumulative effects in their food chain.[37] The only threat to watercourses was perceived as coming from the careless disposal of pesticide containers or spray tank washings which, it was felt, could cause acute, but transient incidents.[38] An absence of good monitoring data on pesticides in water helped generate an atmosphere of complacency. However, this complacency was challenged in the 1980s by the European Drinking Water Directive. The Directive, which became law in Britain in 1985, set a very low maximum admissible concentration level of 0.1 µg/l for any individual pesticide and 0.5 µg/l for total pesticides. These were the first legally enforceable, numerical standards for pesticides in water in Britain. The Directive meant that, for the first time, data were available on the spread of pesticide contamination of water, and it became apparent that water contamination from agricultural pesticides was quite extensive across much of southern England. Friends of the Earth requested data from the then Regional Water Authorities and were able to show that between 1985 and 1987, the limit for any single pesticide had been exceeded in 298 water supplies and 70 times for total pesticides. The report, which subsequently informed a major feature in *The Observer* in August 1989, brought the now measurable problem of pesticide pollution to wider public attention.[39] Over

14 million people were living in water supply areas where drinking water breached the pesticide standard.

The means by which agricultural pesticides pollute ground and surface waters became the subject of much greater scientific effort.[40] A new regulatory system had been introduced under the Control of Pesticides Regulations 1986 which meant any pesticide could be recalled for review if new data came to light about its environmental impacts. The Regulations required that farmers comply with the conditions of approval for the application of pesticides. More significant, however, has been the tightening of the approval process and the withdrawal of the more problematic and persistent pesticides being detected in the water environment. Here the development of the EU's regulatory framework for governing the approval of pesticides became an important driver of a strengthened approach in the UK. For example, one of the most widespread pesticides detected in ground and surface waters in the UK in the 1980s and 1990s was Isoproturon, a relatively cheap and effective pre-emergent herbicide use that had been introduced in the early 1970s for the control of weeds in cereal crops. This was phased out between 2007 and 2009 because of the risks it posed to aquatic life.

Coming in the aftermath of the outcries over landscape change and loss of wildlife due to farming, the water pollution controversies of the 1980s and early 1990s brought cumulative concern about farming's environmental impacts and the weak system of environmental controls. As a result of the 1989 Water Act, agriculture flipped from being one of the least regulated sectors when it comes to water pollution to one of the most regulated.[41] High-profile prosecutions of polluting farmers brought local shame and responsible slurry and livestock effluent management became a much more prominent concern in the livestock sector. In arable production, farmers generally placed their faith in the pesticides approval system, believing that environmentally harmful products would not be permitted for use. Some pesticides have been banned from use, and the Government has developed successive national action plans that seek to reduce dependence on pesticides.[42] The voluntarism of the 1970s and 1980s thus seemed to give way to a stronger regulatory approach when it came to farming's water pollution problems.

There are those who continue to argue that the approach to addressing water pollution from agriculture is inadequate. Almost 145 million tonnes of livestock manure and slurry are produced each year in England and Wales and storage facilities installed in the 1980s and 1990s are becoming obsolete, leaving substantiated pollution incidents from farms stubbornly high. Some farmers acknowledge the possibility of pollution but take a business risk not to spend on expensive pollution control facilities. Although the problems of the 1980s were taken on board at the time, the sticks and carrots approach has not been sufficiently successful to address the fundamental problems with livestock production systems. The years of austerity saw a reduction in regulatory resources given to addressing agricultural pollution such that between 2015 and 2020 fewer than 40 per cent of reported pollution incidents from farms were even attended by the Environment Agency.[43]

Agriculture's contribution to poor river quality continues to exercise policymakers and attract considerable media attention.[44]

Farm Animal Health and Welfare

Alongside increasing controversy about farm pollution, the 1980s also saw a wave of successive problems with farm livestock that raised both public health and animal welfare concerns. British policy for farm animal health and welfare evolved during the twentieth century in response to socio-economic and political change on the one hand and the emergence of disease outbreaks and the scientific understanding of them on the other. By the early 1980s, the prevailing neoliberal political mood was to roll back the state and reduce public expenditure on the eradication of farm animal diseases but by the end of the 1980s, the Government had been forced by events to revise this stance.[45]

In 1988, the discovery of salmonella in eggs caused a major public outcry and the wholesale price of eggs halved in a matter of weeks. It had been known by the Government for some time that poultry contained high levels of salmonella and cases of salmonella enteritidis, the type later associated with eggs, had increased from 1,087 cases in 1981 to 6,858 in 1987.[46] By 1988, the number of cases doubled to more than 13,000. One concern at the time was that recycling slaughterhouse waste could lead to infected birds being returned to the food chain as animal feed. Disagreements between government departments in the handling of the crisis heightened media and political interest and led to the resignation of a junior health minister, Edwina Currie, who had remarked in December 1988 that "most of the egg production in this country, sadly, is now affected with salmonella".[47] Environmental and consumer groups blamed intensive farming systems and the relaxation of the regulatory regime during the 1980s. Farming groups, however, lobbied hard for Currie to be removed for giving inaccurate information and bringing unnecessary economic damage to the egg and poultry industry.[48] Over three and a half million laying hens were slaughtered between 1989 and 1993 under the powers of the 1981 Animal Health Act and the British egg industry contracted significantly in the immediate aftermath of the crisis. The 34,000 holdings with 31 million birds before the crisis shrank by 17 per cent to 28,227 holdings and 28 million birds by 1990, with mainly smaller producers going out of business.[49] The salmonella crisis set off a wave of public controversies about food safety that ran through 1988 and 1989.[50] It also tapped into a vein of concern about so-called factory farming that had been developing since the 1960s.[51] This centred on problems of animal welfare resulting from the huge changes in pig and poultry production and brought considerable pressure on agriculture ministers to improve farm animal welfare standards. The salmonella crisis of the late 1980s helped give some impetus to the growth of free-range egg production during the 1990s and food safety scandals led to the 1990 Food Safety Act that increased penalties for food safety offences.

The rendering or recycling of farm animal waste into feedstuff to be fed back to farm animals was at the root of an even greater controversy with the emergence of Bovine Spongiform Encephalopathy (BSE, or "Mad Cow Disease"). Here the problem was feeding cattle animal feed that contained processed carcasses of scrapie-infected sheep. The first cases were identified in 1985 and the State Veterinary Service acknowledged a new disease in 1986. For ten years, the Government told the public that, although the disease had seemed to have jumped species from sheep to cattle, there was no evidence that BSE could be transmitted to humans, and so it was most unlikely that the disease posed any risk to humans. Put simply, it was safe to eat beef. By 1988, it was clear that large numbers of cases of BSE were being identified throughout the British livestock industry. Once it had embarked on its "beef is safe" narrative, it became difficult for the Ministry of Agriculture, Fisheries and Food (MAFF) to deviate from this course without losing credibility. Its approach to science-based policymaking at this time has been characterised as "policy-based evidence-making".[52] In March 1996, the Government was forced to announce that cases of a new variant of CJD (Creutzfeldt–Jakob Disease), a fatal and degenerative brain disease, had been identified in humans and the most likely explanation was that it had come from eating infected beef. By September 2000, over 80 cases of CJD had been identified in humans.[53]

The Government had first introduced a ruminant feed ban in July 1988, although it gave the animal feed industry a five-week period of grace to clear stocks. All animals showing signs of the disease were compulsorily slaughtered with compensation paid to farmers. During the BSE crisis, over 170,000 animals either died or had to be destroyed. The disease was a peculiarly British disaster. It did not affect many animals in other countries and led to the European Community banning imports of British beef. Those scientists who advocated a precautionary approach in response to BSE and advocated the need to act ahead of any evidence of the risk of the disease jumping to humans were often attacked by supporters of the food and farming industry for scaremongering.[54] A new Meat Hygiene Service was established to regulate hygiene practices at slaughterhouses in the face of concern among some politicians about over-zealous regulation. New sets of requirements were introduced to strengthen the book-keeping for cattle identification and movement, although there were concerns about the level of diligence farmers paid to these rules.[55]

A further animal health crisis occurred in 2001 when Foot and Mouth Disease (FMD) struck. The disease was first spotted in pigs at an abattoir in Essex, but before the original source of infection could be traced to a farm in Northumberland, the disease had already spread extensively around the country via livestock movements and markets. Immediately, an export ban was put in place covering live cattle, sheep, pigs and goats and also of meat, meat products, milk and milk products. National livestock movement restrictions were imposed after three days, although it was later estimated that the three-day delay resulted in the outbreak being two to three times the scale that it would have been if the restrictions had been immediate.[56] A ban was also introduced on swill feeding. More than 6 million animals were slaughtered under the powers of the 1981 Animal Health Act, including not only animals on infected farms but also those on contiguous premises.

Initially, the public were warned not to go to the countryside and the 2001 general election was delayed. The outbreak was the first since 1967 but the effects of the crisis were exacerbated by the changes in the livestock industry that had taken place over the 34 intervening years. The number of sheep and lambs had risen by almost 50 per cent over that period, and subsidy rules required farmers to have a full quota of sheep for which they could claim payments at the inspection period in February/March. This fuelled extensive animal movements, with some sheep subject to several moves in quick succession between different markets. The amount of livestock movement even took MAFF by surprise and during the crisis it had to increase its estimation of livestock movements from 1 million animal movements during the month of February to 2 million. MAFF officials had effectively lost touch with the nature of FMD since the late 1960s. "As time went by, their perceptions of, and policy responses to, FMD became increasingly dated and eventually ceased to make sense".[57] The 2001 crisis was a huge shock to the system and was calculated to have cost £8 billion.[58] It also stood as an indictment of agricultural expansion and the national system of livestock trading and movement.

The 2001 FMD crisis resulted in a much stronger emphasis on biosecurity measures on farms.[59] It also resulted in the 2002 Animal Health Act which strengthened the legal basis for animal disease control including for pre-emptive culling and required that advice and guidance for the maintenance of biosecurity is regularly updated and published. "Biosecurity" was a term that was not widely known until the 2001 FMD crisis. "We used to just call it cleaning and disinfecting", one National Farmers' Union official quipped,[60] but good biosecurity standards became something that was linked to the granting of livestock movement licences. There were attempts to tie the paying of compensation for slaughtered farm animals to good standards of biosecurity, but these were rejected because of concerns that there were no objective measures of what constituted "good biosecurity" that could be enforced.[61]

More recently, livestock farmers have faced additional restrictions because of the spread of Bovine Tuberculosis (TB). Measures to control the disease have attracted some controversy because of the culling of badgers that are thought to contribute to its spread. The number of herds affected by the disease more than doubled from 1,660 in 1999 to 3,512 in 2006.[62] The disease was first concentrated in South West England but has geographically spread, affecting the West Midlands and Wales, and has become "the most pressing animal health problem in the UK".[63] A regional framework was put in place designating areas according to their risk. In 2006, to supplement the existing system of routine testing, Defra introduced an additional system of pre-movement testing of cattle in England to help reduce the risk of spread from herds in high-risk areas, but the spreading continued. By 2010/2011, Bovine TB was costing the taxpayer some £91 million per year for the testing regime and in compensation for cattle slaughtered.[64] In 2016, post-movement testing was also introduced in low-risk areas for cattle moved from other areas of England and from Wales. Livestock farmers are thus subject to an increasingly detailed and prescriptive set of measures to test cattle especially, although not exclusively, when they are being moved and traded. There had been concern that some farmers deliberately send to market animals they fear may prove positive at their next routine test or swap animals' ear tags to hide infection status.[65]

This succession of farm animal health crises contributed to a mounting public anxiety about the risks being generated by the agri-food system. Each crisis left its legacy not only in terms of economic and reputational damage, but also of legislation, rules and regulations governing farming practices that sought to better manage these risks. They each played their part in challenging the faith in, and complacency around, the productivist model, and underlined how it is possible to make a quite radical change to farming practice when necessary, usually under crisis conditions such as BSE or FMD.

Towards a Greener Agriculture: Sustainable Food and Farming Reforms

Successive controversies have left their mark by tightening controls on farming practices. The 1989 Water Act brought much stricter rules on farm pollution control. In 1990, a straw burning ban was introduced to reduce local air pollution, and rules on animal feed, animal movements and animal record-keeping have all tightened as a result of farm animal health crises. From the early 1990s, academics began to characterise the environmental regulation of agriculture as part of an epoch shift from productivism to "post-productivism".[66] The succession of major controversies, national scandals and the scale of some of the shifts in practice, all contributed to a sense of a new age. In each of the three pillars of productivism outlined in Chapter 3, the old order seemed to be being replaced by the new. Much regulation could be enacted under British statute, but the greater influence of European environmental policy through the 1980s and 1990s also stimulated tighter rules for farmers, as evidenced in the pesticides in water controversy.[67] The 1980s and 1990s were also pivotal times in the reform of the CAP as financial and political pressure mounted to manage down surplus production, reduce the distortion of world markets in farm commodities and deal with the environmental criticisms of the CAP.

The first major reform of the CAP came in spring 1984 when, almost overnight, milk quotas were introduced to curb the growth in milk production. The move came as a seismic shock to dairy farmers who found that their milk production was to be restricted to 9 per cent lower than their 1983 level. This radically changed the context for dairy farmers who previously had been investing to expand output. Milk quotas meant the objective now became to produce a fixed quantity of milk at as low cost as possible. A second set of reforms was the introduction of budgetary stabilisers and set-aside to take some land out of production in order to reduce the over-production of cereals and avert budgetary crisis from 1988. The so-called grain mountains had been a mounting problem in the early

1980s and by 1987 the European Community was on the brink of bankruptcy.[68] The European Commission then began working towards a more comprehensive CAP reform, under Agriculture Commissioner Ray MacSharry, which was agreed in 1992. The MacSharry reforms included a marked reduction in support prices for grains, oilseeds and beef in order to bring EU prices closer to world market prices. Quasi-compulsory set-aside was introduced to reduce the over-production of arable crops along with direct payments to arable and beef farmers to compensate for price cuts and a set of "accompanying measures" (to promote agri-environment, agro-forestry and early retirement programmes). The agri-environment schemes proved to be a popular innovation and MacSharry's successor, Franz Fischler, began the work on a subsequent set of reforms and built upon this approach to develop a "second pillar" to the CAP, which would include agri-environmental measures and support for wider rural development.[69] Fischler's Agenda 2000 reforms to the CAP were finally agreed in 1999 and saw a further shift from market support and direct payments to farmers towards second pillar funding. In the UK, the discretionary option to accelerate this reform even further, through the modulation of direct payments, was taken up. The UK ended up advancing a progressive strategy for CAP reform which moved further away from production support and towards environmental payments. Following the 1999 reforms, the amount of money available to support agri-environmental schemes doubled in England. At the next opportunity for reform in 2003, the EU decided to apply the British approach to modulation across the whole of the Union with CAP reformists calling for the second pillar (agri-environment and rural development schemes) to evolve to replace the first (direct payments based on past production). Subsequent reforms saw the progressive greening of the CAP up to the UK's departure after Brexit. Brexit opened new debates about a British agricultural policy now unfettered by the CAP and the Government's 2020 Agriculture Act provides the legislative framework for a new approach to farm payments in England.[70] Its broad approach, "public money for public goods", adopts that advocated by the turn of the century CAP reformists.[71]

Gradually, from the early 1990s, the rhetoric of agricultural productivism began to be replaced with a rhetoric of "sustainable agriculture" and national environmental policy priorities began to bear increasingly upon the agri-food sector and upon the regulations governing farming practice in the field and farmyard. Initially, UK environmental policy for global warming and sustainable development did not treat agriculture as a prominent priority. The first comprehensive environmental policy for the UK, *This Common Inheritance* in 1990, in a chapter on "countryside and wildlife", proclaimed "the Government is working to integrate agricultural and environmental objectives across the whole range of its policies for the next decade".[72] It talked about set-aside, measures to tackle farm pollution and to promote organic farming. However, by 1990, just 3.5 per cent of agricultural land had been designated under Environmentally Sensitive Areas and there was very little sense, if any at all, of agriculture's role in tackling climate change.[73]

Following the Rio Summit, the UK developed a national strategy for sustainable development, which was published to much fanfare in January 1994.[74] It set out the principles of sustainable development and reviewed the pressures and policy frameworks governing different environmental media (global atmosphere, air quality, fresh water, the sea, soil, etc.). A seven-page agriculture chapter, when coupled with the analysis in the sections on water, soil, land use and wildlife, effectively served as the UK Government's first statement on sustainable agriculture and what the implementation of policies for sustainable agriculture might mean.[75] The MAFF civil servant responsible for producing the agriculture section of the sustainable development strategy explained the thinking behind this landmark piece of work in British twentieth-century agriculture and environment policy.[76] Producing the document had been a difficult process. The concept of sustainable development felt ill-defined, and the scientific knowledge about many aspects of agriculture's impact on the environment was partial. Rather than set out to define a sustainable UK agriculture, the civil servants instead sought to identify the general directions in which agriculture needed to move in order to contribute to a more sustainable UK economy. The Strategy expressed four aims for agriculture: adequate, efficient production; minimising resource consumption; safeguarding soil, water and air quality; and preserving biodiversity and the landscape.[77] Of course, these aims could be in conflict, but it was felt that at least some indicators could help guide operational decisions. The Strategy acknowledged that sustainable development would bring changes to how individuals lived but it continued to strongly espouse a preference for voluntarism over regulation or subsidy. From today's perspective, it is striking how limited was the insight into agriculture's contribution to climate change and the implications for the future development of the sector. In its pledges and commitments involving agriculture, the Government makes no mention of greenhouse gases, only committing to "minimise the environmental impacts of agricultural wastes, particularly on water quality and emission to air".[78] One agricultural scientist commenting on the Strategy's implications for climate change pointed out "there do not seem to be any policies being implemented that will lead to stabilisation of carbon emissions within the time-scale that is required".[79] This has been the case for almost three decades since.

The prevalent conceptualisation in the Strategy of environmental damage as unwanted externalities of a production system did not suit agriculture because what farmers do in their fields at one and the same time is produce marketable goods and environmental goods. Farming is not just a form of primary production but is a form of environmental management in its own right. The integrating impulse of sustainable development ought to have brought economy and environment together, but MAFF remained wedded to an "old school", traditional approach which regarded production and environment as separate spheres. Problems like pollution stood as discrete externalities to be solved by end-of-pipe technologies or special protection zones. Indeed, the Strategy implied that environmental protection was a luxury add-on that could only be afforded once the "advanced development of … agriculture and general economic prosperity" had been achieved.[80] The Government placed considerable faith in applying pressure to reduce levels of CAP support, liberalise world trade and encourage an internally competitive agriculture sector as key elements in its sustainability strategy for agriculture. The relationship between price support and trade reforms and environmental impacts was not straightforward, however, and it was just as likely that reducing support and intensifying competition would serve to fuel environmentally damaging practices. The Government pointed to a number of schemes to promote environmentally friendly farming, glossing over the fact that the schemes were voluntary and highly spatially restricted, leaving only very limited possibilities for encouraging environmentally beneficial practices on the majority of farmland. Critics argued that "forty years of 'productivist' agriculture have left their mark ... requiring that attention also be paid to the ingrained values and entrenched practices which underpin a defensive and dismissive reaction to alternative approaches. Such attitudes need to be tackled not only on the farm, but also in advisory services, agricultural research establishments, supply companies and policy-making circles".[81]

The UK's first strategy for sustainable agriculture embodied an individualistic conception of farming emphasising voluntary co-operation and financial incentives. It did not set out a clear vision for how agriculture and land management might develop along a more sustainable path. It was, nevertheless, a landmark document in explicitly committing the UK to the sustainable development of agriculture, and just about every strategy document about agriculture since has at least paid lip service to sustainability as a central goal. However, for the 30 years following Rio, UK agriculture has been slow to respond to climate change and the need to reduce emissions compared to other sectors. Following the FMD crisis, a major review of farming policy was commissioned by Prime Minister Tony Blair and chaired by Sir Don Curry.[82] It talked about food miles and emissions from transport but did not spend much time on greenhouse gas emissions from agriculture. The 2008 Climate Change Act introduced national statutory targets for emissions reductions and Defra, the government department by now responsible for agriculture, did begin to develop a set of indicators around greenhouse gas emissions.[83] The 2008 Act also established the Climate Change Committee, which produced a report in 2013 on climate change and agriculture, but the focus was mainly on the impacts of climate change on the sector, rather than anything the sector might need to do to help combat climate change.[84]

Conclusions

We saw in Chapter 3 how successful agricultural productivism had been in raising productivity and expanding UK farm output. The changes in farming practices came at a cost, however, and from the 1970s onwards, the agri-food system became buffeted by a succession of environmental and health controversies. As evidence of species and habitat loss mounted, a growing and increasingly strident environmental movement began to campaign for reform. Realisation that agricultural policy was in large part fuelling environmental pressures and problems helped undermine the policy framework. As the costs of agricultural support and surplus production became more apparent, so it became clear that the post-war productivist approach would need fundamental reform. The fact that UK agricultural policy had to operate within the framework of the CAP slowed the pace of change, yet even within the CAP, there was scope for the Member States to exercise some discretion and tailor their agricultural support in the light of their own national environmental priorities and problems.

The first phase of the British response to the problems of intensive farming was heavily rooted in a tradition of voluntarism. Farmers could choose, if they so wished, to enter into management agreements to moderate their practices to protect environmental assets and be paid for doing so. Agri-environmental schemes provided a welcome new income stream for some farmers, squeezed by reforms to production subsidies, but they only slowed or halted rates of change initially in delineated geographical areas. Even when such schemes were made available across the whole countryside, take-up was patchy and swathes of farmland could still be farmed according to traditional productivist priorities. The cumulation of pollution and animal health problems did bring elements of a new approach as direct regulation of farming practices was tightened in some areas. Problematic pesticides were taken off the market, standards were set for pollution control facilities and there was a stronger emphasis on prosecuting farmers for pollution. Much more bureaucracy was introduced to maintain the traceability of farm animals for the sake of disease risk management. Yet large elements of voluntarism remained, along with a propensity to pay farmers to change their practices. From the early 1990s, sustainable development began to become more important in the framing of the objectives of food, farming and land use. However, it has taken a period of three decades for the climate change concerns to begin to impinge on farming and land use. Although there were some reductions in greenhouse gas emissions from agriculture due to productivity gains and efficiency of input use, emissions have largely flatlined over the last decade.[85]

The UK is now committed to have fully transitioned to net zero carbon by 2050. As we shall see in Chapter 6, much will need to change in the British agrifood system. Lessons can be drawn from the 40 years from 1940 to 1980 and the experience of improving agriculture's environmental record since the early 1980s. If 1980–2020 is the model, meeting the net zero goal is likely to be a struggle. In contrast, the planned changes and transformation of the sector from 1940 to 1980 was, at least in its own productivist terms, a stunning success. We turn to the current challenge facing food and farming with respect to climate change and net zero in Chapter 6. First, however, there is the question of how climate change has emerged as an issue for food and farming and for other sectors, and it is to the development of climate science and climate policy that we now turn in Chapter 5.

Notes

1 Goodman, D. and Redclift, M. (1991) *Refashioning Nature: Food, Ecology and Culture.* London: Routledge.

2 Carson, R. (1962) *Silent Spring*. Boston, MA: Houghton Mifflin; Lear, L. (1997) *Rachel Carson: The Life of the Author of Silent Spring*. London: Penguin.

3 Lear (1997).

4 Carson (1962), p. 17.

5 Westmacott, R. and Worthington, T. (1974) *New Agricultural Landscapes*. Cheltenham: Countryside Commission.

6 Westmacott and Worthington (1974); Westmacott, R. and Worthington, T. (1984) *Agricultural Landscapes: A Second Look*. CCP168. Cheltenham: Countryside Commission; Barr, C. *et al.* (1986) *Landscape Changes in Britain*. Huntingdon: Institute of Terrestrial Ecology; Countryside Commission/Huntings (1986) *Monitoring Landscape Change*. Cheltenham: Countryside Commission.

7 Shoard, M. (1980) *The Theft of the Countryside*. London: Temple Smith.

8 Shoard (1980), p. 34.

9 Baird, W. and Tarrant, J. (1973) *Hedgerow Destruction in Norfolk, 1946–1970*. Centre of East Anglian Studies. Norwich: University of East Anglia.

10 Ward, N. *et al.* (1990) Farm landscape change: trends in upland and lowland England. *Land Use Policy* 7, 291–302.

11 Shoard (1980), p. 184.

12 Quoted in Shoard (1980), p. 184.

13 Nature Conservancy Council (1984) *Nature Conservation in Great Britain*. London: Nature Conservancy Council, quoted in Lowe *et al.* (1986) *Countryside Conflicts: The Politics of Farming, Forestry and Conservation*. Aldershot: Gower, p. 55.

14 Shoard (1980), p. 185.

15 Lowe, P. *et al.* (1986), p. 114.

16 Lowe, P. and Goyder, J. (1983) *Environmental Groups in Politics*. London: George Allen & Unwin; Dixon, J. (1998) Nature conservation, pp. 214–31 in P. Lowe and S. Ward (eds.) *British Environmental Policy and Europe: Politics and Policy in Transition*. London: Routledge.

17 Cox, G. and Lowe, P. (1983) A battle not the war: the politics of the Wildlife and Countryside Act, pp. 48–76 in A. Gilg (ed.) *Countryside Planning Yearbook*, Vol. 4. Norwich: Geobooks, p. 65.

18 ADAS (1976) *Wildlife Conservation in Semi-natural Habitats on Farms: A Survey of Farmer Attitudes and Intentions in England and Wales*. London: HMSO; MacDonald, D. (1984) A questionnaire survey of farmers opinions and actions towards wildlife on farmlands, pp. 171–7 in D. Jenkins (ed.) *Agriculture and Environment*. Cambridge: NERC; Mori (1987) *Farmers Attitudes Towards Nature Conservation*. A report on qualitative research prepared for the NCC. London: Mori.

19 Potter, C. (1986) Investment styles and countryside change in lowland England, pp. 146–59 in G. Cox, P. Lowe and M. Winter (eds.) *Agriculture, People and Policies*. London: Allen & Unwin.

20 Potter (1986), p. 149.

21 Munton, R. and Marsden, T. (1991) Occupancy change and the farmed landscape: an analysis of farm-level trends, 1970–85. *Environment and Planning A* 23, 499–510; Marsden, T. and Munton, R. (1991) The farmed landscape and the occupancy change process. *Environment and Planning A* 23, 663–76.

22 Baldock, D. *et al.* (1990) Environmentally sensitive areas: incrementalism or reform. *Journal of Rural Studies* 6, 143–62; Baldock, D. and Lowe, P. (1996) The development of European agri-environmental policy, pp. 8–25 in M. Whitby (ed.) *The European Environment and CAP Reform: Policies and Prospects for Conservation*. Wallingford: CAB International.

23 Pye-Smith, C. and North, R. (1984) *Working the Land*. London: Maurice Temple Smith; see also Winter, M. (1985) Administering land-use policies for agriculture: a possible role for County Agriculture and Conservation Committees. *Agricultural Administration* 18, 235–49.

24 Cox, G. *et al.* (1990) *The Voluntary Principle in Conservation*. Chichester: Packard, p. 2.

25 For example, Gates, S. and Donald, P. (2000) Local extinction of farmland birds and the prediction of further loss. *Journal of Applied Ecology* 37, 806–20; Chamberlain, D. *et al.* (2000) Changes in the abundance of farmland birds in relation to the timing of agricultural intensification in England and Wales. *Journal of Applied Ecology* 37, 771–88.

26 Siriwardena, G. *et al.* (1998) Trends in the abundance of farmland birds: a quantitative comparison of smoothed common birds census indices. *Journal of Applied Ecology* 35, 24–43; Chamberlain *et al.* (2000); Goulson, D. (2021) *Silent Earth: Averting the Insect Apocalypse*. London: Jonathan Cape.

27 Department for Environment, Food and Rural Affairs (2020a) *Wild Bird Populations in the UK, 1970–2019*. London: Defra.

28 National Rivers Authority (1992) *The Influence of Agriculture on the Quality of Natural Waters in England and Wales*. Bristol: National Rivers Authority, p. 11.

29 Lowe, P. *et al.* (1997) *Moralising the Environment: Countryside Change, Farming and Pollution*. London: Routledge.

30 Lowe, P. (1992) Industrial agriculture and environmental regulation: a new agenda for rural sociology. *Sociologia Ruralis* 32, 4–10.

31 Department of the Environment & Welsh Office (1986) *River Quality in England and Wales 1985*. London: HMSO.

32 House of Commons Environment Committee (1987) *Pollution of Rivers and Estuaries*. Third Report. Session 1986–87. London: HMSO.

33 Rose, C. (1990) *The Dirty Man of Europe: The Great British Pollution Scandal*. London: Simon and Schuster.

34 Kinnersley, D. (1994) *Coming Clean: The Politics of Water and the Environment*. London: Penguin; Maloney, W. and Richardson, J. (1995) *Managing Policy Change in Britain: The Politics of Water*. Edinburgh University Press.

35 Lowe *et al.* (1997), p. 54.

36 Lowe *et al.* (1997); Ward, N. *et al.* (1998) Keeping matter in its place: pollution regulation and the reconfiguring of farmers and farming. *Environment and Planning A* 30, 1165–78.

37 Royal Commission on Environmental Pollution (1979) *Agriculture and Pollution*. Seventh Report. London: HMSO.

38 Tait, E. J. (1981) The flow of pesticides: industrial and farming perspectives, pp. 219–50 in T. O'Riordan and R. K. Turner (eds.) *Progress in Resource Management and Environmental Planning, Volume 3*. London: John Wiley.

39 The Observer (1989) Poison on tap: the first region by region guide to your drinking water. *The Observer Magazine* 6 August.

40 See, for example, Croll, B. (1991) Pesticides in surface waters and groundwaters. *Journal of the Institution of Water and Environmental Management* 5, 389–95; Greig-Smith, P. *et al.* (eds.) (1992) *Pesticides, Cereal Farming and the Environment: The Boxworth Project*. London: HMSO; Royal Commission on Environmental Pollution (1992) *Freshwater Quality*. Sixteenth Report. London: HMSO.

41 Lowe *et al.* (1997).

42 Department for Environment, Food and Rural Affairs (2013) *The National Action Plan for the Sustainable Use of Pesticides*. London: Defra; Department for Environment, Food and Rural Affairs (2021b) *The National Action Plan for the Sustainable Use of Pesticides – Consultation Document*. London: Defra.

43 Bailey, T. (2021) *Livestock's Longer Shadow: Hope Lives in Kindness*. Gloucester: Choir Press, pp. 112–33; see also Climate Change Committee (2020a) *Land Use: Policies for a Net Zero UK*. London: Climate Change Committee, p. 87; House of Commons Environmental Audit Committee (2022) *Water Quality in Rivers*. Third Report. Session 1986–87. London: The Stationary Office, pp. 45–8.

44 House of Commons Environmental Audit Committee (2022).

45 Woods, A. (2011) A historical synopsis of farm animal disease and public policy in twentieth century Britain. *Philosophical Transactions of the Royal Society* 366, 1943–54.

46 Lancet (1988), Salmonella enteritidis phage type 4: chicken and egg, 11(8613), 24 September, p. 720, quoted in Smith (1991) From policy community to issue network: Salmonella in eggs and the new politics of food. *Public Administration* 69, 235–55, p. 240.

47 Smith (1991).

48 Smith (1991).

49 North, R. (2001) *The Death of British Agriculture: The Wanton Destruction of a Key Industry*. London: Duckworth, p. 91.

50 Tansey, G. and Worsley, T. (1995) *The Food System: A Guide*. London: Earthscan, pp. 243–6.

51 Harison, R. (1964) *Animal Machines: The New Factory Farming Industry*. London: Vincent Stuart.

52 van Zwanenberg, P. and Millstone, E. (2005) *BSE: Risk, Science and Governance*. Oxford University Press, p. 233. van Zwanenberg and Millstone (2005) analysed the large volume of detailed information published as a result of the BSE Inquiry to show how concerns about economic damage to the UK beef industry led to an approach to public health and risk management that was "profoundly misleading and comprehensively flawed" (p. 229). For a more defensive account of MAFF's approach, see Packer, R. (2006) *The Politics of BSE*. Basingstoke: Palgrave Macmillan.

53 The BSE Inquiry (2000) *The BSE Inquiry Report. Sixteen Volumes*. National Archives.

54 See, for example, the hearings of the House of Commons Agriculture Committee (1990) *Bovine Spongiform Encephalopathy*. London: HMSO.

55 See BSE Inquiry (2000), Vol. 12, pp. 16–19.

56 Anderson, I. (2002) *Foot and Mouth Disease 2001: Lessons to Be Learned Inquiry Report*. London: Stationary Office, p. 60.

57 Woods, A. (2004) *A Manufactured Plague: The History of Foot and Mouth Disease in Britain*. London: Routledge, p. 148.

58 Ward, N. *et al.* (2004) Policy framing and learning the lessons from the UK's Foot and Mouth Disease crisis. *Environment and Planning C: Government and Policy* 22, 291–306.

59 Donaldson, A. and Wood, D. (2004) Surveilling strange materialities: categorisation in the evolving geographies of FMD biosecurity. *Environment and Planning D: Society and Space* 22, 373–91; Donaldson, A. (2008) Biosecurity after the event: risk politics and animal disease. *Environment and Planning A* 40, 1552–67.

60 Quoted in Donaldson (2008), p. 1554.

61 Donaldson (2008), p. 1559.

62 House of Commons Environment, Food and Rural Affairs Committee (2008) *Badgers and Cattle TB: The Final Report of the Independent Scientific Group on Cattle TB*. London: The Stationary Office.

63 Defra (2018) *Bovine TB Strategy Review*. London: Defra, p. 18.

64 Defra (2011) *Bovine TB Eradication Programme for England*. London: Defra, p. 6.

65 Defra (2018), p. 51.

66 Marsden, T. *et al.* (1993) *Constructing the Countryside*. London: University College London Press; Ward, N. (1993) The agricultural treadmill and the rural environment in

the post-productivist era. *Sociologia Ruralis* 33, 348–64; Ilbery, B. and Bowler, I. (1998) From agricultural productivism to post-productivism, pp. 57–84 in B. Ilbery (ed.) *The Geography of Rural Change*. Harlow: Longman.

67 Lowe, P. and Ward, S. (eds.) (1998) *British Environmental Policy and Europe: Politics and Policy in Transition*. London: Routledge.

68 Fennell, R. (1997) *The Common Agricultural Policy: Continuity and Change*. Oxford: Clarendon Press, p. 165.

69 Lowe, P. *et al.* (2002) Setting the next agenda? British and French approaches to the second pillar of the Common Agricultural Policy. *Journal of Rural Studies* 18, 1–17.

70 Helm, D. (2017) Agriculture after Brexit. *Oxford Review of Economic Policy* 33, S124–33; Lobley, M. *et al.* (2019) *The Changing World of Farming in Brexit UK*. London: Routledge.

71 Coe, S. and Finally, J. (2020) *The Agriculture Act 2020*. House of Commons Library Briefing Paper No. CPB 8702. London: House of Commons Library.

72 Department of the Environment (1990) *This Common Inheritance – Britain's Environmental Strategy*. London: HMSO, p. 97.

73 Department of the Environment (1990), p. 106.

74 UK Government (1994) *Sustainable Development: The UK Strategy*. Cm 2426. London: HMSO.

75 Whitby, M. and Ward, N. (1994) *The UK Strategy for Sustainable Agriculture: A Critical Analysis*. Centre for Rural Economy Research Report, University of Newcastle upon Tyne.

76 Cann, C. (1994) The background to the agriculture chapter in the Sustainable Development Strategy, pp. 4–6 in M. Whitby and N. Ward (eds.) *The UK Strategy for Sustainable Agriculture: A Critical Analysis*. CRE Report. University of Newcastle.

77 UK Government (1994), para 15.4, p. 106.

78 UK Government (1994), para 15.21, pp. 111–12.

79 Davison, A. (1994) Agriculture, air pollution and sustainability, pp. 43–9 in M. Whitby and N. Ward (eds.) *The UK Strategy for Sustainable Agriculture: A Critical Analysis*. CRE Report. University of Newcastle, p. 48.

80 UK Government (1994), para 15.3, p. 106.

81 Lowe, P. and Ward, N. (1994) Environmental policy and regulation, pp. 85–9 in M. Whitby and N. Ward (eds.) *The UK Strategy for Sustainable Agriculture: A Critical Analysis*. CRE Report. University of Newcastle, p. 87.

82 Policy Commission on the Future of Food and Farming (2002) *Farming and Food: A Sustainable Future*. London: Cabinet Office.

83 Department for Environment, Food and Rural Affairs (2012) *Greenhouse Gas Emissions From Agriculture Indicators*. London: Defra.

84 Climate Change Committee (2013) *Managing the Land in a Changing Climate*. London: Climate Change Committee.

85 See Figure 1.1 in Chapter 1.

5

THE EVOLUTION OF CLIMATE SCIENCE AND CLIMATE POLITICS

Introduction

Until the latter half of the twentieth century, it was generally thought that the Earth's climatic conditions were essentially stable. It took over a century for this assumption to be gradually overturned. From the early nineteenth century, scholars began to observe how the extent of Alpine glaciers appeared to have changed over time. This prompted the realisation that, over the long term, the Earth had experienced intermittent periods of extended glaciation or ice ages. Then in 1859, an Irish scientist, John Tyndall, working at the Royal Institution in London, established through experimentation that different gases found in the atmosphere absorbed different amounts of radiation. His discovery was to provide the scientific foundations for understanding the greenhouse gas effect and anthropogenic climate change.

This chapter describes how climate change emerged as a scientific problem, drawing on literature in the history of climate change and climate science.[1] It tells the story of how we came to be worried about climate change. Our models of social and economic development, through the industrial revolution and since, generated the climate change problem, but it was our growing scientific understanding of the Earth's atmospheric processes and the effects of greenhouse gases that highlighted it. Alongside this interplay between the *causes* of climate change and the development of the science to *understand* climate change is the growth of social and political movements and actions by governments and other organisations focused on tackling the climate change problem.

The Long Discovery of Climate Change, 1850s to 1980s

Although a few individual scientists were interested in the idea that climate may change over time, the general assumption until well into the twentieth century was

DOI: 10.4324/9781003278535-5

that the Earth's climate was essentially stable. Eighteenth-century historians noted that deforestation had warmed the European climate and those who recorded grape ripening dates were able to observe in the 1830s how parts of France seemed cooler than they had previously been. However, it was not until the 1860s, a decade of great scientific tumult in our understanding of the natural world, that the idea that the Earth's climate could change over time began to gain traction among scientific opinion. In 1837, following observations that the limits of glaciers appeared to have moved over time, Jean Louis Rodolphe Agassiz, a Swiss naturalist, presented an "ice age theory" to the Swiss Society of Natural Science. It was a radical new insight in an age dominated by biblical ideas of a created, stable world, but the idea that the limits of glaciation might ebb and flow began to gain acceptance.

Tyndall's 1859 discovery of the greenhouse gas effect introduced the profound idea that by changing the composition of gases in the atmosphere, the overall temperature of the planet could be altered. This realisation opened the door for subsequent work to establish the global warming potential of different gases in the Earth's atmosphere which provides the fundamental basis through which we measure the extent of human impacts upon the world's temperature. Soon after Tyndall published his results, Charles Darwin produced his book, *On the Origin of Species*, which together with ice age theory helped fundamentally challenge prevailing notions of time and stability with respect to both biological and climatic history. Tyndall, "one of the most outstanding scientific personalities of the Victorian age",[2] was involved in the debates about the possible causes of glacial epochs and as a member of the network of scientists around Darwin, played his role in the intellectual ferment of the time. In literature, French writer Eugène Mouton in 1872 and still in the age of steam wrote the first dystopian tale foretelling of the Earth warming and sea-level rising from the burning of fossil fuels.[3]

By the end of the nineteenth century, the nature and extent of previous glaciations had become well established, although the causes of fluctuations in ice cover were not yet clear. In his 1875 book, *Climate and Time*, James Croll set out his astronomical theory that changes in the Earth's orbit and the gravitational pull of the sun and moon might account for ice ages.[4] Others wondered about the changing composition of atmospheric gases. An important breakthrough came with the work of Svante Arrhenius, a Nobel Prize-winning chemist in Sweden, who in 1895 was able to show how doubling the concentration of carbon dioxide in the global atmosphere would increase the Earth's average surface temperature by 4–5°C. This insight quickly took hold so that by the end of the nineteenth century it became more widely accepted, at least among the scientific community, that changing levels of carbon dioxide in the atmosphere could cause global climate change. It opened up questions of whether burning coal could increase concentrations of carbon dioxide and so cause global warming, but these concerns did not gain much traction at the time and the carbon dioxide theory lay dormant for a few decades.[5]

By the mid-1930s, two decades of relatively milder winters in Europe and North America led to suggestions of possible longer term change in climate. Guy Stewart Callendar, an engineer based at Imperial College London, developed an interest in

Arrhenius's carbon dioxide theory of climate change and began collating meteorological data from around the world. He hypothesised that given the rate of change in the composition of the atmosphere as a result of humanity's emissions, a climate change effect might be detectable and he presented his calculations to the Royal Meteorological Society in London in 1938.[6] His paper represented "the first systematic attempt to link together the three pillars of the idea of anthropogenic climate change – the physical theory of carbon dioxide and the greenhouse effect, the rising concentration of carbon dioxide in the atmosphere, and the increase in world temperature".[7] Callendar calculated that world temperatures were increasing at the rate of 0.3°C per century, but his claims were met with general scepticism among his audience. In the 1960s, more than 20 years after he had first set out his calculations, Callendar reflected upon why people were reluctant to accept the carbon dioxide theory of climate change. It seemed unbelievable that a single factor within the vast complexity of climatic systems could cause such warming and many seemed to find the idea that humankind could effect such a change on the planet repugnant.[8] Although his physical reasoning has proved to be broadly correct, Callendar's interpretation of the significance and implications of his findings has not aged well. He felt burning fossil fuels would bring benefits as global warming would expand the northern margins of agricultural production and warming was desirable to prevent the return of glaciation.

The scientific debates prompted by the work of Arrhenius and Callendar could only be resolved if more could be known about the fate of carbon dioxide emitted into the atmosphere, including how much was absorbed by oceans and how much accumulated. Carbon dioxide monitoring sites were established in Hawaii and at the South Pole producing a flow of data and enabling a baseline of carbon dioxide concentrations to be established. In 1959, research scientist, Charles David Keeling showed how carbon dioxide concentration was rising at both sites by between 0.5 and 1.3 parts per million per year. This was another stepping-stone on the path to recognising anthropogenic climate change although its significance was not widely recognised at the time. The idea of global warming began to circulate more widely in society, at least among the intelligentsia. American playwright, Arthur Miller, recalled science-fiction writer Arthur C. Clarke first alerting him to the concept of global warming over breakfast in New York in the early 1960s, for example.[9] Keeling's measurements later showed how carbon dioxide concentrations rose through the 1960s and early 1970s. At the same time, early climate modelling began to produce calculations of climate sensitivity through the emerging technology of supercomputing. Atmospheric scientists Syukuro Manabe and Richard Wetherald at Princeton University produced pioneering new calculations of climate sensitivity, estimating that a doubling of carbon dioxide concentration could lead to warming of 2.3°C and 2.9°C, respectively, representing another significant step, and computer modelling has been a central tool of climate science ever since.

Later developments in environmental science enabled the reconstruction of the long-term climate record. During the 1960s and 1970s, air samples trapped in ice cores from the Greenland ice sheet and later from Antarctica showed changing concentrations of greenhouse gases over a 100,000-year period and revealed how environmental change need not be characterised by smooth long-term oscillations but could also involve short and relatively abrupt shifts in climatic conditions. An influential piece in *Nature* by Wallace Broeker in 1987 challenged the complacency of those who assumed gradual warming over the long term and warned of the potential for "sharp jumps" which could trigger the large-scale reorganisation of the Earth's climate system.[10] Possible rapid changes to the oceanic and atmospheric systems, such as those responsible for the Gulf Stream in the North Atlantic, could lead to catastrophic, sudden change. It became more common to think of the global climate system as potentially fragile and precarious, and vulnerable to a sudden tipping point.

The period from the 1960s to the 1980s saw the rising salience of global climate change as a scientific issue and a popular and political concern. Here, climate change cannot be separated from the general rise in environmental awareness and concern. Rachel Carson's *Silent Spring* in 1962 had highlighted the pervasive effects of chemical pesticides and ignited the world's ecological imagination. The loss of valued species and habitats and the problems of desertification and deforestation all began to attract international attention. There were increasing concerns about industrial pollution and nuclear waste. Together, these issues helped inspire growth in the number and membership of environmental pressure groups and the rise of green parties in many political systems. Environmentalism challenged notions of progress and by the early 1970s, the Club of Rome were pointing to fundamental limits to growth in global population, agriculture, resource-use, industry and pollution.[11]

In this atmosphere of heightened concern, the United Nations hosted its first conference on the environment in 1972 in Stockholm – the UN Conference on the Human Environment. The collapse in the international system of financial regulation and economic crises across much of the western world gave the early 1970s a sense of epoch shift. A deepening environmental critique of industrial models of development gathered pace with twin concerns about uneven development between the world's rich and poor, and the growing pressures on the Earth's environmental systems. In 1980, an independent commission led by former West German Chancellor, Willy Brandt, presented a global analysis of the challenges of economic development and social justice.[12] It emphasised the interconnectedness of the global economy and the need for a concerted effort on the part of the most developed countries to combat poverty and improve the development prospects among the poorest parts of the world. A few years later in 1983, the United Nations established the World Commission on Environment and Development, chaired by Gro Harlem Brundtland, to focus on the world's environmental and development problems. The Brundtland Report popularised the term "sustainable development" as a means of reconciling the challenge of economic development in the face of accelerating ecological degradation.[13] It proposed new guiding principles to bring development within ecological limits and provided a definition of sustainable development as "development that meets the needs of the present without

Since the first wave of widespread popular concern about global warming over the period 1988–1992, people have questioned the data, doubted the evidence and even attacked the scientists who produced the scientific reports. There are at least two categories of scepticism that need to be differentiated. The first comes from relativist social scientists working within the traditions of the sociology of scientific knowledge and science and technology studies. The second comes from conservative sceptics more traditionally associated with right-leaning think-tanks and sometimes funded by economic interests with much to lose from measures to curb greenhouse gas emissions. These are very distinct realms of scepticism and need to be understood separately, although it has been argued there are links between the two worlds.

The sociology of scientific knowledge developed in the 1960s following Thomas Kuhn's pioneering work on the dynamics of paradigm shifts in scientific thought.[29] The insight inspired a great deal of new work on the social practice of science and social influences upon the development of scientific knowledge. This sociology of science applied itself to questions of technological change that were particularly pertinent as the sometimes-unforeseen social, economic and environmental implications of the new technologies of the post-war world became increasingly apparent. In science and technology studies, it has become a mantra that science and technology are socially constructed. Social constructionists also conceptualise the natural world as a social construction that can only be understood through processes that are always susceptible to social shaping, be that through funding decisions, institutional norms, individual or collective ideologies and moral frameworks and so on.[30] Taking the relativism of social constructivism to its logical extreme leads to problems because of its sometimes-antagonistic relationship with the idea of "scientific facts". If anthropogenic climate change is merely a social construction, then it becomes difficult to see why anything should be done about it. Writings in the social sciences over recent years have questioned whether the relativism of postmodern social constructivism in the social sciences might be in part responsible not only for climate change scepticism, but also for the turn to "post-truth", fake news and popularism of the Donald Trump and Boris Johnson political eras.[31] Former British Universities Minister, David Willetts, when commenting on the implications of the UK Brexit referendum and the rise of Trump at a meeting of the Campaign for Social Science in November 2017 argued that postmodern thought in universities had contributed to the intellectual origins of current anti-intellectualism, illustrating how this idea had seeped into the world of politics too.

Early social science work on global environmental change does highlight a critical relativist scepticism. Sven Ove Hansson examined the writings on climate change of a host of sociologists of science including Fred Buttel, Brian Wynne, Mary Douglas, Arron Wildavsky, Steve Yearley and Steve Fuller.[32] An early piece by Buttel and colleagues discussed the "cautionary position" of some climate change sceptics and conceptualised global change as an environmental ideology.[33] In work with the geographer Peter Taylor, Buttel argued that uncritical acceptance of climate science had led to "a premature stress on global change problem amelioration" and the established scientific consensus on global warming had brought "premature closure on stylized facts of global change".[34] From this perspective, the task for social scientists had become to "explain why particular kinds of environmental knowledge claims, in particular those positing a global-level dynamic and constructed at a global level of analysis, tend to be privileged over others".[35] Hansson sets out how these early writings on global change were clearly doubtful and critical of the evidential basis of anthropogenic climate change and were suggesting that the heightened attention to the issue served the interests of some parties, including environmental pressure groups and environmental scientists. The critical relativists over-reached their own expertise when they argued "the current consensus on the greenhouse effect has raced ahead of the quality and quantity of scientific data on the issue, and … scientists and officials of environmental groups have played a major role in this achievement".[36] Buttel did later retract his position when in 1993 he wrote "neither a "strong programme" dissection of environmental knowledge nor a gratuitous postmodern cultural sociology of environmental beliefs will or should change the reality of global environmental problems".[37] Nevertheless, it is clear that in the early days of the widespread recognition of the global warming issue, social scientists were not slow to question the plausibility and legitimacy of climate science. Rather, there was a "stream of criticism against climate science" from relativists, which only petered out towards the end of the 1990s.[38] The scientific consensus had been established in 1988, when the IPCC was formed, and only strengthened thereafter. Notably, the work of these sceptical social science relativists was at times co-opted by the second category of sceptics – those from the conservative right.

The backlash against the claims of climate science lagged behind the exponential growth in coverage and concern about global warming from 1988, but not by far. In the United States, the George C. Marshall Institute was established in the 1980s to defend Ronald Reagan's Strategic Defence Initiative, but with the collapse of the Soviet Union and Eastern Bloc, it began to turn its attention to climate change and what it called "environmental alarmists". The Institute did not deny global warming, but in 1989 pointed to the sun rather than carbon dioxide emissions as the cause.[39] It had quite an impact within the US Government and slowed the momentum that had been building on tackling climate change. The Institute's claims were considered and rejected by the IPCC in its First Assessment, published in May 1990. In the 1992 US presidential campaign, Democratic candidate Al Gore emphasised climate change following publication of his book, *Earth in the Balance*.[40] His position on climate change was attacked by opponents and the evidential basis for claims and counterclaims about climate change and climate science became steeped in controversy over this period.[41]

There was intense wrangling over the wording of the IPCC's Second Assessment as delegates from Saudi Arabia and Kuwait, along with American industry lobbyists, argued about the interpretation of the latest scientific evidence in what became known as "the Chapter 8 controversy".[42] In the Summary for Policymakers part of the report, the dispute boiled down to what adjective should describe human influence on the global climate. After more than twenty different adjectives were tried, the outcome of the exercise was that the Assessment concluded that "the balance of evidence suggests that there is a *discernible* human influence on global climate".[43] Fred Singer attacked the process of producing the IPCC report. The Global Climate Coalition, a sceptical organisation that opposed climate action, accused the IPCC of "institutionalised scientific cleansing".[44] Fred Seitz wrote to the *Wall Street Journal* accusing IPCC author, Ben Santer, of being a fraud. The Marshall Institute's work to challenge the scientific consensus on climate change had a significant impact, was influential in the Bush White House and was published in the *Wall Street Journal* reaching millions of people. Given there were vocal differences, even if they were between the large majority of climate scientists on the one hand and, in comparison, a very small group of dissenters on the other, media outlets tended to air both sides of the argument, thereby giving disproportionate coverage and airtime to the sceptics. "Balanced" coverage leads to informational bias as minority and maverick views are given more credence than they might otherwise warrant.[45]

A key moment in the conflict between climate scientists and climate science sceptics was the Climategate affair, the "last gasp" in hardcore climate change denial.[46] Described in a 2021 BBC Radio 4 investigative series as "The Hack that Changed the World",[47] the controversy was triggered by the hacking of the server at the Climatic Research Unit (CRU) at UEA in November 2009 and the publication of a large cache of e-mails and other documents through climate sceptic websites. Climate sceptic bloggers quickly began suggesting that the stolen and published material contained the smoking gun that proved that scientific claims about anthropogenic climate change were the result of a conspiracy among climate scientists to dupe the rest of the world. This sceptical interpretation framed the way the controversy unfolded. The timing of the hack was significant in that it was just weeks before important international climate negotiations were due to begin at a COP meeting in Copenhagen. Echoing the approach of US sceptics in the 1990s, the CRU material was highly selectively quoted and misleadingly used to convey a sense of climate scientists manipulating data.[48]

A central part of the controversy was an e-mail from Phil Jones, the Director of CRU, in which he wrote he had used "Mike's Nature trick" in a 1999 graph to "hide the decline." The phrases were latched onto by climate change sceptics and by politicians, including Sarah Palin, the former US Vice Presidential candidate, who spoke of "a highly politicised scientific circle" who "manipulated data to 'hide the decline' in global temperatures".[49] Former UK Chancellor of the Exchequer, Nigel Lawson, was also prominent in calling into question the use of, and motives behind, the science. The "decline" in question came from tree-ring data that had been highly correlated with temperature, but the relationship broke down after the 1950s and so more thermometer data had to be merged with the tree ring surrogate data. The practice was justifiable. Out of context, the e-mail was able to be presented as something suspicious and devious when in reality it was a simple, matter-of-fact e-mail conversation between two scientists about the statistical presentation of data. The Climategate affair resulted in several independent inquiries into the integrity of CRU's science and the serious claims made about malpractice. Of eight inquiries, none found any evidence of fraud or scientific misconduct. Fred Pearce of *The Guardian* examined all the e-mails and the claims of those critics of the CRU. He described the CRU's critics as a diverse set. Some "fitted the stereotype of right-wing attack dogs" but others were "amateur scientific sleuths ... with a healthy scepticism for received wisdom".[50] What the private e-mail correspondence between the climate scientists did reveal, though, was their "bunker mentality" as a result of the continual pressure and challenge from climate sceptics.[51]

Climategate was a high-profile global public controversy and well-illustrated the contested nature of climate science and the strength of feeling on each side of the argument. Analysis of media coverage of climate science around the UN Copenhagen conference in December 2009 found that climate contrarians were given disproportionate coverage.[52] Subsequent analysis of a network of 171 blogs and found that three, *Climate Audit, JoNova* and *Watts Up with That* were most central in influencing sceptical opinion and were acting as alternative sites of expertise for climate sceptic audiences.[53] From the media coverage, it would be easy and understandable for an uninformed observer to form the view that the debate about the existence of anthropogenic climate change was taking place between two relatively equally balanced views of the evidence. In fact, the vast majority of the world's climate scientists were of one view and an extremely small minority thought otherwise.

After the election of Donald Trump to the US Presidency in 2016, climate change sceptics had a new friend in the White House. Trump's policy was to strengthen US energy independence through greater fossil fuel use and in June 2017 he announced the withdrawal of the United States from the Paris Climate Change Agreement. With the election of Joe Biden in 2020, the United States began to re-engage with international climate change diplomacy and there was a sense of hope among international climate change scientists and diplomats that the Trump years might be an aberration. Biden and the Americans played a prominent role in pressing the case for climate action at the Glasgow COP in November 2021.

Twenty-First-Century Climate Governance and Governmentalities

As we have seen, 1988 proved a pivotal year in climate politics and international efforts to address the growth of greenhouse gas emissions. A rhythm of IPCC scientific assessments, UN intergovernmental conferences and the annual COP meetings was set in train. Key milestones since 1988 have been the 1992 Rio Summit, the 1997 Kyoto Protocol and the 2015 Paris Agreement. The Rio Summit was the biggest intergovernmental conference of its kind and included the most heads of government. Unexpectedly, the US President, George H.W. Bush attended the conference to sign the agreements which proved an important symbolic and political boost to the event. There were five major outcomes from the meeting: two Conventions (the Framework Convention on Climate Change and the Convention on Biological

Diversity); the Rio Declaration on Environment and Development; the Statement on Forest Principles; and Agenda 21 – an action plan for the years to the twenty-first century and beyond. The Framework Convention on Climate Change came into force in 1994 and established the system of annual COP meetings, the first taking place in Berlin in March 1995. The COP system is open to all parties and operates on a "one country-one vote" system of governance. The COP has the authority to take decisions necessary to promote the effective implementation of the Convention. Signatories to the Convention were required to produce reports on their plans to combat global warming and these were due within six months of the date on which signatories ratified the Convention.

There were immediate controversies about the accuracy of the data in reports, and the assumptions upon which they were based, and efforts commenced to find standardised or comparable methodologies for calculating greenhouse gas emissions. Already by COP 1 in Berlin, pressures were building to try and achieve international agreement on fixed targets for reductions in greenhouse gas emissions, led by the Alliance of Small Island States, some of whom faced the most pressing existential threat from sea-level rise as a result of global warming. A draft protocol ahead of the Berlin COP proposed that developed countries be required to reduce their carbon dioxide emissions by 20 per cent of their 1990 levels by 2005.[54] Several years of negotiations followed Rio as the international community moved through the Framework process and COP meetings towards a global commitment on reducing greenhouse gas emissions along the same lines as the Montreal Protocol on ozone depletion – a targets and timetables approach.

The Kyoto Protocol was adopted in Kyoto, Japan, in December 1997 and entered into force in February 2005. It required that the developed nations reduce their collective greenhouse gas emissions by 5.2 per cent by the period 2008–2012 relative to 1990 levels but permitted that this reduction could be achieved through a range of trading and investment mechanisms. Coming to a deal at Kyoto was a difficult process, and there followed a further period of wrangling as signatory governments sought to protect their national economic interests. Kyoto was a significant moment in setting "quantified limitation and reduction objectives within specific time frames".[55] The Montreal Protocol on Ozone Depletion, on which Rio and Kyoto were modelled, had restricted emissions of a small number of artificial gases released through the production practices of a small number of multinational chemical companies. In contrast, the Kyoto process was restricting emissions that resulted from just about every aspect of social and economic life and involved every individual, company and public institution on the planet. And in the absence of a world government, the framework depends upon sovereign national governments making formal commitments to act, and then delivering on these commitments.

The Kyoto Protocol had its critics. For example, some UK climate scientists soon criticised its targets as insufficient.[56] The reduction commitments only applied to 38 industrialised nations who accounted for over half of all emissions. However, these countries were predicted to contribute only 25 per cent of the anticipated growth in emissions over the next 20 years. Three-quarters of the growth in emissions was expected to come from the less developed countries that were outside the Protocol's commitment to reductions. As a consequence, the scientists concluded, the Kyoto Protocol would do relatively little to draw down the rate of climate change. They argued that given the continuing risks of catastrophic climate change, Kyoto and the subsequent COP in Buenos Aires had to be seen as steps in a longer term process that would need to bring much greater reductions in emissions in future. There were also problems with individual governments becoming sceptical of the Protocol and looking to withdraw from their commitments. In 2001, new US President George W. Bush signalled his dissatisfaction with the Protocol arguing that it was an "unfair and ineffective means of addressing global climate change concerns".[57] The US Senate was concerned that commitments only applied to developed nations and not the less developed. It was felt that the Protocol would unduly harm the US economy and so the United States refused to ratify it. Eventually, a deal was done to enable the Treaty to go into legal effect without the United States.

In the UK, the new Labour Government pledged to go beyond the UK's Kyoto target of a 12.5 per cent reduction on 1990 emissions by 2008–2012 and achieve a 20 per cent reduction by 2010. It introduced a new Climate Change Programme in 2000 and a form of climate change levy in 2001 which targeted the largest energy users. A pilot Emissions Trading Scheme was established in 2002 and a Renewables Obligation was launched to stimulate electricity generation from renewable sources. More radical policy change came between 2006 and 2010. A revised Climate Change Programme in 2006 sought to reinvigorate emission reduction efforts across the Government and the Treasury-commissioned Stern review was published, making the economic case for an ambitious transition to a low-carbon economy.[58] David Miliband's appointment as Secretary of State for Environment, Food and Rural Affairs led to the establishment of the new Office for Climate Change to provide independent cross-departmental advice and analysis and the Government announcing its Climate Change Bill. The subsequent 2008 Climate Change Act has provided the framework for UK climate policy since. The Act established long-term statutory targets for the UK to decarbonise and reduce greenhouse gas emissions, first committing the Government to a target of reducing the UK's net emissions by 80 per cent relative to 1990 levels by 2050. The Act established the Climate Change Committee as an independent statutory body to advise on climate policy and targets. Since 2017, its chair has been Lord Deben who, as John Gummer, served as Secretary of State for the Environment (1993–1997) and for Agriculture, Fisheries and Food (1989–1993). The Committee has established a strong independent reputation, helping strengthen the credibility of the UK's climate targets and bringing a longer-term perspective to bear on climate change policymaking. Crucially, it has developed a series of six carbon budgets covering the period 2008–2037. It does not have any formal powers to change government policy but instead relies on the political embarrassment its assessments may cause. Although the UK Government has not followed the Committee's advice in every detail, its statutory advice on carbon targets has generally been followed.[59]

In international climate science and policy, the construction of a global climate budget has helped guide negotiations on emissions reductions processes. The Global Carbon Project was established in 2001 to track the major carbon fluxes and their trends and has published annual reports on the state of the carbon cycle since 2007.[60] Contemporary carbon governance "hinges on the ability to account for stocks and flows of carbon",[61] and the carbon accounting enabled by the Global Carbon Budget facilitates a new form of climate governmentality in which emissions are rendered measurable and governable. The carbon budget and carbon economy exercises a "systemic structuring condition"[62] upon sociotechnical strategies for lowering emissions.

The next key milestone in international emissions reduction was the Paris Climate Change Conference (COP 21) held in December 2015. Lessons were learned from the difficulties in reaching agreement in Kyoto and considerable preparatory work took place in the run-up to Paris. The IPCC's Fifth Assessment, published in 2014, had concluded that warming of the climate was unequivocal, human influence on the climate was clear, that continued emissions would cause further warming and changes in all components of the climate system, and that substantial and sustained reductions in emissions would be necessary. Governments published "Nationally Determined Contributions" (NDCs) for reducing emissions to limit warming to below 2°C before the 196 countries met in Paris. Analysis suggested the pledges would only reduce expected warming of 4–5°C to around 2.7°C. Outside the COP negotiations, the United States and China, the world's two biggest emitters, issued a joint commitment to reducing emissions. The final agreement was pushed for by a coalition of over 100 countries (the "High Ambition Coalition") which included the United States, the EU and at least 75 developing and least developed countries from the Pacific, Caribbean and Africa. They did not want a minimalist agreement and pressed for a 1.5°C temperature goal, a clear pathway for a low-carbon future, a five-year review process and a climate finance package.[63] The coalition was able to bring pressure to bear on some of the more reluctant signatories such as Saudi Arabia and Australia.

On 12 December 2015, the Paris Climate Agreement was signed to come into force by 2020. Unexpectedly, the Conference agreed the ambition of keeping temperatures "well below 2°C above pre-industrial levels and to pursue efforts to limit the temperature increase to 1.5°C above pre-industrial levels" with a further ambition for emissions to peak "as soon as possible". The Agreement established a process of five-yearly stock-takes with NDCs key to the system's success. The UK Government welcomed the Agreement suggesting it represented a turning point towards a low carbon, sustainable future. It said the long-term goal "sends a strong signal to investors, businesses, and policy-makers about the shift to a low carbon economy and provides confidence that will help drive the scale of investment needed".[64] In June 2019, the UK Parliament passed legislation requiring the Government to reduce emissions by 100 per cent of 1990 levels by 2050 and achieve net zero. It was the first major economy to legally commit to net zero and the step is cited as probably the most significant legacy of then Prime Minister Theresa May's premiership.[65] The Climate Change Committee has described achieving net zero as technically feasible but "highly challenging".[66]

The IPCC's cycle of work between its Fifth and Sixth Assessments has been the most ambitious since its establishment. Since the Fifth Assessment in 2014, it has produced a series of Special Reports on thematic issues such as global warming of 1.5°C, oceans and climate change and land. The Special Report on *Climate Change and Land*, published in August 2019, provided the first comprehensive overview of the entire land-climate system and addressed land itself as a "critical resource". Ahead of COP26 in Glasgow, in August 2021 the IPCC published the first part of its Sixth Assessment, a "Summary for Policymakers".[67] The IPCC's report used blunter terminology than previous assessments. It showed how over the past decade the Earth had been between 0.95°C and 1.2°C hotter than it was in the second half of the nineteenth century, which is 0.2°C higher than the IPCC's previous assessment. Improved science meant the range of the IPCC's measures and predictions were narrowing. It predicted that the world is likely to be 1.5°C warmer than preindustrial levels by 2040, even with planned reductions in emissions, and that the evidence for human-induced warming was "unequivocal". It predicted that temperatures should be expected to continue to rise until at least 2050, bringing more frequent and severe floods and heatwaves. Confidence in its predictions had strengthened from medium confidence to high confidence. Predictions tended to be based on multiple lines of evidence, some from computer models but increasingly from improved physical understanding of the various planetary processes involved and from direct observations. In a much-quoted phrase, the UN Secretary General, Antonio Guterres, said the report signalled "code red for humanity."[68]

The 2021 Glasgow Pact agreed at COP26 was significant because the parties formally took stock of the commitments made through NDCs to emissions reductions under the Paris Agreement. Difficulties arose in the final stages around financial commitments for richer countries to help poorer countries and commitments to phase out coal use in power generation. The culmination of the COP was the last-minute move by India, backed by China, to water down the wording of the commitment to end the use of coal power, which dashed hopes of a more ambitious commitment. The Pact strengthened financial commitments to support mitigation and adaptation in developing countries and finalised rules established in Paris on carbon markets. It committed countries to improve their 2030 emissions targets in their NDCs that had put the world on course only to limit warming to between 2.5°C and 2.7°C. By revising their NDCs over the following 12 months, the Parties agreed to seek to strengthen the prospects of keeping below 2°C by the end of the century and of reaching the target of 1.5°C.[69] However, because the COP process has no legal enforcement mechanism, its primary power rests on the peer pressure and public scrutiny that surrounds the commitments made. Other pledges made at Glasgow included a Declaration on Forest and Land Use which committed countries to halt and reverse deforestation and land degradation by 2030 covering over 85 per cent of the world's forests. In addition, 28 countries representing 75 per cent of global trade in key commodities that threaten forests, such as palm oil, cocoa and soya, signed a trade statement committing to actions to reduce pressure on forests.[70]

Over 100 countries also signed a new Global Methane Pledge orchestrated by the United States and EU. Methane has been estimated to be responsible for about 30 per cent of warming to date and atmospheric concentrations have risen sharply since 2007.[71] The pledge called for countries to reduce methane emissions by 30 per cent between 2020 and 2030. Although criticised for being unambitious, such a reduction would reduce global average temperature by an estimated 0.2°C and the pledge was signed by 15 of the top 30 national emitters, including the United States, EU and Indonesia.[72] At the same time, the United States published its own action plan for reduction in methane emissions, focusing on oil and gas production, landfill sites and agriculture.[73] Although not one of the elements of the COP26 attracting the highest profile coverage, the pledge was hailed as potentially one of the meeting's enduring legacies.[74]

Conclusions

This chapter has traced the evolution of climate science and climate policy over the past century and particularly since the international community were compelled into action in 1988. The strengthening scientific consensus around the evidence of anthropogenic climate change and the target levels by which greenhouse gas emissions will need to be reduced has been achieved through the establishment of international structures and processes of scientific assessment and peer review, especially through the IPCC. Yet the scale of the challenge also prompted a backlash. An international network of maverick dissenting scientists and blogging sceptics, coupled with think tanks and lobby groups backed by economic interests invested in the status quo, have had some success is slowing the momentum and efforts to address climate change, not least in the United States during the George W. Bush and Donald Trump Presidencies. Nevertheless, the process of annual COP meetings and international climate change agreements is, albeit too slowly for many environmental campaigners, committing the governments of the world make the changes necessary to reduce emissions. There remains much debate about whether the agreements go far enough and fast enough, but there is no doubt that efforts to promote the transition to a post-carbon economy now pervade many areas of policymaking across the world. By the end of 2021, four-fifths of the world's economy were subject to net zero emissions targets.

Since the Paris Agreement, extreme weather events around the world have become more common and more widely experienced. Forest fires in the United States and Australia and flooding and heatwaves in Europe have rendered the claims of climate change deniers increasingly implausible. In the run-up to COP26 in Glasgow, less airtime seemed to be given to the sceptical view and a consensus strengthened around the need for action to limit temperature increase to well below 2°C. The IPCC's work on agriculture and land use and the Global Methane Pledge agreed in Glasgow have helped raise the profile of this complex and difficult source of emissions. In the next chapter, drawing on the recent work by the IPCC on climate change and land, we turn to the implications of international climate change commitments for food and farming systems generally, and in the UK in particular.

Notes

1 Fleming, J. (2005) *Historical Perspectives on Climate Change.* Oxford University Press; Weart, S. (2003) *The Discovery of Global Warming.* Harvard University Press.

2 Hulme, M. (2009) *Why We Disagree About Climate Change: Understanding Controversy, Inaction and Opportunity.* Cambridge University Press, p. 45.

3 Mouton, E. (1872) The end of the world, pp. 1–9 in D. Ford (ed.) *Grave Predictions: Tales of Mankind's Post-Apocalyptic, Dystopian and Disastrous Destiny.* New York: Dover Publications.

4 Weart (2003).

5 Hulme (2009), pp. 47–8.

6 Hulme (2009), pp. 48–53.

7 Hulme (2009), p. 50.

8 Hulme (2009), p. 53.

9 Miller, A. (1987) *Timebends: A Life.* London: Bloomsbury, p. 513; Bigsby, C. (2011) *Arthur Millar 1962–2005.* London: Weidenfeld and Nicholson, p. 15.

10 Broeker, W. (1987) Unpleasant surprises in the greenhouse. *Nature* 328, 123–6.

11 Meadows, D. *et al.* (1972) *The Limits to Growth. A Report for the Club of Rome's Project on the Predicament of Mankind.* London: Pan Books.

12 Independent Commission on International Development Issues (1980) *North-South: A Programme for Survival.* Basingstoke: Macmillan.

13 World Commission on Environment and Development (1987) *Our Common Future.* Oxford University Press.

14 World Commission on Environment and Development (1987), p. 43.

15 World Commission on Environment and Development (1987), p. 1.

16 Buttel, F. *et al.* (1990) From limits to growth to global change: constraints and contradictions in the evolution of environmental science and ideology. *Global Environmental Change* 1, 57–66, p. 58.

17 Buttel *et al.* (1990), p. 60, emphasis in original.

18 Hulme (2009), pp. 63–6.

19 Quoted in Hulme (2009), p. 64.

20 Quoted in Hulme (2009), p. 65.

21 Department of the Environment (1990) *This Common Inheritance – Britain's Environmental Strategy.* London: HMSO.

22 Maddison, D. and Pearce, D. (1995) The UK and global warming policy, pp. 123–43 in T. Gray (ed.) *UK Environmental Policy in the 1990s.* Basingstoke: Macmillan.

23 Pearce, D. *et al.* (1989) *Blueprint for a Green Economy.* London: Earthscan.

24 Maddison and Pearce (1995), p. 127.

25 Hulme (2009), p. 291.

26 Quoted in Maddison and Pearce (1995), p. 142.

27 UK Government (1994) *Sustainable Development: The UK Strategy.* Cm 2426. London: HMSO.

28 Quoted in Hulme (2009), p. 51. IPCC conventions are that the term "likely" implies a chance of between 66 and 90 per cent chance that the statement is correct and the term "very likely" implies greater than 90 per cent.

29 Kuhn, T. (1962) *The Structure of Scientific Revolutions.* University of Chicago Press.

30 MacKenzie, D. and Wajcman, J. (eds.) (1985) *The Social Shaping of Technology.* Milton Keynes: Open University Press; Bijker, W. *et al.* (eds.) (1987) *The Social Construction of Technological Systems: New Directions in the Sociology and History of Technology.* Cambridge, MA: MIT Press; Hackett, E. *et al.* (eds.) (2008) *The Handbook of Science and Technology Studies.* Third Edition. Cambridge, MA: MIT Press.

31 See, for example, Hansson, S. O. (2020) Social constructionism and climate science denial. *European Journal for Philosophy of Science*, 10, 37–63.

32 Hansson (2020).

33 Buttel *et al.* (1990), p. 58 and p. 63.

34 Buttel, F. and Taylor, P. (1992) Environmental sociology and global environmental change: a critical assessment. *Society and Natural Resources* 5, 211–30, p. 218.

35 Buttel and Taylor (1992), p. 221.

36 Buttel *et al.* (1990), p. 58.

37 Quoted in Hansson (2020).

38 Hansson (2020), p. 15.

39 Mann, M. (2021) *The New Climate War: The Fight to Take Back Our Planet.* London: Scribe.

40 Gore, A. (1992) *Earth in the Balance: Ecology and the Human Spirit.* New York: Plume.

41 Oreskes and Conway (2020).

42 Lahsen, M. (1999) The detection and attribution of conspiracies: the controversy over Chapter 8, pp. 111–36 in G. Marcus (ed.) *Paranoia Within Reason: A Casebook on Conspiracy as Explanation.* Chicago, IL: Chicago University Press.

43 Quoted in Oreskes and Conway (2020), p. 205, emphasis added.

44 Oreskes and Conway (2020), p. 207.

45 Boykoff, M. and Boykoff, J. (2004) Balance as bias: Global warming and the US prestige press. *Global Environmental Change* 14, 125–36.

46 Mann, M. (2021), p. 36.

47 Corera, G. (2021) *The Hack That Changed the World.* BBC Radio 4 series broadcast 1st to 5th November.

48 Pearce, F. (2010) *The Climate Files: The Battle for the Truth About Global Warming.* London: Guardian Books.

49 Quoted in Pearce (2010), p. 174.

50 Pearce (2010), p. 12.

51 Pearce (2010), p. 13.

52 Gavin, N. and Marshall, T. (2011) Mediated climate change in Britain: Scepticism on the web and on television around Copenhagen. *Global Environmental Change* 21, 1035–44.

53 Sharman, A. (2014) Mapping the climate sceptical blogosphere. *Global Environmental Change* 26, 159–70.

54 Werksman, J. (1995) The United Nations Framework Convention on Climate Change: the first conference of the parties opening in Berlin. *Global Environmental Change* 4, 339–40.

55 Quoted in Hulme (2009), p. 291.

56 Parry, M. *et al.* (1998) Buenos Aires and Kyoto targets do little to reduce climate change impacts. *Global Environmental Change* 8, 285–9.

57 Quoted in Hulme (2009), p. 109.

58 Stern, N. (2007) *The Economics of Climate Change: The Stern Review.* Cambridge University Press.

59 Averchenkova, A. *et al.* (2018) *The Role of Independent Bodies in Climate Governance: The UK's Committee on Climate Change.* London: The Grantham Research Institute on Climate Change and the Environment.

60 Poruschi, L. *et al.* (2010) *Ten Years of Advancing Knowledge on the Global Carbon Cycle and its Management.* Tsukuba: Global Carbon Project; Le Quéré, C. *et al.* (2013) The global carbon budget 1959–2011. *Earth Systems Science Data* 5, 165–85.

61 Lövebrand, E. and Stripple, J. (2011) Making climate change governable: accounting for carbon as sinks, credits and personal budgets. *Critical Policy Studies* 5, 187–8.

62 Low, S. and Boettcher, M. (2020) Delaying decarbonization: climate governmentalities and sociotechnical strategies from Copenhagen to Paris. *Earth Systems Governance* 5, 100073, p. 1.

63 House of Commons Library (2015) *Paris Climate Change Conference*. House of Commons Library Papers CPB 7393. London: House of Commons, p. 18.

64 Department for Energy and Climate Change (2015) World agrees historic global climate deal – a historic new global climate agreement has been struck at the United Nations conference on climate change in Paris. *DECC Press Release*, 12 December. London: DECC.

65 Barwell, G. (2021) *Chief of Staff: Notes from Downing Street*. London: Atlantic, p. 392.

66 Climate Change Committee (2019) *Net Zero: The UK's Contribution to Stopping Global Warming*. London: Climate Change Committee, p. 271.

67 Intergovernmental Panel on Climate Change (2021) Summary for policymakers, in V. Masson-Delmotte *et al.* (eds.) *Climate Change 2021: The Physical Science Basis. Contribution of Working Group I to the Sixth Assessment Report of the Intergovernmental Panel on Climate Change*. Cambridge University Press.

68 IPCC (2021); The Economist (2021) A new reality. *The Economist* 14 August, pp. 65–7; Hodgson, C. (2021) World likely to be 1.5C warmer by 2040, UN's science panel warns. *Financial Times* 19 August, p. 1.

69 Hook, L. (2021) Relief and frustration as climate deal is done., *Financial Times* 15 November, p. 2.

70 Prime Minister's Office (2021) Over 100 leaders make landmark pledge to end deforestation at COP26. *10 Downing Street Press Release*, 2 November.

71 Vaughan, A. (2021) COP26: 105 countries pledge to cut methane emissions by 30 per cent. *New Scientist* 2 November.

72 Clancy, H. (2021) Here's what to make of the COP26 methane moment. *GreenBiz Group Press Release*, 2 November.

73 White House Office of Domestic Climate Policy (2021) *US Methane Emissions Reduction Action Plan: Critical and Commonsense Steps to Cut Pollution and Consumer Costs, While Boosting Good-Paying Jobs and American Competitiveness*.

74 Clancy (2021).

6

REDUCING GREENHOUSE GAS EMISSIONS FROM FOOD, FARMING AND LAND USE

Introduction

Agriculture and the food system contribute around a third of greenhouse gas emissions worldwide. The emphasis on reducing emissions from electricity generation and transport systems to date is, in part, because it is relatively more straightforward to envisage and manage a transition to lower carbon systems in those sectors because of the availability of new, low-emission technologies. Agriculture and food, on the other hand, produce highly diffuse emissions from livestock and land management practices, as well as food distribution, retail and consumption, which make the transition a greater challenge. Although international efforts to tackle climate change and curb emissions can be traced to the late 1980s and early 1990s, it is only in recent years that reducing emissions from agriculture and land use, and the development of measures in response, have begun to come to the fore.[1] The IPCC in 2019 produced a new analysis of the role of land use and the food system in climate change, and research has mapped the changing emissions contributions of different parts of the food system over the past three decades and how these trends vary across different parts of the world.[2] In more rapidly industrialising countries, the proportion of emissions from the food system is diminishing, even if absolute quantities of emissions from the food system are increasing. For example, in Asia between 1990 and 2015, emissions from the food system increased from 5.7 $GtCO_2e$ to 7.1 $GtCO_2e$, although because of the rate of growth of industry and other economic activity, the proportion of total emissions from the food system fell from 58 to 29 per cent.[3] Global emissions from the food system have been generally increasing (Figure 6.1). However, in the UK, since the mid-1990s, total greenhouse gas emissions from the food system have been slowly but steadily declining, although not at a rate yet sufficient for the UK to meet its 2050 net zero target (Figure 6.2).

DOI: 10.4324/9781003278535-6

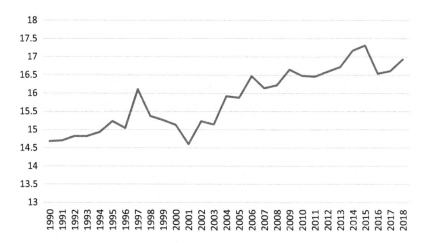

FIGURE 6.1 Total Greenhouse Gas Emissions from the Global Food System, 1990–2018 (GtCO$_2$e)

Source: Data from the EDGAR Emissions Database for Global Atmospheric Research. (https://edgar.jrc.ec.europa.eu/edgar_food); See Crippa *et al.* (2021a,b).

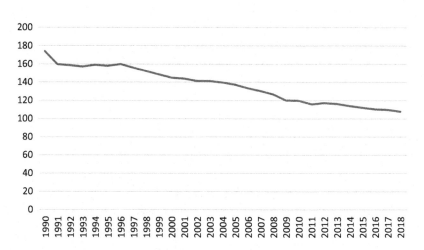

FIGURE 6.2 Total Greenhouse Gas Emissions from the UK Food System, 1990–2018 (MtCO$_2$e)

Source: Data from the EDGAR Emissions Database for Global Atmospheric Research. (https://edgar.jrc.ec.europa.eu/edgar_food); See Crippa *et al.* (2021a,b).

Chapters 3 and 4 considered the rise of agricultural productivism and the post-war transformation of farming and the response to the resultant environmental and public health problems. Chapter 5 explained how climate science came to reveal the problem of climate change and the efforts of the international community, including the UK Government, to begin curtailing emissions. In this chapter, we trace the recent history of thinking about the role of agriculture, food and land management in the context of the climate change challenge and the recent steps towards a net zero world. The chapter explains the IPCC's assessment of the role of land use globally in climate change, before examining recent prescriptions for agriculture and land use in the UK. The most authoritative analysis comes from the UK's statutory advisory body on climate change, the Climate Change Committee, although other organisations, including the National Farmers' Union and the Food, Farming and Countryside Commission, have also set out proposals for the net zero transition. These different sets of prescriptions or pathways are compared before the chapter concludes by explaining the main tensions in different ways of envisaging the agri-food system in the net zero transition.

The IPCC, Land and Agriculture

The IPCC's Sixth Assessment has been the most ambitious period of the IPCC's work. A novel development since 2016 has been the establishment of working groups to produce more specialist reports and the *Special Report on Climate and Land* is an early example.[4] The Special Report, based on an assessment of literature published up to April 2019, estimated that by 2015, about three-quarters of the global ice-free land surface was affected by human use.[5] Humans appropriate between a quarter and a third of global potential net primary production, and cropland covers 12–14 per cent of the global ice-free land surface. Globally, since 1961, the per capita supply of food calories has increased by approximately a third, and the consumption of vegetable oils and meat has more than doubled. Higher levels of production have been aided by the use of inorganic nitrogen fertiliser, which has increased nearly nine-fold since 1961.

Climate change is already impacting upon global land use and food production. The average temperature over land for the period 2006–2015 was 1.53°C higher than for the period 1850–1900 and warmer temperatures are altering growing seasons, reducing some regional crop yields, reducing fresh water availability and putting biodiversity under stress. Nevertheless, the drivers of land-use change, such as technological changes, population growth and increasing per capita demand for ecosystem services are projected to continue and will only accentuate the social and environmental challenges from climate change. Climate change is expected to lead to greater volatility in food production and prices, although trade in food commodities could potentially help buffer some of these effects. Even with a global population forecast to grow to almost 10 billion by 2050, the IPCC were confident that sustainable food supply and food consumption, based on nutritionally balanced diets, could still enhance food security even under expected climate and socio-economic changes. It should be technically feasible to continue to feed the world. However, to do so will require an active change in the global food system including promoting globally equitable diets and tackling food loss and waste, estimated to affect 25–30 per cent of food produced.[6] Rapidly reducing emissions will help in meeting this challenge. The IPCC stressed that restricting warming to well below 2°C would greatly reduce the negative impact of climate change on land ecosystems,[7] but the reverse is also true. Failure to restrict warming to well below 2°C will greatly worsen the damage. Furthermore, those sorts of climate change mitigations that require large land areas (such as growing bioenergy crops or afforestation) will compete with existing uses of land such as growing food. Increased competition for land could increase food prices and bring pressures for further intensification of agricultural land use.

Land use contributes about a quarter of global greenhouse gas emissions, principally carbon dioxide emissions from deforestation, methane emissions from rice and ruminant livestock and nitrous oxide emissions from fertiliser use. However, on the other side of the equation, land ecosystems can take up, or sequestrate, large amounts of carbon. During the period 2007–2016, the agriculture, forestry and other land-use sectors accounted for around 13 per cent of carbon dioxide emissions, 44 per cent of methane and 82 per cent of nitrous oxide emissions from human activities globally. The IPCC emphasise that there are measures that could be taken to reduce emissions from land management practices and enhance the uptake of carbon and these can have broader benefits of enhancing productivity, soil fertility and biodiversity. However, addressing the land-use challenges associated with climate change will require major changes in social and economic systems and these are likely to be just as important, if not more so, than changes in science and technology. While there are some generalisable strategies that will be important to the climate change transition across the globe, land use and ecological dynamics vary considerably. In addition, the social organisation of land management including patterns of local land ownership vary. Strategies, therefore, have to be regionally and locally tailored because these social and economic systems are so crucial in the capacity to respond. Improving food security is influenced by economic drivers such as prices and stability of supply and social and cultural norms around food consumption can be barriers to change. Women play a significant role in food production across large parts of the world and so women's land rights and wider gender relations will also be important in climate change adaptation and mitigation globally.[8] Effecting change to develop a globally sustainable food system, therefore, requires expertise from the social sciences as much as from natural sciences.

Overall, the IPCC's Special Report underlines how land-based mitigation can play an important part in reducing net emissions and limiting future warming, but there will be limits to what land-based mitigation can achieve by itself. Turning to extensive afforestation or growing biofuel crops to replace fossil-fuel-based energy may help mitigate climate change but will bring new pressures upon existing land use for food production and other ecosystems services. The Special Report helped raise global awareness of the implications of climate change for land use but also provided a framework within which national governments and food and farming organisations could develop their own analyses and strategies. One example was the UK's Climate Change Committee which produced its own reports on land-use policies for net zero in the UK in November 2018 and January 2000.[9]

The Climate Change Committee and Land-Use Policies for a Net Zero UK

The UK's Climate Change Committee began producing annual progress reports to Parliament on the Government's work on addressing climate change targets soon after it was established under the 2008 Climate Change Act. This regular scrutiny brought more focus on possible steps to address emissions from agriculture and land use. The Committee reviewed agriculture and land use in its 2011 progress report. An Agriculture Industry Greenhouse Gas Action Plan (for England) had been published in February 2010, but the Committee was sceptical about its scale of ambition. (It sought reductions of 3 million tonnes of carbon dioxide equivalent [$MtCO_2e$] by 2020). Emissions from the UK agriculture sector had fallen steadily from 1990 to 2009 from approximately 54 $MtCO_2e$ to 45 $MtCO_2e$, and this bred a sense of complacency among agricultural policymakers that the sector was broadly going in the right direction. The Action Plan focused on improved nutrition management, improved crop varieties to generate less nitrous oxide, improved feed efficiency and the deployment of more anaerobic digestor systems.[10] It was based on a voluntary approach over three phases. Sector roadmaps were to be developed from 2010 to 2012, followed by the promotion of improvements in farming practice in target sectors (such as in crop nutrition, low emission animal diets and animal health) from 2012 to 2015, and then a third phase from 2015 to 2020 would involve the promotion of a wider range of measures. However, despite some progress in measuring, monitoring and reporting, emissions from the sector did not fall significantly after 2009, and the Committee became increasingly concerned that the reliance on voluntary changes was not delivering the emissions reductions required. By 2016, the referendum vote to leave the EU had introduced some uncertainty into the policy framework for agriculture and land use. The Committee noted there was no progress in most areas relating to agriculture and emphasised the need to move beyond the reliance on a voluntary approach and to develop a more ambitious policy framework for reducing emissions.[11] It also complained about lack of progress and difficulties in monitoring:

> Despite all the programmes and initiatives that the [greenhouse gas] Action Plan has established to date, it has been impossible to appraise its effectiveness with regards to reducing emissions given the lack of an effective monitoring and evaluation framework.[12]

In the aftermath of the Brexit vote, the Committee embarked on a major programme of work to deepen its analysis of the drivers of emissions from agriculture and land use and the effectiveness or otherwise of existing approaches to the issue. The Committee published two reports in November 2018 and January 2020.[13] The first emphasised how a future land strategy that delivers the UK's climate goals will require "a fundamental change" in how land is used. "Incremental changes will not deliver climate goals", it stressed.[14] It identified a set of barriers that need to be addressed.

These include inertia in moving away from the status quo and lack of experience and skills in alternative land uses; long-term under-investment in research and development and bringing new innovation to market; lack of information about new low-carbon farming techniques; high up-front costs of new farming methods and alternative land uses; uncertainty over future markets for new products; and little or no financial support for public goods and services provided by land that do not have a market value.[15]

As the Government considered the possibility of committing to a new target of net zero by 2050, the Committee published a major review in May 2019 across all sectors to support the move. It concluded that net zero is "necessary, feasible and cost-effective, necessary to meet the requirements of the 2015 Paris Agreement, feasible because the technologies and approaches required are understood and can be implemented, and cost-effective because the estimated costs fall within those already accepted by Parliament when it set its existing target in 2008".[16] It was estimated that across the economy about 90–95 per cent of the target could be achieved through improving efficiency, healthier diets, electrification of transport and heating, developing hydrogen as an energy source, carbon capture and storage, and land-use change. The subsequent publication of the Committee's report on land use in January 2020 focused attention on agriculture and land use more specifically. This second report on land use looked in more detail at the kinds of policies and measures that would be required to deliver emissions reductions on the scale the Committee considered necessary. The Committee emphasised that current policies would be insufficient to enable the UK to meet its commitments, noting that "incentives for agricultural land use have not seen fundamental change for decades".[17] What, then, were the fundamental changes that would be required?

The Committee's proposals fell into two groupings, those required to deliver land-based emissions reduction and carbon sequestration, and those required to reduce demand through dietary change and reductions in food waste. The Committee argued that "climate mitigation needs to be at the heart of a new land use strategy".[18] Because agricultural policy had been dominated by encouraging food production, this had "led to a distorted set of uses of land that do not reflect the need to mitigate climate change and reduce the stresses on environmental ecosystems that climate change is causing".[19] The Committee's modelling suggested that 22 per cent of land would have to be released out of traditional agricultural production and into long-term carbon sequestration and this would require a high degree of uptake of low-carbon farming practices.[20] To ensure sufficient food could still be produced, farming practices would need to deliver continual improvements in productivity. Some land would need to be used for carbon sequestration, habitat restoration and bioenergy production. The Committee calculated that tree-planting would need to increase to at least 30,000 hectares per year by 2050 and possibly to 50,000 hectares.[21] In its calculations, average planting rates of bioenergy crops such as miscanthus, short rotation coppice and short rotation forestry would need to be scaled up to reach of the order of 23,000 hectares per year from the mid-2020s.[22] In addition, at least half and potentially three-quarters of upland peat and at least a quarter and potentially a half of lowland peat would have to be restored.[23]

Two key demand-side measures were envisaged. These involve changes in diet and a reduction in food waste across the supply chain, but both require extensive behaviour change among the population at large, rather than just among farmers and land managers. Animal-based protein sources generally generate more greenhouse gas emissions and ruminant meat (beef and lamb) is the worst emitter. However, different types of livestock production system can have an important bearing on emissions. Changing the population's diet will pose a huge behaviour change challenge but some early policy initiatives were suggested such as offering a fully plant-based option on all public sector catering menus, for example. A national strategy would be required to shift diets that would need to include, for example, food labelling, addressing skills gaps, promoting the development of novel protein alternatives, and possibly requiring mandatory reporting against clear metrics for businesses.

Because livestock production accounts for such a significant proportion of UK agriculture's greenhouse gas emissions, reducing domestic demand and similarly reducing the number of livestock being farmed in the UK seemingly offers a direct route to reducing emissions. The climate impact of livestock production is multi-dimensional. Farm animals require land and feed. If livestock farmland was not farmed, this would reduce emissions. Emissions are also produced by applying nitrogen fertiliser to boost crop or grass yields and cows and sheep produce methane through their enteric fermentation, as they chew and digest. Carbon dioxide is also emitted from handling farm animal manure and slurry. The transportation and processing of livestock and livestock products also produce emissions. Different types of livestock system and methods of grassland management can result in different greenhouse gas footprints, but it is clear that ruminant meat is, on average, the most greenhouse gas-intensive source of protein, with beef from dedicated beef herds worse than beef from dairy herds.[24] In light of this, there has been recent interest in developing 'alternative' meats and sources of protein that are associated with much lower levels of emissions. These include plant-based meat substitutes and lab-grown meat. Insects are sources of protein in some parts of the world and could potentially be incorporated into western diets or in animal feed.[25]

The IPCC's 2019 Special Report had pointed to the global potential for dietary change and highlighted stark headline figures. Around 30 per cent of global emissions are from the food system, of which about 50 per cent come from livestock production. Around 50 per cent of global habitable land is currently used for agriculture, with nearly 80 per cent of this used for livestock production, but this 80 per cent of land contributes only 20 per cent of total calorific intake. From a global perspective, there is huge potential in reducing emissions from agriculture if systemic and large-scale shifts in the consumption and production of meat could be achieved. This would also be healthier for consumers of meat. A 2019 study in the Lancet found that a change to "healthy diets" by 2050 would require a more than 50 per cent reduction in global consumption of unhealthy foods such as red meat and sugar and a more than doubling of healthy foods such as nuts, fruits and vegetables (see Chapter 7).[26]

The Climate Change Committee estimated at least a 20 per cent shift away from beef, lamb and dairy protein per person by 2050 in the UK, and possibly as much as 50 per cent. There is some evidence that recent trends in diet are reducing meat consumption, although it is not clear that the rate of change is sufficient. Average per-person meat consumption fell by 6 per cent between 2000 and 2018, for example. Consumption of fresh meat fell by 23 per cent but most meat (around 80 per cent) is now consumed in processed form, and this has remained constant. The consumption of dairy products is also in decline, falling by 16 per cent between 2000 and 2018. Veganism and vegetarianism are increasing, with the proportion of the UK population who are vegetarian or vegan increasing from 1.6 per cent in 2009/2010 to 2.5 per cent in 2015/2016,[27] although surveys suggest a much more widespread willingness to try alternative diets. A 2019 YouGov survey found that almost half the people surveyed were willing or were already committed to reducing their meat consumption or cutting it out altogether.[28] Shifting diets on the scale required to meet climate commitments will not happen if left to markets and individuals' free will, although government moves are likely to be politically highly contentious. The Government established a National Food Strategy to consider these issues which reported in two parts in 2020 and 2021.[29]

Reducing food waste is a less politically contentious issue. Globally, the Food and Agriculture Organisation calculate that over 1 billion tonnes of food are wasted every year. This amounts to one-third of the total food produced for human consumption and equates to 8 per cent of global greenhouse gas emissions.[30] In the UK, annual food wastage is of the order of 13.6 million tonnes, of which just over a quarter is on-farm wastage. Within the food chain, most food is wasted within households, with approximately 14 per cent of food that is taken home being discarded. Reducing such wastage would both reduce greenhouse gas emissions contributing to the net zero target, but also contribute to freeing up agricultural land for other uses including for climate change mitigation.

A strong framework for promoting widespread behaviour change in something as routine, everyday and personal as eating sits uncomfortably with successive governments that have emphasised the values of individual freedom, personal choice and market liberalism. Yet, it is in this political context that the Climate Change Committee advocates an active and sustained push to significantly change consumer behaviour and shift people's eating habits for the sake of meeting the UK's climate emission objectives. The Committee's analysis and proposals are the most authoritative, coming from the Government's own statutory advisory body on climate change. However, its vision is not the only one in circulation. In the next section, we briefly review other visions of how the transition in food and farming might be addressed.

Contrasting Visions of the Transition to Net Zero

Among prescriptions for how food production and environmental imperatives from land management might be reconciled, two broad types of strategies can be identified – land sparing and land sharing. Land sparing has tended to involve the conceptual and managerial separation of food production and ecosystem services. Here some land is dedicated to environmental conservation objectives and the priorities for food production are pursued on separate agricultural land. In order to "free up" land for sparing while still enabling sufficient food production, higher yields have to be achieved on the remaining farmland. In the second strategy, land sharing, conservation and food production objectives are integrated on the same land. This might lead to some reduction of agricultural productivity per hectare. The land sparing – land sharing terminology was first developed in 2005 but has been picked up by a range of organisations seeking to influence agriculture and land management policy.[31] Different individuals and institutions promote each approach, often working within separate networks and with distinctive worldviews.[32] The framework was originally prompted by concerns about biodiversity and conservation rather than reducing greenhouse gas emissions. The concepts have provided a key means of framing discussions about farming, land use and biodiversity over the last decade, and continue to be influential in the way organisations approach questions of climate change mitigation from agriculture and land use.

Food, farming and environmental organisations began to articulate their visions for the net zero transition in 2019, soon after the UK Government announced its new target in June of that year. In late 2018, the Government had asked the Climate Change Committee for a revised recommendation on when it should seek to achieve net zero. In January 2019, the National Farmers' Union (NFU) announced at the Oxford Farming Conference that it would produce its own assessment, from a farming and land-use perspective, of how to reach net zero emissions for England and Wales later in the year. On 27 June, Energy and Clean Growth Minister Chris Skidmore signed the legislation which committed the UK Government to end its contribution to global warming by 2050. Following the NFU's announcement, and soon after the net zero commitment was signed into law, the House of Commons Environment, Food and Rural Affairs Committee announced an inquiry into the implications of the net zero emissions target for British agriculture. The political context in the summer of 2019 was an historic and febrile one. The spring had been dominated by the difficulties in negotiating the Brexit Withdrawal Agreement and gaining Parliamentary approval. Prime Minister Theresa May led a torturous process of failed votes for the Agreement and ultimately resigned as Conservative Party leader and Prime Minister. The political and media establishment were almost wholly focused on Brexit and the Tory leadership question and climate change was not a prominent issue. Notably, on the day after Skidmore signed the UK's net zero commitment, France recorded its hottest ever temperature (44.9°C). Four weeks later Boris Johnson entered Number 10 as the new Prime Minister on 24th July. He sacked 17 members of the Cabinet and reshaped the Conservative Government to focus on the goal of Brexit. The following day was the hottest July day ever recorded in the UK (38.1°C).

In September 2019, the NFU published its own assessment of the net zero challenge, trailed at the Oxford Farming Conference in January that year.[33] It committed to working to achieve net zero agriculture in the UK by 2040, ten years ahead of the UK Government's commitment for the UK economy as a whole. The union set out three pillars key to achieving this goal. Pillar 1 involved boosting productivity through improving soil quality, livestock health and breeding, on-farm anaerobic digestion of farm wastes and improved energy efficiency of vehicles and buildings. This the NFU calculated could save 11 $MtCO_2e$ per year.[34] Pillar 2 covered farmland carbon storage, especially in soils, through hedgerows, woodland, soil management and peatland and wetland restoration. This pillar was calculated to save 9 $MtCO_2e$ per year. Pillar 3 involved coupling bioenergy to carbon capture, utilisation and storage using bio-based materials in industry and applying biochar to soils in the longer term. This was estimated to provide the greatest potential savings of up to 26 $MtCO_2e$ per year. The NFU explained that its policy on emissions from the agricultural sector had evolved significantly, partly in response to growing scientific evidence of the impacts of climate change, and partly because of its membership's experience of weathering extremes of cold, drought and flooding during 2018. Significantly, it now aspired for agriculture to be produc- ing "the most climate-friendly food in the world".[35] Notably, and in contrast to the Climate Change Committee's analysis, the NFU plan involves no reduction in meat consumption.

The NFU's approach emphasises productivity improvements and tends more towards land sparing. An alternative approach, centred on agroecology and land sharing, was developed by the Food, Farming and Countryside Commission. Established in November 2017 by the Royal Society for the Arts, this Commission had sought to "look afresh at the food and farming system" and established six 12-month inquiries across the UK in a broad consultative study.[36] It focused on agroecology, defined as "an integrated approach that applies ecological and social principles to the design and management of food and agricultural systems".[37] It proposed a ten-year transition plan for farming that included universal baseline payments to support gathering data and continuous professional development for farmers, targeted payments to facilitate a shift to farming according to agroecological principles, redirecting fiscal incentives towards emissions-reduction and much more stringent controls on the use of pesticides and antibiotics.

In its planned inquiry, the House of Commons Environment, Food and Rural Affairs Committee asked questions about what should be done to repurpose agri- cultural land and whether there were other practical and economic ways for the sector to achieve net zero. However, a few weeks into the inquiry a snap General Election was called, and the work of the Parliament came to an end. Although the Committee could not complete its inquiry and publish a report, the 41 submissions of evidence were available for a period and provided a useful insight into the range of views among the key interested parties at this pivotal time in 2019 as they were first coming to terms with the national net zero commitment. All the organisations submitting evidence recognised the need for the food and farming system to change in the light of evidence of the climate change problem and welcomed the Government's commitment to net zero in general and the Committee's interest in the food and farming questions in particular.

Agricultural organisations tended to emphasise the sector's potential positive role in addressing the climate change challenge. The NFU estimated that farmers host about 70 per cent of Britain's solar power capacity, over half of its anaerobic digestion capacity and the majority of its wind power.[38] They also presented the sector as a success story when compared to the rest of the world, with UK farming performing well in terms of environmental efficiency. The NFU argued that the carbon footprint of red meat in the UK is only 40 per cent of the world average[39] and Dairy UK, representing dairy processors, companies and farmer-owner dairy co-operatives, claimed that the UK dairy industry's carbon footprint was among the best in the world. Dairy UK calculated that if the rest of the world performed at the same environmental level then global dairy supplies could come from just 73 million cows rather than the current 264 million.[40] Some farming organisations suggested that the sector was being unfairly targeted and that claims about the damaging contribution of food and farming to UK emissions were being overplayed. This was particularly with respect to the livestock industry and questions about red meat and dairy products. The dairy sector was opposed to any reduction in dairy consumption, arguing that the significance of the sector as an emitter had been misrepresented.[41] The Tenant Farmers' Association felt that calls to change diets away from red meat were "unfounded" and complained that meat and dairy production was being unfairly attacked by "uniformed and disingenuous commentators".[42] The organisation argued that agricultural land in the UK was less polluting by a factor of 20 in comparison to non-agricultural land. Farming organisations were unsurprisingly focused on the need for financial support to assist farmers and landowners with the required changes to transition to net zero. All felt that the levels of payments to agriculture needed to be broadly maintained, and the Country Land and Business Association judged that current levels of financial support through agri-environment schemes were insufficient to incentivise farmers to make the changes likely to be required and would need to be increased.[43]

The Department for Environment, Food and Rural Affairs (Defra), the Government department responsible for agriculture, spent much of its submission setting out work that was in hand. It explained that there were currently no sector-specific targets for emissions reduction and expressed scepticism that the agricultural sector as a whole would be able to achieve zero emissions, although it could contribute to a net zero target. Defra rehearsed that there had been progress in some areas, with the emissions from producing a litre of milk reducing by 17 per cent since 1990, and by 40 per cent for the production of a kilogram of pork.[44] It emphasised the potential of "sustainable intensification" through improved animal health, precision farming technologies and improved plant and animal genetics.[45] Its strategy depended heavily upon more environmentally efficient and effective production on a smaller area of land, essentially a land-sparing approach.

Three other statutory bodies – Natural England, the Environment Agency and National Parks England – approached the issue from an environmental perspective. Natural England, the Government's statutory adviser on the natural environment and conservation, warned that there is no "silver bullet" in ensuring food supply is maintained from a smaller area of land. The agency concluded that reaching net zero while maintaining food supply "is possible and very desirable" but that it would be "challenging and will require significant investment and creativity". It warned that "changes in land use take time to implement and the benefits for greenhouse gas balances are slow to develop". It stressed the need to begin the transition as soon as possible.[46] The Environment Agency, the body most experienced in regulating agriculture to address pollution, emphasised that "addressing climate change is going to require a significant step change in farming and rural land use and some changes in farming behaviours can only be achieved through a set of regulatory and fiscal measures".[47] It focused on the need to establish a clear regulatory baseline that removes avoidable climate impacts, although the Agency warned that its own experience showed "a lack of compliance with current legislation on the vast majority of farms".[48] It called for a greater range of agricultural activities to be brought within a regulatory framework where permits are issued so that emissions can be set at appropriate levels and the Agency, as a regulator, can be funded through cost recovery to enforce it.[49] National Parks England, the umbrella body for England's 10 National Park Authorities, called for "well-designed incentives, regulatory structures, collaboration, facilitation and advice" in order to shift agricultural management practices across the UK.[50] On peatlands, National Parks England recommended that future agri-environment schemes should "ensure that marginal hill farmers can afford to leave areas ungrazed and where appropriate can also afford to fence off these special peat areas to help manage the movement of animals around the land".[51] And ruminant livestock production, it was felt, should be based on grass and browse-fed outdoor systems as opposed to grain, with consumers persuaded and incentivised to eat less meat.[52]

Environmental groups generally placed more emphasis on "nature-based" measures. The Royal Society for the Protection of Birds, the UK's largest membership-based environmental group, argued that "converting agricultural land and the consequent impacts on food production should be taken as part of a wider strategy of waste reduction and demand management" and that the focus should be "on providing a strong contribution to sustainable and healthy diets in the UK, rather than simply maintaining current patterns of production".[53] They called for the new Environmental Land Management scheme being developed by Defra to provide measures to support a shift to agroecological practices, but also emphasised the need for "robust and well-enforced regulatory standards based on the polluter pays principle to reduce emissions from inappropriate practices". A question that follows is how will the climate challenge and the Paris Agreement obligations redefine what constitutes "appropriate practices" because, as we saw in Chapter 3, regulatory baselines around acceptable farming practices evolve over time in line with changing public priorities.

Wildlife and Countryside Link, an umbrella organisation for more than 50 environmental and wildlife groups, emphasised the need to restore carbon-rich habitats such as woodlands and peatlands and ensure they are nested within bigger, healthier, more joined-up ecological networks. They argued that agricultural productivity needs to be viewed not just in simplistic economic terms, which can drive unsustainable production, but more broadly in terms of meeting nutritional needs, avoiding uncosted externalities, and restoring nature to support production (e.g. through pollinators, healthy soils and natural predators). Notably, Wildlife and Countryside Link pointed to estimates of the level of funding required to support farmers and land managers to help meet the UK's climate emission commitments (£2.5 billion per year, and not much less than the level of CAP payments). They also highlighted how the system of knowledge, advice and training needs to be improved, arguing for example that "the agricultural education sector is not equipping the next generation of farmers with adequate knowledge on climate change mitigation. It must become a mainstream component on the agricultural college and university curriculum alongside technological solutions".[54]

This brief review of the positions of the key organisations involved in agriculture, food, land use and climate policy in the UK shows how contrasting perspectives on the net zero challenge were beginning to take shape and crystallise in 2019. A set of emerging tensions are apparent. The first of these is around the relative balance of effort and potential between supply-side and demand-side measures to reduce emissions. The agricultural industry, parts of the agri-science establishment and agri-tech companies focus more on the potential of technologies to enable 'sustainable intensification' of farming practice. Their emphasis is on agricultural and agri-tech solutions. Others see afforestation as the most straightforward route to emissions reduction and sequestration and see the encouragement of reduction in demand for red meat and dairy products as a means of reducing the UK livestock population and the need for so much agricultural land. Changing diet will bring wider health benefits, and will mean fewer livestock, and more forestry and energy crops.

A second, and related tension, is around contrasting visions of the relationship between farming's food production and environmental management functions. The farming industry remains heavily invested in UK farming's food-producing role. Furthermore, from a global perspective, the argument goes that British farming is relatively efficient in terms of greenhouse gas emissions, and it could make sense environmentally for the UK to be producing a *greater* proportion of the world's food than it currently does. Farming is all about producing food, and environmental management issues are a by-product of this primary function. In contrast, environmental groups emphasise farming's environmental management role, in managing water quality, biodiversity, flood risk and carbon, all in addition to food production. At times, given the emphasis on vital ecosystem services, it can seem that farming's food production role is a by-product of its environmental management functions. Post-Brexit and post-CAP, British agricultural policy had been trailed to become more significantly oriented to its environmental management functions, with financial support based on 'public money for public goods.' However, the way the economics of food production and carbon reduction interplay will be critical.

A third tension is in the different implicit models of behaviour change among farmers and landowners and of the relationship between the state and individual. Some call for a review and ratcheting up of the regulatory baseline governing farming practices with a stronger and more prescriptive approach to what should count as legal and legitimate farming and land-use practices. As the experience of water pollution and animal disease problems in the past shows, what society judges acceptable can change over time and regulatory regimes can shift, sometimes quite markedly, in response to political pressures. Others, probably the majority, are currently focused much more on the financial framework for agricultural policy to seek to incentivise desirable farming and land-use practices and disincentivise undesirable practices. The current implicit model is for national schemes of agri-environmental measures in England, Scotland, Wales and Northern Ireland to pay farmers to 'green' their practices. Past agri-environment schemes have been based on the principle of compensation for income foregone, so this approach leaves the Government open to the charge that the polluter pays principle is being turned on its head, and instead, the polluter is being subsidised to change rather than being compelled to.

A fourth tension is around the techniques and technologies for measuring and monitoring progress in emissions reduction. The international convention is to convert emissions to carbon dioxide equivalents, and this brings the issue of methane and nitrous oxide emissions into sharp focus as serious problems. Parts of the British agri-food sector argue that the focus should be much more strongly on carbon dioxide, and we should worry about methane less because it does not persist in the atmosphere as long.

Amid these tensions, there are a set of issues that seem to enjoy a strong consensus. It is widely agreed that an integrated approach to greenhouse gas emissions reduction is required that also embraces biodiversity, water quality and other environmental factors. There are calls for a national land-use strategy to help integrate these priorities, including from the Climate Change Committee.[55] Similarly, there is widespread acceptance of the need for a skills and training revolution to support farmers and landowners through the transition. However, within this consensus, there has been relatively less discussion about the role of those large and influential interests in the food system beyond the farm, the food processors and retailers, and how their activities and priorities might relate to a national land-use strategy. Also, there is little discussion of what, practically, a research, education and training system might need to look like to effect a set of changes in food and farming the scale of which we have not seen since the early post-war period.

Conclusions

The UK's commitment to net zero was in part prompted by the Paris Agreement in 2015. Following Paris, the IPCC had embarked upon its most ambitious period of work including the production of its special report on climate and land.[56] This landmark piece of work set the global context for the challenge facing the world's agriculture and food systems, showing how land plays a critical role in generating climate pressures, and will need to play a central role in reducing net emissions in the decades ahead. It also established the headline categories for action (afforestation and land-use change, low-carbon farming practices in food production, and shifting diets towards lower-emission foods). In the UK, the Climate Change Committee also stepped up its work on food, farming and land use, building on its 2018 report and coming up with much more specific and prescriptive recommendations within each of these three spheres by January 2020. During 2019, the likely scale of sectoral emissions reductions in the UK became clearer, along with the realisation that there would have to be a significant policy change. According to the Climate Change Committee, almost a quarter of agricultural land would be taken out of food production by 2050, at least a 20 per cent reduction in red meat and dairy consumption would be required, along with a significant expansion in the area of land under woodland. This "carve up" of contributions to emissions reductions between changing land use, changing farming practices and changing diets has set the broad framework for the subsequent discussions about how the transition to net zero food and farming might be planned and managed. In a bold move, the NFU produced its own preferred pathway to net zero by 2040, setting out a positive agenda for the farming industry, but this emphasised afforestation and capturing carbon through better soil management rather than the need for any change in meat consumption or livestock numbers.

In the debates about how best to proceed in reducing emissions from food and agriculture global, national and sectoral issues interact. Domestic production levels depend on the flows of imports and exports of food. The Climate Change Committee and the House of Commons Environment, Food and Rural Affairs Committee both take as a given that the proportion of the UK's food requirements produced domestically should not change. This makes the subsequent discussions easier. Some argue that increasing domestic self-sufficiency would be highly desirable,[57] not just because of claims that British agriculture is more environmentally efficient than elsewhere, but often also because of an implicit assumption that food produced more locally must inherently be 'greener' than food that has to be transported further.[58] Of course, without protective measures, the UK's agri-food farming system could proceed towards net zero by importing more food and so offshoring our emissions elsewhere. Keeping the ratio of domestic and imported food constant overcomes this problem although the UK's level of domestic self-sufficiency has varied considerable over the past century.

The UK's plans to reduce net emissions from the agri-food system in the coming years will be influenced by the international scientific evidence and an emerging set of international prescriptions about what needs to be done. However, these international processes will interact with a set of national struggles between the main UK protagonists, the farming and landowning lobby, agri-business and food companies, environmental and consumer groups, scientific institutions and government. A key tension is the balance between supply and demand measures – the relative focus on farmers and landowners changing on the one hand or consumers and retailers changing on the other. Another tension is around the nature and balance of interventions between mandatory regulation, financial incentives, and advice and persuasion. As yet, little detailed thought has been given to the structures, systems and processes of knowledge exchange and managing behaviour change on a national scale and among an occupational community facing a wide range of other challenges too. We will consider these tensions and knowledge gaps in the coming chapters. In the next three chapters, we consider a more detailed assessment of the three principal realms of change in the food and farming system – food consumption practices including diet and food waste, the pattern of rural land use including the switch to forestry and bioenergy crops, and the low-carbon farming practices that need to be developed on the remaining land for food production. Each chapter develops its analysis of the UK situation by first reviewing the global context, then the emerging national priorities, before going on to examine the science and politics of the three sets of issues, and the links between them in the UK.

Notes

1　See, for example, Adger, N. and Brown, K. (1994) *Land Use and the Causes of Global Warming*. Chichester: Wiley.
2　Poore, J. and Nemecek, T. (2018) Reducing food's environmental impacts through producers and consumers. *Science* 360, 987–92; Crippa, M. *et al.* (2021a) Food systems are responsible for a third of global anthropogenic GHG emissions. *Nature Food* 2, 198–209; see also Tables 1.1 and 1.2 in Chapter 1.
3　Crippa, M. *et al.* (2021a), p. 204; see also Table 1.1 in Chapter 1.
4　Intergovernmental Panel on Climate Change (2019) *Special Report on Climate Change and Land*. Geneva: IPCC.
5　IPCC (2019), p. 79.
6　IPCC (2019), p. 80.
7　IPCC (2019), p. 79.
8　See Masika, R. (ed.) (2002) *Gender, Development and Climate Change*. Oxford: Oxfam; Chanana-Nag, N. and Aggarwal, P. K. (2018). Woman in agriculture, and climate risks: hotspots for development. *Climate Change* 1–15.
9　Climate Change Committee (2018) *Land Use: Reducing Emissions and Preparing for Climate Change*. London: Climate Change Committee; Climate Change Committee (2020a) *Land Use: Policies for a Net Zero UK*. London: Climate Change Committee.
10　Climate Change Committee (2011) *Meeting Carbon: 3rd Progress Report to Parliament*. London: Climate Change Committee, p. 187.
11　Climate Change Committee (2016), *Meeting Carbon: The 2016 Progress Report to Parliament*. London: Climate Change Committee, p. 189 and p. 172.
12　Climate Change Committee (2016), p. 185.

13 Climate Change Committee (2018, 2020a).

14 Climate Change Committee (2018), p. 9.

15 Climate Change Committee (2018), p. 10.

16 Climate Change Committee (2019) *Net Zero: The UK's Contribution to Stopping Global Warming*. London: Climate Change Committee, p. 8.

17 Climate Change Committee (2020a), p. 8.

18 Climate Change Committee (2020a), p. 20.

19 Climate Change Committee (2020a), p. 21.

20 Climate Change Committee (2020a), p. 30.

21 Climate Change Committee (2020a), p. 33.

22 Climate Change Committee (2020a), p. 34.

23 Climate Change Committee (2020a), p. 34 and p. 67.

24 Climate Change Committee (2020a), p. 110.

25 Goulson, D. (2021) *Silent Earth: Averting the Insect Apocalypse*. London: Jonathan Cape.

26 EAT-Lancet (2019) Food in the Anthropocene: The EAT-Lancet Commission on Healthy Diets from Sustainable Food Systems. *The Lancet* 393, 447–92.

27 Climate Change Committee (2020a), p. 114.

28 Quoted in Climate Change Committee (2020a), p. 115.

29 National Food Strategy (2020, 2021).

30 Climate Change Committee (2020a), p. 119.

31 Green, R. *et al.* (2005) Farming and the fate of wild nature. *Science* 307, 550–555; Balmford, A. *et al.* (2005) Sparing land for nature: exploring the potential impact of changes in agricultural yield on the area needed for crop production. *Global Change Biology* 11, 1594–606; see also Loconto, A. *et al.* (2020) The land sparing – land sharing controversy: tracing the politics of knowledge. *Land Use Policy* 96, 103610; Finch, T, *et al.* (2021) *Assessing the Utility of Land Sharing and Land Sparing for Birds, Butterflies and Ecosystem Services in Lowland England*. Final Report to Natural England.

32 Loconto, A. *et al.* (2020).

33 National Farmers' Union (2019a) *Achieving Net Zero: Farming's 2040 Goal*. London: NFU.

34 NFU (2019a), p. 7.

35 National Farmers' Union (2019b) *Memorandum of Evidence to the House of Commons Environment, Food and Rural Affairs Committee Inquiry into Agriculture – Achieving Net Zero Emissions*, para 3.

36 Food, Farming and Countryside Commission (2019) *Our Future in the Land*. London: Royal Society for the Arts, pp. 6–7.

37 Food, Farming and Countryside Commission (2019), p. 39.

38 NFU (2019b), para 6.

39 NFU (2019b), para 4.

40 Dairy UK (2019) *Memorandum of Evidence to the House of Commons Environment, Food and Rural Affairs Committee Inquiry into Agriculture – Achieving Net Zero Emissions*, para 21.

41 Dairy UK (2019), para 4.

42 Tenant Farmers Association (2019) *Memorandum of Evidence to the House of Commons Environment, Food and Rural Affairs Committee Inquiry into Agriculture: Achieving Net Zero Emissions*, para 6.1.

43 Country Land and Business Association (2019) *Evidence to the House of Commons Environment, Food and Rural Affairs Committee Inquiry into Agriculture: Achieving Net Zero Emissions*, para 34.

44 Department for Environment, Food and Rural Affairs (2019b) *Memorandum of Evidence to the House of Commons Environment, Food and Rural Affairs Committee Inquiry into Agriculture – Achieving Net Zero Emissions*, para 1.4.

45 Pretty, J. and Bharucha, Z.P. (2018) *Sustainable Intensification of Agriculture: Greening the World's Food Economy*. London: Earthscan.

46 Natural England (2019) *Memorandum of Evidence to the House of Commons Environment, Food and Rural Affairs Committee Inquiry into Agriculture: Achieving Net Zero Emissions*.

47 Environment Agency (2019) *Memorandum of Evidence to the House of Commons Environment, Food and Rural Affairs Committee Inquiry into Agriculture: Achieving Net Zero Emissions*, para 11.

48 Environment Agency (2019), para 12.

49 Environment Agency (2019), para 13.

50 National Parks England (2019) *Memorandum of Evidence to the House of Commons Environment, Food and Rural Affairs Committee Inquiry into Agriculture: Achieving Net Zero Emissions*, para 2.

51 National Parks England (2019), para 1.20.

52 National Parks England (2019), para 1.38.

53 Royal Society for the Protection of Birds (2019) *Evidence to the House of Commons Environment, Food and Rural Affairs Committee Inquiry into Agriculture: Achieving Net Zero Emissions*, p. 1.

54 Wildlife and Countryside Link (2019) *Memorandum of Evidence to House of Commons Environment, Food and Rural Affairs Committee Inquiry into Agriculture: Achieving Net Zero Emissions*, para 12.

55 Climate Change Committee (2020a), p. 21.

56 IPCC (2019).

57 For example, Hetherington, P. (2021) *Land Renewed: Reworking the Countryside*. Bristol University Press.

58 See Edward-Jones, G. *et al.* (2008) Testing the assertion that 'local food is the best': the challenges of an evidence-based approach. *Trends in Food Science and Technology* 19, 265–74; Bridle, S. (2020) *Food and Climate Change: Without the Hot Air*. Cambridge: UIT Cambridge.

7

DIET, FOOD AND WASTE

Introduction

The agri-food system will be essential to bringing greenhouse emissions within safe limits. This will mean changes to how farmland is used, with more land given over to afforestation and growing energy crops, and changes to farming practices to ensure sufficient food can be produced with much lower emissions. Steps will also need to be introduced to reduce wastage in the food chain and to reduce emissions from the transport, processing and storage of food products. However, over and above these measures on land use and the resource efficiency of food production – that is, the production side of the equation – it is increasingly acknowledged that there will have to be significant shifts in the consumption of food around the world. This poses difficult problems for policymakers in how to effect behaviour change on a global scale to encourage people to make changes to their diets for the sake of reducing emissions. A public policy-led, managed approach to behaviour change on a global scale has rarely been attempted before. Food consumption habits are often intricately bound up with local and national cultures and identities and seeking to change them opens up profound questions of the relationship between the state and the individual and how markets function. The dilemmas go to the heart of the question of the state's conception of the legitimate scope for state rule and the techniques and technologies of government explored in Chapter 2.

Changes in diet have caused problems for the environment and health, and the unhealthiest diets usually cause the greatest problems for the environment. The increasing reliance on red meat and dairy products, for example, has contributed to problems of obesity and poor diet and at the same time contributed to environmental pressures from food production, including greenhouse gas emissions. This has prompted a quest for both healthier and more sustainable diets around the world and efforts to stipulate what might constitute a "healthy" or "sustainable"

DOI: 10.4324/9781003278535-7

diet. This chapter examines the challenge of changing food consumption patterns to help address climate change. It first explains the global problem of humanity's unsustainable diets before considering the UK case in more detail. It examines behaviour change in relation to diet and the key strategies that have been advocated for what has been called the "great food transformation".

The Global Challenge of Unsustainable Diets

Global food production measured in calories has broadly kept pace with the dramatic population growth of the last half century, although more than 820 million people are estimated to have insufficient food and many more have low-quality diets that are nutritionally deficient.[1] Global population is expected to increase from around 7.8 billion in 2021 to 9.8 billion by 2050 and is expected to reach almost 11 billion people by 2100. A key issue becomes whether it is possible to feed the world, given forecast population growth, and do so within the constraints of reducing greenhouse gas emissions to avoid catastrophic climate change. The United Nations' Sustainable Development Goals, agreed in 2015, address interlinked global challenges to help deliver sustainable development globally. Among these are the goals of ending malnutrition and combating climate change. It is increasingly recognised that the global food system is failing to meet basic nutritional needs for some and to provide healthy diets for others, and is placing pressure on planetary environmental systems.[2] The average diet in most high-income countries is well in excess of World Health Organisation recommendations for calories, meat and sugar consumption and so brings risks of non-communicable diseases such as cancer, stroke and heart disease.[3] Population growth and economic growth risk this problem becoming more acute and widespread over time, with increasing pressures on the intensification of agricultural systems and accentuating climate risks. The global food system, global diets and global warming, therefore, have to be considered hand-in-hand.

National governments and international bodies have begun to develop dietary guidelines. Studies have pointed to the potential for significant greenhouse gas reductions if meat consumption was reduced or meat-intensive diets were replaced with more pescatarian, vegetarian or vegan-type diets.[4] However, there have been no internationally agreed guidelines on a diet that would provide adequate human nutrition *and* might be environmentally sustainable for the world's population. Country-level dietary guidelines and their resultant per capita greenhouse gas emissions can vary widely, with some showing a minimal reduction in emissions relative to the average projected income-dependent diet by 2050.[5] It has become clear that the health and environmental dimensions need to be better brought together. The EAT-Lancet Commission was established to examine the development of a global approach to healthy diets from sustainable food systems, so tackling unsustainable food production practices and unhealthy diets. Drawing upon expertise from 16 countries, it developed the concept of a "universal healthy reference diet" to provide the basis for estimating the health and environmental benefits of the world's population adopting a healthy diet. Particular dietary patterns are more likely to promote overall wellbeing and lower risk of major chronic disease. These patterns have the following characteristics. *First*, they include protein sources primarily from plants, including soy foods, other legumes and nuts, fish or alternative sources of omega-3 fatty acids several times per week with the optional modest consumption of poultry and eggs, and low intakes of red meat, if any, especially processed meat. *Second*, fat is derived mostly from unsaturated plant sources with low intakes of saturated fats and no partly hydrogenated oils. *Third*, carbohydrates are primarily from whole grains with low intake of refined grains and less than 5 per cent of energy from sugar. *Fourth*, such diets include at least five servings of fruits and vegetables per day, not including potatoes. *Finally*, the consumption of dairy products is moderated as an option.[6] These elements of a healthy diet, the Commission argues, have the advantage of allowing flexibility and are compatible with a wide variety of cultural traditions and individual dietary preferences. This definition of a healthy diet was used to quantify human dietary needs and was integrated with global scientific targets for sustainable food systems. The concept of a "safe operating space" was established for six key earth system processes and food production was found to be among the most significant drivers of environmental change.

Future demand for food is affected by the size of the global population and income levels. The Commission's modelling projected that food production could increase greenhouse gas emissions, cropland use, freshwater use, and nitrogen and phosphorus application by 50–90 per cent between 2010 and 2050 if there were no mitigation measures.[7] This increase would push those biophysical processes that regulate the Earth's system beyond the safe operating space for food production. Healthy diets from sustainable food systems are estimated to be possible for a global population of up to 10 billion people but then become increasingly unlikely beyond this population threshold. The Commission emphasised that even a small increase in the consumption of red meat or dairy foods would make the goal of maintaining sustainable food production very difficult or impossible to achieve. This is principally because animal sourced foods have large environmental footprints per serving for greenhouse gas emissions, cropland use, water use, and nitrogen and phosphorous applications. Overall, animal sourced foods are responsible for about three quarters of climate change effects from food production.[8] In order to stay within the safe operating space for food systems, a combination of dietary changes and production-related measures would be required. However, dietary change is likely to be much more significant than changing production practices. Changes in food production practices are estimated to be able to reduce agriculture's greenhouse gas emissions globally by about 10 per cent by 2050, whereas an increased consumption of plant-based diets in place of animal-based foods has the potential to reduce emissions by up to 80 per cent. A further 5 per cent reduction could be achieved if food waste were halved.[9]

The effects of switching from animal-based to more plant-based diets are significant because of the amount of land and agricultural resources taken up by growing animal feedcrops. Currently, almost two-thirds of all soyabeans, maize and barley, and around a third of all grains, are used to feed animals for meat and dairy production. Therefore, any change in diets away from animal products would release agricultural land to grow other crops for more direct human consumption.[10] Global food systems could deliver "win-win" diets that are both healthy and environmentally sustainable for the global population of 2050, although this would require a rapid transformational change in what the Commission calls the "great food transformation" – that is "a substantial change in the structure and function of the global food system so that it operates with different core processes and feedback". However, "this transformation will not happen unless there is widespread, multi-sector, multi-level action to change what food is eaten, how it is produced, and its effects of the environment and health, while providing healthy diets for the global population".[11] It emphasised the evidence-based nature of its analysis and conclusions and the need for urgency. "Data are sufficient and strong enough to warrant action, and delay will increase the likelihood of serious, even disastrous, consequences".[12]

Such a global transformation represents uncharted territory in policy terms. "Humanity has never aimed to change the food system so radically at this scale or speed", the Commission acknowledged.[13] However, there are examples of individual countries experiencing major transformations in the twentieth century, including China, Vietnam, Brazil and Finland, and lessons can be learned from these experiences. Some examples of global system transformations include the modernisation of agriculture and productivity increases during the 1950s and the 1960s, the development of retroviral drugs in the fight against HIV/AIDS and the development of renewable energy. However, none of these examples are as extensive and profound as the great food transformation. It is clear from these other examples that no single actor or breakthrough is likely to catalyse systems change. Because the required change is so extensive, it is likely to require the engagement of actors at all scales and across sectors and the utilisation of a wide range of policy levers. The Commission argued that the evidence base strongly supports specific strategies for transformational change, and international and national commitments should be established to shift towards healthy diets. A range of measures is possible, including reducing portions, choice and packaging, innovating in the preservation of perishable foods and using public and private sector procurement policies to improve diets. Steps can be taken to make healthy food more affordable and accessible and to reduce the volatility of food prices, and the advertising and promotion of unhealthy foods can be tackled and restricted by governments. National dietary guidelines that accord with both health and environmental objectives are a potentially useful tool, as part of wider efforts to promote understanding and behaviour change.

An overarching strategic commitment would be required to reorient priorities to producing healthy food. Such a shift would require accurate data to track diet quality and the development of robust diet quality assessment tools. Crucial is that national agricultural policies should be more explicitly focused on enhancing nutritional outcomes with particularly beneficial plant-based foods incentivised.

Animal production systems would need to be considered in specific environments where they may play a key role in supporting grassland ecosystem services, but this would need to be in the context of an overall shift away from meat production. Alongside this reorientation of agricultural policy, productivity would have to improve sustainably to increase high-quality output. Food losses and waste would have to be at least halved in line with global sustainable development goals. Loss and waste at initial production stages is highest in low-income and middle-income countries and can be the result of poor infrastructure. Food waste reduction will require the co-operation of different actors across the food system and will be complex, but the benefits in reducing greenhouse gas emissions are significant. In higher-income countries, proportionately more food waste arises closer to the point of consumption and so requires behaviour change at the level of domestic households and individuals.

The Commission concluded: "the food we eat and how we produce it will determine the health of people and planet, and major changes must be made to avoid both reduced life expectancy and continued environmental degradation".[14] Its integrated framework, which has informed the work of the UK's Climate Change Committee, is "universal and provides boundaries that are globally applicable with a high potential of local adaptation and scalability".[15] Crucially, the combination of the universal healthy reference diet and the set of safe planetary boundaries for the key Earth systems processes have enabled the Commission to show how it could be possible to feed the world's global population of nearly 10 billion with a healthy diet from sustainable food systems by 2050. The great food transformation is, therefore, necessary and achievable, albeit a hugely complex and ambitious challenge for humanity.

The UK Food System and British Diet

As elsewhere, UK food policy has been the subject of heightened debate in recent years as the climate crisis has intensified and the role of food consumption patterns in driving environmental pressures has become clearer. There have been growing concerns about the poor quality of British diets and the mounting health problems associated with unhealthy eating. British diets are too rich in sugar, fat and meat and too low in fruits and vegetables. In 2019, a health survey for England found that almost two-thirds of the adult population were either obese or overweight.[16] The UK's dietary crisis is not simply the result of the consumption practices and choices of individuals. What people eat is influenced by their individual preferences, but also family and domestic circumstances, cultural factors, daily working lives and time availability, and the provision and promotion of food products by manufacturers and retailers. Therefore, to understand the evolution of British diets, we must consider the structure and evolution of the food system.[17]

The UK agri-food sector is a significant component of the national economy contributing about 6.4 per cent to Gross Value Added (GVA).[18] Food and drink account for approximately 20 per cent of all manufacturing and employ over

400,000 people. The largest share of GVA in the food system comes from non-residential catering (30 per cent) followed by food and drink retailing (25 per cent), while wholesaling generates 11 per cent. Agriculture accounts for the smallest proportion of GVA in the food system, with just 8 per cent of total GVA.[19] Typically, models of the food system start with the farm. However, farmers are themselves part of a chain, and to fully understand their role in the food system, we must also look upstream of the farm to the industries that supply the sector with inputs. UK agriculture spent approximately £17.3 billion on inputs in 2020.[20] Of this, £5.6 billion (a third) was spent on animal feed, £1.1 billion (6 per cent) on pesticides and £1.0 billion on seeds.[21] These sectors show high degrees of market concentration. For seeds and plant breeding, for example, the top four companies cover 58 per cent of the market for fodder and oilseeds and 95 per cent for barley.[22]

Market concentration has been a continuing feature of the British food system for more than half a century. By the late 1980s, the two largest companies accounted for almost half the UK animal feed market, and the five largest companies controlled two-thirds of pesticide sales. Over three-quarters of agricultural machinery sales were from the four largest manufacturers.[23] British farmers are, therefore, dependent upon agricultural inputs from markets dominated by large, often global, companies who hold large market share. This constrains farmers' options when it comes to large parts of farming practice including the choice of seeds and animal feeds, pesticides and fertilisers, and agricultural machinery. In contrast, individual farm businesses are likely to produce only very small proportions of total supply of most crops and livestock products.[24] Farmers also sell into markets that are often dominated by small numbers of very large food processors and manufacturers. Together the top five food manufacturing companies in the UK now have a turnover of £30 billion, which is more than the total gross output from the whole of British agriculture.[25] The dairy sector accounts for about £8.8 billion of sales each year and meat processing is worth £8.2 billion.[26] Levels of market concentration remain very high across many key categories of groceries. For example, in the £1.4 billion breakfast cereals market, four companies account for 60 per cent of sales. Similarly, in the £1.4 billion market for butter and spreads, the top four companies account for 65 per cent of sales, while in the £1.3 billion market for bread the proportion is over 70 per cent.[27]

The UK food system is highly internationalised with flows of imports and exports. On balance, the UK is a net importer and is only 60 per cent self-sufficient in all food and 74 per cent in indigenous food.[28] In 2020, UK food exports were valued at £21.4 billion, while imports were £48.0 billion. The trade deficit in food and drink has widened by over 40 per cent from £18.8 billion in 2005 to £26.6 billion in 2020.[29] In international terms, the UK's food trade gap is sizable, with fruit and vegetables making up the largest component. Imports exceed exports in most food and drink categories except for beverages where the importance of Scotch Whisky helps contribute to a trade surplus.[30] In meat, beef accounts for half of meat imports, pork accounts for nearly 30 per cent and lamb nearly 20 per cent. Road haulage is crucial in the transport of food to and within the UK. In 2017,

287 million tonnes of food products were transported by heavy goods vehicles registered in Britain, some 21 per cent of all goods,[31] and it is estimated that food lorries account for around a fifth of all UK truck traffic.[32]

Consumer expenditure on food, drink and catering totalled £234 billion in 2019, an increase of 2.7 per cent on the previous year.[33] The proportion of total household consumption expenditure spent on household food decreased from 17.8 to 7.7 per cent between 1980 and 2019. In contrast, the proportion of total household consumption expenditure spent on food eaten out increased from 4.1 to 4.8 per cent over the same 1980–2019 period.[34] Food retailers have become an important influence over what British people eat, replacing food manufacturers and processors as the most influential force in the food system. Since the 1964 Resale Prices Act prohibited resale price agreements between manufacturers and retailers, food and drink retailers have competed on cost and through aggressively seeking to build market share. The result has been an increasingly concentrated food retailing sector with the largest supermarket chains holding a significant proportion of the total market (see Table 7.1). Over the past two decades, the large supermarket chains have also developed a strong presence among smaller convenience stores in town and city centres.[35]

Notably, the UK has the third highest volume of sales of ultra-processed foods per capita of 80 high- and middle-income countries and the most processed diet in Europe.[36] The most highly processed foods make up more than half the total dietary energy consumed in the UK, which contributes to the UK's higher average body mass index and chances of obesity. In 2018, only 28 per cent of UK adults consumed the recommended five portions of fruit and vegetables a day.[37] National Health Service surveys find that the intake of free sugars exceeds

TABLE 7.1 British Food Retail Market Share, Ownership Structure and Base, 2018

Company	Ownership structure	Country base	British market share, %
Tesco	FTSE 100	UK	27.7
Sainsbury	FTSE 100	UK	15.7
Asda	Walmart	USA	15.5
Morrisons	FTSE 100	UK	10.5
Aldi	Albrecht family	Germany	7.6
Co-op	Non-profit	UK	5.9
Lidl	Schwartz Gruppe (family)	Germany	5.2
Waitrose	Employee share partnership	UK	5.2
Iceland	Management buy-out plus Brait SE	UK	2.2
Symbols and independents	Private	UK	1.6
Other outlets	n/a	UK	1.8
Ocado	FTSE 100	UK	1.2

Source: Lang (2020, p.357). Reproduced by permission of Tim Lang.

government recommendations for all age groups and genders. The average consumption of saturated fats exceeds government recommendations (less than 11 per cent of calorific intake) for all ages, and the average daily consumption of oily fish is below the recommended amount for all ages.[38] The average weight of the UK population has increased steadily since the 1950s. While the rise of sedentary jobs and the proliferation of labour-saving devices are part of the explanation, changes in diet and the availability of cheaper food play a significant role too.[39] Over-consumption of red and processed meats is associated with cardiovascular disease, type 2 diabetes, and bowel cancer as well as climate change. More food consumed is in highly processed form, although the consumption of red meats has been falling. In 2012, 75 per cent of adults ate beef, lamb or pork once a week. By 2018, this proportion had declined to 55 per cent.[40] There is some evidence of heightened interest in improving diets too. A survey in March 2017 found that 28 per cent of British people had reduced or limited their meat consumption in the previous six months and 44 per cent reported being willing or already committed to reducing or cutting out meat. Since 2017, surveys report significantly increased awareness of livestock's environmental impacts.[41] Some 96 per cent of survey respondents shop for food in large supermarkets, although the proportion of the population buying food online is increasing. In January 2020, online spending on food reached 5.4 per cent, although this will have increased as a result of the Covid-19 crisis.[42]

Post-farmgate food waste amounted to 9.5 million tonnes in 2018 and most of this waste, some 70 per cent, was intended to be consumed by people. This wastage was valued at £19 billion and represented 25 million tonnes of greenhouse gas emissions. Over 85 per cent of this waste occurs in the household and food manufacturing sector. UK households threw away 6.6 million tonnes of food in 2018, although this annual amount of waste had reduced from 8.1 million in 2007. Of the 6.6 million tonnes, 4.5 million was food that could have been eaten. Almost 40 per cent of waste by weight is fruit, vegetables, salads and drink, which is paradoxical given a healthy diet requires more of the first three. If purchases of these were reduced, this would have only a small impact on UK agricultural land use because most fruit consumed in the UK is imported and UK horticulture accounts for only 3 per cent of cropland.[43] A much smaller amount, some 700,000 tonnes, is surplus food from the manufacturing, retail and hospitality sectors, and this is donated to charities to distribute or diverted to produce animal feed.[44] A constellation of local food redistribution networks has developed in recent years with charities taking surplus food from retailers and manufacturers to distribute via food banks and other local schemes to feed the poor and disadvantaged. Surplus food redistribution trebled between 2015 and 2020. Total food redistributed over that period amounted to 320,000 tonnes worth almost £1 billion and equivalent to 760 million meals.[45] The Climate Change Committee assumed a 20 per cent reduction in food waste by 2050, but recognised a more ambitious reduction may be necessary.[46]

Overall, then, a set of key trends shape the British food system. Beyond the farm, market power upstream and downstream is dominated by a small group of large companies, often multi-national corporations, who supply agriculture with its inputs and process and sell its outputs. The increasing significance of highly processed foods, higher in sugar and saturated fat has been a key contributor to poor diet in the UK. Food waste has been a growing problem in the food system, but recent years have seen a gradual reduction in waste, especially from retailers and manufacturers. There is also some evidence of a shift away from red meat in diets. However, this trend cannot be relied upon to deliver sufficient benefit in terms of reduced greenhouse gas emissions. Indeed, if other measures in the transition to net zero fail to deliver sufficient progress, it is possible that more will be required from changes to British diets. In this context, then, what are the key considerations in addressing behaviour change in British eating habits to address climate change?

The Net Zero Challenge: Corporate and Consumer Behaviour

The Climate Change Committee estimates that the UK needs to cut some 69 $MtCO_2e$ of emissions from agriculture and land use by 2050. About 7 $MtCO_2e$ (or 10 per cent) of this saving comes from changing diet by reducing consumption of the most carbon-intensive foods (red meat and dairy) by at least 20 per cent and reducing food waste by 20 per cent, although it acknowledged that more significant reductions may be necessary.[47] These dietary changes would have two further beneficial effects. First, diets would be healthier, and this would improve wellbeing and reduce pressure on health services. Second, reduced consumption of red meat and dairy products would free up agricultural land for other land uses such as forestry and energy crops. Dietary change on the scale required is not unheard of, and there are examples of dietary change being positively affected by governments. For example, changes in alcohol duties between weaker and stronger beers reduced the consumption of alcohol units by 1.9 billion between 2011 and 2013.[48]

As international bodies increasingly call for radical change in diet to address the climate and sustainability challenge, so a few national governments have begun to respond.[49] Often, there is resistance and challenge from food and farming bodies, but there are examples where healthier diet initiatives have been welcomed by such groups and food manufacturers and retailers are increasingly conscious of changing consumer trends.[50] Food companies are also exploring the development of alternative proteins intended as substitutes for meat, milk and other animal products.[51] Decisions about what we eat are seen as deeply personal choices, and there is a reluctance by many politicians to intervene. Nevertheless, there is evidence that the public expect governments to lead on action for the global good.[52] The Covid-19 pandemic has also altered prevailing public and political values around the scope and limits of government action to protect the public.[53]

According to the Behavioural Insights Team, despite a widely prevailing view that our food choices reflect an "indelible, immutable and sovereign set of tastes that are our 'own'",[54] there is plenty of evidence to show how tastes are shaped by economic, material and socio-cultural influences. Food manufacturers and retailers spend considerable sums on marketing food products and the science of shaping choice among supermarket shoppers has become increasingly sophisticated.[55] Individuals' food choices are not generated wholly from within and are shaped by those with an interest in selling. Therefore, it should be possible for government to play a role in influencing diet for the public good. Yet influencing food choices is not straight-forward because consumers often struggle to define and act upon their true preferences. "Present bias" can favour short-term over long-term desires, and there are plenty of examples of consumers acting against their better judgement. A survey of over 6,000 consumers across the United States, China, Brazil, Germany and the UK found that two-thirds wanted to consume less and to consume more sustainably, but most admitted failing to act on this expressed preference.[56] Interest in "nudge theory" was driven by the view that the public good could be served in ways that need not give the appearance of restricting liberties or choice.[57] A key political concern around measures to induce or stimulate behaviour change is that they are rarely popular ahead of being implemented, even though they can become widely appreciated after the event. The British experience of smoking bans, plastic bag levies and congestion charges are echoed around the world. A month before the introduction of the London congestion charge in early 2003, public opposition outstripped support by 5 percentage points. Yet a month after its introduction, once its impacts and effectiveness became apparent, public support for the charge outstripped opposition by almost 30 percentage points.[58] Future potential benefits can seem vague and unproven and so feel harder to appreciate than the tangible experience of the privileges that will be lost. This all serves to reinforce faith in the status quo and queasiness about change.

Governments legitimately intervene to protect citizens from harms such as smoking, drink-driving and so on. The rationale is both paternalistic, in that individuals' free choice is restricted for their own good, and for the public good in that society benefits. Because of the combination of health and environmental benefits, reducing red meat and dairy consumption is both paternalistic and for the public good. Public acceptance of government intervention to reduce red meat consumption is found to be stronger when the rationale concerns individual health rather than environmental sustainability.[59] The Behavioural Insights Team consider this to be because interventions that are "pro-self", that is in our own interests and thus not paternalistic, tend to be more acceptable.[60] They warn it may be hard to build public support purely on the environmental case because it appears to go against the self-interest of those who consume unsustainably. However, the debate about the merits and limits of state action is a product of its time and place. The interest of the Coalition and Conservative Governments of 2010–16 in the "nudge" approach was the result of a timidity about restricting choice after three decades of neoliberal politics around consumer sovereignty and celebrating choice. Viewed from the perspective of the UK in the aftermath of Covid-19 restrictions, the situation feels less stable. During the Covid-19 pandemic, the Government severely restricted choice among its citizens to protect the public good.[61] A key question will be whether saving the planet from the effects of catastrophic climate change will come to be viewed in the same way as protecting populations from a coronavirus that by spring 2022 had killed over 165,000 British people and over 6 million worldwide.[62]

In June 2019, Defra commissioned restaurateur and businessmen, Henry Dimbleby, to lead a National Food Strategy, the first for 75 years.[63] The purpose was to address the environmental and health problems caused by the food system, to ensure the security of food supply and to maximise the benefits of the coming revolution in agricultural technology. The Covid-19 crisis ended up framing the work, which was published in two parts in July 2020 and July 2021, but it does consider behaviour change around diet in the context of Covid.[64] The Strategy used the Behavioural Insights Team's "ISM" (Individual, Social, Material) model to understand the drivers of food choice. Conceptually, dietary trends are a product of consumer choices, but rooted in collective tastes, preferences and habits. Individual choices cannot be separated from the contexts in which they are made, and this context influences individual preferences and choices. Understanding decisions in context is, therefore, crucial to behaviour change. The ISM model identifies the dominant factors shaping diets at three levels. The *individual level* involves the "inner" psychological drivers of our behaviour, both conscious and unconscious. This includes our tastes and preferences, values and beliefs, but also ingrained habits, emotions, mental shortcuts and cognitive bias. The *social level* involves others' influence on our behaviour, including cultural norms and narratives, peer influence and social identity. Finally, the *material level* includes the physical environment and the manner in which options are made available and presented to us, including pricing and promotions, and technological factors that all shape our food environment.[65]

At the individual level, consumer preferences, awareness and values around food and climate change depend on consumers understanding the complex relationship between diet and the environment. Although most people profess to care about the environment, the relationship between meat consumption and climate change is not generally well understood. A survey of UK consumers in 2018 found only 17 per cent associated meat with climate change, a much lower proportion than associated meat with negative health effects.[66] Health concerns are driving a move from meat to plant-based proteins, but only among the most health-literate groups, and most people see meat as essential for a healthy diet and vegetarian diets as inadequate.[67] Raising awareness can help shift behaviour, but it is usually not sufficient on its own. A systematic review of awareness-raising interventions in 2018 found that although they affected self-reported intentions to act, there was little evidence they affected actual behaviour.[68] Motivation is usually more significant than awareness, and here taste, cost and convenience of food usually rank higher than health considerations, let alone climate impacts. Put simply, "expecting consumers to care about the environment *enough to compromise enjoyment, cost, or convenience* is a big ask".[69] This points to strategies to make sustainable food more appealing. In any case, there can be a gap between our values and actions, which means despite the best of intentions, behaviour does not change.[70] Much of our behaviour is intuitive and habitual rather than carefully considered, and this is generally thought to be particularly so when it comes to food choices.[71]

A focus on social drivers helpfully shifts attention from the individual to the effects of the context they are in.[72] Although cooking for, and eating with, other people is central to social life, the UK does not seem to place as high a social value on food and cooking as the rest of Europe and the UK spends a smaller proportion of household income on meals at home than any other European country.[73] Nevertheless, social norms can be harnessed to promote more sustainable practice. Research has found that messaging to promote behaviour change is more effective when it conveys what others are doing. The normative beliefs of peers can be an important influence on becoming a vegetarian, for example.[74] Our sense of social etiquette, trust, fairness and status is a product of our social relations and provides another means by which behaviour may be influenced. Similarly, social identities and culture have a bearing on our food choices and the choice to eat healthily, ethically or sustainably is, in part, an expression of our sense of identity and belonging. This can work both for against the grain of sustainable diets.[75] Eating meat is associated with masculinity and gender has been found to be the strongest demographic predictor of meat consumption.[76] Vegetarianism is associated with perceived seriousness, higher socio-economic status, arrogance and leftist/green politics.[77] Such stereotypical identities can be potent and breaking them can be difficult. It has been found that the strongest predictor of meat consumption among men is the number of vegetarian friends they have.[78] In much of the world, meat consumption is a sign of affluence and so is taken as a sign of wealth and status. In many cultures across the anglophone world and northern Europe, meat is seen as the mainstay of most meals, which would be considered incomplete without it. A radical reduction in meat consumption would require either that what counts as traditional in these cultures has to be reimagined and reinvented, or the influence of other cultures and cuisines lower in ruminant meat would have to be amplified. Empathy for the planet and each other would need to triumph in reconciling what Rob Percival calls the meat paradox.[79] Conventional meat-eaters tend to associate plant-based foods as attached to the vegetarian social identity which they do not subscribe to. As the Behavioural Insights Team put it, "in short, plant-based food is weird".[80]

The third level on which to consider drivers of dietary choices is the material level that is the physical and economic context. The National Food Strategy is clear that "the single most important force that shapes our food environment is the free market".[81] Economically, meat consumption is affected by prices and the cheap availability of meat represents an obstacle to more sustainable diets. Consumer studies have found meat to be among the most price-elastic of foods,[82] suggesting that taxing meat or removing subsidies for its production could reduce consumption. There are strong material forces supporting consumption, however. Agricultural production is still subsidised in many parts of the world, including Europe and North America, which can distort the kinds of crops and animals being grown. In addition, meat producers and processors marshal resources to lobby to protect their interests and advertise and promote their products. In 2015, UK supermarket promotions were the highest in Europe, with almost two-thirds of our food expenditure going on promoted products.[83] The average UK adult spends five hours a week looking at food-related content on social media and more than an hour and a half watching food-related TV. Famously, the Huffington Post reported that we now spend more time watching other people cook on TV and social media than doing it ourselves.[84] It has been found that 47 per cent of young people in the UK consider themselves a "foodie", almost two-thirds aged 13–32 post pictures of food on social media, and there were 23 billion views of online food videos, a number that has been steeply rising.[85]

As we saw in Chapter 2, behavioural insights suggest that our choices are affected by the micro-environment, or "choice architecture", within which they are made. For example, we tend to stick to the default option, so editing the default option to be a desirable one can be effective. We are more likely to pick the first option in canteens, and putting meat-free and other sustainable options first has proved successful in work-place canteens. There is also evidence that certain positions in supermarkets attract shoppers' attention more easily.[86] The Behavioural Insights Team developed 12 strategies for promoting sustainable diets and these are set out in Table 7.2. They involve making sustainable food appealing, normal and easy. Nevertheless, public policy to influence diet can be difficult politically, given the neoliberal emphasis on consumer choice and sovereignty and a deep queasiness about accusations of "nanny statism". A result of this difficulty has been the prominence of work on behavioural science, which considers decision-making by individual consumers. Rather less social science attention seems to have been focused on the roles, influence and decision-making of those companies in food manufacturing, processing and retailing who play such a crucial role in meeting, and shaping, consumer demand.[87] A reluctance to regulate the food industry to improve the national diet has left the debate confined to the narrow territory of nudging.

Irrespective of governmental efforts to manage behaviour, consumption patterns are changing. Consumer preferences are evolving as more people become aware of climate change problems and more deeply motivated to alter their practices. Consumer choices around more sustainable foods have been aided by the publication of popular but scientifically robust guides to the emissions footprint of different food products.[88] At the same time, food companies are embracing the net zero challenge, in response to their customers and to develop their brand identities as responsible and ethical companies. Market research data are revealing growing demand for food and drink products with organic, Fairtrade, Rainforest Alliance or Marine Stewardship Council certification, for example. The UK market was estimated at some £9.7 billion in 2020 and has grown by nearly 60 per cent since 2015. A key driver has been the expansion of own-label food and drink products with these certifications. Mintel forecast the value of sales of food and drink with these certifications to grow further. Some 85 per cent of surveyed consumers had bought food and drink with some form of ethical certification in the six months to April 2021. The proportion buying LEAF (Linking Environment and Farming)-certified products rose from 8 to 12 per cent between 2019 and 2020, while products assured by the Royal Society for the Prevention of Cruelty to Animals rose from 17 to 23 per cent and Rainforest Alliance-assured rose from 25 to 30 per cent.[89] There

TABLE 7.2 Strategies for Promoting Sustainable Diets

Who?	Strategy	Expected impact
	Make sustainable food more APPEALING	
Government	Drive product reformulation and innovation with a carbon tax targeting producers	High
Industry	Market plant-based food as aspirational, delicious and indulgent	Medium
Industry	Use novel in-store/in-app promotions, incentives and games	Modest
Civil society	Campaign with pride, positivity and pragmatism	Modest
Government, industry and civil society	Raise awareness, and build a mandate for strong policy	High
	Make sustainable food NORMAL	
Civil society and government	Publicise the desirable norm, and lead by example	Medium
Industry and civil society	Re-brand plant-based food towards mainstream identity, and promote more mainstream dishes	Medium
Industry	Integrate (don't segregate) the plant-based produce	Medium
	Make sustainable food EASY	
Government	Ecolabels and supermarket ratings	Modest/High
Government, industry and civil society	Ease the change with "rules of tumb", tips and recipes	Medium
Industry and civil society	Prompt sustainable choices at timely moments	Medium
Industry	Edit the choice architecture, to make sustainable options more prevalent, more prominent, and the default choice	High/Modest/Medium

has also been spectacular growth in non-cow's milk, in part fuelled by its greater availability through larger coffee chains. The UK market grew from £333 million in 2019 to £428 million in 2020, a 28.5 per cent growth in one year, and plant-based milks made up over half of all new milk and cream category launches in 2020. The proportion of consumers who had bought plant-based milk increased from 25 per cent in 2019 to 32 per cent in 2020, and 62 per cent of consumers of milk say they feel it is worth paying more for cows' milk that has a sustainable farming guarantee.[90] In addition, growth in the market for meat substitutes accelerated in 2019 with volume and value sales up by 11.5 and 21.4 per cent, respectively. Mintel estimated the UK market to be £549 million in 2020 and forecast it to grow to £824 million by 2025 (with a best case forecast of £1.18 billion).[91]

Supermarket chains are responding to this ethical impulse among their customers by strengthening their own commitments to reduce their greenhouse gas emissions. In January 2020, Sainsbury's pledged to spend £1 billion to meet the company's net zero pledge to support a programme of changes to reduce carbon emissions, food waste, plastic packaging and water usage. In June 2021, Asda announced that it had reduced greenhouse gas emissions by 16 per cent in 2020 as part of its strategy to halve its direct carbon emissions by 2025 and become a net zero business by 2040. In September 2021, Tesco's announced that it would be aiming for net zero emissions across its entire supply chain by 2050 and to become net zero in its own operations by 2035. In October 2021, Morrison's announced that they were bringing forward their net zero commitment by five years from 2040 to 2035. The company is aiming to reduce its net emissions from its own supply chains by 30 per cent by 2030 and is hoping to achieve its goals by working with "net zero" farms as well as by reducing food waste and food miles across its business.

Conclusions: Strategies for a "Great Food Transformation"

There is increasing realisation among food industry executives and senior policymakers in the UK that more radical change in food provision is likely to be required. The National Food Strategy has helped give force to this view.[92] The work represents the most comprehensive effort to plan a path for the "great food trans-formation" for the UK, what the report calls a "feat of acrobatics".[93] In its introduction, Dimbleby emphasised the urgency of the situation. Over the last decade or so, the food system has decarbonised at half the rate of the economy as a whole and the agriculture sector has hardly reduced emissions at all. Most of the decline in emissions from the food system has come through changes in energy sources and resource efficiency within food manufacturing, transport, retail and catering.[94] We have become trapped in a vicious circle, the "Junk Food Cycle". Eighty per cent of processed food is unhealthy, but because there is a bigger market for unhealthy food, companies invest more into developing and marketing it, comforted by the fact that they are meeting consumer demand. However, the Covid crisis has opened a window of opportunity and created momentum for change. As one major food company Chief Executive put it, "something has to change fundamentally".[95] Food companies are reported as recognising the need for legislation to improve diet and reduce consumption of unhealthy food while maintaining a level playing field for competition.

The Strategy set out four objectives for transforming the food system: escape the junk food cycle; reduce diet-related inequality; make the best use of land and create a long-term shift in food culture. It is admittedly interventionist and recognises that some companies have business models shaped to fit the current food system. Its recommendations included proposals for a tax on sugar and salt to stimulate food manufacturers to reduce their use in food products. It suggested mandatory reporting by food companies on sales of product types and on food waste. It made recommendations on free school meals and educational initiatives about food and proposed measures on public procurement and to support those on low incomes to improve their diets. It pressed the Government to extend the guarantee of the budget for agricultural payments from 2024 to 2029 to smooth the transition to a support system for net zero. It also proposed a national land-use framework and suggested food standards be incorporated within any trade deals.

The report was praised for the quality of its analysis and the way it grappled with complex and interconnected issues in an holistic way. Immediate coverage was overshadowed by Prime Minister Boris Johnson saying on the morning of publication of the report that he was "not in favour of extra taxes on working people", but the Government committed to consider all the recommendations and produce a White Paper on the food system in 2022. Critics were mainly from the libertarian right. Charles Moore in the *Daily Telegraph* was concerned that the strategy was over-reliant on government control. "If government tries … to tell our farmers what to produce and what we must eat or not eat, it will get it all wrong", he complained. Moore also found the repeated link between the ills of the food system and climate change distasteful. Fatalistically, he wrote: "the concept of Net Zero by 2050 does terrible damage to clear thought because it insists on an emergency without having proved one. The demand to do something big, now, at once, is a hustler's trick. The likelihood is that we cannot hit the Net Zero target without doing ourselves terrible damage (and we probably cannot hit it at all). If we really have so little time, it is too late to learn to eat well".[96] *Farmers Weekly* covered the report as an important contribution to the debate about the future of food and farming but dwelt on criticisms about the relative merits of intensively versus extensively reared meat, the assumptions about carbon dioxide equivalent emitted per units of beef and dairy, and the question of handling methane as a carbon dioxide equivalent.[97]

Globally, there is a scientific consensus that bringing human activity to within safe limits of the Earth's biosphere is likely to require a significant change to the operation of food systems around the world. While reducing food waste in the food system is probably the least contentious of the measures to address greenhouse gas emissions from the food system, any measures by government to influence dietary choices are among the most contentious. This is particularly the case where neo-liberal values have been most dominant, such as the UK. The broad range of international expertise brought to bear in the EAT-Lancet study called for an ambitious approach to systems change under the banner of the "great food transformation". International bodies increasingly insist that it will only be possible to feed the world's population of 2050 in an environmentally sustainable way if diets change towards foodstuffs that involve lower greenhouse gas emissions.

In the UK, the climate crisis coincides with a mounting public health crisis as a result of poor diet. Dietary choices are shaped by personal preferences and habits but also by the products developed and sold by food manufacturers and retailers. The UK food system is characterised by higher degrees of corporate concentration, such that a relatively small number of very large companies have a significant influence upon the nation's diet. For the food system to play its part in delivering net zero emissions by 2050 in the UK, both consumers and companies will need to change their ways. Dietary choices have been the subject of much consideration by exponents of behavioural science. An acute sheepishness about government taking a more active approach to intervening means that it is food companies themselves who have begun to set the pace in developing strategies for transitioning to meet net zero targets in their activities, although this commitment does not yet extend to interfering in consumers' ability to purchase high-emission foods if they wish to. We will return to the question of what sorts of approaches might help support a transition to a lower-emission food system in Chapter 10, reflecting on the respective contributions of farmers, consumers, companies and government. However, first we turn to the other two components of the transformation, land-use change and then changing farming practice.

Notes

1 EAT-Lancet (2019) Food in the Anthropocene: the EAT-Lancet Commission on healthy diets from sustainable food systems. *The Lancet* 393, 447–92, p. 447.
2 Ritchie, H. *et al.* (2018) The impact of global dietary guidelines on climate change. *Global Environmental Change* 49, 46–55.
3 World Health Organization (2015) *Healthy Diet Fact Sheet No. 394*. Geneva: WHO.
4 See, for example, Tilman, D. and Clark, M. (2014) Global diets link environmental sustainability and human health. *Nature* 515(7528), 518–22; van Dooren, C. *et al.* (2014) Exploring dietary guidelines based on ecological and nutritional values: a comparison of six dietary patterns. *Food Policy* 44, 36–46; Scarborough, P. *et al.* (2014) Dietary greenhouse gas emissions of meat-eaters, fish-eaters, vegetarians and vegans in the UK. *Climate Change* 125(2), 179–92; Springman, M. *et al.* (2016) Analysis and valuation of the health and climate change co-benefits of dietary change. *Proceedings of the National Academy of Sciences USA* 113(15), 4146–51; Bridle, S. (2020) *Food and Climate Change: Without the Hot Air*. Cambridge: UIT Cambridge.
5 Ritchie *et al.* (2018).
6 EAT-Lancet Commission (2019), p. 459.
7 EAT-Lancet Commission (2019), p. 471.
8 EAT-Lancet Commission (2019), p. 471.
9 EAT-Lancet Commission (2019), p. 472; see also Springman *et al.* (2018).
10 EAT-Lancet Commission (2019), p. 472; see also Erb *et al.* (2016).
11 EAT-Lancet Commission (2019), p. 476.
12 EAT-Lancet Commission (2019), p. 476.
13 EAT-Lancet Commission (2019), p. 476.
14 EAT-Lancet Commission (2019), p. 484.
15 EAT-Lancet Commission (2019), p. 485.
16 Balogun, B. *et al.* (2021) *Obesity*. House of Commons Library Briefing Paper No. 9049, 26 May. London: House of Commons.
17 Tansey, G. and Worsley, T. (1995) *The Food System: A Guide*. London: Earthscan.
18 Hasnain, S. *et al.* (2020) *Mapping the UK Food System – A Report for the UKRI Transforming UK Food Systems Programme*. Oxford: Environmental Change Institute, University of Oxford, p. 9; Department for Environment, Food and Rural Affairs (Defra) (2021a) *Agriculture in the United Kingdom 2020*. London: Defra, p. 144.
19 Defra (2021a), p. 145.

20 Defra (2021a), p. 94.

21 Defra (2021a), p. 99.

22 Hasnain *et al.* (2020), p. 23.

23 Ward, N. (1990) A preliminary analysis of the UK food chain. *Food Policy* 15, 439–41.

24 The poultry sector is an exception where there is a much higher level of market concentration among a small number of large broiler companies.

25 Hasnain *et al.* (2020), p. 5; see also Defra (2021a).

26 Hasnain *et al.* (2020), p. 25.

27 *The Grocer*, 18 December 2021. The Grocer's Top Products Survey uses data from NielsenIQ's Scantrack service that monitors weekly sales from a nationwide network of checkouts in grocery multiples, co-ops, independents, garages, off-licences convenience stores and online grocery retailers. Data are for the 52 weeks to 11 September 2021. The multiple retailers own-label products are included in the total market size, but the market concentration share does not include own label products.

28 Defra (2021a), p. 148.

29 Hasnain *et al.* (2020), p. 29; see also Defra (2021), p. 133.

30 Hasnain *et al.* (2020), p. 29.

31 Hasnain *et al.* (2020), p. 27.

32 Lang, T. (2020) *Feeding Britain: Our Food Problems and How to Fix Them*. London: Pelican.

33 Defra (2021a), p. 145.

34 Defra (2021a), p. 146; Statistics are also from the tables supporting Defra's *Agriculture in the UK 2019* report.

35 Wrigley, N. *et al.* (2019). Corporate convenience store development effects in small towns: convenience culture during economic and digital storms. *Environment and Planning A 51*(1), 112–32.

36 Hasnain *et al.* (2020), p. 33.

37 Hasnain *et al.* (2020), p. 34.

38 National Health Service (2020) *Statistics on Obesity, Physical Activity and Diet, England*. Leeds: NHS Digital.

39 National Food Strategy (2020) *National Food Strategy – Part One*. London: National Food Strategy, p. 32.

40 Hasnain *et al.* (2020), p. 34.

41 Behavioural Insights Team (2020) *A Menu for Change: Using Behavioural Science to Promote Sustainable Diets Around the World*. London: Behavioural Insights Team, p. 16.

42 Hasnain *et al.* (2020), p. 36.

43 Climate Change Committee (2020a) *Land Use: Policies for a Net Zero UK*. London: Climate Change Committee, p. 119.

44 Hasnain *et al.* (2020), p. 37; see also WRAP (2021) *Food Surplus and Waste in the UK – Key Facts*. www.wrap.org.uk.

45 WRAP (2021), p. 9.

46 Climate Change Committee (2020a), p. 120.

47 Climate Change Committee (2020a), p. 9.

48 Behavioural Insights Team (2020), p. 21.

49 Vermeulen, S. *et al.* (2020) Changing diets and the transformation of the global food system. *Annals of the New York Academy of Sciences* 1478, 1–15.

50 For example, Sainsbury's (2019) *Future of Food Report*. London: Sainsbury's.

51 Sexton *et al.* (2019) Framing the future of food: the contested promises of alternative proteins. *Environment and Planning E: Nature and Space* 2, 47–72.

52 Behavioural Insights Team (2020), p. 22.

53 Tooze, A. (2021) *Shutdown: How Covid Shook the World's Economy*. London: Allen Lane.

54 Behavioural Insights Team (2020), p. 22.

55 Wrigley, N. (1998) How British retailers have shaped food choice, pp. 112–28 in A. Murcott (ed.) *The Nation's Diet: The Social Science of Food Choice*. London: Longman.

56 BBMG, GlobeScan, and SustainAbility (2012), quoted in Behavioural Insights Team (2020), p. 23.

57 Jones, R. *et al.* (2013) *Changing Behaviours: On the Rise of the Psychological State*. Cheltenham: Edward Elgar.

58 Behavioural Insights Team (2020), p. 24.

59 Wellesley, L. *et al.* (2015) *Changing Climate, Changing Diets: Pathways to Lower Meat Consumption*. Chatham House; Hoek, A. *et al.* (2017) Shrinking the food-print: a qualitative study into consumer perceptions, experiences and attitudes towards healthy and environmentally friendly food behaviours. *Appetite* 108, 117–31; Stoll-Kleemann, S. and Schmidt, U. (2017) Reducing meat consumption in developed and transition countries to counter climate change and biodiversity loss: a review of influence factors. *Regional Environmental Change* 17, 1261–77.

60 Behavioural Insights Team (2020), p. 26; see also Hagman, W. *et al.* (2015). Public views on policies involving nudges. *Review of Philosophy and Psychology* 6, 439–53.

61 Tooze, A. (2021) *Shutdown: How Covid Shook the World's Economy*. London: Allen Lane.

62 These figures are as at 5 April 2022.

63 Department for Environment, Food and Rural Affairs (2019a) *National Food Strategy – Call for Evidence*, 17 August. London: Defra.

64 National Food Strategy (2020), pp. 29–49.

65 National Food Strategy (2020), p. 33; Behavioural Insights Team (2020), p. 28.

66 Behavioural Insights Team (2020), p. 30.

67 Stoll-Kleemann and Schmidt (2017).

68 Bianchi, F. *et al.* (2018) Interventions targeting conscious determinants of human behaviour to reduce the demand for meat: a systematic review with qualitative comparative analysis. *International Journal of Behavioral Nutrition and Physical Activity* 15, 102.

69 Behavioural Insights Team (2020), p. 31, emphasis in original.

70 Moser, S. and Kleinhückelkotten, S. (2018). Good intents, but low impacts: diverging importance of motivational and socioeconomic determinants explaining pro-environmental behaviour, energy use, and carbon footprint. *Environment and Behaviour* 50, 626–56.

71 Kahneman, D. (2011) *Thinking Fast and Slow*. London: Allen Lane; Behavioural Insights Team (2020), p. 33.

72 For example, Hargreaves, T. (2011) Practice-ing behaviour change: applying social practice theory to pro-environmental behaviour change. *Journal of Consumer Culture* 11, 79–99.

73 National Food Strategy (2020), p. 35.

74 Wyker, B. and Davison, K. (2010) Behavioral change theories can inform the prediction of young adults' adoption of a plant-based diet. *Journal of Nutrition Education and Behaviour* 42, 168–77.

75 Stoll-Kleemann and Schmidt (2017).

76 Brough, A. *et al.* (2016). Is eco-friendly unmanly? The green-feminine stereotype and its effect on sustainable consumption. *Journal of Consumer Research* 43, 567–82; Tobler, C. *et al.* (2011) Eating green. Consumers' willingness to adopt ecological food consumption behaviours. *Appetite* 57, 674–82.

77 Behavioural Insights Team (2020), p. 35.

78 Behavioural Insights Team (2020), p. 35.
79 Percival, R. (2022) *The Meat Paradox: Eating, Empathy and the Future of Meat.* London: Little Brown.
80 Behavioural Insights Team (2020), p. 35.
81 National Food Strategy, (2020), p. 38.
82 Andreyeva, T. *et al.* (2010). The impact of food prices on consumption: a systematic review of research on the price elasticity of demand for food. *American Journal of Public Health* 100, 216–22.
83 National Food Strategy (2020), p. 39.
84 Moss, R. (2016) We now spend more time watching other people cook than doing it ourselves. *Huffington Post* 22 September.
85 World Business Council for Sustainable Development (2018) *The Future of Food: A Lighthouse for Future Living, Today,* 23 October, quoted in Behavioural Insights Team (2020), p. 37.
86 Bucher, T. *et al.* (2016). Nudging consumers towards healthier choices: a systematic review of positional influences on food choice. *British Journal of Nutrition* 115, 2252–63.
87 A project with Peter Jackson and Polly Russell is an exception and studied the motives and values of food company managers in the sugar and chicken supply chains. See Jackson, P. and Ward, N. (2008). Connections and responsibilities: the moral geographies of sugar, pp. 235–52 in A. Nützenadel and F. Trentmann (eds.) *Food and Globalisation.* Oxford: Berg; Jackson, P. *et al.* (2007) The appropriation of 'alternative' discourses by 'mainstream' food retailers, pp. 309–30 in D. Maye *et al.* (eds.) *Alternative Food Geographies: Representation and Practice.* Amsterdam: Elsevier; Jackson, P. *et al.* (2010) Manufacturing meaning along the chicken supply chain, pp. 163–87 in D. Goodman *et al.* (eds.) *Consuming Space: Placing Consumption in Perspective.* Aldershot: Ashgate; Jackson, P. *et al.* (2011) Brands in the making: a life history approach, pp. 59–74 in A. Pike (ed.) *Brands and Branding Geographies.* Cheltenham: Edward Elgar.
88 Berners-Lee, M. (2010) *How Bad Are Bananas? The Carbon Footprint of Everything.* London: Profile; Bridle (2020).
89 Baker, A. (2021) *The Ethical Food Consumer – UK – 2021.* London: Mintel.
90 Price, A. (2021) *Dairy and Non-Dairy Drinks, Milk and Cream – UK – 2021.* London: Mintel.
91 Clifford, N. (2020) *Meat Substitutes: Including Impact of Covid-19 – UK – 2020.* London: Mintel.
92 National Food Strategy (2021).
93 National Food Strategy (2021), p. 11.
94 National Food Strategy (2021), p. 21.
95 National Food Strategy (2021), p. 10.
96 Moore, C. (2021) Eating up your greens is not very much to do with saving the planet. *Daily Telegraph* 17 July, p. 18.
97 Clarke, P. (2021) The meat of the argument about nation's diet. *Farmers Weekly* 23 July, pp. 12–3.

8

LAND-USE CHANGE AND GREENHOUSE GAS REMOVAL

Introduction

The destruction of the rainforests is one of the most iconic symbols of the causes of climate change. Cutting down trees and expanding farmland at the expense of woodland has been a feature of agricultural expansion for centuries, but it is only in the last half-century that the connection has been established in the popular imagination between forests, carbon and global warming. As national governments have wrangled with the climate change problem, so it has become increasingly apparent that stopping net deforestation and planting new forests will have to be an important part of mitigating climate change across the world. In some sectors such as aviation, it is likely to be difficult to eliminate greenhouse gas emissions entirely, and so achieving net zero means that there will be a need to remove greenhouse gases from the atmosphere.

The Paris Agreement requires rapid and dramatic decreases in emissions and the removal of greenhouse gases from the atmosphere, beginning in the 2020s. Scientists and policymakers have been examining options, and large-scale greenhouse gas removal is currently seen as essential to the transition to net zero.[1] Of the integrated assessment models considered at the time of the Paris Agreement, almost nine out of ten of those that expect to limit warming to 2°C and all of those that expect a 1.5°C limit assume some greenhouse gas removal as well as emission reductions. Methods involve the removal of greenhouse gases from the atmosphere and their storage for long periods of time, a process that works best for carbon dioxide rather than other greenhouse gases such as methane or nitrous oxide. Approaches to greenhouse gas removal generally fall into two categories. First are nature-based approaches such as afforestation and soil carbon sequestration. Second are engineering-based approaches such as direct air carbon capture and bioenergy with carbon capture and storage (BECCS). For the purposes of our

DOI: 10.4324/9781003278535-8

interest in land-use change and the agri-food system, this chapter focuses on afforestation, BECCS and other methods of sequestration on rural land such as peat restoration. Because some methods are already used and are relatively straightforward (e.g. planting trees), their early deployment and expansion may make it easier to achieve overall net zero targets. There are some technical challenges of engineering, especially around BECCS, but also social, economic and institutional challenges around large-scale, land-use change.[2] Indeed, some are cautious about the emphasis on greenhouse gas removal, fearing it risks reducing pressures on governments to cut emissions in the first place and gives a sense of complacency around a technical fix to solve climate change.[3] Nevertheless, it has been estimated that greenhouse gas removal would need to remove about one quarter of the world's annual emissions each year.[4]

In the UK and across the EU, changing what the agricultural sector produces (to replace higher emitting products with lower emitting products) and changing production practices to increase the per unit greenhouse gas efficiency of production will not be enough to reduce emissions sufficiently. Greenhouse gas removal methods to capture and store carbon in the soil and biomass will be an important contributor, as will larger-scale, land-use change where any surplus agricultural land is turned over to grassland and forestry.[5] In the UK, the Climate Change Committee recommends a reduction of 69 $MtCO_2e$ by 2050 from agriculture and land use, half of which comes forestry and agro-forestry.[6] This would increase the UK's forestry cover from 13 to around 18–19 per cent by 2050. Such expansion would require the planting of at least 30,000 hectares of broadleaf and confider woodland each year as possibly as much as 50,000 hectares. To achieve such large-scale land-use change would require an economic incentive system through some form of carbon pricing. In addition to afforestation, wetland, peatland and coastal habitat are high-carbon-density ecosystems whose restoration can serve as a means of greenhouse gas removal. Peatlands and coastal wetlands have been estimated to store 44–71 per cent of the world's terrestrial biological carbon.[7] The UK is relatively well placed to pursue wetland and peatland restoration as a greenhouse gas removal strategy. It has 0.45 Mha of saltmarsh, 0.8 Mha of fresh water wetland and 2.7 Mha of peatland, up to 15 per cent of Europe's total peatland area, and 80 per cent of its peatland is currently in a poor condition.

This chapter examines in more detail the scale and nature of changes to land use potentially required by the UK's commitment to net zero emissions. It first looks at the role of greenhouse gas removal and land-use change as a means of mitigating climate change globally. It goes on to examine the context for managed land-use change in the UK. Expanding forestry by 30,000–50,000 hectares each year until 2050 is itself a significant change. In addition, the switch to energy crops (perhaps of the order of an extra 23,000 hectares each year) and reductions in the number of farm livestock would also change the way land is used. The chapter explores the debates about how best this part of the UK's shift in land use can be managed, with a twin emphasis on the science and politics of land-use change.

Climate Change and Land Use in a Global Context

A key strategy globally in addressing climate change is to rapidly reduce and then halt the net loss of forest. At the Glasgow COP26 meeting in November 2021, over 100 countries signed an agreement pledging to end deforestation by 2030. Deforestation accounts for a significant proportion of global greenhouse gas emissions and erodes the Earth's capacity to capture and store carbon. Efforts to tackle deforestation and improve tropical forest management were made during the negotiation of the Kyoto Protocol but had to be dropped. However, eventually the REDD+ framework was negotiated under the United Nations Convention on Climate Change in 2005. (REDD+ stands for reducing emissions from deforestation and forest degradation and the role of conservation, sustainable management of forests and enhancement of forest carbon stocks in developing countries.) Greenhouse gas removal through afforestation poses significant implications for land use globally because it requires such large-scale change. Globally, several hundred GtCO$_2$ would need to be removed by the end of the century to meet the target of 2°C warming and almost a thousand GtCO$_2$ would need to be removed to reach 1.5°C. The most commonly considered form of greenhouse gas removal is growing forests and using bioenergy, coupled with carbon capture and storage. There are a range of other technological possibilities for greenhouse gas removal too, but these are generally less well developed. Greenhouse gas removal must involve the capture and removal and storage of greenhouse gases in a form that prevents them returning to the atmosphere. Although other approaches such as increasing inorganic reactions with rocks and engineering direct capture from the atmosphere are potentially possible, enhancing biological uptake currently looks to have the most promise.

Planting and replanting forests capture carbon because trees absorb carbon dioxide as they grow. The uptake of carbon dioxide slows as trees reach maturity, but forest management can help ensure some additional capture gains. Harvested wood from mature forests can be used for long-life wood products or for bioenergy with the emissions captured. Forest regrowth or replanting then means further carbon dioxide removal. Forests take about ten years to reach the maximum sequestration rate, and trees then reach maturity after between 20 and 100 years. Globally, the potential for greenhouse gas removal from afforestation is estimated to range from 3 to 18 GtCO$_2$ per annum.[8] Land availability is a key limitation to afforestation. Then, there is the question of whether landowners have sufficient incentive to switch to this use over others. However, many countries have included forestation or forest management in their Nationally Determined Contributions under the Paris Agreement, and forests (and avoided deforestation) are planned to meet around a quarter of the total pledged mitigation.[9]

BECCS combines biomass combustion to generate energy with carbon capture and storage. It therefore has the advantage of providing both an alternative energy source to fossil fuels and greenhouse gas removal. Carbon capture and storage comprises the technologies that capture carbon dioxide emissions from power stations and other industrial sources and then handles, transports and stores the carbon dioxide in safe ways that do not contribute to emissions. Although BECCS is currently seen as green energy production with carbon capture and storage as a by-product, this may be reversed in the long run and the approach will become principally about greenhouse gas reduction with green energy as a by-product.[10] Currently, the technology for bioenergy and biomass power plants is mature, but carbon capture and storage technology is still largely in the demonstration phase. At the time of writing, there is one BECCS demonstration plant running in Decatur, Illinois in the USA, which is producing ethanol rather than electricity. A gas processing plant is under construction in Australia and will be the largest carbon dioxide storage project, up to four times the scale of Decatur, with an expected storage rate of 3.4–4 $MtCO_2$/yr.[11] BECCS has been estimated to have the potential to remove around 10 $GtCO_2$ per annum globally.[12] Storage capacity ought not to be a limiting factor for BECCS globally, and in the UK, there is probably storage potential of the order of 20 $GtCO_2$.[13] BECCS ought to be a net energy generator, producing 0.8–10 gigajoules of power per tonne of carbon dioxide removed from energy crops.[14]

BECCS will have significant implications for land-use change globally. The integrated assessment models used by the IPCC typically assume that 300–600 Mha of land is available for energy crop production, which represents a significant change in land use of an area similar to the size of the whole EU, or around 40 per cent of the current global area of arable production.[15] Such large-scale growth of energy crops will impact local water environments and may affect albedo – the reflectivity of the Earth's surface. There is also the potential conflict in land use between growing food crops and growing crops to capture carbon and produce energy. A key challenge is the scale of ramping up biomass production and carbon capture and storage infrastructure. BECCS plants are estimated to have electrical efficiencies of 22–33 per cent but could improve to 38 per cent, which are broadly comparable to coal-fired power stations if less efficient than combined-cycle gas turbines. There remain significant knowledge gaps in the development of greenhouse gas removal technologies, including BECCS.[16] Overall, the main concerns with BECCS lie in the carbon capture and storage side of the system and in the potential public controversy around the technology. Oxfam, for example, have been sceptical about the use of carbon removal approaches because of the risk of being seen to allow powerful interests to continue to pollute.[17] The scale of the change in land use and the need for new large-scale infrastructure to transport and store carbon dioxide may prompt public opposition.[18] Nevertheless, the potential contribution of BECCS to greenhouse gas reduction is significant, and greenhouse gas removal is becoming hardwired into assumptions and models of the pathway to limiting global temperature rise.[19]

The IPCC's integrated assessment modelling and analysis of the most cost-effective pathways to safe levels of emissions suggest that large-scale greenhouse gas removal has to be a prominent part of international mitigation efforts. When large-scale greenhouse gas removal proposals were first developed, they were principally framed as a geoengineering technological solution to a problem of policy-failure to address rising emissions.[20] Some global assessments have raised serious concerns about the physical, technical and economic feasibility of large-scale greenhouse gas removal approaches.[21] For example, up to a billion small farmers worldwide may be implicated in the land-use changes anticipated by models of greenhouse gas removal potential.[22] Greenhouse gas removal, therefore, needs to be considered not just as a purely technical issue, but as a change that has important social and political dimensions that could be crucial to its success. A review of the social and political dimensions of greenhouse gas removal identified six sets of issues: economics and economic incentives; innovation; societal engagement; governance; complexity and uncertainty; and ethics, equity and justice.[23]

Most literature is premised on the notion that a system of carbon pricing would be required to incentivise the adoption of greenhouse gas removal. Commonly, IPCC Fifth Assessment Report scenarios assume a carbon price of around 100 US$ per tonne of carbon dioxide, which is widely considered a precondition for large-scale delivery of BECCS. Economies of scale would be important to viability and BECCS power plants could produce carbon-free electricity and negative emission permits, which would be doubly attractive. Afforestation would be relatively more attractive on more marginal agricultural land where there may be environmental co-benefits such as biodiversity and flood risk reduction. Innovation will be crucial both to reduce the costs of greenhouse gas removal schemes and to increase demand and returns. Generally, the literature focuses on the supply side, and on why carbon capture and storage has failed to take off to date. The complexities of schemes require that disparate components have to be made to work not only technically but also organisationally. In general, assessments of innovation focus narrowly on the likelihood of developing effective technologies and less on wider desirability of societal ends and values. Studies of societal engagement with greenhouse gas removal schemes range from those driven by an instrumental, normative concern with securing public acceptance to wider questions of trust in institutions and the use of lay knowledge. Communities' responses to land-use change proposals can be complex. Some argue that the perceived "naturalness" of BECCS technologies seems to help make them more publicly acceptable.[24] However, there remains suspicion about what can be cast as a large-scale technical fix.

In terms of governance, it is generally assumed that there needs to be strong international agreement and commitment to greenhouse gas removal in order to establish legitimacy and spur national and sub-national policymaking. International rules are also crucial in establishing a reliable system of carbon accounting. For BECCS, carbon accounting is particularly significant in including the land sector in new market mechanisms required to mobilise international financial flows on a sufficiently large scale, while the REDD+ framework can operate as a global framework for afforestation.[25] There are concerns, however, that cap-and-trade systems could lead to BECCS being treated simply as an offsetting device.[26] The prospects for greenhouse gas removal are, therefore, shrouded in uncertainties as a result of the interplay between technical, social and institutional factors, and this makes integrated assessment modelling difficult.[27] Concerns about the experience with developing bioenergy are often cited prompting fears that BECCS strategies could even increase greenhouse gas emissions through indirect land-use changes.[28] And even before coming into operation, BECCS can be used by policymakers to potentially avoid tougher mitigation decisions elsewhere.[29] Additional complexity comes from the potential trade-offs between greenhouse gas removal and other environmental goals such as protecting biodiversity or water quality.

Greenhouse gas removal clearly raises questions of ethics, equity and justice. These may vary through different stages in the development of strategies from research to deployment and beyond. Local questions about who benefits from changes in forest ownership and access in afforestation projects can be difficult to solve when governments have their own ways of valuing forests.[30] The experience with REDD+ is that social safeguards are not always effective. Improving the economic valuation of carbon will be dependent upon institutions that support livelihoods and land tenure security in developing countries. A range of social and political dimensions, therefore, frame the context for greenhouse gas removal. Three main framings can be identified.[31] A *techno-economic framing* is based on an instrumental and utilitarian sense of innovation and a centralised global policy-making process. At its heart is a concern over whether greenhouse gas removal techniques are technically feasible and cost-effective, and any wider social science input is limited to supporting adoption. A *social and political acceptability framing* centres on the question of the social and political acceptability of greenhouse gas removal measures. Even though the vast majority of research on greenhouse gas removal is carried out in the natural and physical sciences, concern about public acceptability is widespread. Demonstration projects are likely to be important to the reception and promotion of greenhouse gas removal strategies in future, as is a more open debate about the range of options for how to marketise and financially incentivise greenhouse gas removal. Finally, a *responsible development framing* opens up broader questions of acceptability, including questioning the feasibility of greenhouse gas removal pathways. Public controversies, instead of being antithetical to technology assessment, can broaden appraisals of greenhouse gas removal and open issues of governance. In this, greenhouse gas removal looks similar to other emerging technologies where public engagement and participatory approaches can help enrich insight and sometimes reshape and redirect innovation. This third framing is the weakest and least developed in studies of greenhouse gas removal to date, however.[32]

Managing Land Use and Land-Use Change in the UK

Current visions for the transition to net zero imply significant land-use change in the UK. Today's pattern of land use reflects a legacy of past priorities. Only around 10 per cent of land is developed, and although the UK was the first country in the world to experience the industrial revolution and its associated rapid urbanisation, the growth in the urban area has generally been slower in the last half-century than the 50 years before.[33] Most residential development has been concentrated in cities, and planning approaches have prioritised the development of brownfield sites and increased residential densities in urban areas. With rural land, the main change has been the growth of woodland at the expense of farmland. The proportion of land covered by woodland has more than doubled since the 1920s and now covers approximately 13 per cent of the UK land area.[34] The level of forest cover varies between the different parts of the UK, with 19 per cent of Scotland forested, 15 per cent of Wales, 10 per cent of England and almost 9 per cent of Northern Ireland. This is low compared to other European countries with France and Germany having 31 and 33 per cent of forest cover, respectively, and the proportion being 46 per cent for the European continent as a whole.[35]

Town planning emerged in the nineteenth century in response to growing problems of poor health and squalor in cities. A major housebuilding programme was introduced following the First World War and the spread of suburbs during the inter-war years prompted concerns about urban sprawl and the need for stronger planning control. The planning system developed to help plan and accommodate the growing needs for housing, infrastructure and economic development, but also to control development to protect green land and prevent sprawl. Gradually, planning in urban and rural areas began to diverge, with the former more focused on growth and development and the latter dominated by preservationism and protection. The 1947 Town and Country Planning Act established a new approach to development planning and development control by local authorities that has broadly endured for more than 70 years. The rise in personal mobility with the growth of car ownership brought challenges and pressures as people began to live further from where they worked, and supermarkets and retail centres developed at the edges of urban areas, so causing new patterns of mobility and congestion and undermining town and city centres.

In 2010, the Government published a major report on land-use and future challenges for the twenty-first century.[36] It highlighted how the UK population was forecast to grow by 9 million by 2031 and 15 million by 2051, but that growth pressures would not be evenly distributed.[37] It highlighted three key cross-sectoral challenges at that time: the rising demand for land in and around the south east of England; the needs of climate change adaptation and mitigation for land use; and the delivery of public goods and services, including amenity and ecosystem services. The planning system has been largely successful at containing urban sprawl, but social and economic changes have meant that the system has come under increasing pressure. In particular, the absence of a strong national strategic framework has made it difficult to deal with large national infrastructure projects. In 2020, the Government published proposals for a major reform of the planning system to simplify and speed planning decisions.[38] This prompted a political backlash from its Members of Parliament and supporters in the south of England where development pressures are most acute, and the Government has since backtracked from the proposals, although pressure for reform is likely to continue.

Addressing climate change will bring pressures and change to UK land use the like of which have not been seen since the Second World War. Most significant will be the repositioning of agricultural land use, including the likely shrinkage of land given over to conventional food production and the growth in land used for climate change mitigation such as energy crops and forestry. While changes to cropping patterns may not require planning permission, the infrastructure to support large-scale BECCS is likely to, and the physical appearance of significant swathes of the countryside will alter. The Climate Change Committee is calling for significant growth in land under forestry and woodland and admits that there is uncertainty about how far its levels of ambition can be achieved in practice. However, the success of afforestation is critical because it makes up around half of all reductions from agriculture, food and land use in the Climate Change Committee's proposed pathway. Moreover, if other aspects of the transition to net zero are less successful than it intends, then more may have to be asked of the afforestation of rural land.[39] The Committee's speculative scenario, for example, assumes even greater reductions in ruminant meat and dairy consumption and so would release up to 30 per cent of agricultural land for afforestation.[40]

The Committee's proposed pathway requires an increase in tree-planting to at least 30,000 hectares per year to 2030 and its more speculative option is to increase planting rates to 50,000 per year.[41] It usually assumes a split of 60:40 broadleaf to conifers. Improved forestry yields of 10 per cent would be expected by 2050 through improved breeding and management techniques. The Committee calculates that improved woodland and forestry management would yield 14 $MtCO_2$ emission sequestration by 2050, with an additional 14 $MtCO_2$ from harvested materials by 2050. Together, these 28 $MtCO_2$ represent the largest proportion of emission reduction from agriculture, food and land use.

Forestry currently covers approximately 3.2 Mha of UK land, of which 27 per cent is owned by state forestry agencies. The area of forested land in the UK has been steadily growing for the past century (see Table 8.1). From 2000 to 2018, the annual average increase in land under forestry was approximately 10,000 hectares per year, although rates are beginning to increase. Around 13,000 hectares of new woodland were planted in the UK in the year 2020–2021, of which just over half was conifers.[42] The industry employs around 18,000 people including in around

TABLE 8.1 Changing Woodland Cover in the UK

Year	England		Scotland		Wales		Northern Ireland		UK	
	Area (000 ha)	%	Area (000 ha)	%	Area (000 ha)	%	Area (000 ha)	%	Area (000 ha)	%
1924	660	5.1	435	5.6	103	5.0	13	1.0	1211	5.0
1980	948	7.3	920	11.8	241	11.6	67	4.9	2175	9.0
2008	1127	8.7	1342	17.2	285	13.7	87	6.4	2841	11.7
2021	1320	10.1	1480	19.0	310	15.0	119	8.6	3229	13.3

Source: Forest Research statistics. Reproduced by permission of Forest Research.

200 sawmills and other wood processing businesses. The forestry sector plays several roles including the production of forest products, carbon sequestration and the provision of valued habitats and sites for public recreation. Almost 70 per cent of respondents in a UK wide survey had visited forests or woodlands in the last few years, and of these, 35 per cent reported an increase in the number of visits in the last 12 months. There were an estimated 368 million visits to woodlands in England in 2018–2019.[43] New woodland planting is heavily focused on Scotland, Wales and Northern Ireland, with the Climate Change Committee in 2020 anticipating that 300,000 hectares of new mixed woodland will be planted by 2035 across the three countries.[44] The UK Net Zero Strategy, published in October 2021, contained commitments to plant an additional 18,000 hectares of woodland in Scotland by 2024/2025 and to increase forest cover from 19 to 21 per cent by 2032.[45] It also pledged 9,000 hectares of new planting in Northern Ireland by 2030.[46] The Welsh Government's Net Zero Strategy is to plant 43,000 hectares of new woodland by 2030 and 180,000 by 2050 contributing to a National Forest for Wales.[47]

The next biggest contributor to savings is bioenergy crops, where the Committee suggests that average planting rates for miscanthus, short rotation coppice and short rotation forestry might scale up to reach 23,000 hectares per year from the mid-2020s. Estimated savings here are 2 $MtCO_2$ in the land sector and a further 11 $MtCO_2$ from harvested products (through, for example, carbon capture and storage). Further savings can be generated from agro-forestry and hedgerow expansion where the area of cropland and grassland planted with trees would need to increase to 10 per cent by 2050, and the area of hedgerows would increase by 181,000 hectares by 2050 delivering 6 $MtCO_2$. The Committee also assumes that at least 50 per cent of upland peat and 25 per cent of lowland peat are restored. Peatland restoration would yield 5 $MtCO_2$ by 2050. These are ambitious targets, and there is uncertainty about how far they can be achieved. The implications of the hedgerow target would be a more than doubling of the UK's current total length of hedgerows, more than compensating for all the loss since the Second World War. The fact that the targets stretch over a period of three decades means that there will be scope for learning and innovation along the way and the balances between different measures can be adjusted in the light of experience. They appear cost-effective from a carbon perspective and have the advantage of bringing other benefits. Hedgerows, for example, help sequester carbon and also help reduce diffuse water pollution, provide shelter for livestock and support biodiversity.

BECCS is also anticipated to be instrumental in offsetting the UK's remaining emissions from those sectors where decarbonisation is most difficult. The UK's large offshore storage capacities in the North Sea, experience in large-scale bioenergy deployment and strong research base in bioenergy and carbon capture and storage leave it well positioned. Of the 23 large-scale carbon capture and storage projects under development worldwide, none are in the UK, although the UK Government's Net Zero Strategy committed to several land-based greenhouse gas removal demonstrator projects.[48] BECCS has been estimated to have the potential to remove up to 60–70 $MtCO_2$ per annum in the UK by 2050. Examples of potential land-based supply chains include sawmill residues to generate electricity with carbon capture and storage, energy crops such as miscanthus to produce combine heat and power with carbon capture and storage, and gasification of willow to produce electricity and carbon capture and storage. Around 90 per cent of carbon dioxide from the biomass could potentially be captured, although energy is expended and emissions are generated in the supply chains which reduces the overall net negative emissions delivered through BECCS. Crucially, levels of greenhouse gas removal vary across different types of supply chain.[49] The Net Zero Strategy envisages the deployment of mature BECCS technologies with potentially significant contributions to the UK's NDC commitments by 2030.[50] A technical review for the Department of Business, Energy and Industrial Strategy estimated that land-based BECCS could operate in the UK at a scale of up to around 10 $MtCO_2$ by 2030 and up to 60 $MtCO_2$ by 2050.[51]

Given the scale of change required, the Climate Change Committee has called for a bold national land-use strategy to balance the needs of the net zero transition with those of other land uses. This call has been echoed by other organisations including in the independent National Food Strategy produced in 2021.[52] The need for reducing carbon emissions and greenhouse gas removal will have to be managed alongside the need for improved agricultural productivity to maintain food supplies from a reduced land area. The relationships between net emission savings from agriculture, food and land use and other sectors of the economy could therefore be significant. If, for example, it becomes clear that emission reduction targets for, say, aviation, look less likely to be achieved, then more could be required from land use.

Delivering such marked expansion in forestry and agro-forestry would require a carbon-trading scheme or auctioned contract system (similar to those for renewable energy) in order to attract private sector investment. The Committee suggests that such schemes could be funded through a levy on greenhouse gas–emitting industries such as fossil fuel providers or airlines.[53] Public funding could also help support the non-carbon benefits of afforestation, agro-forestry and hedgerows (such as flood-risk mitigation, for example). There is also the need to guard against the risk of offshoring, where the UK meets carbon objectives from land and agriculture but imports more food produced less sustainably from elsewhere.

As we saw in Chapters 3 and 4, land-use policy in the UK was oriented to clear national strategic objectives for the three decades after the Second World War, with impressive results in terms of both food production and the protection of the most cherished landscapes. From the 1980s onwards, the strategic priorities have been less clear, and there has been a long period of flux. It is now more than three decades since a House of Lords Select Committee highlighted the strategic dilemmas around the uses of rural land and the future of rural society.[54] The needs of climate change mitigation only add to the policy dilemmas. The Climate Change Committee argues that the complex influences upon land use have "rewarded food production over other services that land can provide including climate change mitigation and adaptation and wider environmental benefits".[55] It points out that currently there are no national or UK-wide policies that directly seek to reduce greenhouse gas emissions in the land-based industries other than those providing information and advice. Support for planting energy crops is minimal and piecemeal, and the existing policy framework is insufficient to meet the emission reductions that are required. It advocates a new policy framework with three components: regulation to establish a strong regulatory baseline through legislation; financial support to address financial barriers; and non-financial support including enabling policies to address non-financial barriers.

The Committee estimated that a net additional £0.5 billion per year would be required to support the planting of 30,000 hectares per year and £0.2 billion for growing trees on farms.[56] A secure income stream would be required to provide long-term certainty through a Feed-in-Tariff scheme or a trading scheme, along the lines of that used for low-carbon electricity generation. A reverse auction mechanism allows for a price to be settled upon and a guarantee of a fixed payment offers an insurance against a variable market price. It is also open to the UK to develop an emission trading scheme similar to that in New Zealand, which does include forestry credits. Such a scheme would put a price on the carbon stored by forestry and encourage landowners to manage forests to maximise carbon storage. Owners would receive carbon credits which could be held or traded, although they should not be allowed to offset emissions from elsewhere in the economy. Such a scheme would require robust monitoring, reporting and evaluation but, over time, could be extended to peatland restoration and other emission removal technologies. A trading scheme for afforestation would provide long-term support for tree planting and allow price uncertainty to be managed. It ought also to reduce overall costs as the market would seek out the most cost-effective ways to reduce emissions. Public funding would still be required to support the land-use transition. For example, there might be advantages to having trees planted in some places rather than others because of wider benefits such as amenity or flood risk. Here public funding could be used as a top up to provide incentives. Similarly, public funding could help bring neglected broadleaf woodland back into sustainable management.

The Science and Politics of Land-Use Change

Meeting the UK's net zero objectives for food, farming and land use can, at first sight, look like a huge and intractable problem. The potential controversy around the various measures varies. The measures to reduce agricultural emissions (as we shall see in Chapter 9) will look like technical issues to many and may only be of interest to those most directly affected. Dietary changes are at the other end of the spectrum. They affect the whole population in the intimate and everyday sphere of eating and so provoke heightened interest and reaction. The land-use changes lay in between. They are generally seen as challenging because they require a sustained change, at historically high rates, over a period of three decades. They provoke interest, but also general approval, with the main concerns being about the possible changes in appearance of valued landscapes and the economics of bioenergy.

The Climate Change Committee appointed a Land Use Advisory Group to examine policies for agriculture, forestry and land use.[57] It reported that climate action must be the key strategic priority, and the goals of climate policy should be prioritised over other agriculture and land-use policy goals. Food security always underpins agricultural policy, and the UK has signed international commitments on biodiversity. However, because climate change is an emergency and, without corrective action, will pose the principal threat to food security, biodiversity and ecosystems in the long term, a clear, sustained message is needed that climate change is the key priority. Such clarity of purpose and priority would help build momentum for large-scale, enduring and transformational change and help overcome inertia. The implementation of climate action will need to be conducted at levels below the UK state. On land use, siting will be important and large-scale, land-use change will need to be planned holistically to optimise potential gains for landscapes, water catchments and biodiversity and to be sensitive to the cultural landscape.

The Land Use Advisory Group emphasised the need for sufficient institutional capacity, strong coherence and co-ordination, and strong, clear leadership, especially in the face of defensive or oppositional attitudes. This is potentially hampered by the UK's complex governance arrangements with the devolved administrations and many statutory bodies operating in this field across the different parts of the UK. Agriculture, environment, food and land use are all largely devolved matters in Scotland, Northern Ireland and Wales. Government departments and agencies include Defra, Natural England and its devolved counterparts, the Environment Agency, Rural Payments Agency and the Forestry Commission. Landscape and other conservation bodies include National Park Authorities, Areas of Outstanding Natural Beauty, nature reserves, local planning authorities and a host of third sector trusts and voluntary bodies. The "highly fragmented and confused" institutional landscape outlined above is not likely to be able to adapt simply or quickly.[58] It is not surprising that there have been calls for a UK-wide body to oversee climate action for agriculture, forestry and land use. The Climate Change Committee is a UK statutory body and helps underpin the thinking, planning and delivery of obligations that the UK makes as a national state in international climate negotiations. However, the UK is made up of four nations that face very different challenges and opportunities with respect to the net zero transition. Nearly 60 per cent of all the abatement in Scotland, Wales and Northern Ireland is in sectors where key powers are partially or mostly devolved. Table 8.2 shows how emissions per person and per unit of GDP are higher in Scotland, Wales and Northern Ireland compared to England, although emissions are lower when compared by land area. Scotland has legislated for a net zero target by 2045, five years ahead of the UK target, and helped by its greater potential for afforestation. Wales will find it more difficult to reach net zero by 2050 and is currently committed to a 95 per cent reduction on 1990 levels by 2050.[59] Policies for agriculture, environment, food and land use have long been distinctive in the different parts of the UK, but the devolution reforms of 1999 have given greater expression to this diversity.[60] Although

TABLE 8.2 Greenhouse Gas Emissions Relative to Population, Economic Activity and Land Area Across the UK

		UK	Scotland	Wales	Northern Ireland
GHG emissions in 2018 (MtCO$_2$e)		539	55	42	25
Population	Population in 2018 (million)	67	5	3	2
	GHG emissions per person (tCO$_2$e/person)	8	10	13	13
Economic activity	GDP in 2018 (£billion)	2,140	160	70	50
	GHG emissions per GDP (tCO$_2$e/£)	252	340	562	505
Land area	Land area (km^2)	250,000	80,000	21,000	14,000
	(tCO$_2$e/km^2)	2,200	700	2,000	1,700

Source: Climate Change Committee (2020b), p. 209. Reproduced by permission of the Climate Change Committee.

the pragmatic concerns about co-ordination and accounting for emission reduction might suggest a stronger UK–wide approach seems desirable, the fragile politics of devolution and the Union make this difficult.

The planting of an additional hundreds of thousands of hectares of forestry will bring challenges for the various actors involved in forestry and land management. A key issue is the financial incentives to make forestry worthwhile. Financial support is likely to be required to support the upfront planting costs, and then to cover income foregone for a period, perhaps until wood products can be sold from thinning. As the forests grow, so carbon will be sequestered, and income can be derived from fuelwood and biomass from forest management. Eventually the forest will produce a yield from its timber. There are bureaucratic obstacles in obtaining a licence to plant and fell trees, and limitations in expertise. Some landowners may be holding off on plans for afforestation until the details of the new post-Brexit subsidy schemes become clearer and there are risks that there might be a lack of confidence in the longer-term durability of any schemes or public funding commitments. Given afforestation is such a significant part of the UK's plan to transition to net zero, a new scheme will need to be signalled as a centrepiece, with vigour and determination. Woodland management advice and training will need to be expanded to help ensure the right trees get planted in the right places and are properly managed, including the technicalities of the density and mix of broadleaf and conifer trees. Investment will also be required to build up capacity among tree breeding and nursery stock sectors, given that future plans mean a three- to five-fold increase in planting trees. And if the supply of timber is going to increase significantly in future, then encouragement will need to be given over the long term to stimulate the uptake of timber and wood fibre products to replace more emission dense material such as steel, concrete and plastics in construction.

Long-term stability and clarity are important, and UK forestry has suffered as a result of the frequency of changes in support over recent decades. There is some concern about the pace at which planting can be increased to achieve at least 30,000 additional hectares each year,[61] and it is possible that there will have to be sub-target planting for the first few years and then higher levels of planting in later years. In the context of this challenge, the role of public funding can be to "set the ball rolling at the desired pace".[62] Any new system of support for afforestation could then learn from experience and adapt accordingly.

Private investors may be willing to support investment in forestry, and there is some evidence of increasing private sector interest. Some £200 million of forestry properties were traded in 2020, which made it the "biggest year on record". The average value of commercial forestry per hectare also increased by 39 per cent.[63] Public and private funding would need to be sufficiently co-ordinated to avoid public money being used unnecessarily. It is possible, given the effects of Brexit and the UK's withdrawal from the CAP, that significant farm occupancy change could follow as farmers sell up. This provides a potential opportunity for the state to invest in expanding the nationally owned forest, as well as allowing other landowners and institutional investors to expand their land holdings. Landowners and farmers are increasingly being presented with the option of creating and selling carbon credits, and a voluntary carbon market already exists in the UK principally in the form of the Woodland Carbon Code. Approximately 15,500 hectares of woodland have been planted under the Code since its introduction in 2012, with a further 24,000 in process. Although these are relatively small amounts of land, the area registered with the Code more than doubled between March 2020 and March 2021 signalling increasing interest.[64]

There is scope for planting more smaller woodlands on farmland and more purposefully managing existing woodland for greenhouse-gas removal. Farm woodland expansion currently tends to be constrained by low financial returns, but also problems of physical access and poor infrastructure. The Climate Change Committee suggested that a target of ensuring 80 per cent of existing broadleaf woodland is brought under management to UK Forest Standard.[65] This would require a campaign of information and advice to promote understanding among land managers of additional management requirements to deliver carbon seques-tration and biodiversity benefits. There would also be a need for additional infra-structure to enable the harvesting and sale of woodland products such as fuel wood. The Committee envisages enhanced sequestration through improved management of hedgerows. The new Environmental Land Management (ELM) scheme ought to be able to compensate farmers for income foregone and facilitate the expansion of hedgerows.

A switch in land use from arable or grassland to the production of energy crops such as miscanthus and short rotation coppicing and forestry would also help green-house gas reduction. Although these are relatively low-input, low-output systems, they may require some new specialist knowledge for farmers and access to infra-structure to enable harvesting and use of biomass.[66] It would be helpful if energy generators were obliged to incorporate a proportion of such renewable sources which might help expand the market and reduce risk for growers. Similarly, advice, information and demonstration projects might help further stimulate adoption. Wider biodiversity and possible amenity benefits could be recognised within the ELM scheme, although landscape concerns may militate against large monocultures of such energy crops.

Carbon capture and storage technology is likely initially to develop as a means of decarbonising heavy industry in the UK, and so it is near the clusters of heavy industries such as iron and steel and chemical processing that capacity will first emerge. The UK Government's Net Zero Strategy is for 20–30 $MtCO_2$ to be captured and stored annually across four industrial clusters. BECCS remains a technology at the planning stage, and there is a risk that misconceptions develop about its potential in the balance of measures to reduce net emissions. The first misconception is that BECCS is all about growing and burning energy crops. Although, in the Climate Change Committee's proposal, BECCS is largely associated with the additional 23,000 hectares of energy crops required annually in the Committee's modelling to help sequester carbon, it need not be confined to energy crops grown on agricultural land. There are a range of waste biomass streams that could potentially produce bioenergy and supply carbon capture and storage systems, including tree management waste, waste products from the forestry and wood processing industries and other agricultural wastes such as straw. The second misconception is that a tonne of carbon dioxide captured from the atmosphere is a tonne safely stored. Supply chains and capture-and-storage processes use energy and generate emissions themselves, and so only a proportion of carbon dioxide captured will be able to be safely stored and so count as negative emissions.

One comparative analysis investigated three potential BECCS supply chains for development in the UK using process modelling and lifecycle analysis. The first used sawmill residues, in pelletised form, for direct combustion to generate electricity in combination with carbon capture and storage. The pellets were assumed to be imported from the timber industry in North America. A second example was based on miscanthus, an energy crop grown in the UK on marginal land, and used to generate combined heat and power, in combination with carbon capture and storage. The third was based on the gasification of willow feedstock, with willow grown in 20-year rotations and producing hydrogen to generate electricity. Net energy efficiency levels were satisfactory and compared reasonably well to other studies, with some evidence that miscanthus can potentially yield higher energy conversion efficiencies. In terms of carbon capture, the modelling suggested that all three supply chains would be able to reach capture rates of 90 per cent or above. When it came to the overall capacity to deliver greenhouse gas removal, amounts differed. While the sawmill residue model has the most robust and proven business model, it delivered the lowest greenhouse gas removal potential. The miscanthus model removed about two-thirds more carbon dioxide than the willow model and three quarters more than the sawmills residue model per unit of energy generated. The analysis estimated that in order to achieve an annual greenhouse gas removal of 20 MtCO2$_e$, as set out by the Climate Change Committee, 10 facilities processing sawmill residues, 32 processing miscanthus or 18 processing willow would be required.[67]

Even when the carbon capture and storage part of BECCS technology becomes more strongly proven and cost-effective, there will remain important dilemmas to be resolved. For example, in capturing carbon, the energy crop miscanthus is more effective than growing trees but brings fewer biodiversity benefits. Furthermore, social science research has highlighted some public anxieties around large-scale carbon capture and storage, with some people associating the technology with the experience of shale gas fracking in the UK.[68] Even with technologies that capture and store carbon while producing green energy, there will be a need to consider and manage questions of public acceptability.

Peatland restoration represents a further opportunity for emission-reducing land-use change. Drained peatland soils used for agriculture and forestry are currently a major emitter of carbon as soils are oxidised. Restoration involves rewetting the land, usually through drain-blocking, and encouraging peat-forming vegetation to return. While full restoration to establish natural peatland habitat might not be appropriate on all peat soils, even partial rewetting yields carbon benefits. There is greatest potential in the uplands. There, peatlands had been "improved" and brought into use for grazing cattle and sheep, but such farming systems are not viable without subsidies, and declining red meat consumption might undermine their viability further. It is generally acknowledged that the move from the CAP to the post-Brexit system of agricultural support will pose the most acute financial challenge for upland farmers.[69] The attachment to what have become seen as "traditional" upland farming systems may be a barrier to restoring peatland, along with limited expertise and human resources. There is some potential to become more directive and use the regulatory baseline to compel land managers to bring those areas designated as Sites of Special Scientific Interest into (ecologically) favourable condition. Grouse moor burning could also be banned. The scale of land-use change required of upland areas could lead to local economic changes and even further depopulation of already sparsely populated areas. Upland landscapes are much more likely to be designated as National Parks, and there is the potential for the social fabric as well as the landscape fabric to change significantly as a result of the needs for climate change mitigation. In contrast, some lowland peat soils support the most productive agricultural systems in the UK with high yielding vegetable crops. (Other lowland peat soils are used for grazing or for natural or semi-natural habitat.) Soil management practices to minimise carbon loss on these lowland peatlands could be encouraged through cross-compliance-type mechanisms (whereby farm payments are conditional on appropriate environmental practices).

Conclusions

Land-use change is going to play a significant role globally in the reduction of net emissions and any transition to net zero. All IPCC-assessed modelled pathways that bring warming to within 2°C require land-based mitigation and land-use change, and afforestation and avoiding deforestation feature prominently in the Nationally Determined Contributions under the Paris Agreement.[70] The IPCC suggest many of the land-related responses that contribute to climate change adaptation and mitigation have other positive benefits for desertification and land degradation.[71] While some measures need not increase competition for land, others such as afforestation and the growth of energy crops including with carbon capture and storage will increase demand for land. Growth in these land uses therefore needs to be accompanied by new agricultural practices and dietary changes to reduce the demand for land for food production. It is also clear that a widespread shift to greater use of land for afforestation and energy crops could have other implications for biodiversity and other ecosystem services from land. This is why the large-scale shifts envisaged for land use to mitigate climate change often come with calls for holistic and nationally integrated approaches to land-use change. Some of these shifts require the development of whole new socio-technical systems such as BECCS. These bring not only technical challenges around the development of new supply chains and carbon capture and storage technologies, but also complex socio-economic challenges around how carbon capture is measured, accounted for and financed. They are not likely to be making a significant contribution to greenhouse gas reductions until the 2030s.

In the short term, afforestation looks to be the most straightforward way to reduce net emissions, and the Climate Change Committee assumes afforestation to be the UK's most significant contributor to net emission reductions. Requiring an additional 30,000–50,000 hectares per year to 2050 to be planted annually will see the UK's area of woodland rise from 3.2 Mha to of the order of between 4 and 4.5 Mha, a significant proportion of which will be concentrated in more sparsely populated areas, including in Scotland, Wales and England's northern uplands. These major land-use changes will need to be managed alongside changes in farming practices on remaining farmland, which is forecast by the Climate Change Committee to take up just 77 per cent of today's agricultural land area in 2050. It is to the question of changing farming practices to meet the demands of the net zero age that we now turn.

Notes

1 Greenhouse gas removal (GGR) is also sometimes referred to a Negative Emission Technologies (or NETs).
2 Sen, A. and Darbi, N. (2021) *Tightening the Net: Net Zero Climate Targets – Implications for Land and Food Quality.* Oxford: Oxfam International.
3 Hulme, M. (2014) *Can Science Fix Climate Change?* Cambridge: Polity Press; McClaren, D. *et al.* (2021) Attractions of delay: using deliberative engagement to investigate the political and strategic impacts of greenhouse gas removal technologies. *Environment and Planning E: Nature and Space* (Online first).
4 Royal Academy of Engineering and Royal Society (2018) *Greenhouse Gas Removal.* London: Royal Society and Royal Academy of Engineering.

5 Lóránt, A. and Allen, B. (2019) *Net Zero Agriculture in 2050: How to Get There.* London: Institute for European Environmental Policy.

6 Climate Change Committee (2020a) *Land Use: Policies for a Net Zero UK.* London: Climate Change Committee, p. 9.

7 Zedler, J. and Kercher, S. (2005) Wetland resources: status, trends, ecosystem services, and restorability. *Annual Review of Environment and Resources* 30, 39–74.

8 Royal Academy of Engineering and Royal Society (2018), p. 26.

9 Royal Academy of Engineering and Royal Society (2018), p. 28.

10 Royal Academy of Engineering and Royal Society (2018), p. 39.

11 Gough, C. *et al.* (2018) Challenges to the use of BECCS as a keystone technology in pursuit of 1.5°C. *Global Sustainability* 1, e5, 1–9, p. 3.

12 Smith, P. *et al.* (2016) Preliminary assessment of the potential for, and limitations to, terrestrial negative emission technologies in the UK. *Environmental Science: Processes & Impacts* 18(11), 1400–5.

13 Royal Academy of Engineering and Royal Society (2018), p. 40.

14 Royal Academy of Engineering and Royal Society (2018), p. 40.

15 Gough *et al.* (2018), p. 4.

16 Minx, J. *et al.* (2018) Negative emissions – part 1: research landscape and synthesis. *Environmental Research Letters* 13, 063001; Fuss, S. *et al.* (2018) Negative emissions – part 2: costs, potentials and side effects. *Environmental Research Letters* 13, 063002; Nemet, G. *et al.* (2018) Negative emissions – part 3: innovation and upscaling. *Environmental Research Letters* 13, 063003.

17 Sen and Darbi (2021), p. 7.

18 Fridahl, M. and Lehtveer, M. (2018) Bioenergy with carbon capture and storage (BECCS): global potential, investment preferences, and deployment barriers. *Energy Research & Social Science* 42, 155–65.

19 Minx *et al.* (2018).

20 See National Academy of Sciences *et al.* (1992). *Policy Implications of Greenhouse Warming: Mitigation, Adaptation, and the Science Base.* Washington, DC: The National Academies Press; Waller, L. *et al.* (2020) Contested framings of greenhouse gas removal and its feasibility: social and political dimensions. *Wiley Interdisciplinary Reviews: Climate Change* 11, e649.

21 Courvoisier, T. *et al.* (eds.) (2018) *Negative Emission Technologies: What Role in Meeting Paris Agreement Targets?* EASAC Policy Report 35. Halle (Saale): EASAC Secretariat, Deutsche Akademie der Naturforscher Leopoldina.

22 Fuss, S. *et al.* (2014) Commentary: betting on negative emissions. *Nature Climate Change* 4(10), 850–3.

23 Waller *et al.* (2020).

24 Thomas, G. *et al.* (2018) Ambivalence, naturalness and normality in public perceptions of carbon capture and storage in biomass, fossil energy, and industrial applications in the United Kingdom. *Energy Research and Social Science* 46, 1–9.

25 Honegger, M. and Reiner, D. (2018) The political economy of negative emissions technologies: consequences for international policy design. *Climate Policy* 18, 306–21; Ehrenstein, V. (2018) Carbon sink geopolitics. *Economy and Society* 47, 162–86.

26 Geden, O. *et al.* (2018) Integrating carbon dioxide removal into EU climate policy: prospects for a paradigm shift. *WIREs Climate Change* 9(4), e521.

27 Merk, C. *et al.* (2019) Do climate engineering experts display moral-hazard behaviour? *Climate Policy* 19(2), 231–43.

28 Vaughan, N. and Gough, C. (2016) Expert assessment concludes negative emissions scenarios may not deliver. *Environmental Research Letters* 11(9), 095003.

29 Geden *et al.* (2018).

30 Ehrenstien (2018).

31 Waller *et al.* (2020).

32 Waller *et al.* (2020).

33 Foresight Land Use Futures Project (2010) *Land Use Futures: Making the Most of Land in the 21st Century.* Final Project Report. London: Government Office for Science, p. 61.

34 Foresight Land Use Futures Project (2010); Climate Change Committee (2020a).

35 International comparative statistics on forest cover are from Forest Research. www. forestresearch.gov.uk/tools-and-resources/statistics/forestry-statistics/forestry-statistics-2018/international-forestry/forest-cover-international-comparisons/.

36 Foresight Land Use Futures Project (2010).

37 Foresight Land Use Futures Project (2010), p. 12.

38 Garton Grimwood, G. (2021) *Planning for the Future: Planning Policy Changes in England in 2020 and Future Reforms.* House of Commons Library Briefing Paper No. 8981. London: House of Commons.

39 Climate Change Committee (2020a), p. 33.

40 Climate Change Committee (2020a), p. 114.

41 Climate Change Committee (2020a), p. 33.

42 Forest Research (2021) *Forestry Statistics 2021.* Edinburgh: Forest Research.

43 Forest Research (2021).

44 Climate Change Committee (2020b), p. 208.

45 UK Government (2021) *Net Zero Strategy: Build Back Greener.* London: Stationary Office, p. 182.

46 UK Government (2021), p. 183.

47 Welsh Government (2021) *Net Zero Wales Carbon Budget 2021–25.* WG42949. Cardiff: Welsh Government, p. 161.

48 García-Freites, S. *et al.* (2021) The greenhouse gas removal potential of bioenergy with carbon capture and storage (BECCS) to support the UK's net-zero emission target. *Biomass and Bioenergy* 151, 2.

49 García-Freites *et al.* (2021), p. 13.

50 UK Government (2021), p. 189.

51 Element Energy and UK Centre for Ecology and Hydrology (2021) *Greenhouse Gas Removal Methods and their Potential UK Deployment.* Report for the Department for Business, Energy and Industrial Strategy. London: BEIS, pp. iii–v.

52 National Food Strategy (2021) *National Food Strategy – Independent Review: The Plan.* London: National Food Strategy, pp. 232–6.

53 Climate Change Committee (2020a), p. 76.

54 House of Lords Select Committee on the European Communities (1990) *The Future of Rural Society.* HL Paper 80-I. London: Stationery Office.

55 Climate Change Committee (2020a), p. 77.

56 Climate Change Committee (2020a), p. 90.

57 Buckwell, A. (2019) *Policies for Agriculture, Forestry and Land Use: Chair's Report of the CCC Land Use Advisory Group.* London: Climate Change Committee.

58 Buckwell (2019), p. 8.

59 Climate Change Committee (2020b) *The Sixth Carbon Budget: The UK's Path to Net Zero.* London: Climate Change Committee, p. 206.

60 Ward, N. and Lowe, P. (2002) Devolution and the governance of rural affairs in the UK, pp. 117–39 in J. Adams & P. Robinson (eds.) *Devolution in Practice: Public Policy Differences within the UK*. London: IPPR.

61 Buckwell (2019), p. 18.

62 Buckwell (2019), p. 19.

63 Millard, R. (2021) City investors planning to turn reforestation into a growth industry. *The Sunday Telegraph* 17 October. Business Section, p. 8.

64 Elliott, J. *et al.* (2022) *The Opportunities of Agri-Carbon Markets: Policy and Practice*. London: Green Alliance, p. 33.

65 Climate Change Committee (2018).

66 Buckwell (2019), p. 22.

67 García-Freites *et al.* (2021).

68 Cox, E. *et al.* (2021) But they told us it was safe! Carbon dioxide removal, fracking, and ripple effects in risk perceptions. *Risk Analysis* (Online early view); McClaren, D. *et al.* (2021).

69 House of Commons Environment, Food and Rural Affairs Committee (2021) *Environmental Land Management and the Agricultural Transition*. Second Report, Session 2021–22. London: House of Commons.

70 Intergovernmental Panel on Climate Change (2020) *Climate Change and Land: Summary for Policymakers*. Geneva: IPCC, p. 24.

71 IPCC (2020), p. 20.

9

FARMING PRACTICE AND CLIMATE CHANGE MITIGATION

Introduction

Agricultural production is estimated to account for at least 10 per cent of the world's greenhouse gas emissions.[1] In the UK, agriculture makes up just 0.5 per cent of the UK's Gross Domestic Product and produces more emissions for the size of its economic contribution than any other sector.[2] As we have seen in Chapter 7, addressing climate change globally will bring pressure for significant changes to diet to reduce the consumption of red meat from ruminant livestock in particular. This will have consequences for patterns of land use as less land would be required for livestock. Alongside dietary changes and reductions in food waste, mitigating climate change will mean other changes to land management across the world. Changes in farming practices will be required to improve productivity and reduce emissions. This is a twin challenge because the world's population will continue to grow and reducing greenhouse gas emissions will need to be accompanied by a continual improvement in the amount of food that can be produced globally per unit of land, per unit of labour and now per unit of carbon equivalent emitted.

Demand for food is expected to increase by more than 50 per cent by 2050 as the global population grows to 9.8 billion. Climate change will impact upon agricultural productivity and if no adaptation takes place global crop yields are anticipated to decline by at least 5 per cent by 2050.[3] Improvements in crop and pasture productivity will need to exceed historical rates of yield gain if there is to be no expansion of agricultural land. Without such improvements, land conversion to agriculture would be five times greater by 2050 compared to 2010 and an additional 593 Mha would be required to meet expected food demand.[4] In addition to these productivity gains, emissions need to be reduced. In the UK, the Climate Change Committee set out a proposed pathway for agriculture's transition to support the national net zero target. This informed the Committee's Sixth

DOI: 10.4324/9781003278535-9

Carbon Budget, which proposes a 78 per cent in total emissions compared to 1990 levels by 2035.[5] It envisages that by 2035, 460,000 hectares of new mixed woodland are planted to remove carbon dioxide and deliver wider environmental benefits, 260,000 hectares of farmland shifts to producing energy crops, and woodland cover rises from 13 per cent of UK land today to 15 per cent by 2035 and 18–19 per cent by 2050. It envisages that farming practices reduce emissions by 10 $MtCO_2e$ by 2050, a reduction of just over 20 per cent of the 46 $MtCO_2e$ emitted in 2017.[6]

This chapter examines in more detail the changes to UK farming practice that will be required by these emissions-reduction plans. Given the future potential switch of current farmland to forestry and energy crops, the equivalent of current levels of food production will have to be delivered from less land. This challenge is prompting a debate about "sustainable intensification" or land sparing, on the one hand, with the adoption of ever-more sophisticated yield-boosting and emission-reducing farming techniques and, on the other, agro-ecology or high-nature-value farming, which represents a more ecologically-driven, land sharing approach rooted in appreciation of environmental constraints. This binary reproduces ideas that have featured in arguments about farming and environment for the past half-century which have sometimes been characterised as agri-centric or ecocentric. The chapter examines the main arguments and the institutions and networks that seek to advance them.

Climate Change and Farming Practices in a Global Context

Globally, changing farming practices needs to meet the twin goals of helping improve productivity without expansion of the area of agricultural land and reducing emissions of greenhouse gases per unit of food produced. These twin challenges have stimulated a huge global scientific effort.[7] The significant global yield gains since the 1960s were largely achieved by doubling the irrigated area and extending the use of more productive seed varieties and commercial fertiliser. Although it looks to be possible to continue to achieve higher yields, other approaches will be required to ensure sufficient food is produced sustainably. The World Resources Institute identify five key strategies for improving agricultural productivity: raise livestock and pasture productivity; improve crop breeding to boost yields; improve soil and water management; plant existing cropland more frequently; and adapt to climate change.[8] In addition, there is the prospect of more radical change in food production through the industrial and lab-based development of novel foods such as "lab-grown meat". Here, we first consider conventional agriculture.

Pasture makes up two-thirds of all agricultural land globally so its productivity will critically affect future land use and emissions. Pork and poultry are reaching their biological limits of productivity improvement in developed countries and expansion in their production in developing countries will intensify environmental pressures because of increasing emissions and demands on land. Ruminant systems do have potential for productivity improvements, however. The greenhouse gas emissions from producing a kilogram of beef varies significantly around the world because of different production and feeding systems and cattle breeds. Land requirements can be 100 times greater in some places compared to others and quantities of feed can vary by 20 times. Improved feed quality, breeding and animal health can all increase livestock productivity. Improved fertilisation and crop rotations can benefit pastures with good rainfall, and supplementary feeds can help in dry seasons. The main challenge lies in the scale of the improvements required. Almost every hectare of wetter, accessible and environmentally appropriate land would need to achieve close to its maximum potential to meet expected global demand without the requirement for any additional land.

Crop breeding has historically been a key source of agricultural productivity gain. Those countries that have invested more over recent years in crop breeding, including Brazil and China, have seen significant improvements in their yields. Although crop breeding has traditionally been incremental, new crop cycles could be speeded up. Genetic modification has attracted controversy in some parts of the world, but gene editing has the potential to make crops more efficient at absorbing nitrogen or suppressing methane and nitrous oxide emissions. Geonomics allows the mapping of plants' entire genetic code and purifying crop strains more quickly. Further investment in crop breeding could bring significant opportunities for productivity improvements. Improved soil and water management can also help. African farmers have been increasingly encouraged to adopt no-tillage or reduced tillage systems which reduce soil erosion risks and can help boost yields in drier areas. Agroforestry also has promise and is boosting yields in Africa's Sahel region.

Some gains may be possible through cropping intensity. Food and Agriculture Organisation (FAO) data suggest that more than 400 Mha of cropland are unharvested each year, while approximately 150 Mha are double-cropped. Increasing double cropping could boost production without needing extra land. However, roughly half of today's double-cropped land is irrigated, and water will limit the extent to which the practice can be expanded. Nevertheless, greater cropping intensity has some promise, especially in Latin America. If cropping intensity was to improve from the FAO's current estimate of 82 to 92 per cent, the gap between the current agricultural land area and that required to feed the world's population in 2050 would shrink by 81 Mha or 14 per cent.[9] At the same time, climate change will increasingly affect world agricultural production. Growing periods will change, and rainfall may become more variable, and so adapting to climate change will need to be an integral feature of efforts to improve productivity.

The World Resources Institute estimate that global emissions from agricultural production need to fall to 4 $GtCO_2e$ by 2050. However, their baseline scenario is for emissions to grow to 9 $GtCO_2e$ by 2050 with productivity gains, or 11 $GtCO_2e$ with no productivity gains. With productivity gains, this still leaves a 5 $GtCO_2e$ mitigation gap. A range of management practices are proposed to help narrow this gap. Ruminant livestock generates roughly half of global agricultural emissions, and productivity improvements can help reduce emissions per unit produced with the greatest potential for improvement in the poorest countries. Among the least efficient producers, as milk production becomes more efficient so emissions intensity falls dramatically.[10] Special feeds or supplements can also help reduce emissions, with some reporting reductions of up to 30 per cent, and more research funding is now being directed to better understanding enteric fermentation and its emissions.[11]

Similarly, manure management in confined systems can reduce emissions. Roughly half of emissions from managed manure comes from pigs, with dairy cows just over one-third and beef cows around 15 per cent.[12] (Manure deposited in fields is treated as "unmanaged"). Wet systems can produce emissions 20 times higher than dry systems and so systems that separate and dry out manure are beneficial. In intensive pig units in developed countries, it can be possible to eliminate virtually all water and air pollution from manure using treatment tanks. Anaerobic digesters can be used to convert manure into methane for energy use, although the capital costs of the technology can be prohibitively high in developing countries. Technologies under development may be able to lower emissions from manure deposited on pasture, and savings can also be derived from improving the efficiency of nitrogen use. Globally, crops absorb less than half the nitrogen applied to land, but this can be significantly improved if farmers take more care to assess nitrogen needs and apply only what is needed. Nitrogen efficiency can be improved through nitrification inhibitors and other enhanced fertilisers, but globally these technologies are currently only used with 2 per cent of fertilisers. Agriculture's use of fossil fuels can be reduced through increasing energy efficiency and through switching to renewable energy sources. The World Resources Institute estimated that 65 per cent of expected agricultural energy emissions in 2050 will result from on-farm energy use.[13] Solar and wind sources can replace fossil fuels for electricity generation, although replacing diesel fuel for agricultural machinery may be more difficult and take longer.

Soil carbon sequestration is estimated to have considerable potential for reducing greenhouse gas emissions globally, but there are high degrees of uncertainty. One estimate of the mean global potential for agricultural soil carbon sequestration is 1.5 $GtCO_2e$ per year at US$20 per tonne and 2.6 $GtCO_2e$ per year at US$100 tonne.[14] Estimates of the economic mitigation potential of supply-side measures will be upper limits. Social and political constraints such as concerns about food security, distributional impacts and distributional leakages (or countries exporting their carbon problems) will reduce this potential. Given these considerations, the OECD consider that "achieving the necessary global uptake of mitigation policies in the agricultural sector ... is likely to be an enormous political and technical challenge".[15] Nevertheless, most countries of the world have pointed to the agriculture sector as a key source of their planned emissions reductions under the Paris Agreement. Of the 185 states that signed the agreement, over 100 of these identify agriculture as a contributing sector in their NDCs. However, progress in implementing concrete measures lags other sectors such as energy and transport.[16]

A range of countries have developed mitigation policies and targets. These generally tend to involve voluntary schemes which pay farmers to mitigate emissions by adopting management improvements that go beyond "business as usual" farming practice. For example, the California Air Resources Board introduced a compliance offset programme and Australia have an Emissions Reduction Fund, most of which is orientated to supporting vegetation projects that enhance or protect carbon stocks.[17] The Alberta Emissions Offset System purchases offsets from increased soil carbon sequestration as a result of zero tillage methods and anaerobic digestion. In California, targets have been set for cutting dairy and livestock manure methane emissions by 40 per cent by 2030 from 2013 levels, equivalent to 12 $MtCO_2e$ per year in 2030.[18] In New Zealand, the Emission Trading Scheme exempts non-carbon dioxide emissions from agriculture, but its Zero Carbon Amendment Bill sets separate targets for reducing methane emissions, which come mainly from ruminant livestock, by 10 per cent by 2030 and to 24–47 per cent by 2050.[19]

In the EU, targets have been set for non-Emission Trading Scheme sectors such as transport, agriculture, buildings and waste to reduce emissions from 2005 levels by 10 per cent by 2020 and 30 per cent by 2030.[20] Most EU Member States do not have sector-specific targets for agriculture, but some do. The Netherlands has proposed a target of 3.5 $MtCO_2e$ per year by 2030, an 18 per cent reduction on 2016 levels.[21] In its National Low Carbon Strategy, France has established a carbon budget for agriculture with a reduction in emissions of 8 per cent by 2023, 13 per cent by 2028 and 20 per cent by 2033, compared to 2015 levels. Germany's ambitions for reducing agricultural emissions go further, aiming for 31–34 per cent reductions on 1990 levels by 2030.[22] Finland targeted a 13 per cent reduction in agricultural emissions between 2005 and 2020 and Ireland is aiming for net zero overall by 2050, with cumulative methane and nitrous oxide emissions reductions of 16.5 to 18.5 $MtCO_2e$ between 2021 and 2030.[23] Industry-led initiatives have emerged in some OECD countries, often in response to consumer pressure and acting ahead of government. One ambitious example is the Australian red meat and livestock industry's goal to become carbon neutral by 2030.[24] According to the OECD, "there are nevertheless limitations to all voluntary approaches such as these, and in most countries stronger incentives will be needed to underpin large-scale mitigation ambitions that are commensurate with the targets of the Paris Agreement".[25] Where initiatives have been launched, they have yielded important new insights and lessons about efficacy. Methane reduction from manure on more intensive and confined livestock systems such as piggeries and dairy farms have been relatively more straightforward as they more closely resemble point sources of pollution. However, this is only a small proportion of total global emissions from agriculture. And after experimenting with mitigation schemes, it is not uncommon for forestry options to be found to be relatively more straightforward than adaptations to farming practices.

Around the world, agriculture remains a highly subsidised sector. Those countries that accounted for two-thirds of the world's agricultural output together provided US$600 billion per year in financial support to agriculture between 2014 and 2016, with half of this through direct government payments or targeted tax benefits. Agricultural subsidies amount to almost a third of the total value added by agriculture across these countries. There is considerable scope to reform and redirect this spending towards mitigating climate change.[26] The OECD concludes that progress in developing mitigation for the agriculture sector has been uneven across countries and tends to rely on voluntary policies, including payments to farmers, green finance schemes and modest target setting. "This amounts to an aggregate global level of policy ambition that is out of step with the agricultural sector's potential to address climate change".[27] Without accelerated progress, wider efforts to limit global warming could be stifled. Some scenario modelling suggests that non-carbon dioxide emissions from agriculture could become the largest source of greenhouse gas emissions by mid-century if other sectors succeed in their decarbonisation strategies. Indeed, emissions of methane, which is the second most important greenhouse gas after carbon dioxide, have risen much faster than expected.[28] This makes meeting the Paris Agreement targets more urgent, and if similar scientific evidence emerges, pressure will build to go further and faster to reduce emissions.

Changing Farming Practices in the UK

In the UK, agriculture accounted for 10 per cent of total greenhouse gas emissions in 2018, although its contribution to some individual greenhouse gases is much higher, at 70 per cent of nitrous oxide and 49 per cent of methane emissions. Methane has a global warming potential 25 times higher than carbon dioxide, while the warming potential of nitrous oxide is almost 300 times that of carbon dioxide. UK agriculture's emissions come mostly from livestock and manure (56 per cent), the use of inputs such as manufactured fertilisers (31 per cent) and fuel and machinery (12 per cent). We have seen how UK agriculture can contribute to emissions reduction through afforestation and growing energy crops, but there remains the question of the farming practices on the remaining farmland. Here potential measures include: more efficient use of fertilisers to reduce loss to the environment; improved manure management; using monitoring data to manage and improve efficiency and emissions; and reducing emissions from buildings and machinery.

Total greenhouse gas emissions from UK agriculture declined by 16 per cent, from 54 $MtCO_2$ equivalents in 1990 to 45.2 $MtCO_2$ in 2009. However, since 2009 emissions have broadly flatlined (see Figure 1.1 in Chapter 1). Measures to reduce emissions have been largely voluntary and the flatlining since 2009 suggests the need for a stronger approach. The emissions challenge coincides with other significant changes for British agriculture. The UK's departure from the EU and its CAP means new national frameworks for agricultural policy are being introduced in the four parts of the UK. There is a general commitment to continuing to support agriculture's role in producing public goods, although there is uncertainty about precisely how new arrangements will work.[29] Measures to reduce emissions from farming practices focus on promoting improvements in productivity and resource use. These are estimated by the Climate Change Committee to be able to reduce emissions from the sector by approximately 20 per cent by 2050.[30] Estimates for the abatement rates of different types of farming practice are set out in Table 9.1.

TABLE 9.1 Abatement Rates for Measures to Reduce Emissions from Agriculture

Measure	Estimate of abatement rate (tCO_2e), per hectare and per year
Using biological fixation to provide Nitrogen (N) inputs (*e.g.* using clover)	0.5
Reducing N fertiliser	0.5
Improving land drainage	1.0
Avoiding N excess	0.4
Fully accounting for manure and slurry N	0.4
Introducing species such as legumes	0.5
Improving management of N mineral fertiliser	0.3
Applying controlled release fertilisers	0.3
Utilising nitrification inhibitors	0.3
Improving the management of slurry and manure	0.3
Adopting farming practices and systems that are less reliant on inputs (nutrients, pesticides, etc.)	0.2
Using plant varieties with improved N use efficiency	0.2
Separating slurry/manure applications from fertiliser applications by several days	0.1
Adopting reduced or no till practices	0.15
Using compost or straw based manures instead of slurry	0.1

Source: MacLeod *et al.* (2010) and Ortiz *et al.* (2021), p. 16. Reproduced by permission of Carole Dalin, Institute for Sustainable Resources, University College London.

Careful steps in fertiliser use can help. For example, controlled-release fertilisers and inhibitors[31] can increase the efficiency of nitrogen use and reduce emissions. Improved use of weather forecasting, including seasonal forecasting, can also assist more timely fertiliser application and precision farming technologies can help deliver nutrients more accurately within fields. More accurate and efficient fertiliser application has the additional benefit of reducing the risk of water pollution and with soil management, reducing the risk of soil compaction can mean less need for cultivation, also reducing emissions.

Because livestock farming is the biggest source of emissions, any measures that can reduce problems in this part of the sector have disproportionate impact. Improving the digestibility of animal feed is one such step along with improving the feed conversion ratio, which has the effect of less feed being required. For sheep, the use of legumes in pasture reseed mixes has been found to reduce emissions along with using organic sources of nitrogen rather than mineral fertilisers. Animal breeding can also contribute to emissions reduction. Faster growing breeds have a shorter age to slaughter which means they do not eat as much food nor emit as much pollution. Animal breeding can also help improve the functioning of animals' digestive systems so that fewer emissions are produced.

Manure management is another area for improvement, especially through improved handling, storage and application. British livestock farming has been through considerable change in the management of farmyard manure and slurry since the 1980s to reduce water pollution risks. Lower emissions can result from a more careful and rigorous approach. Stored slurry can be treated with additives to reduce nitrous oxide emissions and anaerobic digestion systems can convert animal manures and crop by-products into renewable energy. The design of farm buildings can also contribute to reducing emissions including the use of air scrubbers. More energy-efficient buildings reduce energy use and costs, and sometimes animal welfare benefits can be generated alongside emissions reductions. Agricultural vehicles are another source of emissions, and improvements in engines and fuels will help reduce their impact. Smaller machines such as drones and robots may also help to reduce emissions in future. Crucial in bringing about reductions in emissions is the ability to measure and monitor performance over time. There are several emission or footprint calculators available to British farmers that help estimate emissions. Examples include Cool Farm Tool, Agrecalc and the Farm Carbon Toolkit. Establishing a baseline is an important first step, but such tools can then help guide investment decisions and changes in farming practice.

In England, Defra run an annual survey of farming practices including practices associated with managing greenhouse gas emissions.[32] The most recent survey found that 56 per cent of farmers had a nutrient management plan, a proportion that had not changed significantly since 2011. These tended to be larger farms and the 56 per cent of farmers accounted for 74 per cent of the farmed area covered by the survey. Over a third of farmers (38 per cent) keep track of soil organic matter and almost two thirds (63 per cent) know the soil types for each field on their farm. Three in ten farmers calculate a whole farm nutrient balance every year. Just 8.9 per cent of farmers surveyed said they used anaerobic digestion, although this was an increase on 2020 when the figure was 6.6 per cent and significantly higher than 2015 when the proportion was just 1.5 per cent. Fifty-six per cent of farmers said they were taking action to reduce greenhouse gas emissions from their farms. Of those taking action, the most common measures were recycling waste materials (83 per cent), improving energy efficiency (79 per cent) and improving nitrogen fertiliser application (62 per cent). The biggest increase between 2013 and 2020 was in the proportion of farmers improving the efficiency of their slurry and manure application, which rose from 28 per cent in 2013 to 51 per cent in 2021. Generally, the most common motivation for greenhouse gas emission reduction measures were that they were good business practice (80 per cent), followed by concern for the environment (75 per cent). Farmers were surveyed about what prevented them from taking action to reduce greenhouse gas emissions. Reasons varied according to whether farmers were taking any action or not. For those not taking any action, the most common explanation was that they did not think it was necessary as the farm did not produce many emissions. Some 41 per cent, however, said they were inhibited because they were not sure what to do.

Over three-quarters of farmers (79 per cent) spread slurry or manure on their land and 84 per cent spread fertilisers. Notably, for 43 per cent of those who do spread slurry or manure, the spreader is never calibrated. Almost all dairy farms spread slurry or manure and the majority (60 per cent) of grazing livestock farms in the uplands spread slurry or manure. Temporary muck heaps in fields remain the most common form of storage for solid manures (72 per cent) although over a fifth of livestock farmers store slurry in a tank (22 per cent) while 13 per cent use a lagoon. In 2021, 20 per cent of livestock farmers with storage facilities intended to enlarge or upgrade them, compared to 16 per cent in 2020. The proportion of holdings that had up to six months storage capacity for slurry had decreased slightly to 76 per cent, with almost all the remaining holdings having 7–12 months capacity. Of those farmers who had livestock, 71 per cent had a farm waste (slurry and manure) management plan and these respondents tended to be larger farms and covered 82 per cent of the farmed area.

Sowing temporary grassland with a clover mix or high sugar grasses can improve production and also help reduce greenhouse gas emissions.[33] Although not suitable on all soil types, clover can fix nitrogen and so reduce the need for nitrogen fertilisers. In 2021, 76 per cent of livestock holdings had at least some of their temporary grassland sown with a clover mix and high sugar grasses were sown on 65 per cent of livestock holdings that had some temporary grassland. Farmers are also taking up new practices in livestock feeding regimes and livestock breeding. Some 54 per cent of livestock farmers used a ration formulation based on nutritional advice when planning their feeding regime. Almost a quarter (23 per cent) offered some alternative forages other than conserved grass to their animals, the most common being whole crop silage and maize.

Soil management also has a potentially important role to play in capturing and storing carbon both in the short and long term.[34] On deforested land, soils lose their source of organic carbon from leaf litter and carbon can be depleted as organic matter decomposes, so releasing emissions. Stocks of soil organic carbon have been depleted but can be built up through lower impact tillage and the use of soil amendments such as compost, paper crumble, manure and biochar. Initiatives to recarbonise global soils have highlighted how soils can be in the forefront of climate change mitigation. The NFU's plan for reaching net zero by 2040 includes enhancing soil carbon as a significant feature, capturing around 5 $MtCO_2$ per year.[35] Effective soil carbon management also involves using information technologies and analytics. Precision agriculture technologies can help improve the efficiency and effectiveness of input use and farming practices can be promoted to prevent nutrient losses such as no or low tillage, using nitrogen-fixing cover crops and field margin management.

Post-Brexit, the 2020 Agriculture Act provides the framework for England's new agricultural policy to replace the CAP. Further measures will come as Statutory Instruments. The current system of direct payments to farmers will be phased out over a seven-year period to be replaced by support for the provision of public goods. A new Environmental Land Management scheme will be introduced in stages, first with a pilot from 2022. From Autumn 2024, the scheme will be expanded and fully rolled out and there are expected to be nine options for farmers, which will include support for measures relating to soil and nutrient management, tree and woodland management and livestock management. Climate change mitigation is likely to be a prominent feature of the new regime for agricultural support in all parts of the UK. This will be a challenging process of change for farmers and land managers. Practical tips for UK farmers include the importance of advice and monitoring, but also the valuable role that experimentation, risk-taking and leadership can play.[36] It is clear from Defra's survey work that the most successful uptake of measures occurs when there is an economic benefit to the farmer as well as an environmental benefit from reduced emissions.

The Science and Politics of Changing Farming Practices

As we saw in Chapter 6, two approaches frame current debates about how farming practices will need to change in order to deliver sufficient emissions reductions for a net zero UK. The first emphasises the need for "sustainable intensification" to maintain food production levels from a smaller area of agricultural land. Here the focus is on techniques and technologies to make farming practice more efficient and boost productivity. Under this "land sparing" approach, land is freed up for other purposes such as carbon sequestration, or for enhancing biodiversity. The second emphasises the need for farming to work in closer harmony with nature. This agroecological approach focuses on "high nature farming" and is particularly espoused by environmental organisations and by some enthusiastic farmers. It was also the approach emphasised by the Royal Society for Arts' Food, Farming and Countryside Commission and its subsequent modelling of the development of UK agriculture to 2050.[37]

Reducing emissions is going to involve complex changes to farming practices and this is at a time when scientific knowledge of the precise relationships between specific practices and their emissions is still developing. There are dilemmas around the balance of measures between the voluntaristic approach, involving giving farmers advice and encouragement to alter practices, and strengthening regulation to stipulate what can and cannot be done. Between the two extremes, desirable practices can be incentivised through farm and land management payments. The issue is made more complex by the different greenhouse gases emitted by farming practices. In addition to carbon dioxide are methane and nitrous oxide. It is not straightforward to measure these emissions at the farm level which makes it harder to establish ways to reduce them. Defra's own work into reducing emissions had by 2019 identified over 30 potential measures.[38]

The Government's Net Zero Strategy has a target of 75 per cent of farmers in England engaging with low-carbon practices by 2030 rising to 85 per cent by 2035.[39] Surveys suggest there is a significant challenge in explaining to farmers emissions processes and what might need to be done. Defra's recent survey found that only 19 per cent of farmers said it was "very important" to consider greenhouse gas emissions when making decisions about their land, crops and livestock with a further 46 per cent considering it "fairly important".[40] The proportion of farmers who consider climate change to be important is increasing over time, but there remain 26 per cent of farmers who place little or no importance on greenhouse gas emissions when making decisions about their farming. Fifty-six per cent report they are taking action to reduce emissions, but for those who do not, a substantial proportion (over 40 per cent) do not believe it to be necessary. Another key challenge is greenhouse gas accounting at the farm level. A high proportion of farmers do not use basic cost accounting in running their businesses, so moving to a system of carbon accounting is unlikely. Larger and more commercial farmers are much more likely to have a good command of their business and management accounts and use performance benchmarking, but there is still a dearth of accepted environmental accounting systems for farms. As farming practice needs to be increasingly integrated with emissions reduction, so there will be a need for an authoritative, standardised and officially endorsed methodology for greenhouse gas accounting.[41]

A new clear regulatory baseline ought to be the first step in developing policy governing farming practice to reduce emissions. It can sometimes be assumed that this baseline can be objectively and technically set. However, what society judges as acceptable and unacceptable changes over time and so baseline-setting is an inherently social and political act and not merely a technical one. As we saw in Chapter 4, what counts as acceptable farming practice in relation to water pollution or managing biosecurity and animal health shifts over time in response to scientific evidence of environmental and animal health risks but also changing public values. Economic theory would suggest applying the polluter pays principle, with a clear regulatory baseline and then taxing producers on their emissions or developing a cap-and-trade scheme to financially incentivise emissions reduction. The biggest burden would fall upon the biggest emitters who would be more strongly incentivised to reduce pollution. However, disentangling carbon dioxide, methane and nitrous oxide emissions and administering such a system at the farm level is likely to be prohibitively complex. Taxing pollution would probably raise food prices and this may be politically uncomfortable, although economists increasingly point to the fact that farming's externalities are not currently incorporated in food prices.[42] Shaping discussions about the balance between regulation, voluntary schemes and farm payments are implicit assumptions about the relationship between agricultural production and environmental resources. One perspective sees production as separate and in opposition to the environment. Under this model, reductions in intensity of production automatically lead to improvements in environmental quality, and environmental impacts are conceptualised as "externalities". A second perspective sees environmental attributes as jointly produced public goods arising from production systems that have co-evolved with their environments. Under this model, the relationship between production practices and environmental assets is more complex and indeterminate.[43]

Another concern is around international competitiveness. Farming interests often warn that if environmental or animal welfare rules are tougher in the UK than elsewhere, then this will undermine international competitiveness. The argument was applied during debates about paring back CAP direct payments in the late 1990s.[44] In other words, if direct payments were reduced in the UK ahead of other Member States, as had been permitted by the 1999 CAP reform, then this would undermine the competitiveness of British farmers compared to their European counterparts. A counterargument is that agriculture in all countries will have to adapt to the needs of climate change mitigation and by reforming early British farmers would be better prepared for the new competitive environment. Given global environmental change is a global challenge, there might be a case for seeking to co-ordinate basic rules on emissions internationally, but this would be a hugely complex task given the diversity of farming systems and environments. The OECD estimated that if greenhouse gas taxes were applied in all OECD countries but not elsewhere, the leakage from importing food from elsewhere could amount to a third of the emissions reduction.[45]

In the UK, the most likely approach is to develop a suite of measures to stimulate the uptake of specific practices and technologies to reduce farm emissions and develop a complementary set of measures to improve agricultural productivity. The Environment Agency has called for a firmer regulatory approach.[46] However, the Land Use Advisory Group informing the Climate Change Committee concluded that adding to the regulatory baseline "is not likely to be fruitful".[47] They directed attention instead to using cross-compliance requirements to encourage farmers to adopt emission-reducing practices. However, as direct farm payments gradually decrease as the UK transitions from the CAP, the leverage of cross-compliance is likely to diminish. It would be administratively cumbersome, with teams of inspectors required to effectively police farming practices and measuring and monitoring would be difficult given our current state of knowledge about emissions and the link to particular farming practices. Developing farmers' own skills in monitoring and benchmarking was felt by the group to be the most fruitful way forward. However, the experience of other initiatives to modify farming practices such as for animal health do not inspire confidence in self-regulation. Other regulatory systems could be developed to help contribute to greenhouse gas reduction. For example, the regime around water pollution advises and supports catchment sensitive farming practices that could potentially have greenhouse gas benefits too. The more careful spreading of slurry with low-level spreaders helps with both goals. Around 58 per cent of agricultural land in England is designated as Nitrate Vulnerable Zones where Defra guidance limits the use of fertilisers. Farm Waste Regulations have existed for more than three decades but could be more effectively enforced if there were more regulatory capacity.[48]

The Land Use Advisory Group preferred to seek changes in farmer behaviour through new payment schemes. The new post-Brexit agricultural policy is to reward farmers for delivering environment public goods, an approach encapsulated in the mantra coined by Michael Gove when Secretary of State for Environment, Food and Rural Affairs, "public money for public goods". A key part of the new Environmental Land Management (ELM) scheme is to facilitate farm-level environmental planning, which should include those practices which cause greenhouse gas emissions. Crucially, participation in the scheme will be voluntary. Although it turns the polluter pays principle on its head by paying polluters not to pollute, using farm environmental payments to reduce greenhouse gas emissions seems to be being accepted by British policy analysts. "If it succeeds in inducing the necessary changes it could be money well spent", they argue.[49] There could potentially be a differentiated system where farms not in the ELM system were subjected to greater levels of regulatory enforcement.

Alongside the challenge of changing farming practices in order to reduce emissions through regulation, incentive schemes or persuasion, is the question of maintaining levels of food production on a smaller area of available farmland. On this question, the agricultural policy community seems much more comfortable. There is strong rhetoric from Defra and from food and farming bodies which resonates with a narrative that has prevailed since the 1940s. Farmers need to become more productive and should take up the latest technologies to help improve the amount of food they can produce from a given area of land. In this context, the message of the 2020s differs little from that of 1947. British agriculture is perceived to have a poor record of productivity growth compared to other countries[50] and exiting the CAP may, it is argued, be a stimulus to productivity improvements. Under a new regime, productivity ought to be measured against emissions per tonne of output and emissions accounting of agricultural productivity does complicate the usual equations. "The more efficient the conversion of forage and feeds into meat and milk, the less time to fatten an animal, the higher yield per animal, then the lower the emissions per kg of meat or milk. Similarly, the higher the nitrogen use efficiency of crops through soil management, crop breeding and nutrition, the lower the emissions per tonne of crop".[51] However, such a perspective on efficiency does not incorporate biodiversity, landscape or animal welfare considerations. We are left again faced by the two different visions of sustainable intensification or a more ecological approach.

Technological optimists point to the revolution in artificial intelligence and the use of big data, combined with the revolution in molecular genetics and gene editing to suggest a high-technology, hyper-efficient agriculture of robotics, satellite-guided agricultural machinery and super-productive crops and animals resistant to disease and pests. Narratives about the wonders of this fourth agricultural revolution have proliferated over recent years. There are also the prospects of biotechnological innovations including vertical farming and hydroponics, lab-grown meat and the industrial production of proteins which could reduce the need for agricultural land even further than the Climate Change Committee's most speculative scenarios. The counter view comes from the exponents of "agroecology" uneasy at the seeming blind faith in the technoscience approach to food and farming, arguing that this way of thinking led to the over-simplified, over-industrialised approaches to intensive farming that caused the landscape, biodiversity, pollution and health problems described in Chapter 4.[52] They worry that the "sustainable intensification" approach is more about the "intensification" and less about the "sustainable".

They argue that sustainable intensification prioritises off-farm biodiversity, while much valuable biodiversity is found on agricultural land. Agroecology systems, it is argued, will have lower input and output densities by design. They may mean lower levels of food produced, but when linked to more sustainable diets, agroecology has the advantage of delivering marked benefits in biodiversity and other ecosystem services.[53]

It is possible we will see a combination of the two, and a twin-track approach could be seen as an extension of that of the past 40 years. Agriculture continues to intensify and increase its output in some places, and on some farms, while elsewhere, a different path is taken where practices are supported by agri-environmental schemes to protect and enhance valued environments. This twin-track approach can operate at the farm level, with parts of farms under agri-environmental agreements and managed to protect the environment, while the cutting-edge productive agriculture takes place on other land. As the Land Use Advisory Group points out, "a key issue in understanding these tensions is whether we continue to measure productivity by only including the marketed outputs of land management (*i.e.* the provisioning ecosystems services) and not all the goods and services too".[54]

Markets and Morality

In the dynamics of changing farming practices, it has long been recognised that farmers do not make decisions based on economic rationality alone. Sometimes maximising outcomes is not an important motivation compared to just coming to a satisfactory solution. Because farms are not just businesses but also households with families, social and family objectives can moderate or interfere with economically optimising behaviour. Social norms within the farming community can also be important, with farmers reporting their keen interest in what their neighbours do in their fields and farmyards. Comparing farming practices has most commonly been based on how productive and well-managed other farms look – the health of stock, tidiness of fields, who is cutting silage first, the types of machinery and so on. In thinking about how farming practices might be actively encouraged to change in particular ways to reduce emissions, this sense of the social formation of what constitutes a "good farmer" can be an important influence on, or barrier to, change.[55] A commonly-expressed motive in agriculture concerns farm improvement, the notion of maintaining the land "in good heart", and passing on the farm, its land and buildings, to the next generation in a better condition than when it was taken on.[56] Farms and land are productive assets and the logic of farm improvement is often expressed as a responsibility to the land, to "not take more out of the soil than gets put back in".[57] Climate sensitive farming involves a more complex ethic than the logic of farm improvement as the critical test involves not only questions of agricultural productivity and a duty of care to one's land and animals, but also the wider social responsibility of emissions. It is less straightforward for farmers to look over the hedge and form a view of a neighbour's greenhouse gas emissions.

When farming systems come under pressure or criticism from beyond agriculture, then different moral frameworks are drawn upon. Farming interests may articulate the moral rationale for the status quo in the face of what are often morally charged assertions about farming needing to change. In the 1980s and 1990s, we saw how spillages of livestock effluents into watercourses shifted from being an unfortunate technical side-effect of modern dairy farming to being something cast as morally reprehensible, a form of environmental crime for which farmers could be hauled before the courts and prosecuted. Farmers may complain that the pollution was unintentional, an 'act of God', resulting from sudden heavy rain which overwhelmed storage facilities. Yet, the pollution could cause serious damage to river water quality, and serious incidents could wipe out fish stocks. "For farmers, *the morality of the pollution comes from the morality of the deed* – whether the pollution was deliberate or accidental. Their sense of personal worth, responsibility and circumstances all come into play around the morality of farming and the morality of pollution".[58] In contrast, from an environmental perspective, the morality of the pollution comes from the effect – damage to river environments and ecosystems. The new regulatory regime around water pollution, which reflected changing social values in wider society, changed the way farmers thought about and understood water pollution and they largely took pollution control on board. Notably, the new regulatory framework did not advance fundamental system-level transformation. Pollution control was a technical add-on to the existing production system. Feed and animal housing systems remained the same, with the stores, tanks and pumps added-on in attempts to reduce pollution risk, and herds became ever larger and more concentrated. More than 30 years after the huge efforts to address British agriculture's water pollution problems, in January 2022, the House of Commons Environmental Audit Committee reported livestock farming to still be a key contributory factor damaging river water quality through pollution.[59] Even if a new environmental morality around greenhouse gas emissions were to develop among British farmers, it is likely to require a more fundamental approach to systems transformation than even the efforts of the 1980s and 1990s to solve the water pollution problem. New notions of what is right and wrong may help in effecting changes in farming practice but are not enough to deliver sustainable systems on their own.

Of course, for many, the answer to changing farming practices centres on economics, and what makes good business sense. It is a question of markets as much as morality. Markets can be developed to help drive practices that reduce net emissions, including through carbon sequestration on farmland. Chapter 8 examined the prospects for land-use change through afforestation and growing energy crops for carbon capture and storage, but there are additional practices on farmland that can potentially have beneficial net effects in sequestering carbon. These include grazing management, no and low till, planting cover crops, hedgerow planting, incorporating crop residues, agroforestry (*i.e.* combining trees and shrubs with arable or pastoral uses), or adding biochar to soil. Carbon markets can be either voluntary or regulatory and in regulatory markets the regulated industries are required to reduce or compensate for their emissions or face financial penalties for polluting. There has been recent growth in global voluntary carbon markets from 46 $MtCO_2e$ in 2017 to 104 $MtCO_2e$ in 2019 and it is predicted that demand will continue to grow steeply.[60] There is increasing interest in producing carbon credits by sequestering carbon on farmland through increasing soil carbon storage[61] and several international initiatives have sought to draw attention to the potential.[62] Globally, the capacity for soil carbon sequestration is estimated at between two and seven $GtCO_2e$ per year while UK estimates vary considerably from 1 to 30 $MtCO_2e$ million tonnes. The NFU's net zero strategy assumes some 5 $MtCO_2e$ sequestered in this way, and the Royal Society estimates that 10 $MtCO_2e$ are potentially achievable. A review for the Green Alliance is more cautious, with an estimate of 3.5 $MtCO_2e$ of sequestration per year based on regenerative practices such as no till and incorporating organic matter.[63] In addition to these methods, carbon can be sequestered on farmland in the biomass of trees and hedgerows. Demand for carbon offsetting by UK companies is estimated to be between 14 and 42 $MtCO_2e$ a year by 2030 and between 16 and 228 $MtCO_2e$ a year by 2050, so there is predicted to be more demand than capacity. UK companies are already the third-largest buyers of voluntary carbon offset credits globally and bought almost 6 $MtCO_2e$ of offsets in 2019.[64]

For markets for on-farm carbon sequestration to work effectively there needs to be confidence in the credibility of the system. Carbon credits or certificates must be additional to what would have happened anyway and there needs to be permanence to the carbon storage so that emissions do not leak and so nullify the credit. In addition, the full greenhouse gas impacts of the activity need to be considered in the round, otherwise, storage activities may generate emissions elsewhere. Finally, a credible and accurate monitoring, reporting and verification system is required for the stored carbon. A review for the Green Alliance examined twelve different soil carbon standards and protocols from eight different organisations and found wide variations in their scope and practice. These complexities are sufficient to leave the Climate Change Committee cautious about the prospects of carbon sequestration in soil. A study for Defra concluded that reduced tillage did not increase soil organic content consistently enough and that any soil organic carbon benefits from increased use of crop residues would be outweighed by nitrous oxide emissions and nitrate run off.[65] In any case, building up carbon storage in soils could not continue inexorably and would only represent a relatively short-term opportunity of up to around 20 years, with limited greenhouse gas abatement after this. The Committee concluded that the net benefits of these land and carbon management practices would be small compared to more straightforward land-use changes such as afforestation. Soil carbon sequestration has not therefore been incorporated within the Climate Change Committee's suggested pathways to net emissions reduction. Nevertheless, efforts continue to develop a credible UK Farm Soil Carbon Code.

The Green Alliance's review of agri-carbon market opportunities concluded that selling agri-carbon offset credits could limit farmers' future options in managing their land. Furthermore, any potential for trading credits across countries brings the risk of failing to reduce global emissions through offshoring. "If buyers of offset credits are using offsets instead of emissions reductions they would otherwise have made, it will be harder for the UK to achieve its net zero target as further carbon removals will be necessary to compensate for the emissions that should have been reduced".[66] A market-driven "dash for carbon" may also lead to unanticipated consequences that undermine other environmental priorities such as by rendering afforestation less attractive. Market approaches to carbon offsetting based on changing practices on farmland therefore face a set of difficulties in ensuring that activities generate real and meaningful net emissions reductions that are measurable and verifiable.

Conclusions

While the growth of the world's population to almost 10 billion people by 2050 is one important driver of the likely development of farming practices in the UK and around the world over the next three decades, climate change mitigation is going to become an increasingly important counter-driver. Increasing the resource efficiency of production is one important means by which emissions can be reduced and farmers can benefit. International bodies such as the IPCC and FAO increasingly assert the need to address the problems of ruminant livestock production in particular, although there is more resistance to this among some farming organisations. While health and environmental bodies call for less meat to be consumed, there is common ground around the need to develop technologies and practices that reduce emissions from livestock production. The considerable investment going into the development of plant-based alternatives to meat may also prove influential. The high levels of financial support to agriculture around the world also provides a potential set of levers to influence farming practices to mitigate climate change.

In the UK, over half of agricultural emissions of greenhouse gases come from livestock and manure, with fertiliser use comprising a further third. While there was some decline in emissions in the period 1990–2009, levels have stubbornly flatlined since, suggesting that the current reliance on voluntary measures by farmers is not proving effective. A wide range of practical prescriptions are available for things farmers might do to reduce emissions. These range from managing soil organic carbon through improving fertiliser, slurry and manure management and adopting improved breeds and varieties. Crucially, climate-sensitive farming requires more sophisticated monitoring and analysis alongside conventional farm accounting practices. And then there is the question of the economic viability of different approaches to farming practice. The insights and prescriptions arising from the evolving science of climate-sensitive farming practice are born into a world of competing visions and ideologies around what the net zero transition might look like for farming. Sustainable intensification competes with agroecology, land sharing competes with land sparing. It is questionable whether any of these perspectives will ever wholly win the day. In Chapter 10, we turn in more detail to the question of the dynamics of change in the net zero transition, and the factors that might help or hinder reducing the agri-food system's emissions.

Notes

1 Tubiello, F. *et al.* (2021a) Greenhouse gas emissions from food systems: building the evidence base. *Environmental Research Letters* 16(6); Tubiello, F. *et al* (2021b) *Methods for Estimating Greenhouse Gas Emissions from Food Systems, Part III: Energy Use in Fertilizer Manufacturing, Food Processing, Packaging, Retail and Household Consumption.* FAO Statistics Working Papers Series, 21–9.

2 Helm, D. (2020) *Green and Prosperous Land: A Blueprint for Rescuing the British Countryside.* London: William Collins, pp. 164–6.

3 World Resources Institute (2018) *Creating a Sustainable Food Future: A Menu of Solutions to Feed Nearly 10 Billion People by 2050.* Synthesis Report. Washington, DC: World Resources Institute, p. 27; Ortiz-Bobea, A. *et al.* (2021) Anthropogenic climate change has slowed agricultural productivity growth. *Nature Climate Change* 11, 306–12.

4 World Resources Institute (2018), p. 22.

5 Climate Change Committee (2020b) *The Sixth Carbon Budget: The UK's Path to Net Zero.* London: Climate Change Committee.

6 Climate Change Committee (2020a) *Land Use: Policies for a Net Zero UK.* London: Climate Change Committee, p. 8.

7 See, for example, World Resources Institute (2018); World Resources Institute (2019) *Creating a Sustainable Food Future: A Menu of Solutions to Feed Nearly 10 Billion People by 2050.* Full Report. Washington, DC: World Resources Institute; Intergovernmental Panel on Climate Change (2019) *Special Report on Climate Change and Land.* Geneva: IPCC; OECD (2019) *Enhancing Climate Change Mitigation Through Agriculture.* Paris: OECD; Benton, T. and Bailey, R. (2019) The paradox of productivity: agricultural productivity promotes food system inefficiency. *Global Sustainability* 2, e6, 1–8.

8 World Resources Institute (2018).

9 World Resources Institute (2018), p. 26.

10 World Resources Institute (2018), p. 45.

11 Terazono. E. and Hodgson, C. (2021) Raising climate friendly cows. *Financial Times* 11 October, p. 23.

12 World Resources Institute (2018), p. 46.

13 World Resources Institute (2018), p. 50.

14 Smith, P. (2016) Soil carbon sequestration and biochar as negative emission technologies. *Global Change Biology*, 22, 1315–24; Keenor, S. *et al.* (2021) Capturing a soil carbon economy. *Royal Society Open Science* 8, 202305.

15 OECD (2019), p. 14.

16 OECD (2019), p. 15.

17 OECD (2019), p. 15; California Air Resources Board (2019) *Compliance Offset Program.* Sacramento, CA: California Air Resources Board.

18 Lee, H. and D. Sumner (2018) Dependence on policy revenue poses risks for investments in dairy digesters. *California Agriculture* 72, 226–35.

19 New Zealand Ministry for the Environment (2019) *Climate Change Response (Zero Carbon) Amendment Bill: Summary.*

20 European Commission (2019) *Effort sharing: Member States' Emission Targets.* Brussels: European Commission.

21 Klimaatakkoord (2018) *Proposal for Key Points of the Climate Agreement,* 10 July.

22 Federal Ministry for the Environment, Nature Conservation, Building and Nuclear Safety (2016) *Climate Action Plan 2050: Principles and Goals of the German Government's Climate Policy.* Berlin: BMUB.

23 OECD (2019), p. 17.

24 Meat and Livestock Australia (2020) *The Australian Red Meat Industry's Carbon Neutral by 2030 Roadmap.* Sydney: Meat and Livestock Australia.
25 OECD (2019), p. 17.
26 Searchinger, T. *et al.* (2020) *Revising Public Agricultural Support to Mitigate Climate Change.* Development Knowledge and Learning. Washington, DC: World Bank.
27 OECD (2019), p. 18.
28 Nisbet, E. *et al.* (2019) Very strong atmospheric methane growth in the 4 years 2014–2017: implications for the Paris Agreement. *Global Biogeochemical Cycles* 33(3), 318–42.
29 House of Commons Environment, Food and Rural Affairs Committee (2021) *Environmental Land Management and the Agricultural Transition.* Second Report, Session 2021–22. London: House of Commons.
30 Climate Change Committee (2020a), p. 8 and p. 20.
31 Inhibitors are added to fertilisers and generally inhibit soil enzymes and reduce nitrous oxide emissions and nitrate losses from leaching.
32 See Defra (2021d) *Greenhouse Gas Mitigation Practices – Farm Practices Survey England 2021.* London: Defra; (2021c) *Agri-climate Report 2021.* London: Defra.
33 High sugar grasses are grasses that have been bred to express elevated concentrations of water-soluble carbohydrates. This helps utilisation of nitrogen from forage digested by ruminant livestock.
34 Keenor, S. *et al.* (2021) Capturing a soil carbon economy. *Royal Society Open Science* 8, 202305.
35 Keenor, S. *et al.* (2021).
36 Ortiz, M. *et al.* (2021) *Towards Net Zero in UK Agriculture: Key Information, Perspectives and Practical Guidance.* London: University College London Institute for Sustainable Resources; Innovation for Agriculture (2022) *Reducing Greenhouse Gas Emissions at Farm Level.* Stoneleigh: Innovation for Agriculture.
37 Food, Farming and Countryside Commission (2019) *Our Future in the Land.* London: Royal Society for the Arts; Poux, X. *et al.* (2021) *Modelling an Agroecological UK in 2050.* Paris: IDDRI, Sciences Po.
38 Buckwell, A. (2019) *Policies for Agriculture, Forestry and Land Use: Chair's Report of the CCC Land Use Advisory Group.* London: Climate Change Committee, p. 12.
39 UK Government (2021) *Net Zero Strategy: Build Back Greener.* London: Stationary Office.
40 Defra (2021a,b).
41 Buckwell (2019), p. 9.
42 Helm, D. (2021) *Net Zero: How We Stop Causing Climate Change.* London: William Collins; see also Helm (2020).
43 Lowe, P. *et al.* (1999) *Integrating the Environment into CAP Reform*, CRE Research Report. Newcastle University.
44 Falconer, K. and Ward, N. (2000) Using modulation to green the CAP: the UK case. *Land Use Policy* 17, 269–77.
45 OECD (2019).
46 Environment Agency (2019) *Memorandum of Evidence to the House of Commons Environment, Food and Rural Affairs Committee Inquiry into Agriculture: Achieving Net Zero Emissions.*
47 Buckwell (2019), p. 13.
48 Bailey, T. (2021) *Livestock's Longer Shadow: Hope Lives in Kindness.* Gloucester: Choir Press; House of Commons Environmental Audit Committee (2022) *Water Quality in Rivers*, Third Report, Session 1986–87. London: The Stationary Office.
49 Buckwell (2019), p. 14.
50 Buckwell (2019), p. 14; See also CCC (2020a).

51 Buckwell (2019), p. 14.
52 Booth, R. (2021) Pathways, targets and temporalities: Analysing English agriculture's net zero futures. *Environment and Planning E: Nature and Space* (Online first); International Panel of Experts on Sustainable Food Systems and ETC Group (2021) *A Long Food Movement: Transforming Food Systems by 2045*. Brussels: IPES-Food.
53 Poux, X. *et al.* (2021).
54 Buckwell (2019), p. 14.
55 Burton, R. *et al.* (2021) *The Good Farmer: Culture and Identity in Food and Agriculture.* London: Routledge; Burton, R. (2004) Seeing through the 'good farmer's' eyes: towards developing an understanding of the social symbolic value of 'productivist' behaviour. *Sociologia Ruralis* 44, 195–215.
56 Lowe *et al.* (1997) *Moralizing the Environment: Countryside Change, Farming and Pollution.* London: UCL Press, pp. 134–6.
57 Lowe *et al.* (1997), p. 125–7.
58 Lowe *et al.* (1997), p. 204, emphasis in original.
59 House of Commons Environmental Audit Committee (2022) *Water Quality in Rivers.* Third Report, Session 1986–87. London: The Stationary Office.
60 Donofrio, S. *et al.* (2020) *State of the Voluntary Carbon Markets 2020: Voluntary Carbon and the Postpandemic Recovery.* Washington, DC: Forest Trends.
61 Elliott, J. *et al.* (2022) *The Opportunities of Agri-Carbon Markets: Policy and Practice.* London: Green Alliance; Soil Association (2021) *The Roadmap to a Soil Carbon Marketplace.* Bristol: Soil Association.
62 Elliott *et al.* (2022), p. 34.
63 Elliott *et al.* (2022), p. 34.
64 Elliott *et al.* (2022), p. 35.
65 Elliott *et al.* (2022), p. 64.
66 Elliott *et al.* (2022), p. 55.

10

THE DYNAMICS OF TRANSITIONING TO NET ZERO

Introduction

The EAT-Lancet Commission's review called for a great food transformation across the world. There is a consensus among independent scientific opinion that addressing climate change requires dietary change to reduce our consumption of lower-emission food products. Mitigating climate change will require changes to land use across the world, including afforestation and growing energy crops, and in the UK will mean significant changes to land use. In addition, agricultural productivity will have to improve markedly if levels of UK domestic food production are to be at least maintained and the problem of offshoring emissions from food production is to be avoided. Defra and the Climate Change Committee take the view that it will be impossible to eliminate all emissions from agriculture by 2050 so the aim is to reduce them as much as is feasible, reduce the land area on which agriculture takes place, and promote afforestation and energy crops. The three strategies are interdependent. If dietary change reduces demand sufficiently, less land may be needed for food, and more can be given over to forestry and energy crops.

It is clear from Chapters 7 to 9 that transitioning to a net zero world is going to require significant behaviour change. In the agri-food system, farmers and land managers will be making decisions about their everyday practices and the development of their enterprises. Bringing emissions reduction much more strongly to bear on farmer decision-making is a significant challenge for those developing policies for agriculture, land use and land management. Consumer behaviour will have to change if consumption of higher-emitting foodstuffs is to be reduced. While there is evidence of some decline in the consumption of red meat, for example, the rate of change needs to accelerate to contribute enough to meet the Climate Change Committee's pathways or healthy diet targets. Changing food consumption practices is a particularly difficult area for governments sensitive to the accusation of

DOI: 10.4324/9781003278535-10

"nanny-state-ism". Understanding the forces at play in shaping commercial behaviour and decision-making is therefore important in any analysis of what might help or hamper the transition. Finally, government plays a key role in setting the regulatory framework, shaping how markets work, and providing information to citizens. Though politicians may emphasise the importance of markets, the state's role is fundamental.

This chapter considers the factors likely to advance the transition and those more likely to pose obstacles to progress. The chapter maps the landscape for emissions reduction, explaining how the Climate Change Committee have determined the proposed pattern of emissions reductions from different sectors. It then examines the balance of push and pull factors helping and hindering the net zero transition for those groups of actors for whom change will be necessary – farmers, consumers, companies and government.

"Chunking Up" the Challenge

The 2008 Climate Change Act requires that the Climate Change Committee produce carbon budgets to help the Government plan reduced emissions over the medium term and that it sets out opportunities to reduce emissions in particular sectors. The first interim carbon budget was legislated for in May 2009 with a target of a 34 per cent cut in emissions by 2020 from 1990 levels. The budget put the UK on a path to 80 per cent reduction by 2050. The Climate Change Committee issued its first progress report to Parliament in October 2009 in the run-up to the Copenhagen COP meeting and highlighted three sectors where it judged that new approaches were required – electricity generation, residential energy efficiency and electric cars.[1] It has produced progress reports each year since, and its presentation of key sectors evolves over time. Its third report in 2011 sub-divided its analysis into four key sectors: power; buildings and industry; transport; and agriculture.[2] The chapter on agriculture was the first independent comprehensive assessment of UK emissions from the sector since the 2008 Act. By 2016, the Committee was dividing its analysis into seven main sectors: power; buildings; industry; transport; agriculture, land use and forestry; waste; and fluorinated gases.[3] In breaking down its analysis by sectors in this way, sectors and the boundaries between them must be set to avoid double-counting emissions and reduction targets. Rates of emissions reduction have looked particularly impressive for electricity generation, where the shift from coal to gas and then the growth of renewables have gathered pace. Over time, agriculture has come to stand out as lagging, as emissions levels have flatlined since 2009. Sometimes agriculture is treated alongside land use and forestry, but agriculture and land use are not usually combined with the food industry. Agriculture and land use form part of a supply chain that involves food processors, manufacturers and retailers, and involves the packaging and transport of agricultural products, processed foodstuffs and food products. Although the agrifood system might be a relatively coherent and easily understood object of analysis, the emissions associated with different aspects of the system are accounted for in different places, and reductions in those emissions will be the responsibilities of different parts of government.

To achieve net zero for the whole of the UK will require a coherent plan based on a thorough appraisal of the practical options, set out sector by sector, and which gives businesses and other institutions some degree of certainty. It will also require some consistency of policy and regulatory frameworks in each sector, and the capacity to co-ordinate action across the whole of government, and to make key decisions, even when technological options remain uncertain. The Council for Science and Technology, the Prime Minister's independent scientific group, suggested that the Government should take a "whole systems approach" to help decision-makers manage uncertainty and complex interactions between systems.

> A whole systems approach enables decision makers to understand the complex challenges posed by the net-zero target and devise solutions and innovations that are more likely to succeed. It is a discovery process combining structured approaches to understanding and managing physical factors (such as infrastructure and novel/advanced technologies) with broader perspectives on economic, behavioural and other issues, taking into account complex interactions. [4]

Carbon budgets serve as an "ordering device" to help track progress, set objectives and highlight where sectors might be most "off-track" in their contribution to reducing emissions. The UK is on track to meet its third carbon budget (2018–2022) but, according to the Climate Change Committee, it is off-track to meet its fourth and fifth (2023–2027 and 2028–2032).[5] The Sixth Carbon Budget (for 2033–2037) was published in December 2020 and was the first to be produced since the UK's commitment to a net zero target. It considers emissions across eleven sectoral pathways: surface transport; buildings; manufacturing and construction; electricity generation; fuel supply; agriculture and land use, land-use change and forestry; aviation; shipping; waste; fluorinated gases; and greenhouse gas removals.[6] As the budgets move off track, so the problematic nature of the agri-food system becomes more apparent.

In 2019, the UK's greenhouse gas emissions amounted to 522 $MtCO_2e$. They must be radically reduced to achieve net zero, with any residual emissions offset by measures that remove carbon dioxide from the atmosphere. Over the last three decades, emissions have fallen by 44 per cent, or an average of 13 $MtCO_2e$ per year, with much of the fall coming from electricity generation. Although overall progress has been more rapid in the last decade, this is because of the pace of progress in electricity generation. Beyond that, emissions must fall more quickly to meet the Sixth Carbon Budget.[7] The UK is currently off track because it has been failing to make sufficient progress in those sectors other than energy and decarbonising these sectors will be much more difficult in future than the progress made to date.

The Department for Business, Energy and Industrial Strategy co-ordinates action across government in meeting the net zero target and leads on the regulation of the energy industry. The Department for Transport and Defra are other key delivery departments, while the Cabinet Office and Treasury at the centre of Government also have a co-ordinating role. In October 2021, a couple of weeks ahead of the COP26 summit in Glasgow, the UK Government published its new Net Zero Strategy. It divided emissions reductions across the economy into seven categories: power; fuel supply and hydrogen; industry; heat and buildings; transport; natural resources, waste and fluorinated gases; and greenhouse gas removals.[8] Much of the response to the publication of the Strategy focused on heating homes and the switching from domestic gas boilers to electricity-powered heat pumps. Notably, and largely unremarked upon, the Strategy had very little to say about agriculture and food. An associated publication on behaviour change for net zero was published and then swiftly retracted because of concerns about the potentially controversial nature of efforts to influence consumer behaviour around food consumption in particular.[9] The Climate Change Committee welcomed the Government's Net Zero Strategy but drew attention to the lack of detailed planning on agriculture and land use. Its most prominent criticism was "Few details have been set out for delivery mechanisms in the agriculture sector – a combined decarbonisation strategy for agriculture and land is needed urgently".[10]

Farmers

As we saw in Chapter 9, mitigating climate change poses serious implications for farming practices, which will have to change significantly to ensure emissions are sufficiently reduced. To understand how changing farming practices might be helped or hindered requires a clear understanding of what influences the way farmers farm. This is not straightforward. Agriculture is a highly heterogenous sector and although it can be tempting for policymakers and lobbyists to generalise about farmers and farming, circumstances and options vary considerably according to farm type and geography as well as other economic and social factors.[11] Farms are often social units as much as economic units and most farms in the UK can still be called "family farms". This means that the farm may be being managed according to social and family priorities and not always necessarily in ways that economic models assume to be profit maximising.[12] Farms with an identified successor can be managed in different ways to those without. For example, a dairy farmer in their fifties without a successor may be less likely to invest in expensive pollution control facilities than one managing the business to pass on to the next generation. Farms and land are managed according to a mixed set of social and economic motivations. Furthermore, the stereotypical full-time family farm where agricultural production accounts for all the family's income is today a small minority of the sector. According to Defra's most recent published data, over 90 per cent of farm businesses with a standard output of at least €25,000 covered by the annual Farm Business Survey had non-agricultural sources of income and, on average, non-agricultural income made up a third of household income.[13] Farms are often, therefore, managed in conjunction with other economic enterprises or sources of livelihood.

What might help encourage the adoption of farming practices that reduce greenhouse gas emissions? The answer to this question has economic, technological and social dimensions. In economic terms, prevalent models of behaviour and decision making by farmers and land managers see them as rational actors optimising economic welfare. This underpins neoclassical agricultural economics, the discipline most associated with understanding farming behaviour and change. It will, of course, help if tackling greenhouse gas emissions improves the economic viability of farming practices. This may often be the case where mitigation measures involve improved efficiency of input use or improved productivity of animal breeds and crop varieties. A common mantra at net zero agriculture conferences is that "you cannot go green if you're in the red", implying economic viability must come before environmental sustainability. However, not all emissions-reducing measures automatically mean improved cost-effectiveness or economic viability. Some may require capital investment or may mean increased costs and pressure on margins. Investing in an anaerobic digester, for example, can run into millions of pounds.

There has been considerable focus in recent years on the prospects for the new post-Brexit agricultural policy to serve as a framework for a payment system that helps incentivise farming practices with lower greenhouse gas emissions. In the EU, the direction of CAP reform is to place more emphasis on climate change objectives, but the scope will be potentially even greater in a British system that does not have to be negotiated with 27 other Member States. The UK has embarked on a seven-year transition out of the CAP. The details of the new Environmental Land Management scheme (ELM) that will replace the previously CAP-funded Basic Payments Scheme are under development, but the farming and environmental lobbies are focusing their attention on the size, coverage and details of this scheme, which is to be piloted from 2022.[14] Part of the rationale for Brexit was to "take back control" of spending such as that under the unpopular CAP and the Treasury has long viewed farm payments as an area of potential savings post-Brexit. It is, therefore, likely that no more than £3.5 billion will be available to support farming and land management across the UK. In a sector that produces of the order of £9.5 billion gross value added, there is a question of the extent to which a new scheme will provide sufficient incentive to shift farming practice. The scheme is likely to be voluntary and farmers will take a view of the balance of costs from changing farming practices against the benefits of the payments they would receive. If the financial allocation is lower, the scope of influence will be reduced.

Technological advances in lower-emission farming can also help. In biotechnology, genetic innovation is likely to bring major changes in breeds and varieties that can sustainably increase yields per hectare or strengthen resilience to the impacts of climate change. The genome sequencing of hundreds of crop varieties over the past two decades has underpinned an information revolution in plant biotechnology which can reduce dependence upon manufactured pesticides. Research is currently underway to determine whether the capacity of legumes to fix nitrogen from the air can be genetically transferred to cereals and so avert the need for manufactured nitrogen fertilisers.[15] As well as cutting-edge biotechnological research, innovation in information systems for emissions monitoring and accounting could prove pivotal in helping farmers and land managers navigate the net zero transition. Part of the precision farming revolution is the much greater scope for environmental monitoring of agricultural land and buildings, and the harnessing of data science and development of "computational agriculture" may prove important in facilitating emissions reduction.[16] To inform national monitoring and reporting, the knowledge base and data infrastructure for measuring greenhouse gas emissions are continually being developed, although a high proportion of estimates use non-UK-specific data.[17] At the farm level, improvements in data analytics will strengthen our understanding of local emissions over the coming years.

As we saw in Chapter 4, past efforts to change farming practices have included voluntary agri-environmental schemes, but other types of measures too. Farming practices on Sites of Special Scientific Interest are regulated by management agreements to protect highly valued habitats. Animal health and traceability rules have been tightened as a result of BSE, FMD and Bovine TB. Straw burning and some problematic pesticides have been banned, and slurry management is subject to tougher regulations. Some regulatory authorities such as the Environment Agency argue that reducing British agriculture's greenhouse gas emissions would be helped by a tougher regulatory approach.[18] Often, new regulatory frameworks are accompanied by new moral frameworks as the rights and wrongs of what constitute "good farming practice" change over time. It is also possible that the transition to a post-Brexit agricultural policy framework, coupled with the new emphasis on cutting greenhouse gas emissions, may prompt a significant structural change in the industry. The average age of farmers in the UK is 59 and almost 40 per cent are aged over 65. It is possible that many are waiting to review the shape and prospects of the new framework before deciding whether to continue or not. We may be on the cusp of an agricultural version of the so-called great resignation. An increase in agricultural land for sale may open opportunities for new entrants to agriculture, the consolidation of existing farms wanting to grow, or for institutions buying land to farm or to plant trees. Around the world, there has been a steady increase in investment by financial institutions in buying farmland.[19] Structural change has been a continual feature of British agriculture since the Second World War and is likely to accelerate.[20]

What factors, then, may hinder change among farmers? Most obviously, if changing farming practices are voluntary and do not make financial sense, then it is unlikely that large numbers of farmers will make the switch if it costs them money. This is the challenge for those designing the new farm support framework. Over and above this basic economic issue is the difficulty farmers face when wanting to make decisions about the medium to longer term. Changing crop rotations requires planning over a cycle of a few years and switching between enterprises can take longer. The five years since the Brexit vote have been dominated by uncertainty for farmers, and prolonging that uncertainty only makes things more difficult. There is, therefore, an urgency given the 2050 target for net zero and the relatively poor progress of agriculture in reducing emissions over the last decade.

In any case, relying on a wholly voluntary system brings risks of its own. Farmers will be free to have nothing at all to do with agri-environment schemes if they wish and may prefer to free themselves from the rules and restrictions that go with them. From an emissions reduction point of view, a largely voluntary approach may not encourage sufficient change and the Climate Change Committee has repeatedly flagged its concerns about relying on a tradition of voluntarism. A further factor potentially hindering the transition for farmers is the wide variety of advice and information now being proffered about "climate-sensitive agriculture". Compared to the heydays of productivism, there is no unified vision of the trajectory agriculture needs to take, and little sense of the state having a clear vision and actively orchestrating the development of the sector in the ways that it did through research and development, education and training, and practical advice under productivism. The contrasting discourses of regenerative agriculture or agroecology on the one hand and sustainable intensification on the other lead to potentially quite different farming practices and trajectories. Where under productivism there looked to be one main path, now there seem several.

Consumers

The Climate Change Committee's pathway to net zero currently assumes some change in consumer behaviour to reduce demand for some high-emission practices such as flying and eating ruminant meat and dairy. This is recognised as one of the more challenging components of the net zero transition and the Government's Net Zero Strategy was notable for its silence on dietary change. The sensitivities around behaviour change were only underlined by the swift withdrawal of a review of what works for behaviour change, produced by the Behavioural Insights Team.[21] The study set out an upstream-downstream model of behaviour change using a metaphorical river where upstream represents systemic factors, midstream represents the "choice environment" and downstream represents individual agency. Downstream interventions focus on the attitudes, choices and actions of individuals and depend on the clarity and effectiveness of communications. Evidence suggests downstream interventions are rarely enough on their own, especially when it comes to more ambitious, transformational change. Midstream interventions move away from individual agency and instead act on the context – or "choice environment" – within which consumer choice is exercised. They might involve infrastructure changes to improve convenience, or changes to advertising. Using the river analogy, they seek to change the features of the river to help make the flow and currents more navigable. Upstream interventions are at a greater scale and more fundamentally alter the "flow" of the social or economic system, and so help carry people in the desired direction. These interventions tend to be in the functioning of markets which incentivise businesses to help generate transformational change. Examples would include the UK Soft Drinks Levy on Sugar Content ("sugar levy") which incentivised the widespread reformulation of sugary drinks.[22] Therefore, narrow views of behaviour change that focus on awareness raising and calls to action are unlikely to succeed by themselves. As the Behavioural Insights Team put it:

> Though everyone has a degree of agency in changing their behaviour, and well-crafted messages from government can certainly be influential, behaviour is simply too profoundly driven by factors in the environment rather than in hearts and minds. As it stands, low-carbon behaviours are often more costly, less convenient, less available, less enjoyable, and rarely the default choice.[23]

Thus, what was once called the "Nudge Unit" now acknowledges that "as a general rule, acting further upstream will tend to be more effective"[24] and concludes that more profound systems change is required rather than a focus on individual behaviour, which all too often is rather hopelessly seeking to encourage individuals to "swim against the current". Instead, attention should focus on the most foundational changes "that allow most people to 'go with the flow'".[25]

> Individuals have some agency, and varied preferences and attitudes, but are contextually constrained, and are enmeshed in a system characterised by commercial incentives and norms which are more readily changed by institutions and businesses than by individuals.[26]

The report sets out a behavioural approach to dietary change. Because food consumption is a largely automatic, habit-based behaviour, with cues in the environment playing an important role in shaping choices, making changes to the choice environment is seen as much more likely to be successful than simply prompting or imploring people to make more sustainable food choices. The proposed approach, therefore, centres on upstream and midstream strategies and is rooted in the UK's experience with obesity policy.

Upstream, it suggests, the success of the sugar levy could be replicated through a producer or retailer-facing tax to incentivise reformulating high-emission foods. In obesity policy, 30 years of information campaigns encouraging healthy eating and exercise had met with very little impact. Then in 2018 the sugar levy was introduced and led to a dramatic reduction in sugar consumption as it incentivised businesses to reformulate drinks to avoid the tax. The total volume of sales of sugary drinks fell by 50 per cent and the volume of sugar sold from soft drinks dropped 30 per cent between 2015 and 2018.[27] A further upstream measure would be to "de-shroud" the environmental performance of food retailing. Consumers currently have no easy way of knowing which supermarket is most effectively helping their customers to eat sustainably, which leaves the marketplace open to "greenwashing" – or the heavy marketing and "spinning" of environmental claims without independent audit and accreditation. This can be addressed through government endorsement of official comparison tools such as kitemarks and rating systems to help consumers make more informed choices. It only requires a minority of consumers to start making different choices to incentivise food retailers to compete on promoting more climate-friendly food.

The Government is ultimately responsible for £2.4 billion spending each year on food procurement in schools, hospitals, prisons, military services and so on.[28] Midstream interventions include raising the profile of more plant-based foods in public sector canteens and promoting sustainable consumption practices among key groups such as students who may be buying groceries for the first time. Consumption of highest emission foods can also be reduced through developing substitutes that can be blended, such as blended beef and mushroom replacing minced beef. The Behavioural Insights Team's proposals recognise that government cannot implement such changes directly through retailing or catering, but upstream changes can help reinforce these sorts of midstream options and increase the prospects of successful dietary shifts.

Downstream, simply asking people to eat less red meat and dairy is seen as a major political challenge, although highlighting the health benefits of more sustainable diets does at least help shift from a moralistic message to one focused on self-interest. Tax measures such as the meat tax suggested by the National Food Strategy are likely to look regressive and unfair and there will be sensitivities around not wanting to demonise the livestock sector among consumers, as the sector will be being required to make significant changes in its farming practices under its own contribution to the net zero transition.

The ambiguous position of behaviour change in the UK undermines the delivery of dietary change. The "Nudge Unit" attracted much attention when it was established, and politicians were initially attracted to the idea of "gently" persuading consumers to make changes in a "non-paternalistic" way but under the auspices of a neoliberal approach to markets, "consumer sovereignty" and choice. As the Government put the final touches on its long-awaited Net Zero Strategy in the autumn 2021, it seemed to be doubly timid around dietary behaviour change. First, rather than look to regulate food manufacturing and retailing by setting direct product standards or developing economic incentives such as taxes, it instead looked to the neoliberal art of behavioural science. A locus of nudging has been the personal choices and preferences of the individual consumer. Paradoxically, those working in behaviour change were becoming increasingly of the view that to effect change on the scale and at the pace required necessitates fundamental regulation and resetting of the market and institutional context for food manufacturing and retailing. In the foreword to the Net Zero Strategy, the Prime Minister offered an optimistic view that the target could be met without much pain. He wrote: "For years, going green was inextricably bound up with a sense that we have to sacrifice the things we love. But this strategy shows how we can build back greener, without so much as a hair shirt in sight".[29] So there is little mention of food and dietary change in the Strategy, and once it was realised that the Behavioural Insights Team's analysis had been published with the Strategy's accompanying documents, it was quickly withdrawn. The National Food Strategy set out a much more proactive and interventionist approach to dietary change for the sake of public health and the environment. However, the current political reluctance to intervene to change the commercial context within which food is manufactured and sold or to actively promote dietary change remains a barrier.

Companies

Food manufacturers and retailers clearly play a formative role in producing the "choice environment" within which consumers buy food. As the Behavioural Insights Team's analysis shows, behavioural change specialists are increasingly acknowledging the need for, and value of, governments engaging directly with food companies to regulate and reconstruct markets and reformulate food products. Businesses are sensitive to changing social values and consumer attitudes and beginning to innovate and compete in terms of their climate change and net zero credentials. Sainsbury's, one of the UK's largest supermarket chains, published an analysis of the possible evolution of food production and consumption over 5-, 30- and 150-year timescales to understand the potential implications of social and technological trends. Published in 2019, Sainsbury's Head of Quality and Innovation, Claire Hughes, said: "In the last 18 months we have introduced over 100 alternative protein products led by our *Love Your Veg* range. However, we know that we have a role to play in expanding the nation's diets as the current foods we eat aren't sustainable for a global population that will increase by 50 per cent in the next 30 years".[30]

Nestlé, who work in 186 countries and source directly from over 700,000 farmers, have committed to net zero by 2050, globally. The company calculates that 70–90 per cent of its emissions are generated in the supply chain. It has three main strategies. The first is to support regenerative agriculture through making investments with farmers to adopt new technologies and practices that reduce emissions in agricultural production. Nestlé are investing 1.2 billion Swiss francs (almost £1 billion) from 2020 to 2025 in this sphere. They are particularly focused on farm-level calculators of environmental impacts, covering water, biodiversity and other environmental impacts as well as greenhouse gas emissions. The company committed in 2010 to be deforestation-free by 2020 but were only able to progress 90 per cent of the way towards that target, which they now aim to meet by 2022. The second set of measures concern manufacturing and logistics, where the company has more direct control over systems, practices and emissions. A key focus has been on reducing food waste from manufacturing processes. The third area has been the development of recyclable packaging.[31] Nestlé are also heavily dependent upon dairy products in manufacturing but are reducing this dependence through moving to greater use of plant-based options.

Similarly, Unilever in 2010 launched its Sustainable Living Plan which aimed to double the size of its business in home care, personal care and food products while halving its environmental impact by 2020. It claimed to have reduced its in-house greenhouse gas emissions by 62 per cent between 1995 and 2014 and developed a comprehensive Environmental Performance Reporting system to capture data on energy and water use, waste and other environmental impacts. Half of Unilever's raw materials come from agriculture and so the agri-food supply chain, and particularly the practices that take place on farms, was a key focus of its strategy. In assessing greenhouse gas emissions from its agricultural supply chain, the company developed three levels of assessment. First was its own operations including manufacture and transportation. The second level was to include modelled data on supply chain activities and so included individual product life cycle assessments scaled up to the portfolio and then company level. The third level of analysis includes emissions from the company's own operations but adds monitoring data from supply chain operations. Moving to this third level poses challenges for large food companies. For example, Unilever's work found that greenhouse gas emissions calculators are increasingly used by food companies in their supply chain management. However, different calculators produce different results, and different methods of implementation of the same calculator also produces variation.[32]

Food manufacturers like Nestlé and Unilever have to manage emissions from their own logistics and manufacturing and distribution processes but also take an active interest in what happens in primary production. Food companies play an increasingly influential role in shaping agricultural production practices. This is through contracting arrangements and product and production standards that stipulate in detail how foodstuffs are to be produced.[33] Innovating to develop new food products could potentially play a transformational role in the net zero transition, especially in alternatives to conventional meat. Plant-based food producers are already rapidly gaining market share and include foods such as *Beyond Burger* and *Impossible Burger*. Meat substitutes exist for chicken, pork, beef and seafood. Animal-free product lines have also been developed in snacks, pet-food and baby-food. There is also a rapidly expanding market for plant-based milk drinks. Milk from soya beans has a long history in China, as does almond milk in the Middle East. Growing awareness of lactose intolerance during the 1970s and 1980s stimulated some demand, but the recent interest in plant-based milks has seen very rapid growth linked to wider social changes around avoiding saturated fats but also sustainability concerns. Vegan drinks are now available from oats, cashews, coconut, hemp, peas, barley, rice and chia seeds. Although non-animal, non-dairy is an important ethical driver, there is also a turn from soya milk. The global annual market for dairy is $650 billion, but alternative plant milk products have already grown to $17 billion globally.[34] Swedish company Oatly is reported to be valued at $10 billion and is being listed on the Nasdaq index. Its Chief Executive, Toni Peterson, explained "our aim is to disrupt one of the world's largest industries – dairy – and in the process lead a new way forward for the food system".[35] In May 2021, Nestlé launched its *Wunda* yellow pea milk brand. Demand for plant milk products is being driven in part by café culture with plant-based milks being promoted in global coffee chains such as Starbucks. Large food companies are seeing this growth as a lasting trend rather than a passing middle-class fad, and such sharply growing demand is attracting interest among investors. Venture capital investment in plant-based dairy and egg alternatives rose from $64 million in 2015 to $1.6 billion in 2020 and it is estimated there are more than 120 stand-alone plant-based dairy companies globally. Sustainability is becoming an increasingly important feature of the market. Oatly, for example, labels the carbon footprint on each of their products, and Nestlé have a carbon-neutral certification for Wunda from the Carbon Trust. The established dairy industry is challenging whether plant-based products can legitimately be called "milk" using European Union law, but nevertheless plant-based milks are taking market share from dairy in the UK, Denmark and Sweden.[36]

Cellular agriculture producing so-called lab-grown meat is seen as the cutting edge of the new agrarian revolution.[37] It uses biotechnology, typically cell culture, to replicate meats, seafoods and dairy products. The techniques involved in cultivated meat production come from the biotech industry. Biopsies are taken from animals whose meat is to be replicated. The appropriate cells are isolated and used to establish stable cell lines which can be grown in a bioreactor. The cells are then differentiated into muscle fibres that aggregate into a material equivalent to meat in a process that takes two to three weeks. This sector is at an earlier stage of development than plant-based proteins but around 50 companies are engaged in the sector and expect its products to be widely adopted by 2030.[38] In December 2020, San Francisco-based Eat Just launched the first commercially available cell-based meat – a protein-based chicken nugget. The Dutch company, Mosa Meat, working in cellular agriculture has been developing a lab-produced burger since 2013, and Shiok Meats of Singapore are cultivating shrimp without shrimp.[39] Cellular agriculture is being driven by a rapidly growing number of technology start ups concentrated in the world's high-technology hubs. They are also attracting the attention of financial capital and investors,[40] and it has been estimated that more than $7 billion has been invested in alternative proteins over the past decade, including approximately $900 million into cultured meat.[41]

> That private capital is working overtime to disrupt farming with synthetic biology is likely all that boosters and critics alike need to know about the technology. Techno-optimists see a future of widely available "clean meat", as ecologically and ethically superior to the original as solar power is to coal. Opponents see corporate-controlled lab meat that slots all too comfortably into a broken capitalist food system.[42]

Jim Mellon calls his study of cellular agriculture's growth Moo's Law™ signifying the meaty equivalent of Moore's Law in computing processing. His argument is that the success of the cultured food industry will depend on its ability to scale up production and to lower costs. Also vitally important is the extent to which the new products reach an equal or lower price than conventional meat, while retaining the various health, environmental and ethical benefits. Crucially, cellular agriculture produces something more closely akin to real meat and so may begin to compete in the $1 trillion global meat industry. Mallon produced a directory of details of almost 140 companies active in these areas globally. The drive to develop plant-based proteins and cellular agriculture comes from more than simply a concern about climate change. Mellon sets out seven drivers of what he calls the new agrarian revolution, which include the risk of future zoonotic disease pandemics from the current intensive model of animal agriculture as well as animal welfare and water resource concerns.[43] In his research, he found that entrepreneurs were highly committed and passionate about their cause, and that tackling animal cruelty was the most cited motivation, followed by reducing farming's environmental impacts and then by health benefits.[44] The cause also has its own pressure groups. For example, the Good Food Institute, established in 2016, has more than 100 staff. Centred on the United States, it has global affiliates in the Asia Pacific, Brazil, Europe, India and Israel. It describes its mission as: "developing the roadmap for a sustainable, secure, and just protein supply. We identify the most effective solutions, mobilize resources and talent, and empower partners across the food system to make alternative proteins accessible, affordable, and delicious".[45]

To conclude, commercial firms and organisations have a key role to play in helping advance the transition to a more sustainable food and farming system in a net zero world. This is not only because of their vital role in shaping consumer choice in the marketplace, but also because of the control and influence they exert over whole supply chains through contracting arrangements and standard setting. In addition, there are signs of significant investment and market growth around new food products such as plant-based proteins and lab-cultivated meat that could potentially significantly disrupt food product markets, capitalising on the increasing interest in more ethical consumption for the sake of animal welfare and climate change.

Government Behaviour

In a speech to the Global Investment Summit, held at the Science Museum in London in October 2021, Prime Minister Boris Johnson controversially claimed that the success in developing the Covid-19 vaccine at Oxford University was the result of "free market capitalism". It was a story of great companies, supported by investors and shareholders and "a willingness to spend massive sums at risk on something that might never come off". He went on to say "there is a force out there stronger than government. And actually a force that is stronger than business. And that force is consumer choice. That force is the market. And the market is going green".[46] There is plenty of empirical evidence to demonstrate that climate change and sustainability are increasing features of consumer choice and that the market could be said to be "going green". The claim that the Covid-19 vaccine was the result of free-market capitalism prompted scientists and commentators to point to the large proportion of research funding for the Oxford University team that had come from public and philanthropic sources. The contradiction highlights a paradox at the heart of contemporary government in the UK. A blistering rhetoric around neoliberal free-market ideology has been accompanied by increased taxes, public spending and a significant expansion in the role of the British state, prompting *The Economist* to go so far as to talk of a new age of interventionism.[47] More than this, the drive to reduce emissions to meet the net zero target has also led to a significant change in the machinery of government to marshal the power of the state more effectively.

In addressing climate change and net zero it is difficult for the machinery of government to co-ordinate the central state. Setting clear and ambitious targets is one way in which government can be given clarity, purpose and direction. Strong and visible leadership from the Prime Minister and other central figures in the Government can also help. A key problem, though, is interdepartmental co-ordination. David Miliband, when Environment Secretary responsible for climate change from 2006 to 2007, established the Office for Climate Change as an independent unit that served as a precursor to the Climate Change Committee.[48] The Office for Climate Change carried out the "ground-clearing" work so that ministers could be presented with worked-out options. Since 2016, climate policy has been the responsibility of the Department for Business, Energy and Industrial Strategy (BEIS) and this Department plays a key co-ordinating role. A difficulty is when other Departments with important roles to play in addressing climate change such as, for example, Defra and the Department of Transport have competing policy priorities. Sometimes individual departments tend to prioritise their departmental targets over cross-departmental targets. The co-ordinating department, in this case, BEIS, can struggle as it will not have the levers to compel other Departments to act differently. Cross-departmental coordination can depend on the goodwill of other departments. The challenge is to establish a sense of collective responsibility across government. Without strong central leadership and good "ground-clearing work" in advance, cross-cutting issues can suffer from lowest-common-denominator decisions, where the line of action is just the one with the least resistance across departments. Another difficulty can be the power and influence of the Treasury. The Treasury and its Comprehensive Spending Reviews can be important in signalling and demonstrating the prioritisation of cross-cutting issues such as net zero across government. When more pressing immediate concerns arise, the Treasury can become deflected from the cross-government agenda.[49]

The Conservative Government has reshaped the central machinery of government to drive the net zero agenda across Whitehall departments. A Cabinet Committee on Climate Change was announced in October 2019 to much fanfare (although it did not meet until early March 2020). In June 2020, it was split into a smaller and tighter Cabinet Climate Action Strategy Committee chaired by the Prime Minister and a larger Cabinet Climate Action Implementation Committee chaired by the Business Secretary. This model was found to work in managing the approach to Brexit and the Covid-19 crisis and is now being used for net zero. The Climate Action Strategy Committee and bilateral meetings are used to "knock heads together" when differences emerge or there are problems of strategy or implementation. It is notable that BEIS has been the lead department on net zero and the pace of progress has been fastest in transforming electricity generation. The Department of Transport has adopted net zero enthusiastically, but there have been more concerns about the level of prioritisation given in the Department for Levelling Up, Housing and Communities (formerly the Department for Communities and Local Government). Co-ordination also extends beyond central government to embrace the work of regulatory and arm's length public bodies and others.[50]

The Covid-19 crisis disrupted the operation of government in the UK and across the world. The population was more strictly regulated in its everyday conduct than at any time since the Second World War and the scope and limits of state power were redefined as the virus swept around the world. An array of new calculative technologies of government were developed and deployed.[51] There are key differences between Covid-19 and climate change – one is a health issue while the other is environmental, and one is acute and relatively short term while the other is chronic and extends over a longer term. Nevertheless, there are important commonalities. Both issues span local, national and global scales, both require urgency of action in response, and both face the challenge of exponential escalation without state-led intervention.[52] One lesson from Covid that can equally be applied to net zero is that the framing of the issue as health or environment in opposition to economic welfare is a false trade-off. Those countries that acted quickly and robustly in response to Covid tended to suffer less damage to their economies than those that delayed for fear of the economic consequences.[53] The same is likely to apply to the net zero transition. Although tackling climate change does involve incurring costs, it is generally more cost-effective to act sooner rather than later. The simplistic link between economy and environment is beginning to be broken by the length of experience of addressing climate change. The UK has reduced its emissions by half since 1990 while its economy has grown by 75 per cent over that period.

The value of a clear strategic approach has also been underlined by the Covid experience. The UK's response to Covid was at times characterised by mixed messages (on shaking hands, working from home, the safety of schools and so on). Maintaining a clear strategic vision and persisting through political leadership will help a national economy and society make sense of and navigate the transition. It has been argued that the lack of clearly communicated strategy contributes to deeper polarisation of public views and the culture wars that can accompanying this.[54] A clear strategy, coupled with open and transparent treatment of risks can help give individuals and businesses a better sense of direction and foresight which can aid business planning. Although it was a Conservative Government that legislated for the net zero commitment, signs emerged in 2021 that net zero was becoming an axis of internal opposition and pressure within the UK's governing party with the formation of the "Net Zero Scrutiny Group" of backbench Conservative Members of Parliament.[55] A clear strategic vision may help provide a unifying voice and agenda for government.

Covid also triggered a wave of innovation in businesses, households and public bodies as new products and services were developed and new ways of working and interacting were quickly adopted. The crisis helped highlight the importance of the capacity of the state and public sector in managing and co-ordinating a pandemic crisis. In applying the lessons of Covid to the net zero transition, there is a need to more clearly define the role and capacities of state actors. There has been a significant "hollowing out" of the public sector since the 1980s, but the net zero transition is likely to require new roles and functions for public bodies. Governance arrangements are already complex and there would be value in reviewing state responsibilities in the context of net zero. In the sphere of food, farming and forestry, insights from the experience of the early post-war years could help in designing the governance arrangements for the transition. Clarity and consistency of messaging from government are also important, as is reacting to misinformation. Extensive behaviour change will be required, although it is not likely to be as urgent and acute as that required during the Covid crisis. Behaviour change for net zero will also bring wider benefits such as improved public health. Crucially, the Government needs to be seen to be ensuring the net zero transition is a just transition, which means having a clear sense of the socio-economic distributional consequences of changes.

Conclusions

The "great food transformation" called for by the EAT-Lancet Commission represents the single greatest project for social, economic and technological transformation in the history of humanity. The energy transition to move away from fossil fuels poses a major challenge, but a significant proportion of the energy supply comes from either the state or from large and technology-intensive energy companies, and the shift to renewable energy now involves a technological transformation that is not only technically possible but also economically cost-effective. In contrast, transforming the global agri-food system requires changes in the husbandry and land management practices of hundreds of millions of farmers and the food consumption practices of all humankind. And there is not the relatively simple technical fix that now looks to be viable in both energy and transport. The EAT-Lancet Commission were effectively calling for a global and government-led strategic approach to active agri-food system transformation, and with urgency. It is an awesome challenge, in the sense that awesome means "extremely impressive or daunting".

In the UK, from a technical perspective, the change required might feel more manageable. We saw that the last revolution in the British agri-food sector took place during the Second World War and in the decades after. This period saw transformational change in the pattern of land use and cropping, and the techniques and technologies used to produce food. Productivity radically improved and much more of the nation's indigenous foodstuffs were produced at home. The huge effort to transform agriculture and food supply was orchestrated by the central state, which governed through a powerful institutional architecture of public scientific institutions, advisory services and county bodies with a unity of purpose and a mission to modernise agriculture and increase its output.

Since that time, the state has become larger and, in many ways, more powerful. It spends more money. It has a larger number of Whitehall Ministries. It can harness all the power of the information revolution to "know" its population and to render measurable and calculable an ever-widening array of aspects of social and economic life. The big shift over the 80-year period since the early 1940s is in the received wisdom and prevailing assumptions around the legitimate scope of government and state action. Although the state has got bigger and more powerful, what political opinion imagines it should and should not do has shrunk. The pivotal moment in this shift took place around the early 1980s. Over the most recent four decades, the grip of neoliberalism has meant it appears absurd to look to the ideas, strategies and ambitions of the Second World War and early post-war period for inspiration in how to address the climate challenge. They were wartime conditions. It was an emergency situation. There was an existential threat. In the 12 years since Climategate, the increasing visibility of the effects of climate change has altered the dynamics of climate scepticism. It now seems less histrionic, and has even become commonplace, to talk in terms of the climate crisis and climate emergency. It is an interesting question to consider at what point between 2022 and 2050 will it feel uncontroversial to look to the experience of government in the 1940s and 1950s and see the challenge in comparable terms. For now, although there are those advocating for a mission approach to innovation and addressing climate change, to suggest a more active, Government-led, actively planned approach to transforming the UK agri-food system is still to swim against prevailing norms, to paraphrase a Government-commissioned report on behaviour change deemed too sensitive and politically uncomfortable to publish.[56]

The chapter has explored the dynamics of the transition, from the perspective of the key groups of actors that are in the frontline of change – farmers, consumers, companies and the Government. There is a push-and-pull effect of factors helping and hindering the transition and these effects differ across the groups. Farmers need to make a living and may be aiming to pass on their businesses in a healthy state to their successors. If reducing emissions costs them money, then the question becomes one of the balance between payment schemes and regulation. For voluntary payment schemes to work from an emissions point of view, participation levels will need to be very high. That farming leaders currently refuse to accept that there may need to be any reduction in livestock numbers does not bode well. For consumers, companies and government, the paradox is that some companies and some consumers are already on track and ahead of the Government in the transition. An ideological antipathy and political nervousness around regulating the food industry and interfering in dietary choices hinders progress, but food companies ratchet up their own net zero targets, and the meat-free sections expand along supermarket aisles, and the financial pages of newspapers fill with coverage of investment in alternative proteins and cultured meat.

Notes

1 Climate Change Committee (2009) *Meeting Carbon Budgets – The Need for a Step Change: Progress Report to Parliament.* London: Climate Change Committee.

2 Climate Change Committee (2011) *Meeting Carbon: 3rd Progress Report to Parliament.* London: Climate Change Committee.
3 Climate Change Committee (2016) *Meeting Carbon: The 2016 Progress Report to Parliament.* London: Climate Change Committee.
4 Council for Science and Technology (2020) *A Systems Approach to Delivering Net Zero: Recommendations from the Prime Minister's Council for Science and Technology.* London: Council for Science and Technology, p. 2.
5 Institute for Government (2020) *Net Zero: How Government Can Meet Its Climate Change Target.* London: Institute for Government, p. 16.
6 Climate Change Committee (2020b) The Sixth Carbon Budget: The UK's Path to Net Zero. London: Climate Change Committee.
7 CCC (2020b), p. 60.
8 UK Government (2021) *Net Zero Strategy: Build Back Greener.* London: The Stationary Office, p. 5.
9 Londakova, K. *et al.* (2021) *Net Zero: Principles for Successful Behaviour Change Initiatives.* BEIS Research Paper No. 2021/063. London: Department for Business, Energy and Industrial Strategy.
10 Climate Change Committee (2021b) *Independent Assessment: The UK's Net Zero Strategy.* London: Climate Change Committee.
11 Lobley, M. *et al.* (2019) *The Changing World of Farming in Brexit UK.* London: Routledge.
12 Gasson, R. and Errington, A. (1993) *The Farm Family Business.* Wallingford: CAB International; van der Ploeg, J. D. (2018) *The New Peasantries: Rural Development in Times of Globalisation.* London: Earthscan.
13 Defra (2016) Farm household income and household composition: results from the farm business survey, England 2014/15. *Defra Statistical Release.* London: Defra. This will be an underestimate of the proportion for all registered farm businesses.
14 House of Commons Environment, Food and Rural Affairs Committee (2021) *Environmental Land Management and the Agricultural Transition.* Second Report, Session 2021–22. London: House of Commons.
15 Royal Society (2021) *Nourishing Ten Billion Sustainably: Resilient Food Production in a Time of Climate Change.* Climate Change: Science and Solutions Briefing 10. London: Royal Society; see also Agri-TechE (2020) Nitrogen fixation for cereals to sustainably increase yields in Africa.
16 Gabrys, J. (2016) *Program Earth: Environmental Sensing Technology and the Making of a Computational Planet.* Minneapolis: University of Minnesota Press; see also Donaldson, A. (2021) Digital from farm to fork: infrastructures of quality and control in food supply chains. *Journal of Rural Studies* (Online first).
17 Kmietowicz, E. and Thillainathan, I. (2020) *The Smart Agriculture Inventory: Technical Annex.* London: Climate Change Committee.
18 Environment Agency (2019) *Memorandum of Evidence to the House of Commons Environment, Food and Rural Affairs Committee Inquiry into Agriculture: Achieving Net Zero Emissions.*
19 Ouma, S. (2020) *Farming as a Financial Asset: Global Finance and the Making of Institutional Landscapes.* Newcastle upon Tyne: Agenda Publishing.
20 Lobley *et al.* (2019).
21 Londakova *et al.* (2021).
22 Londakova *et al.* (2021), p. 8.
23 Londakova *et al.* (2021), p. 11.
24 Londakova *et al.* (2021), p. 18.
25 Londakova *et al.* (2021), p. 18; see also Whitmarsh, L. *et al.* (2021) Behaviour change to address climate change. *Current Opinion in Psychology* 42, 76–81.

26 Londakova *et al.* (2021), p. 18.

27 Bandy, L. *et al.* (2020) Reductions in sugar sales from soft drinks in the UK from 2015–18. *BMC Medicine* 18(1), 1–10.

28 Londakova *et al.* (2021), p. 43.

29 UK Government (2021) *Net Zero Strategy: Build Back Greener.* London: Stationary Office, p. 9.

30 Sainsbury's (2019) *Future of Food Report.* London: Sainsbury's, p. 9.

31 Keller, E. (2021) Decarbonisation in the food and drink sector – implementing greener processes, supporting innovation in technology, and priorities for investment, presentation to the Westminster Food & Nutrition Forum '*Net-Zero, Climate Change and the Food, Drink and Agriculture Sector*' conference, 23 June.

32 Keller, E. (2015) *Greenhouse Gas Management in Agri-food Supply Chains: A Focus at the Farm Level.* PhD thesis. University of Surrey, Centre for Environmental Strategy.

33 Jackson, P. *et al.* (2010) Manufacturing meaning along the chicken supply chain: consumer anxiety and the spaces of production, pp. 163–87 in M. Goodman *et al.* (eds.) *Consuming Space: Placing Consumption in Perspective.* Farnham: Ashgate. See also Howard, P. (2021) *Concentration and Power in the Food System: Who Controls What We Eat?* Revised Edition. London: Bloomsbury Academic.

34 Evans, J. and Terazono, E. (2021) Peas add froth to the milk market. *Financial Times* 8/9 May, p. 9.

35 Quoted in Evans and Terazono (2021).

36 Evans and Terazono (2021).

37 Dutkiewicz, J. and Rosenberg, G. (2021) Can lab-grown meat really solve our food problems? *The Guardian* 29 July (The long read), pp. 6–8; Evans and Terazono (2021); Hayward, T. (2021) Lab-grown meat isn't about sustainability, it's big business. *Financial Times* 18 September, p. 12.

38 Mellon, J. (2020) Moo's LawTM: An Investor's Guide to the New Agrarian Revolution. Sudbury: Fruitful Publications.

39 Dutkiewicz and Rosenberg (2021).

40 Mellon (2020); Hayward (2021).

41 Dutkiewicz and Rosenberg (2021), p. 6.

42 Dutkiewicz and Rosenberg (2021), p. 6.

43 Mellon (2020), pp. 29–31.

44 Mellon (2020), p. 73.

45 https://gfi.org/.

46 Johnson, B. (2021) Prime Minister's speech at the Global Investment Summit, 19 October.

47 The Economist (2022) The new interventionism, special report – business and the state. *The Economist* 15 January, pp. 3–12.

48 Lorenzoni, I. and Benson, D. (2014) Radical institutional change in environmental governance: explaining the origins of the UK Climate Change Act 2008 through discursive and streams perspectives. *Global Environmental Change* 29, 10–21.

49 Rutter, J. (2021) *Evidence to the House of Common Business, Energy and Industrial Strategy Committee inquiry into Net Zero Governance* 21 September.

50 For a discussion of the efficacy of these arrangements, see Rutter (2021).

51 Jayasinghe, K. *et al.* (2021) Biopolitics and calculative technologies in Covid-19 governance: reflections from England. *International Journal of Health Policy and Management* 10, 1–9. doi: 10.34172/IJHPM.2021.134.

52 Lord, T. (2021) *Covid-19 and Climate Change: How to Apply the Lessons of the Pandemic to the Climate Emergency.* London: Tony Blair Institute for Global Change, 7 April.

53 Tooze, A. (2021) *Shutdown: How Covid Shook the World's Economy*. London: Allen Lane.
54 Lord (2021).
55 Ivers, C. (2022) Bereft without Brexit, the Tories have a new bone to fight over: net zero. *The Sunday Times* 16 January, p. 7.
56 Londakova *et al.* (2021), p. 7.

11
CONCLUSIONS
Net Zero, Food and Farming

Introduction

International media coverage of the Glasgow COP was heightened by the increasingly widespread and acute effects of climate change since the 2015 Paris meeting and the strengthening scientific evidence around the risks of catastrophic climate change. Many participants commented on a strong sense of focus, consensus and resolve. During the COP, the Food and Agriculture Organisation published research showing that agriculture and the food system was now contributing around a third of all global emissions.[1] As the COP process moved on to Egypt and COP 27 in 2022, so agriculture and food loomed larger as a focus of attention, helped by Glasgow's Global Methane Pledge. It is in this context of the growing focus on reducing emissions from farming and the agri-food system, that this chapter draws out the conclusions of the study. It first highlights the lessons from the UK's experience of twentieth-century change in the agri-food system to guide thinking on the transition required during the 2020s, 2030s and 2040s. It considers the implications of a whole-systems approach to the agri-food transition, and especially the role of technological change. It then reflects on the question of changing behaviours among different actors and institutions and the ways in which various framings of the net zero transition might lead to different types of strategies. It concludes with a discussion of the question of a just transition, and the significance of the social dimensions of sustainability when faced with what at first may seem like a set of environmental and technical issues around transitioning to net zero.

Learning from the Past

The UK is not alone in having a contemporary agri-food system that has been heavily shaped by state priorities over the past century. After decades of a laissez-faire

DOI: 10.4324/9781003278535-11

policy of importing cheap food and leaving domestic farming to the vagaries of the world market, the experience of the Second World War ushered in a radically different model centred on the expansion of domestic production through financial support and guaranteed prices for farmers, coupled with the energetic technical transformation of the industry. The mechanical and chemical revolutions brought the replacement of the horse with the diesel-powered tractor and the widespread use of herbicides to transform crop rotations, save labour and improve productivity. The adoption of new techniques in animal feeding and breeding brought similarly transformational improvements in productivity in livestock sectors too. As in the United States and the rest of Western Europe, the character of farming was actively transformed through the promotion of an ideology of progressive, modernised farming, supported by public investment in an extensive network of agricultural research institutions and a public advisory service. Farmers were not only financially subsidised and celebrated for following a particular path of development but were actively cajoled through the powers of the state. The system of County Agricultural Executive Committees policed the transformation of farming and deployed strong powers to compel farmers to up their game where productivist goals were not being sufficiently pursued. The Committees' powers to actively direct farming practices and even dispossess farmers were extended beyond wartime and continued to be used into the 1950s. The powers of dispossession were not withdrawn until 1958 with the Committees carrying on their advisory and co-ordinating work into the 1970s. The popular narrative of farming's post-war revolution in productivity suggests it was simply the ingenuities of science and technology that enabled such transformational change. However, the success of the productivist model was underpinned by the active role of the state in designing the economic framework and encouraging and exhorting change along particular technological paths. Beyond farming, changes to the competitive regime governing food retailing in the 1960s also brought about the rapid rise of the supermarket chain and the steady decline in small independent grocer's shops which changed the balance of power in the food system from manufacturers to retailers.

The state's central role in the development and maintenance of productivism helped ensure the model endured for more than four decades. The rise of neoliberal ideologies of government, coupled with increasing evidence of the problems arising from modern farming practices, began to call into question the prevailing model in the 1980s. Entry into the CAP in the early 1970s had rendered reform of subsidies a matter of negotiation among Member States, but the burgeoning costs of agricultural support brought pressures on the whole functioning of the then European Community. The result was that the productivism of the 1950s–1970s was gradually modified to bring budgets into balance, reduce incentives for over-production, and develop measures to support less environmentally destructive farming methods. While successive CAP reforms facilitated the expansion of agri-environmental policy from the mid-1980s onwards, the UK also developed a stronger approach to the regulation of agricultural pollution and animal health. Changing farming practice through "sticks and carrots" is a debate that extends back to the 1940s, although the terms of this debate have shifted as national priorities around food production weakened and an increasingly professionalised environmental lobby pressed the Government for agricultural reform. For many aspects of farming that impacted upon biodiversity (and greenhouse gas emissions) environmental policy remains largely voluntary. Furthermore, since the growth of agri-environmental schemes from the mid-1980s, an expectation has built up that if the state requires farming practices to be modified for the sake of reducing environmental harm, then farmers should be compensated for making those changes. The "polluter pays principle" has not fared well when it comes to agriculture.

The implications of the net zero transition for the agri-food system are preoccupying policy-makers around the world. The EU's European Green Deal is an effort to mobilise €100 billion to transition to net zero, including support for reskilling and innovation.[2] In the Netherlands, a proposed new "National Programme for Rural Areas" includes national targets for nature restoration and a 50 per cent reduction in nitrogen use by 2030. The Plan also envisages significant reductions in livestock numbers with funds to be spent compensating farmers.[3] The EU's "Farm to Fork Strategy" includes 27 initiatives to promote the development of a more environmentally sustainable food system, with targets for 2030 including cutting nutrient losses by 50 per cent, reducing fertiliser use by 20 per cent and halving food waste.[4]

Brexit has freed the UK to develop its own approach to agriculture and environmental policy and because these areas are largely devolved matters, frameworks can increasingly diverge between England, Scotland, Northern Ireland and Wales. Since the Brexit vote in 2016, there has been a growing sense of urgency around the climate change challenge and the commitment to net zero, as well as mounting evidence of the breadth of measures necessary to bring emissions from agriculture and land use into alignment with the UK's carbon budgets. However, debate continues to centre on the overall level of financial support for farmers and the potential financial impacts of phasing out direct payments for different parts of the agricultural industry.[5] Those calling for any measures other than a large-scale, country-wide payment scheme to pay farmers to "green" their farming practices are marginal and minority voices. Furthermore, the demands of the new, post-Brexit, English, Scottish, Welsh and Northern Irish agricultural policies are complex and multifaceted. Land ownership and reform have traditionally been more salient in Scotland and thinking there about what a "just transition" to net zero might mean is more advanced. Protecting the Welsh language remains a distinctive concern in agriculture and land-use policy in Wales. The main British environmental groups engaging on agricultural policy tend to be instinctively most interested in species, habitats and landscapes with less of a tradition of focusing on greenhouse gas emissions. There have been calls from the Climate Change Committee and its advisory bodies for net zero and emissions reduction to become the key, central and unifying focus of agriculture and land management policy.[6] This would resemble the unified approach of the productivist period, when increasing productivity provided strategic clarity and unity of purpose. Currently, environmental interests worry about the tensions between the climate crisis and the nature and biodiversity crisis, fearing that focusing heavily on the former may compromise efforts to address the latter.

Arguments about how British agricultural policies might be developed to address climate change invariably get played out through the prism of pre-existing frameworks and prejudices. These include the land sharing and land sparing perspectives, which evolved in response to the loss of species and habitats but begin to feature in debates about the climate change challenge. The most high-profile prescriptions circulating, such as those from the Climate Change Committee and the National Food Strategy, can be broadly mapped onto the land sparing and land sharing model. The Climate Change Committee looks more to land sparing. Food will have to be grown as productively as possible on a reduced land area, so that carbon sequestration activities (afforestation and energy crops) can take place on a share of current farmland, and there is less hope or confidence that soil carbon sequestration can be actively managed and marketed as a measurable contribution. The alternative approach, land sharing, where farmers deliberately share their land with nature, has been described by the National Food Strategy as farming "in a gentler way".[7] Fewer manufactured inputs are applied, yields are lower, and more land is needed. The National Food Strategy favoured a mixed model, combining rewilded land for sequestration, low-intensity farmland and higher-intensity farmland. Like "sustainable intensification versus agroecological farming", the "land sharing versus land sparing" debate can become unnecessarily polarised, and the two approaches need not be mutually incompatible. However, to ensure that agriculture and land use make a sufficient contribution to reducing emissions will require a national vision and strategy for land use and active planning by the state to ensure that sufficient land is managed either wholly for sequestration and biodiversity purposes or as low-intensity farming; otherwise, the national net zero goal will be compromised. In any case, given the structure of the political lobbies around farming, with the farming industry engaging with, and responding to, a nature conservation and biodiversity-oriented environmental lobby, it is likely that the debates around emission reductions will continue to play out through these dichotomous perspectives born out of the struggles of the last half-century. One potentially disruptive strategy is to adopt a public health or emissions reduction starting point when approaching the agriculture and land-use question. This would serve in contrast to, say, the profitability, productivity or competitiveness of the agricultural industry, or the desired proportion of indigenous food produced within the UK.

Systems Change, Net Zero and the Agri-food Transition

The UK agri-food system can be understood as a socio-technical system. This is to recognise that the way the land is used, and food is produced, is influenced by complex networks that include both social and technical elements. These include individuals, small and large businesses and regulatory frameworks that manage the growth and flow of food and biomass through supply chains. There has been a historical tendency in traditions of land use, environmental management, pollution control and food logistics to turn first to engineering and physical sciences, then the natural sciences. However, the mix of expertise accessed is now much more likely to include the social sciences of not just economics but also sociology, psychology, geography and planning. Understood as a socio-technical system, the UK agri-food system can be seen to have evolved through the post-war decades shaped by social, economic and political priorities as well as the development of important new technologies. The revolutionary technological changes in agricultural production are well rehearsed. In addition, there are many innovations in food processing and retailing including, for example, the "cold chain" technique introduced by Marks and Spencer in the early 1960s that preserved quality and freshness, extended shelf life and revolutionised the supermarket supply chain.[8] Technological changes have helped shape the structure of farming, reduced its workforce and transformed food supply chains which in turn have revolutionised how we shop and eat.

Analyses of socio-technical systems have identified the ways in which technologies become obdurate, paradigms come to dominate, systems evolve along pathways, and show characteristics of momentum. While technology is not autonomous from society, momentum, inertia and lock-in are features of systems that can make it difficult to move from one technological paradigm to another. In agriculture, since the emergence of environmental problems in the 1970s and 1980s, the dominance and intractability of certain technological systems have made the development of more sustainable means of production difficult. These include the replacement of mixed farming systems with specialist arable or livestock farms, the centrality of pesticides and especially herbicides in arable cropping and the development of silage and slurry-based systems in dairy and beef farming. Often, attempts to address the unfortunate environmental side effects of these production systems quickly encountered the obduracy of the system itself. Problems were fundamentally systemic rather than simply the consequence of careless or malevolent behaviour of individual farmers. Indeed, a popular metaphor for understanding the farmer's lot in agriculture's environmental difficulties has been that they are caught on a treadmill.[9] The socio-technical systems that evolved around the supply chains for our principal foodstuffs have been all the more powerful and enduring because of the fact that they were instigated and developed through a public infrastructure that advanced the application of science and technology to the twentieth-century revolution in food and farming. The farming leaders and senior civil servants of the 1980s and 1990s had cut their teeth during the hey-days of productivism in the 1960s and 1970s. Technological paradigms bring with them powerful mindsets that can be difficult to change. British efforts to curb productivist agriculture's environmental excesses since the 1980s have not amounted to a paradigm change. They have tinkered with socio-technical systems but fallen short of effecting planned and purposeful paradigmatic change.

The public infrastructure that proved so effective in orchestrating agricultural productivism has largely been dismantled since the 1980s. There are fewer centres of agricultural research, either under the auspices of the Biotechnology and Biological Sciences Research Council or in universities. Land-based colleges are fewer in number and those that remain have pursued strategies that reflect those of the industry they served. They have diversified into sport, equestrianism and training young people to work in pet shops. The former public advisory service, ADAS, is now a privatised commercial consultancy with 400 staff. (In 1970, there were 2,000.)[10] Where during the productivist period a central government ministry, the Ministry of Agriculture, Fisheries and Food, headed by a Cabinet minister, was responsible for overseeing the interests and development of the sector, now agriculture is part of the responsibilities of a Department for the Environment, Food and Rural Affairs. Compared to the three decades from the 1940s to 1970s, the last three decades have been a period of strategic drift in agriculture and land use, with little sense of a long-term vision and no national framework to aid planning and prioritisation. It is in this context of a weakened and fragmented public institutional infrastructure around land, farming and the food system that the net zero challenge has to be faced.

Since 2019 and the UK's statutory net zero commitment, attention is gradually turning to the need for transformational system change in the agri-food system. In transforming electricity generation, the UK is well-advanced along a path, and banning the sale of petrol and diesel-engine cars from 2030 is an example of a regulatory forcing of transformational systems change in private road transport. In advice to the Prime Minister, the Council for Science and Technology set out the case for a "disciplined and rigorous whole systems approach" to support a successful transition to net zero.[11] Drawing on science and engineering expertise, but with an appreciation of the role of social science too, a whole systems approach combines structured ways of understanding and managing physical factors (such as physical infrastructure and novel or advanced technologies) with broader social science perspectives on economic, social and behavioural issues. It helps identify elements or pressures in the system that might inhibit progress as well as points of greatest leverage where measures can have the most impact. It can identify important synergies or interdependencies between emissions reduction and other priorities as well as understanding issues of time pressures and sequencing. It can also help manage the risks of unintended consequences and develop adaptive approaches to deal with uncertainties. Achieving net zero by 2050 is a socio-technical systems transformation challenge, but the agri-food system has distinctive features compared to other key systems such as its role in producing valued landscapes, habitats and ecosystem services and the role of food consumption in public health.

A long-term vision is required for the whole agri-food system that embraces both the territorial dimension of rural land use with a more sectoral approach that extends through whole supply chains from the production of agricultural inputs through primary production, processing, retailing and consumption. A system-wide perspective also involves the way different supply chain processes may interact with each other, and the ways changing demand may shape and influence production and processing. It is only in this way that the potentially competing priorities around food production, net emissions reduction, biodiversity protection and other land uses can be considered together and in the context of the technological and socio-economic processes reshaping the functioning of the agri-food system. A clear, long-term vision allows the development of timescales for change and key decision points and is, in any case, necessitated by the time lag between a decision to plant some trees and their full potential for sequestration being realised. A systems approach also allows some of the key systems-level trade-offs and dilemmas to be reconciled, such as the mix between land-sharing and land-sparing with its implications for how much land is required to produce how much food, along with the balance between plant and animal production and between reducing livestock emissions and the demand for meat and dairy products.[12]

System transformation in agri-food will require a range of different measures that are complementary and mutually reinforcing and aligned with wider national objectives. They will include tax, regulation, standards, financial instruments, research and innovation and efforts to alter the social and moral frameworks around some behaviours. There will be a place for experimentation and iteration, although the timeline to net zero by 2050 does bring some urgency. Analytics and monitoring will be crucial in supporting the state and other institutions in advancing the transition. Technological developments in monitoring environmental effects in socio-technical systems are advancing rapidly.[13] We are in the midst of a data revolution in agriculture and food chain supply management, for example.[14] The extent to which data is publicly available for interrogation is variable, but systems transformation will require both widespread access and sharing and national analytical capability. The data-gathering machine for agricultural productivism, through the national farm surveys of the Second World War and the decades afterwards, provided a valuable data infrastructure that underpinned the national effort to modernise farming.[15] National information on farmers' adoption of emissions-reducing practices is patchy and limited by comparison. In Foucauldian terms, a net zero governmentality of the agri-food system would require a system that instrumentalises the self-governing properties of the array of actors involved. Emissions-reduction needs to be realised with the same success as the productivist framework and the efforts of agricultural science and advisory services and the County War Agricultural Executives of the 1940s and 1950s in modernising farming and revolutionising productivity.

There are risks in placing too much faith in new technologies that will save the day. This is the concern of many of those who are sceptical of geo-engineering solutions in general, and BECCS in particular. When it comes to technology, the Council for Science and Technology advocate a triple track approach. This involves deploying at scale those technologies that are ready, developing those that are not, and researching solutions to the problems we cannot solve yet.[16] Marshalling effective research and innovation for the net zero transition will require rich networks of interaction between business and industry on the one hand and public and third sector research funders and institutions on the other. Mariana Mazzucato's mission-oriented approach to transformational innovation comes with a broader and more ambitious vision of the role of government that goes beyond the neoliberal idea of just fixing market failures. It starts by recognising that markets are the outcome of how socio-technical systems are organised and governed, rather than the cause.[17]

An active approach to system transformation in the UK agri-food system cannot treat the UK as a separate island state, insulated from the rest of the world. A third of food is imported, many food supply chains are global in reach and there will be much to learn from experience in reducing emissions from food and farming around the world. Because the UK's net zero commitment centres on the *production* of emissions from domestic activities, emissions from the UK *consumption* of imports are not included within the UK's emissions accounts or net zero targets. It remains an act of faith that other countries will similarly comply with the commitments of the Paris Agreement and be reducing emissions from their own agri-food systems. In the post-Brexit quest to strike free trade agreements with other countries, this is becoming an issue of some contention. The UK–Australia trade deal announced in June 2021 will remove tariffs on most goods from Australia. Although full access to Australian beef and sheepmeat will take 15 years, UK farming groups have complained about the risk of importing products subject to lower environmental standards.[18] The Australian government has been notably sceptical in its approach to international climate change commitments over recent years and is a key nation in what is sometimes called the "coalition of the unwilling".[19] The deal was criticised by the Chair of the Climate Change Committee for being "entirely unaccept-able for climate change purposes". He said "You cannot ask farmers to do in this country what we are going to ask them to do and import goods from people who are not [meeting the same standards]. The Government promised it wouldn't do that – and it is doing it".[20]

Food, Farming and Behaviour Change

It is not surprising that such a vital part of our economy and way of life as the agri-food system, responsible for around a third of climate change emissions, has been the subject of strong contestation. There have been concerns about the oligopolistic behaviour of the large supermarkets and the increasing control exerted by large corporations over the rest of the food supply chain. Campaigning groups have pointed to the cost and quality of food, with poor access to fresh and healthy food and the active promotion and ready availability of highly processed and unhealthy foods. From an environmental perspective, concerns about greenhouse gas emissions sit alongside those about biodiversity decline and water pollution. Others bemoan the loss of smaller family farms and the rise of large-scale agribusiness, others still the lot of farmed animals. A 30-year quest to bring the UK's 435 MtCO$_2$e of annual emissions down to net zero by 2050 requires systems change with far-reaching implications. In the agri-food system the "climate change agenda" must occupy its place in relation to these other agendas. The scale of the transformation and the existential threat posed by catastrophic climate change suggest that net zero might have some primacy over other causes. However, there are those that fear that tackling greenhouse gas emissions will overwhelm other priorities, while others see the net zero transition as an opportunity to increase leverage for their own preoccupations around food, farming and land use. This strategic framing of net zero as the number one priority or as one driver among several has important implications for the different types of prescriptions and solutions in circulation, and for whose behaviour might need to change and in what ways.

The Climate Change Committee has a clarity of focus in its analysis. The Committee's goal is to present credible pathways through successive carbon budgets to ensure that greenhouse gas emissions are on track to comply with the UK's statutory net zero target by 2050. This clarity of purpose with just two elements to measure – net emissions and time – render other concerns secondary. From this perspective, it is not surprising that its advisors advocate making emission reduction unambiguously the key strategic priority governing all matters of land use and agricultural policy or that greater powers of control and co-ordination might be taken at the national (UK) level, even when many of the levers currently lie in devolved administrations in Scotland, Wales and Northern Ireland. Significant changes to rural landscapes, whole new bioenergy and sequestration supply chains, and behaviour change in food consumption become the order of the day when the starting point is "net zero by 2050". This approach means the only "wiggle room" is the extent to which some emissions from food production might be tolerated as necessary and offset by the net sink of afforestation and the hopes of greenhouse gas removal through carbon capture and storage. The Climate Change Committee's pathway tends more towards land sparing than land sharing, with less demand for higher-emission foods freeing up space for forestry and energy crops and improvements in agricultural productivity ensuring the same amount of food comes from less land.

The National Farmers' Union (NFU) offers an alternative set of proposals where UK agriculture reaches net zero by 2040. Its starting point is the interests of its members. Its three pillars see 25 per cent of reductions (11.5 $MtCO_2e$ per year) coming from improving productivity and reducing emissions, 20 per cent (9 $MtCO_2e$) coming from enhanced farmland storage including soil sequestration, and 55 per cent (up to 26 $MtCO_2e$) coming from BECCS. Although this is a radically ambitious vision, it has two critically distinctive features compared to the Climate Change Committee's proposals. First, it assumes no contribution from the farming and land-use sector to mitigating the necessary emissions from other sectors such as, for example, aviation or iron and steel. Second, it makes no provision for any dietary change including any decline in the production of meat and dairy products. Dietary change is a highly sensitive issue in an industry where livestock farmers are a prominent political force. Under the NFU's vision, agriculture, therefore, continues to use a greater proportion of land than under the Climate Change Committee's proposals, and any land sparing is given over to energy crops and forestry.

The Food, Farming and Countryside Commission (FFCC) offer a further scenario from a new European modelling platform used to assess the expansion of agroecology.[21] It concluded that agroecological approaches (*i.e.* high nature value or in the National Food Strategy's terms, "gentler" farming) would see reduced use of manufactured inputs, strong and positive biodiversity outcomes and reduced crop yields of 17–25 per cent. This would require dietary change to halve consumption of animal products and see the return of more mixed farming instead of specialised arable and livestock production. Emissions from agriculture would only be reduced by 32–38 per cent, although net annual carbon sequestration could increase by 36–55 per cent.[22] The National Food Strategy looked at these approaches and summed up:

> None of these three models quite succeeds in keeping all the necessary balls in the air. The [Climate Change Committee's] model is strong on carbon but says little about biodiversity. The NFU model is not ambitious enough on carbon and says little about nature. And the FFCC model is strong on farm-land biodiversity but falls short on carbon.[23]

And there are significant variations in assumptions about diet and land use. Meat and dairy consumption fall by a fifth to a third in the Climate Change Committee's approach, but do not change at all in the NFU's, while the FFCC assumes the most significant dietary changes of a third less beef, chicken halved, two-thirds less pork and an 80 per cent reduction in sugar. When the UK Government published its Net Zero Strategy in the run-up to the Glasgow COP26 meeting, it was almost silent on the question of dietary change. Its response to the National Food Strategy, due in 2022, maybe an opportunity to take a view on these trade-offs.

Currently absent from much of this modelling and scenario-building is the potential for transformational technological change. Envisioning the nature and direction of technological trajectories can be notoriously difficult and some transformational changes can seem to come "out of the blue". There are voices of caution among climate scientists and campaigners about placing undue faith in technological change unleashing a wave of greenhouse gas removal.[24] A principal concern is that the prospect of a technical fix avoids the need to face some of the other potentially uncomfortable, or for some unprofitable, socio-economic and systems changes. Two areas of potential technological change are most pertinent to the UK agri-food system's pathway to net zero. The first is BECCS as a form of carbon capture and storage and the second is novel foods and sources of protein.

A range of carbon capture and storage technologies are under exploration although knowledge is diffuse and incomplete.[25] Keeping to a below 1.5°C target is likely to require large-scale deployment although policy and action have been limited to date. Four clusters are now planned to be developed in areas of existing heavy industry in the UK and it could be that between 10 and 30 facilities need to be developed to meet the Climate Change Committee's proposal that at least 20 $MtCO_2e$ is saved through greenhouse gas removal. The greenhouse gas removal potential of different BECCS supply chains can vary significantly. Public anxieties about the technology are emerging through its perceived association with systems like shale gas fracking. There will also be trade-offs between the biodiversity value of different land uses and the greenhouse gas removal potential of the biomass being grown.

Likely to be even more contentious than carbon capture and storage are issues of novel foods. This is for several reasons. First is the threat to the livestock industry and livestock farmers whose representative bodies challenge the very notion that any reduction in meat and dairy products or the development of lower-emitting alternatives is necessary. Second is the potential public antipathy to seemingly "unnatural" processes of production associated with, for example, "lab-grown meat" that reflects public caution around food biotechnology in general. The "promissory narratives"[26] around clean foods propagated by venture capitalists and biotechnology companies are seen as attempts to radically disrupt the global agri-food system for purposes of profit and control. We tend to feel there are good and bad ways to feed ourselves, and so eating has "an inescapably ethical dimension"[27] and food politics can be highly morally charged.

Farming groups question the need to develop any alternative proteins and defend the current size of the livestock industry. In a revealing exchange during the COP26 conference Minette Batters, President of the National Farmers' Union, was interviewed by BBC Radio 4 about possible changes to livestock farming and rejected the idea that addressing climate change and transitioning to net zero necessarily meant any need to reduce UK livestock numbers. She said "we absolutely categorically would never have committed to achieving net zero by 2040, which we said back in 2019, if we felt we had to lower our livestock numbers. We can retain the same number of livestock here, but we can farm much more efficiently". When pressed on whether UK consumers should eat less meat to help the environment, she challenged the motives of those pressing for less meat consumption.

> This situation with "meat-versus-plant" is fundamentally flawed. It's driven by people who are looking to make major, major money out of plant-based diets, or else looking for the extinction of livestock and dairy businesses.[28]

Innovation in climate-friendly foods continues apace, supported by food manufacturers and retailers acting ahead of a government acutely cautious about promoting dietary change.[29] The large investments pouring into alternative proteins are likely to continue and the chilled "meat-free" sections will extend further along supermarket aisles. Questions of public acceptability will continue to surround technological changes in the agri-food system, and the debate about genetically modified foods shows how public feeling can sometimes trump scientific consensus around health and environmental risks. When it comes to the future of the agri-food system and the possible emergence of new socio-technical systems, there remain some big differences of view at the heart of the net zero transition.

Social Sustainability and a Just Transition

The structure and dynamics of the UK agri-food system are the product of a set of national priorities put in place in the mid-twentieth century. These led to the modernisation and specialisation of production and the move away from mixed farming systems. The manufacture of inputs to agriculture became concentrated into oligopolistic markets as did the processing and retailing of food products for consumers. The economic drivers of the food system lay beyond agricultural policy, in national security and the balance of payments concerns, and as the expansionist aims of productivism waned so farming was increasingly squeezed. Farmers' scope for action to bring down greenhouse gas emissions needs to be understood in the context of their constrained position in a highly corporatised food chain. Although the state played a crucial role in the construction of the modern food system, ideas among the political establishment about the scope for state action are still heavily influenced by neoliberal views of the relationship between the state and markets. This shapes the way questions of system-transformation and the net zero transition are approached.

Crises can prompt radical change. The Great Depression prompted the New Deal in the United States and the Second World War brought the welfare state and the managed, productivist approach to food and farming in the UK. More recently, the countries of central and eastern Europe experienced profound structural change in their economies, including their agri-food systems, following the breakdown of the Soviet bloc after 1989. The Covid pandemic shook the world economy but also unsettled many taken-for-granted assumptions about the limits of government and the capacity of the state to intervene in markets and everyday life. One lesson of Covid is that, perhaps more than had been expected, people generally welcome the state extending its powers if it meant keeping them safe. Following Covid, tax increases to fund extra spending in the National Health Service and interest in intervening in energy markets suggest a more interventionist regime is emerging.[30] Banning the sale of petrol and diesel vehicles from 2030 is an example of the state taking regulatory action to force the pace of innovation and build new markets to drive the transition to net zero, but the boldness of this move has not yet been matched in the agri-food system.

Net zero poses difficulties for politicians, as the population must be incentivised, encouraged and cajoled out of high-carbon forms of living into a net zero world over three decades. Evidence from citizens assemblies and other participatory forums suggest that people increasingly understand the climate crisis and recognise the need for change. Critical is the sense of fair play, and so the net zero transition must be, and be seen to be, a just transition. Even in these neoliberal times, a Prime Minister who hails the market and "the unique creative power of capitalism" in the Foreword to the Government's Net Zero Strategy has also to emphasise how the Government will strive to make these "historical transitions" fair.[31] Likewise, the EU has committed to the concept of a just transition to a net zero Union.[32] Social justice and fairness already feature in international climate policy. At the Glasgow COP, the obligations of the richest countries to the poorer were a prominent part of the negotiations and the public discussion around the conference. The richest and most industrialised countries are responsible for most of the emissions that have accumulated in the atmosphere since the industrial revolution, and it is accepted that there is an obligation to support adaptation and mitigation among less developed nations, an expression of climate cosmopolitanism. The recent track record of donor countries in failing to meet the commitment of the 2009 Copenhagen COP to provide $100 billion a year was an embarrassment that the Glasgow Pact committed to revisit and address. This cosmopolitan ethic of obligation, care and mutuality pervades thinking on the international and national response to climate change.[33]

Social and economic inequality represents a key challenge of our time, but one that is increasingly recognised as a problem of not only our social systems but also the sustainability of our economic systems. Thomas Piketty's path-breaking work showed how returns to capital are greater than the rate of growth so that wealth inequality not only increases but becomes a more significant driver of inequality than income.[34] While addressing inequality has long been a guiding principle of the political left, the concern now extends more broadly. In his major analysis of inequality, Mike Savage shares his initial bemusement on finding that his topic was exercising and animating the audiences of business elites he was addressing.

> Inequality mattered to this privileged audience, because it spoke to a world they could no longer predict or control. They no longer knew what lay in store for their loved ones, what world their children would inherit, whether their best-laid plans would deliver. The rules of the game, oriented towards a market-driven business logic (that had shaped the world since the 1980s) could no longer be taken for granted. Their familiar world was disintegrating around them.[35]

Henry Dimbleby writes of how the chief executives of major food companies were similarly worried about the dynamics of the food system and the implications for health and environment. He suggests that the Covid pandemic opens a once-in-a-lifetime opportunity to reshape the food system, an opportunity recognised by those that lead the largest and most influential food businesses. They find themselves caught in a business-performance context that emphasises and incentivises margins and profits and so drives the development of ultra-processed foods (what Dimbleby calls the "junk food cycle"). They appear ready to accept the need to make changes and innovate but ask that the Government sets the rules to ensure a level playing field and fair competition.[36] In the transition to net zero, the dynamics between government and large food businesses look to be shifting with the sector calling for government action to force change.

Food companies are taking their own initiatives to improve environmental performance and reduce emissions from their supply chains. This is in large part because they recognise that customer loyalty is increasingly associated with the trust and reputation of their brands as socially and ethically responsible. Critical to the politics of food in Britain in the net zero transition is for food consumption to be shifted from an issue of individual choice to one of social responsibility, for the cosmopolitan impulse more strongly to counter the neoliberal. This does require a new awareness and articulacy about food provenance, attributes and environmental impacts. It is why one of the National Food Strategy's recommendations was an accredited "eat and learn" initiative to make understanding of food and the food system a more prominent feature of the curriculum and school life. Consumers are ever better provided with the means to come to informed judgements about the implications of their food choices for climate change, as the latest science gets translated into handy consumer guides.[37] Carolyn Steel suggests "food's effects are so ubiquitous that they can be hard to spot, which is why learning to see through the lens of food can be so revelatory".[38]

To reconnect people with the agri-food system, and reshape the system to meet food, health, climate and social sustainability goals will require a paradigm shift. Long-term fundamental assumptions about the functioning of the agri-food system are being unsettled and the net zero commitment coupled with the Covid pandemic experience make this a propitious moment. A question becomes how are paradigms disrupted and replaced? Thomas Kuhn wrote about how conventional thinking gets overturned by revolutionary paradigmatic change. An anomaly does not fit with the conventional thinking. A "different kind of thinking cap" must be put on to accommodate and make sense of the anomaly, and a new order is born.[39] We saw in Chapter 2 that socio-technical transitions accelerate when three mutually reinforcing processes bear on them – increasing momentum around niche innovations, weakening of existing systems, and strengthening external pressure – all features of the current juncture.

The agri-food system is a fundamental part of the economy and its greenhouse gas emissions. The centrality of food to life means the agri-food system reflects contemporary society but also shapes society. The structure and functioning of the system are coming to be seen as anomalous and the net zero challenge is forcing questions of technology, production practices, and consumption habits, but also power and control.[40] Transformational systems change prompted by net zero must be planned and managed to deliver a just transition and a new system that is socially sustainable. The dimensions of a socially-just transition involve land, supply chains, consumer choice and welfare, international trade and public voice and influence. When it comes to land, reshaping the agri-food system will produce differential opportunities for farmers on different types of farms, in different places, and with different farming systems. There will be winners and losers. Among the winners will be those best able to adopt lower-emission technologies or capitalise on new markets for environmental services such as carbon sequestration. Among the potential losers could be those less adaptable to change or particularly dependent on producing higher-emission foodstuffs.[41] Furthermore, agriculture's place among rural land uses will be repositioned as peatlands are restored, land is rewilded for biodiversity and forests are planted. There will be social and distributional questions about structural change in the sector, the differing fortunes of smaller, family oriented farm businesses and larger agribusinesses. Similarly, the question of the land ownership structure for forestry and the capturing of carbon credits for forested land is already becoming contentious in some parts of the UK, such as Wales.

The social sustainability of the agri-food system during the net zero transition will also depend on the economic relations between its different component parts. Supply chains operate on the basis of costs, prices, margins and product standards, but also increasingly in terms of ethics and emissions. Carbon accounting in supply chain management will have implications for power relations between buyers and suppliers and could yet lead to even greater control exerted by larger companies over smaller businesses. Life cycle analysis can be as much a governance tool within supply chains as an instrument of emissions reduction.[42] The development of new food products and food and farming technologies will produce new patterns of winners and losers and new questions about the ethics and ownership of intellectual property rights.[43] In addition, there will be risks around the increasing social differentiation of diets and nutrition as food retailers respond to changing patterns of demand but also promote new consumer choices. Potentially transformational new technologies in areas such as carbon capture and storage or novel foods will excite public interest and may prompt calls for stronger controls over innovation and public health risks. A further challenge for a socially just transition centres on the moral responsibilities around international trade in foodstuffs.[44] It would be a fundamental flaw in the UK's Net Zero Strategy if it focused solely on addressing emissions from the domestic agri-food system only to "offshore" emissions through imported food. International trade arrangements will therefore need to incorporate greenhouse gas emissions to help ensure this is not the case. There are many who would like to see the UK produce a greater proportion of its food domestically, but there are popular foods that cannot be grown in the UK. There is also the wider, cosmopolitan question of the ethics of those trading arrangements with distant others whose livelihoods depend on the non-temperate foods we will still want to enjoy.

Avoiding catastrophic climate change is a race against time but the net zero transition is an opportunity to plan change over a three-decade period. The lessons of the past eight decades are that the agri-food system can be actively transformed to deliver new national priorities. It has been before. For the transition to succeed will require a reimagination of the importance of food and the food system in society and a reshaping of that system to ensure not just that catastrophic climate change is avoided, but that the wider benefits to health and biodiversity are also realised, and in a way that is socially just.

Notes

1 Food and Agriculture Organisation (2021) *The Share of Agri-food Systems in Total Greenhouse Gas Emissions – Global, Regional and Country Trends 1990–2019*. Rome: FAO
2 European Commission (2019b). The European Green Deal sets out how to make Europe the first climate neutral continent by 2050, boosting the economy, improving peoples' health and quality of life, caring for nature and leaving no one behind. *European Commission Press Release* 11 December. European Commission https://ec.europa.eu/commission/presscorner/detail/en/ip_19_6691

3 Baldock, D. and Buckwell, A. (2022) *Just Transition in the EU Agriculture and Land Use Sector*. London: Institute for European Environmental Policy, p. 14.

4 Baldock and Buckwell (2022), p. 21; see also Baldock, D. and Hart, K. (2021) *Pathways Towards a Legislative Framework for Sustainable Food Systems in the EU*. London: Institute for European Environmental Policy.

5 House of Commons Environment, Food and Rural Affairs Committee (2021) *Environmental Land Management and the Agricultural Transition*. Second Report, Session 2021–22. London: House of Commons.

6 Buckwell, A. (2019) *Policies for Agriculture, Forestry and Land Use: Chair's Report of the CCC Land Use Advisory Group*. London: Climate Change Committee.

7 National Food Strategy (2021) *National Food Strategy – Independent Review: The Plan*. London: National Food Strategy. p. 98.

8 Goldenberg, N. (1987) *Thought for Food: A Study of the Development of the Food Division, Marks and Spencer*. Orpington: Food Trade Press.

9 Friends of the Earth (1991) *Off the Treadmill: A Way Forward for Farmers and the Countryside*. London: Friends of the Earth; Ward, N. (1993) The agricultural treadmill and the rural environment in the post-productivist era. *Sociologia Ruralis* 33, 348–64.

10 McCann, N. (1989) *The Story of the National Agricultural Advisory Service: A Mainspring of Agricultural Revival, 1946–1971*. Ely: Providence Press, p. 80.

11 Council for Science and Technology (2020) *A Systems Approach to Delivering Net Zero: Recommendations from the Prime Minister's Council for Science and Technology*. London: Council for Science and Technology, p. 1.

12 Benton, T. and Thompson, C. (2016) Food system resilience. *Food Science and Technology* 30(3), 20–4; Pretty, J. *et al.* (2018). Global assessment of agricultural system redesign for sustainable intensification. *Nature Sustainability* 1(8), 441–6; Canales Holzeis, C. *et al.* (2019) Food systems for delivering nutritious and sustainable diets: perspectives from the global network of science academies. *Global Food Security* 21, 72–7; Herrero, M. *et al.* (2021). Articulating the effect of food systems innovation on the Sustainable Development Goals. *The Lancet Planetary Health* 5(1), pp. e50–62.

13 Gabrys, J. (2016) *Program Earth: Environmental Sensing Technology and the Making of a Computational Planet*. Minneapolis: University of Minnesota Press.

14 Donaldson, A. (2021) Digital from farm to fork: infrastructures of quality and control in food supply chains. *Journal of Rural Studies* (Online first).

15 Murdoch, J. and Ward, N. (1997) Governmentality and territoriality: the statistical manufacture of Britain's "national farm". *Political Geography* 16, 307–24.

16 Council for Science and Technology (2020).

17 Mazzucato, M. (2021) *Mission Economy: A Moonshot Guide to Changing Capitalism*. London: Allen Lane, pp. 205–6.

18 National Farmers' Union (2021) Australia trade deal: five questions the UK government must answer. *NFU Press Release* 15 June; see also Webb, D. (2021) *UK-Australia Free Trade Agreement*. House of Commons Library Paper 9204. London: House of Commons Library.

19 Mann, M. (2021) *The New Climate War: The Fight to Take Back Our Planet*. London: Scribe.

20 Quoted in The Observer (2021) New trade deals "are unfair on farmers and won't help emissions". *The Observer* 21 October, p. 19.

21 Poux, X. *et al.* (2021). *Modelling an Agroecological UK in 2050*. Paris: IDDRI, Sciences Po.; See also Food, Farming and Countryside Commission (2019) *Our Future in the Land*. London: Royal Society for the Arts.

22 Poux *et al.* (2021), p. 22.

23 National Food Strategy (2021), p. 88.

24 See, for example, Hulme, M. (2014) *Can Science Fix Climate Change?* Cambridge: Polity Press; Mann (2021).

25 Minx, J., *et al.* (2018) Negative emissions – part 1: research landscape and synthesis. *Environmental Research Letters* 13, 063001; Fuss, S., *et al.* (2018) Negative emissions – part 2: costs, potentials and side effects. *Environmental Research Letters* 13, 063002.

26 Sexton, A. *et al.* (2019) Framing the future of food: the contested promises of alternative proteins. *Environment and Planning E: Nature and Space* 2, 47–72.

27 Steel, C. (2021) *Sitopia: How Food Can Save the World.* London: Penguin, p. 13.

28 BBC Radio Four (2021) *Farming Today* 4 November.

29 In February 2022, the *Financial Times* reported that Prime Minister Boris Johnson asked Tory MPs for a show of hands on whether they supported a government obesity strategy that would ban "buy-one-get-one-free" offers on unhealthy foods. Most Conservative MPs opposed the idea. Payne, S. and Parker, G. (2022) Stage set for Downing Street makeover. *Financial Times* 2 February, p. 2.

30 The Economist (2022) The new interventionism, special report – business and the state. *The Economist* 15 January, pp. 3–12.

31 UK Government (2021) *Net Zero Strategy: Build Back Greener.* London: Stationary Office, p. 8.

32 Baldock and Buckwell (2022), p. 10.

33 Morgan, K. (2010) Local and green, global and fair: the ethical foodscape and the politics of care. *Environment and Planning A* 42, 1852–67.

34 Piketty, T. (2014) *Capital in the Twenty-First Century.* Cambridge, MA: Harvard University Press.

35 Savage, M. (2021) *The Return of Inequality: Social Change and the Weight of the Past.* Cambridge, MA: Harvard University Press, p. 14.

36 National Food Strategy (2021), p. 10.

37 Bridle, S. (2020) *Food and Climate Change: Without the Hot Air.* Cambridge: UIT Cambridge.

38 Steel (2021), p. 23.

39 Kuhn, T. (1962) *The Structure of Scientific Revolutions.* University of Chicago Press, quoted in Savage (2021), p. 3.

40 Tansey, G. (2008) Food, farming and global rules, pp. 3–4 in G. Tansey and T. Rajotte (eds.) *The Future Control of Food: A Guide to International Negotiations and Rules on Intellectual Property, Biodiversity and Food Security.* London: Earthscan; International Panel of Experts on Sustainable Food Systems and ETC Group (2021) *A Long Food Movement: Transforming Food Systems by 2045.* Brussels: IPES-Food.

41 Baldock and Buckwell (2022), pp. 39–42.

42 Freidberg, S. (2013) Calculating sustainability in supply chain capitalism. *Economy and Society* 42, 571–96.

43 Tansey, G. and Rajotte, T. (2008) (eds.) *The Future Control of Food: A Guide to International Negotiations and Rules on Intellectual Property, Biodiversity and Food Security.* London: Earthscan.

44 Jackson, P., Ward, N. and Russell, P. (2009) Moral economies of food and geographies of responsibility. *Transactions of the Institute of British Geographers* 34, 12–24.

ACKNOWLEDGEMENTS

I sat at a desk in a small spare bedroom at home under the 2021 Covid lock-down and started writing the first draft of this book. There were no seminars, visits to Aberystwyth and the like to try out preliminary ideas, or coffee room chats with colleagues. It was just me, my archive and the internet. However, as the project began to take shape people have been very helpful in pointing me to source material, sharing thoughts and commenting on a draft manuscript. Because the book draws on experience from across my academic career, I would like to record my thanks here to those who have supported me along the way. Chapter 3 and parts of Chapter 4 revisit and update the research I originally conducted while at University College London (UCL) in the early 1990s. I was extremely fortunate at that time to be able to work with Richard Munton and Terry Marsden. Their patience and generous mentoring left a lasting imprint and more than three decades later I still find myself drawing on insights from the academic training ground they provided me with and for which I remain profoundly grateful. At UCL, I also worked with Philip Lowe, to whom this book is dedicated, and was able to continue to do so for much of the next 25 years. He was an inspirational colleague and immense fun to work with, and his wisdom and enthusiasm are missed terribly since his death in 2020. Also missed is Jonathan Murdoch, who died in 2005, from whom I learned a great deal about thinking and writing and many other things. Jon's approach to knuckling down and writing first draft material left its mark and has served me well. As Director of the Centre for Rural Economy at Newcastle University from 2004 to 2008, I worked with a wonderful team including Jane Atterton, Terry Carroll, Andrew Donaldson, Carmen Hubbard, Jane Midgley, Jeremy Phillipson and Nicola Thompson, and it has been a real pleasure to be able to keep in touch with former colleagues at Newcastle since I left.

In developing the project, I have incurred many debts. First, I am grateful to David Richardson and Frances Bowen at UEA for providing me with a sabbatical to conduct the research for the book. Christopher Brown in UEA's Library was a big help with sourcing archive materials and John Reardon in UEA's IT team kindly helped me navigate the constraints of the Microsoft printing lockdown of 2021. Chris Bigsby helped me find when and where Arthur Miller discussed global warming with Arthur C. Clarke in the early 1960s and introduced me to Eugène Mouton's remarkable 1872 account of climate catastrophe in *The End of the World*. David Harvey, Jeremy Phillipson, Chris Ritson and Robert Shiel at Newcastle and David Stead in Dublin joined the fun and helped with my investigations into late nineteenth-century agricultural research and education, all to get a sentence right in Chapter 3. I am grateful to those who gave permission for me to use their tables, figures and data including Behavioural Insights Ltd, Paul Brassley and Boydell Press, the Climate Change Committee, Monica Crippa, Forest Research, Tim Lang, the Royal Agricultural Society of England and UCL's Institute for Sustainable Development. I would like to thank those who shared thoughts and ideas with me during autumn 2021 that helped inform my thinking – Tim Bailey, Christopher Darby, Paul Dobson, Janet Dwyer, Gareth Enticott, Andrew Fearne, Corrine LeQuéré, Jeremy Phillipson, Polly Russell, Dale Sanders and Naomi Vaughan. Late in the book's development, I was able to have some useful conversations with a new set of collaborators on the agri-food system for which I am grateful to Angelina Sanderson Bellamy, Tim Benton, Sarah Bridle, Stefan Kepinsky, Jacqueline McGlade, Tom Macmillan, Simon Pearson and Pete Smith. I would also like to thank Hannah Ferguson and Katie Stokes at Routledge for their help and support. Most of all, I am extremely grateful to those who generously read draft material. All errors in the text are my responsibility alone, but my sincere thanks go to David Baldock, Andrew Donaldson, Bethan Gulliver, Carmen Hubbard, Kevin Morgan and Geoff Tansey. Finally, Bethan, Daniel and Polly gave me the space and support at home to indulge myself and fill my head with net zero, food and farming so that there is, at last, another book with a cow on the cover to go alongside the one about slurry.

BIBLIOGRAPHY

Achilladelis, B., Schwarzkopf, A. and Cines, M. (1987) A study of innovation in the pesticide industry: analysis of the innovation record of an industrial sector. *Research Policy* 16, 175–212.

Adam, B. and Groves, C. (2007) *Future Matters: Action, Knowledge, Ethics.* Leiden: Brill.

ADAS (1976) *Wildlife Conservation in Semi-natural Habitats on Farms: A Survey of Farmer Attitudes and Intentions in England and Wales.* London: HMSO.

Adger, N. and Brown, K. (1994) *Land Use and the Causes of Global Warming.* Chichester: Wiley.

Agricultural and Food Research Council, Economic and Social Research Council and Natural Environment Research Council (1994) *Joint Agriculture and Environment Programme: The JAEP Report.* Swindon: The Research Councils.

Agricultural Research Council (1982) *Weed Research Organisation, Ninth Report, 1980–1981.* Oxford: Agricultural Research Council.

Agri-TechE (2020) Nitrogen fixation for cereals to sustainably increase yields in Africa. www.agri-tech-e.co.uk/nitrogen-fixation-for-cereals-to-sustainably-increase-yields-in-africa/ (Accessed 3 January 2022).

Alexander, A. and Phillips, S. (2006) "Fair play for the small man": perspectives on the contribution of the independent shopkeeper 1930–c.1945. *Business History* 48 (1), 69–89. doi:10.1080/00076790500204743

Anderson, I. (2002) *Foot and Mouth Disease 2001: Lessons to Be Learned Inquiry Report.* London: Stationary Office.

Andreyeva, T., Long, M. and Brownell, K. (2010). The impact of food prices on consumption: a systematic review of research on the price elasticity of demand for food. *American Journal of Public Health* 100, 216–22. doi:10.2105/AJPH.2008.151415

Arthur, W.B. (2009) *The Nature of Technology: What It Is and How It Evolves.* London: Penguin.

Averchenkova, A., Fankhauser, S. and Finnegan, J. (2018) *The Role of Independent Bodies in Climate Governance: The UK's Committee on Climate Change.* London: The Grantham Research Institute on Climate Change and the Environment. www.lse.ac.uk/granthaminstitute/wp-content/uploads/2018/10/The-role-of-independent-bodies-in-climate-governance-the-UKs-Committee-on-Climate-Change_Averchenkova-et-al.pdf (Accessed 3 January 2022).

Bailey, T. (2021) *Livestock's Longer Shadow: Hope Lives in Kindness.* Gloucester: Choir Press.

Baird, W. and Tarrant, J. (1973) *Hedgerow Destruction in Norfolk, 1946–1970.* Norwich: Centre of East Anglian Studies, University of East Anglia.

Baker, A. (2021) *The Ethical Food Consumer – UK – 2021.* London: Mintel. (Accessed Business and IP Centre, British Library, 9 November 2021).

Baldock, D. and Buckwell, A. (2022) *Just Transition in the EU Agriculture and Land Use Sector.* London: Institute for European Environmental Policy. https://ieep.eu/publications

Baldock, D. and Hart, K. (2021) *Pathways Towards a Legislative Framework for Sustainable Food Systems in the EU.* London: Institute for European Environmental Policy. https://ieep. eu/publications/agriculture-and-landmanagement/pathways-towards-a-legislative-framework-for-sustainable-food-systems-in-the-eu

Baldock, D. and Lowe, P. (1996) The development of European agri-environmental policy, pp. 8–25 in M. Whitby (ed.) *The European Environment and CAP Reform: Policies and Prospects for Conservation.* Wallingford: CAB International.

Baldock, D., Cox, G., Lowe, P. and Winter, M. (1990) Environmentally sensitive areas: incrementalism or reform. *Journal of Rural Studies* 6, 143–62.

Balmford, A., Green, R. and Scharlemann, J. (2005) Sparing land for nature: exploring the potential impact of changes in agricultural yield on the area needed for crop production. *Global Change Biology* 11, 1594–606. doi:10.1111/j.1365-2486.2005.01035.x

Balogun, B., Baker, C., Conway, L., Long, R. and Powell, T. (2021) *Obesity.* House of Commons Library Briefing Paper No 9049, 26 May. London: House of Commons. https://com monslibrary.parliament.uk/research-briefings/cbp-9049/ (Accessed 3 January 2022).

Bandy, L., Scarborough, P., Harrington, R., Rayner, M and Jebb, S. (2020) Reductions in sugar sales from soft drinks in the UK from 2015–18. *BMC Medicine* 18(1) 1–10. doi:10.1186/s12916-019-1477-4

Barr, C., Benefield. C., Bunce, B., Ridsdale, H. and Whittaker, M. (1986) *Landscape Changes in Britain.* Huntingdon: Institute of Terrestrial Ecology.

Barwell, G. (2021) *Chief of Staff: Notes from Downing Street.* London: Atlantic.

BBMG, GlobeScan, and SustainAbility. (2012) *People Say They Want Sustainable Consumption But Do They Mean It? Summary of Survey Results.* www.fastcompany.com/1681019/people-say-they-want-sustainable-consumption-but-do-they-mean-it/ (Accessed 3 January 2022).

Beck, U. (2000) The cosmopolitan perspective: sociology of the second age of modernity. *British Journal of Sociology* 51, 79–105. doi:10.1111/j.1468-4446.2000.00079.x

Beck, U. (2006) *Cosmopolitan Vision.* Cambridge: Policy Press.

Beck, U. and Grande, E. (2007) *Cosmopolitan Europe.* Cambridge: Polity.

Behavioural Insights Team (2020) *A Menu for Change: Using Behavioural Science to Promote Sustainable Diets Around the World.* London: Behavioural Insights Team. www.bi.team/publications/a-menu-for-change/ (Accessed 3 January 2022).

Bell, W. and Mau, J. (eds.) (1971) *The Sociology of the Future.* New York: Russell Sage.

Benton, T. and Bailey, R. (2019) The paradox of productivity: agricultural productivity promotes food system inefficiency. *Global Sustainability* 2, e6, 1–8. doi:10.1017/sus.2019.3

Benton, T. and Thompson, C. (2016) Food system resilience. *Food Science and Technology* 30(3), 20–4. doi:10.1002/fsat.3003_4.x

Berners-Lee, M. (2010) *How Bad Are Bananas? The Carbon Footprint of Everything.* London: Profile.

Bianchi, F., Dorsel, C., Garnett, E., Aveyard, P. and Jebb, S. A. (2018) Interventions targeting conscious determinants of human behaviour to reduce the demand for meat: a systematic review with qualitative comparative analysis. *International Journal of Behavioral Nutrition and Physical Activity* 15, 102. doi:10.1186/s12966-018-0729-6

Bigsby, C. (2011) *Arthur Millar 1962–2005*. London: Weidenfeld and Nicholson.

Bijker, W., Hughes, T. and Pinch, T. (eds.) (1987) *The Social Construction of Technological Systems: New Directions in the Sociology and History of Technology*. Cambridge, MA: MIT Press.

Body, R. (1982) *Agriculture: The Triumph and the Shame*. London: Temple Smith.

Body, R. (1984) *Farming in the Clouds*. London: Temple Smith.

Body, R. (1991) *Our Food, Our Land: Why Contemporary Farming Practices Must Change*. London: Random.

Booth, R. (2021) Pathways, targets and temporalities: Analysing English agriculture's net zero futures. *Environment and Planning E: Nature and Space* (Online first). doi:10.1177/25148486211064962

Bowers, J. (1985) British agricultural policy since the Second World War. *Agricultural History Review* 33, 66–77.

Bowler, I. (1986) Intensification, concentration and specialization in agriculture – the case of the European Community. *Geography* 71, 14–24.

Boykoff, M. and Boykoff, J. (2004) Balance as bias: Global warming and the US prestige press. *Global Environmental Change* 14, 125–36. doi:10.1016/j.gloenvcha.2003.10.001

Brandt, K. (1945) *The Reconstruction of World Agriculture*. New York: Norton.

Brassley, P. (1996) Silage in Britain, 1880–1990: the delayed adoption of an innovation. *Agricultural History Review* 44, 63–87. www.jstor.org/stable/40275066

Brassley, P. (2000a) Agricultural science and education, pp. 594–649 in E. Collins (ed.) *The Agrarian History of England and Wales Volume VII 1850–1914*. Cambridge: Cambridge University Press.

Brassley, P. (2000b) Output and technical change in twentieth century British agriculture. *Agricultural History Review* 48, 60–84. www.jstor.org/stable/40275614

Brassley, P., Harvey, D., Lobley, M. and Winter, M. (2021) *The Real Agricultural Revolution: The Transformation of English Farming 1939–1985*. Woodbridge: Boydell Press.

Braunholtz, J.T. (1982) Crop protection: The evolution of a chemical industry, in D. Sharp and T. West (eds.) *The Chemical Industry*. Chichester: Ellis Horwood.

Bridle, S. (2020) *Food and Climate Change: Without the Hot Air*. Cambridge: UIT Cambridge.

Broeker, W. (1987) Unpleasant surprises in the greenhouse. *Nature* 328, 123–6. doi:10.1038/328123a0

Brough, A., Wilkie, J., Ma, J., Isaac, M. and Gal, D. (2016). Is eco-friendly unmanly? The green-feminine stereotype and its effect on sustainable consumption. *Journal of Consumer Research* 43, 567–82. doi:10.1093/jcr/ucw044

Bucher, T., Collins, C., Rollo, M., McCaffrey, T., De Vlieger, N., Van der Bend, D., Truby H. and Perez-Cueto, F. J. (2016). Nudging consumers towards healthier choices: a systematic review of positional influences on food choice. *British Journal of Nutrition* 115, 2252–63. doi:10.1017/S0007114516001653

Buckwell, A. (2019) *Policies for Agriculture, Forestry and Land Use: Chair's Report of the CCC Land Use Advisory Group*. London: Climate Change Committee. www.theccc.org.uk/wp-content/uploads/2020/01/Professor-Allan-Buckwell-2019-Summary-report-CCC-land-use-advisory-group.pdf (Accessed 3 January 2022).

Burton, R. (2004) Seeing through the "good farmer's" eyes: towards developing an understanding of the social symbolic value of "productivist" behaviour. *Sociologia Ruralis* 44, 195–215.

Burton, R., Forney, J., Stock, P. and Sutherland, L.A. (2021) *The Good Farmer: Culture and Identity in Food and Agriculture*. London: Routledge.

The BSE Inquiry (2000) *The BSE Inquiry Report. Sixteen Volumes*. https://webarchive.nationalarchives.gov.uk/20060802142310/ www.bseinquiry.gov.uk/ (Accessed 7 June 2021).

Buttel, F. and Taylor, P. (1992) Environmental sociology and global environmental change: a critical assessment. *Society and Natural Resources* 5, 211–30.

Buttel, F., Hawkins, A. and Power, A. (1990) From limits to growth to global change: constraints and contradictions in the evolution of environmental science and ideology. *Global Environmental Change* 1, 57–66.

California Air Resources Board (2019) *Compliance Offset Program*. Sacramento, CA: California Air Resources Board. www.arb.ca.gov/cc/capandtrade/offsets/offsets.htm (Accessed 16 January 2022).

Callon, M., Millo, Y. and Muniesa, F. (eds.) (2007) *Market Devices*. Oxford: Blackwell.

Canales Holzeis, C., Fears, R., Moughan, P., Bentone, T. Hendriksf, S., Cleggg, M., Meulenb, V. and von Braun, J. (2019) Food systems for delivering nutritious and sustainable diets: perspectives from the global network of science academies. *Global Food Security* 21, 72–7. doi.org/10.1016/j.gfs.2019.05.002

Cann, C. (1994) The background to the agriculture chapter in the Sustainable Development Strategy, pp. 4–6 in M. Whitby and N. Ward (eds.) *The UK Strategy for Sustainable Agriculture: A Critical Analysis*. CRE Report. Newcastle upon Tyne: University of Newcastle.

Carson, R. (1962) *Silent Spring*. Boston, MA: Houghton Mifflin.

Castells, M. (1996) *The Rise of the Network Society*. Oxford: Blackwell.

Chamberlain, D., Fuller, R., Bunce, R., Duckworth, J and Shrubb, M. (2000) Changes in the abundance of farmland birds in relation to the timing of agricultural intensification in England and Wales. *Journal of Applied Ecology* 37, 771–88. doi:10.1046/j.1365-2664.2000.00548.x

Chanana-Nag, N. and Aggarwal, P. K. (2018). Woman in agriculture, and climate risks: hotspots for development. *Climatic Change* 1–15. doi:10.1007/s10584-018-2233-z

Cialdini, R. (1984) *Influence: The Psychology of Persuasion*. New York: Harper Collins.

Clancy, H. (2021) Here's what to make of the COP26 methane moment. *GreenBiz Group Press Release*, 2 November. www.greenbiz.com/article/heres-what-make-cop26-methane-moment (Accessed 3 January 2022).

Clarke, P. (2021) The meat of the argument about nation's diet. *Farmers Weekly* 23 July, pp. 12–13.

Clifford, N. (2020) *Meat Substitutes: Including Impact of Covid-19 – UK – 2020*. London: Mintel (Accessed Business and IP Centre, British Library, 9 November 2021).

Climate Change Committee (2009) *Meeting Carbon Budgets – The Need for a Step Change: Progress Report to Parliament*. London: Climate Change Committee. www.theccc.org.uk/publication/meeting-carbon-budgets-the-need-for-a-step-change-1st-progress-report/ (Accessed 3 January 2022).

Climate Change Committee (2011) *Meeting Carbon: 3rd Progress Report to Parliament*. London: Climate Change Committee. www.theccc.org.uk/publication/meeting-carbon-budgets-3rd-progress-report-to-parliament/ (Accessed 3 January 2022).

Climate Change Committee (2013) *Managing the Land in a Changing Climate*. London: Climate Change Committee. www.theccc.org.uk/publication/managing-the-land-in-a-changing-climate/ (Accessed 3 January 2022).

Climate Change Committee (2016) *Meeting Carbon: The 2016 Progress Report to Parliament*. London: Climate Change Committee. www.theccc.org.uk/publication/meeting-carbon-budgets-2016-progress-report-to-parliament/ (Accessed 3 January 2022).

Climate Change Committee (2018) *Land Use: Reducing Emissions and Preparing for Climate Change*. London: Climate Change Committee. www.theccc.org.uk/publication/land-use-reducing-emissions-and-preparing-for-climate-change/ (Accessed 3 January 2022).

Climate Change Committee (2019) *Net Zero: The UK's Contribution to Stopping Global Warming*. London: Climate Change Committee. www.theccc.org.uk/wp-content/uploads/2019/05/Net-Zero-The-UKs-contribution-to-stopping-global-warming.pdf (Accessed 3 January 2022).

Climate Change Committee (2020a) *Land Use: Policies for a Net Zero UK*. London: Climate Change Committee. www.theccc.org.uk/publication/land-use-policies-for-a-net-zero-uk/ (Accessed 3 January 2022).

Climate Change Committee (2020b) *The Sixth Carbon Budget: The UK's Path to Net Zero*. London: Climate Change Committee. www.theccc.org.uk/publication/sixth-carbon-budget/ (Accessed 3 January 2022).

Climate Change Committee (2020c) *Policies for the Sixth Carbon Budget and Net Zero*. London: Climate Change Committee. www.theccc.org.uk/wp-content/uploads/2020/12/Policies-for-the-Sixth-Carbon-Budget-and-Net-Zero.pdf (Accessed 3 January 2022).

Climate Change Committee (2021a) *Progress in Reducing Emissions: 2021 Report to Parliament*. London: Climate Change Committee. www.theccc.org.uk/publication/2021-progress-report-to-parliament/ (Accessed 3 January 2022).

Climate Change Committee (2021b) *Independent Assessment: The UK's Net Zero Strategy*. London: Climate Change Committee. www.theccc.org.uk/publication/independent-assessment-the-uks-net-zero-strategy/ (Accessed 3 January 2022).

Cochrane, W. (1979) *The Development of Industrial Agriculture: A Historical Analysis*. Minneapolis: University of Minnesota Press.

Coe, S. and Finally, J. (2020) *The Agriculture Act 2020*. House of Commons Library Briefing Paper No. CPB 8702. London: House of Commons Library. https://commonslibrary.parliament.uk/research-briefings/cbp-8702/

Collingham, L. (2011) *The Taste of War: World War Two and the Battle for Food*. London: Allen Lane.

Collins, E. (2000) *The Agrarian History of England and Wales Volume VII 1850–1914, Parts I & II*. Cambridge: Cambridge University Press.

Corera, G. (2021) *The Hack That Changed the World*. BBC Radio 4 series broadcast 1st to 5th November. www.bbc.co.uk/programmes/m00114bd

Council for Science and Technology (2020) *A Systems Approach to Delivering Net Zero: Recommendations from the Prime Minister's Council for Science and Technology*. London: Council for Science and Technology. https://assets.publishing.service.gov.uk/government/uploads/system/uploads/attachment_data/file/910446/cst-net-zero-report-30- january-2020.pdf

Country Land and Business Association (2019) *Evidence to the House of Commons Environment, Food and Rural Affairs Committee Inquiry into Agriculture: Achieving Net Zero Emissions*. https://data.parliament.uk/writtenevidence/committeeevidence.svc/evidencedocument/environment-food-and-rural-affairs-committee/agriculture-achieving-netzero-emissions/written/ (Accessed May 2021).

Countryside Commission/Huntings (1986) *Monitoring Landscape Change*. Cheltenham: Countryside Commission.

Courvoisier, T. J., European Academies Science Advisory Council and Deutsche Akademie der Naturforscher Leopoldina (eds.) (2018). *Negative Emission Technologies: What Role in Meeting Paris Agreement Targets?* EASAC Policy Report 35. Halle (Saale): EASAC Secretariat, Deutsche Akademie der Naturforscher Leopoldina. https://easac.eu/fileadmin/PDF_s/reports_statements/Negative_Carbon/EASAC_Report_on_Negative_Emission_Technologies.pdf (Accessed 3 January 2022).

Cox, E., Pidgeon, N. and Spence, E. (2021) But they told us it was safe! Carbon dioxide removal, fracking, and ripple effects in risk perceptions. *Risk Analysis* 41. doi:10.1111/risa.13717

Cox, G. and Lowe, P. (1983) A battle not the war: The politics of the Wildlife and Countryside Act. pp. 48–76 in A. Gilg (ed.) *Countryside Planning Yearbook*,Vol. 4. Norwich: Geobooks.

Cox, G., Lowe, P. and Winter, M. (1990) *The Voluntary Principle in Conservation.* Chichester: Packard.

Crippa, M., Solazzo, E., Guizzardi, D., Montforti-Ferrario, F., Tubiello, F. and Leip, A. (2021a) Food systems are responsible for a third of global anthropogenic GHG emissions. *Nature Food* 2, 198–209. doi:10.1038/s43016-021-00225-9

Crippa, M., Guizzardi, D., Solazzo, E., Muntean, M., Schaaf, E., Monforti-Ferrario, F., Banja, M., Olivier, J.G.J., Grassi, G., Rossi, S. and Vignati, E. (2021b) *GHG Emissions of All World Countries – 2021 Report.* EUR 30831 EN. Luxembourg: Publications Office of the European Union. doi:10.2760/173513, JRC126363

Croll, B. (1991) Pesticides in surface waters and groundwaters. *Journal of the Institution of Water and Environmental Management* 5, 389–95.

Dairy UK (2019) *Memorandum of Evidence to the House of Commons Environment, Food and Rural Affairs Committee Inquiry into Agriculture – Achieving Net Zero Emissions.* https://data.parliament.uk/writtenevidence/committeeevidence.svc/evidencedocument/environment-food-and-rural-affairs-committee/agriculture-achieving-netzero-emissions/written/ (Accessed May 2021).

Dancey, R. (1993) The evolution of agricultural extension in England and Wales. *Journal of Agricultural Economics* 44, 375–93.

Davison, A. (1994) Agriculture, air pollution and sustainability, pp. 43–9 in M. Whitby and N. Ward (eds.) *The UK Strategy for Sustainable Agriculture: A Critical Analysis.* CRE Report. Newcastle upon Tyne: University of Newcastle.

deJager, T. (1993) The origins of the Agricultural Research Council, 1930–37. *Minerva* 31, 129–50.

Department for Business, Energy and Industrial Strategy (2019) *Final UK Greenhouse Gas Emissions National Statistics. Data Tables.* https://data.gov.uk/dataset/9568363e-57e5-4c33-9e00-31dc528fcc5a/final-uk-greenhouse-gas-emissions-national-statistics (Accessed 3 January 2022).

Department for Business, Energy and Industrial Strategy (2021) *Provisional UK Greenhouse Gas Emissions National Statistics.* https://data.gov.uk/dataset/9a1e58e5-d1b6-457d-a414-335ca546d52c/provisional-uk-greenhouse-gas-emissions-national-statistics (Accessed 3 January 2022).

Department for Energy and Climate Change (2015) World agrees historic global climate deal – a historic new global climate agreement has been struck at the United Nations conference on climate change in Paris. *DECC Press Release*, 12 December. London: DECC. www.gov.uk/government/news/world-agrees-historic-global-climate-deal (Accessed 3 January 2022).

Department for Environment, Food and Rural Affairs (2011) *Bovine TB Eradication Programme for England.* London: Defra. https://assets.publishing.service.gov.uk/government/uploads/system/uploads/attachment_data/file/69443/pb13601-bovinetb-eradication-programme-110719.pdf (Accessed 3 January 2022).

Department for Environment, Food and Rural Affairs (2012) *Greenhouse Gas Emissions from Agriculture Indicators.* London: Defra. www.gov.uk/government/statistical-data-sets/greenhouse-gas-emissions-from-agriculture-indicators (Accessed 3 January 2022).

Department for Environment, Food and Rural Affairs (2013) *The National Action Plan for the Sustainable Use of Pesticides*. London: Defra. www.gov.uk/government/publications/pesticides-uk-national-action-plan (Accessed 3 January 2022).

Department for Environment, Food and Rural Affairs (2016) Farm household income and household composition: results from the Farm Business Survey, England 2014/15. *Defra Statistical Release*. https://assets.publishing.service.gov.uk

Department for Environment, Food and Rural Affairs (2018) *Bovine TB Strategy Review*. London: Defra https://assets.publishing.service.gov.uk/government/uploads/system/uploads/attachment_data/file/756942/tb-review-final-report-corrected.pdf (Accessed 3 January 2022).

Department for Environment, Food and Rural Affairs (2019a) *National Food Strategy – Call for Evidence*, 17 August. London: Defra. https://consult.defra.gov.uk/agri-food-chain-directorate/national-food-strategy-call-for-evidence/ (Accessed 3 January 2022).

Department for Environment, Food and Rural Affairs (2019b) *Memorandum of Evidence to the House of Commons Environment, Food and Rural Affairs Committee Inquiry into Agriculture – Achieving Net Zero Emissions*. https://data.parliament.uk/writtenevidence/committeeevidence.svc/evidencedocument/environment-food-and-rural-affairs-committee/agriculture-achieving-netzero-emissions/written/ (Accessed May 2021).

Department for Environment, Food and Rural Affairs (2020) *Wild Bird Populations in the UK, 1970–2019*. London: Defra. https://assets.publishing.service.gov.uk/government/uploads/system/uploads/attachment_data/file/938262/UK_Wild_birds_1970-2019_final.pdf (Accessed 3 January 2022).

Department for Environment, Food and Rural Affairs (2021a) *Agriculture in the United Kingdom 2020*. London: Defra. www.gov.uk/government/statistics/agriculture-in-the-united-kingdom-2020 (Accessed 3 January 2022).

Department for Environment, Food and Rural Affairs (2021b) *The National Action Plan for the Sustainable Use of Pesticides – Consultation Document*. London: Defra. https://consult.defra.gov.uk/pesticides-future-strategy/sustainable-use-of-pesticides-national-action-plan/ (Accessed 3 January 2022).

Department for Environment, Food and Rural Affairs (2021c) *Agri-climate Report 2021*. London: Defra. www.gov.uk/government/statistics/agri-climate-report-2021/agri-climate-report-2021 (Accessed 3 January 2022).

Department for Environment, Food and Rural Affairs (2021d) *Greenhouse Gas Mitigation Practices – Farm Practices Survey England 2021*. 24 June 2021. London: Defra. www.gov.uk/government/statistics/farm-practices-survey-february-2021-greenhouse-gas-mitigation-practices (Accessed 3 January 2022).

Department of the Environment (1990) *This Common Inheritance – Britain's Environmental Strategy*. London: HMSO.

Department of the Environment and Welsh Office (1986) *River Quality in England and Wales 1985*. London: HMSO.

Dixon, J. (1998) Nature conservation, pp. 214–31 in P. Lowe and S. Ward (eds.) *British Environmental Policy and Europe: Politics and Policy in Transition*. London: Routledge.

Dolan, P., Hallsworth, M., Halpern, D., King, D. and Vlae, I. (2010) *MINDSPACE: Influencing Behaviour Through Public Policy*. London: Institute for Government and Cabinet Office. www.instituteforgovernment.org.uk/sites/default/files/publications/MINDSPACE.pdf (Accessed 3 January 2022).

Donaldson, A. (2008) Biosecurity after the event: risk politics and animal disease. *Environment and Planning A* 40, 1552–67. doi:10.1068/a4056

Donaldson, A. (2021) Digital from farm to fork: infrastructures of quality and control in food supply chains. *Journal of Rural Studies* (Online first). doi:10.1016/j.jrurstud.2021.10.004

Donaldson, A. and Wood, D. (2004) Surveilling strange materialities: categorisation in the evolving geographies of FMD biosecurity. *Environment and Planning D: Society and Space* 22, 373–91. doi:10.1068/d334t

Donofrio, S., Maguire, P., Zwick, S. and Merry, W. (2020) *State of the Voluntary Carbon Markets 2020: Voluntary Carbon and the Postpandemic Recovery*, Washington, DC: Forest Trends. www.foresttrends.org/publications/state-of-voluntary-carbon-markets-2020-voluntary-carbon-andthe-post-pandemic-recovery/

van Dooren, C., Marinussen, M., Blonk, H., Aiking, H. and Vellinga, P. (2014) Exploring dietary guidelines based on ecological and nutritional values: a comparison of six dietary patterns. *Food Policy* 44, 36–46. doi:10.1016/j.foodpol.2013.11.002

Dosi, G. (1982) Technological paradigms and technological trajectories: a suggested interpretation of the determinants and directions of technical change. *Research Policy* 11, 147–62.

Dutkiewicz, J. and Rosenberg, G. (2021) Can lab-grown meat really solve our food problems? *The Guardian* 29 July (The long read), pp. 6–8. www.theguardian.com/news/2021/jul/29/lab-grown-meat-factory-farms-industrial-agriculture-animals (Accessed 30 October 2021).

EAT-Lancet (2019) Food in the Anthropocene: the EAT-Lancet Commission on healthy diets from sustainable food systems. *The Lancet* 393, 447–92. www.thelancet.com/journals/lancet/article/PIIS0140-6736(18)31788-4/fulltext (Accessed 3 January 2022).

Edward-Jones, G., Canals, L., Hounsome, N., Truniger, M., Koeber, G., Hounsome, B., Cross, P., York, E., Hospido, A., Plassman, K., Harris, I., Edwards, R., Day, G., Tomos, A., Cowell, S. and Jones, D. (2008) Testing the assertion that "local food is the best": the challenges of an evidence-based approach. *Trends in Food Science and Technology* 19, 265–74. doi:10.1016/j.tifs.2008.01.008

Ehrenstein, V. (2018) Carbon sink geopolitics. *Economy and Society* 47(1), 162–86. doi:10.1080/03085147.2018.1445569

Element Energy and UK Centre for Ecology and Hydrology (2021) *Greenhouse Gas Removal Methods and Their Potential UK Deployment.* Report for the Department for Business, Energy and Industrial Strategy. London: BEIS. https://assets.publishing.service.gov.uk/government/uploads/system/uploads/attachment_data/file/1026988/ggr-methods-potential-deployment.pdf (Accessed 11 January 2022).

Elliott, J. (1980) Weed control: past, present and future – a historical perspective, pp. 285–95 in R. Hurd, P. Biscoe and C. Dennis (eds.) *Opportunities for Increasing Crop Yields.* London: Pitman.

Elliott, J., Ritson, J., Reed, M and Kennedy-Blundell, O. (2022) *The Opportunities of Agri-Carbon Markets: Policy and Practice.* London: Green Alliance. https://green-alliance.org.uk/resources/The_opportunities_of_agri-carbon_markets.pdf (Accessed 7 January 2022).

Environment Agency (2019) *Memorandum of Evidence to the House of Commons Environment, Food and Rural Affairs Committee Inquiry into Agriculture: Achieving Net Zero Emissions.* https://data.parliament.uk/writtenevidence/committeeevidence.svc/evidencedocument/environ (Accessed May 2021).

European Commission (2019a), *Effort Sharing: Member States' Emission Targets.* Brussels: European Commission. https://ec.europa.eu/clima/eu-action/effort-sharing-member-states-emission-targets_en (Accessed 3 January 2022).

European Commission (2019b). The European Green Deal sets out how to make Europe the first climate neutral continent by 2050, boosting the economy, improving peoples' health and quality of life, caring for nature and leaving no one behind. *European Commission Press Release*, 11 December. Brussels: European Commission. https://ec.europa.eu/commiss ion/presscorner/detail/en/ip_19_6691 (Accessed 10 February 2022).

Evans, J. and Terazono, E. (2021) Peas add froth to the milk market. *Financial Times* 8/9 May, p. 9. www.ft.com/content/da70e996-a70b-484d-b3e6-ea8229253fc4 (Accessed 3 January 2022).

Falconer, K. and Ward, N. (2000) Using modulation to green the CAP: the UK case. *Land Use Policy* 17, 269–77. doi:10.1016/S0264-8377(00)00036-3

Farrar, J. (2021) *Spike: The Virus vs the People*. London: Profile Books.

Federal Ministry for the Environment, Nature Conservation, Building and Nuclear Safety (2016) *Climate Action Plan 2050: Principles and Goals of the German Government's Climate Policy*. Berlin: BMUB. www.bmu.de/fileadmin/Daten_BMU/Pools/Broschueren/ klimaschutzplan_2050_en_bf.pdf (Accessed 3 January 2022).

Fennell, R. (1997) *The Common Agricultural Policy: Continuity and Change*. Oxford: Clarendon Press.

Finch, T., Gillings, S., Massimino, D., Brereton, T., Redhead, J., Pywell R., Field, R., Balmford, A., Green, R. and Peach, W. (2021) *Assessing the Utility of Land Sharing and Land Sparing for Birds, Butterflies and Ecosystem Services in Lowland England*. Final Report to Natural England. http://publications.naturalengland.org.uk/publication/6157279470813184 (Accessed 3 January 2022).

Fleming, J. (2005) *Historical Perspectives on Climate Change*. Oxford: Oxford University Press.

Food and Agriculture Organisation (2021) *The Share of Agri-food Systems in Total Greenhouse Gas Emissions – Global, Regional and Country Trends 1990–2019*. Rome: FAO. www.fao. org/3/cb7514en/cb7514en.pdf (Accessed 3 January 2022).

Food, Farming and Countryside Commission (2019) *Our Future in the Land*. London: Royal Society for the Arts. https://ffcc.co.uk/library/our-future-in-the-land (Accessed 3 January 2022).

Foresight Land Use Futures Project (2010) *Land Use Futures: Making the Most of Land in the 21st Century*. Final Project Report. London: Government Office for Science. www.gov. uk/government/publications/land-use-futures-making-the-most-of-land-in-the-21st-century (Accessed 3 January 2022).

Forest Research (2021) *Forestry Statistics 2021*. Edinburgh: Forest Research. www. forestresearch.gov.uk/tools-and-resources/statistics/forestry-statistics/ (Accessed 3 January 2022).

Foucault, M. (1991) Governmentality, pp. 87–104 in Burchell, G., Gordon C. and Miller, P. (eds.) *The Foucault Effect*. London: Harvester Wheatsheaf.

Freidberg, S. (2013) Calculating sustainability in supply chain capitalism. *Economy and Society* 42, 571–96. doi:10.1080/03085147.2012.760349

Fridahl, M. and Lehtveer, M. (2018) Bioenergy with carbon capture and storage (BECCS): global potential, investment preferences, and deployment barriers. *Energy Research & Social Science* 42, 155–65. doi:10.1016/j.erss.2018.03.019

Friedman, M. (1982) *Capitalism and Freedom*. Chicago, IL: University of Chicago Press.

Friends of the Earth (1991) *Off the Treadmill: A Way Forward for Farmers and the Countryside*. London: Friends of the Earth.

Fuss, S., Canadell, J. G., Peters, G. P., Tavoni, M., Andrew, R. M., Ciais, P., … Yamagata, Y. (2014). Commentary: Betting on negative emissions. *Nature Climate Change* 4 (10), 850–3. doi:10.1038/nclimate2392

Fuss, S., Lamb, W., Callaghan, M., Hilaire, J., Creutzig, F., Amann, T., Beringer, T., de Oliveiora Garcia, W., Hartmann, J., Khanna, T. … Minx, J. (2018) Negative emissions – part 2: Costs, potentials and side effects. *Environmental Research Letters* 13, 063002. doi:10.1088/1748-9326/aabf9f/meta

Gabrys, J. (2016) *Program Earth: Environmental Sensing Technology and the Making of a Computational Planet*. Minneapolis: University of Minnesota Press.

García-Freites, S., Gough, C. and Röder, M. (2021) The greenhouse gas removal potential of bioenergy with carbon capture and storage (BECCS) to support the UK's net-zero emission target. *Biomass and Bioenergy* 151. doi:10.1016/j.biombioe.2021.106164

Garton Grimwood, G. (2021) *Planning for the Future: Planning Policy Changes in England in 2020 and Future Reforms*. House of Commons Library Briefing Paper No 8981. London: House of Commons. https://commonslibrary.parliament.uk/research-briefings/cbp-8981/ (Accessed 3 January 2022).

Gasson, R. and Errington, A. (1993) *The Farm Family Business*. Wallingford: CAB International.

Gates, S. and Donald, P. (2000) Local extinction of farmland birds and the prediction of further loss. *Journal of Applied Ecology* 37, 806–20. www.jstor.org/stable/2655927

Gavin, N. and Marshall, T. (2011) Mediated climate change in Britain: scepticism on the web and on television around Copenhagen. *Global Environmental Change* 21, 1035–44. doi:10.1016/j.gloenvcha.2011.03.007

Geden, O., Scott, V. and Palmer, J. (2018). Integrating carbon dioxide removal into EU climate policy: prospects for a paradigm shift. *WIREs Climate Change* 9(4), e521. doi:10.1002/wcc.521

Geels, F., Sovacool, B., Schwanen, T. and Sorrell, S. (2017) Sociotechnical transitions for deep carbonization. *Science* 357(6357), 1242–4 doi:10.1126/science.aao3760

Giddens, A. (2009) *The Politics of Climate Change*. Cambridge: Polity.

Goldenberg, N. (1987) *Thought for Food: A Study of the Development of the Food Division, Marks and Spencer*. Orpington: Food Trade Press.

Goodman, D. and Redclift, M. (1991) *Refashioning Nature: Food, Ecology and Culture*. London: Routledge.

Gore, A. (1992) *Earth in the Balance: Ecology and the Human Spirit*. New York: Plume.

Gough, C., Garcia-Freites, S., Jones, C., Mander, S., Moore, B., Pereira, C., Röder, M., Vaughan, N. and Welfle, A. (2018) Challenges to the use of BECCS as a keystone technology in pursuit of 1.5°C. *Global Sustainability* 1, e5, 1–9. doi:10.1017/sus.2018.3

Goulson, D. (2021) *Silent Earth: Averting the Insect Apocalypse*. London: Jonathan Cape.

Green, R., Cornell, S., Scharlemann, J. and Balmford, A. (2005) Farming and the fate of wild nature. *Science* 307, 550–5. doi:10.1126/science.1106049

Greig-Smith, P., Frampton, G. and Hardy, T. (eds.) (1992) *Pesticides, Cereal Farming and the Environment: The Boxworth Project*. London: HMSO.

Hackett, E., Amsterdamska, O., Lynch, M. and Wajcman, J. (eds.) (2008) *The Handbook of Science and Technology Studies*. Third Edition. Cambridge, MA: MIT Press.

Hagman, W., Andersson, D., Västfjäll, D. and Tinghög, G. (2015). Public views on policies involving nudges. *Review of Philosophy and Psychology* 6, 439–53. doi:10.1007/s13164-015-0263-2

Halpern, D. (2015) *Inside the Nudge Unit: How Small Changes Can Make a Difference*. London: Penguin.

Halpern, D., Bates, C., Mulgan, G., Aldridge, S., Beales, G. and Heathfield, A. (2004) *Personal Responsibility and Changing Behaviour: The State of Knowledge and Its Implications for Public Policy*. London: Cabinet Office Strategy Unit. https://webarchive.nationalarchives.gov.uk/ukgwa/+/www.cabinetoffice.gov.uk/media/cabinetoffice/strategy/assets/pr2.pdf (Accessed 3 January 2022).

Hamby, A. (2004) *For the Survival of Democracy: Franklin Roosevelt and the World Crisis of the 1930s*. New York: Free Press.

Hansson, S. O. (2020) Social constructionism and climate science denial. *European Journal for Philosophy of Science* 10, 37. doi:10.1007/s13194-020-00305-w

Hargreaves, T. (2011) Practice-ing behaviour change: applying social practice theory to pro-environmental behaviour change. *Journal of Consumer Culture* 11, 79–99. doi:10.1177/1469540510390500

Harison, R. (1964) *Animal Machines: The New Factory Farming Industry*. London: Vincent Stuart.

Harvey, D. (2003) The fetish of technology: causes and consequences. *Macalester International* 13, Article 7, 2–30.

Harvey, D. (2005) *A Brief History of Neoliberalism*. Oxford: Oxford University Press.

Harvey, D. (2009) *Cosmopolitanism and the Geographies of Freedom*. New York: Columbia University Press.

Harvey, D. R. (1996) The role of markets in the rural economy, pp. 19–39 in P. Allanson and M. Whitby (eds.) *The Rural Economy and the British Countryside*. London: Earthscan.

Harwatt, H. and Hayek, M. (2019) *Eating Away at Climate Change with Negative Emissions: Repurposing UK Agricultural Land to Meet Climate Goals*. Harvard Law School. https://animal.law.harvard.edu/wp-content/uploads/Eating-Away-at-Climate-Change-with-Negative-Emissions%E2%80%93%E2%80%93Harwatt-Hayek.pdf (Accessed 3 January 2022).

Hasnain, S., Ingram, J. and Zurek, M. (2020) *Mapping the UK Food System – A Report for the UKRI Transforming UK Food Systems Programme*. Oxford: Environmental Change Institute, University of Oxford. www.eci.ox.ac.uk/research/food/downloads/Mapping-the-UK-food-system-digital.pdf (Accessed 3 January 2022).

Hayward, T. (2021) Lab-grown meat isn't about sustainability, it's big business. *Financial Times* 18 September, p. 12. www.ft.com/content/f22b4ace-5276-45fa-9810-4a50427e6b7b (Accessed 3 January 2022).

Helm, D. (2017) Agriculture after Brexit. *Oxford Review of Economic Policy* 33, S124–33. doi:10.1093/oxrep/grx010

Helm, D. (2020) *Green and Prosperous Land: A Blueprint for Rescuing the British Countryside*. London: William Collins.

Helm, D. (2021) *Net Zero: How We Stop Causing Climate Change*. London: William Collins.

Herrero, M., Thornton, P., Mason-D'Croz, D., Palmer, J., Bodirsky, B., Pradhan, P., Barrett, C., Bentoin, T., Hall, A., Pikaar, I., Bogard, J., Bonnett, G., Bryan, B., Campbell, B., Christensen, S., Clark, M., Fanzo, J., Godde, C., Jarvis, A., Loboguerrero, A., Mathys, A., McIntyre, L., Naylor, R., Nelson, R., Oberstein, M., Paroidi, A., Popp, A., Ricketss, K., Smith, P., Valin, H., Vermeulen, S., Vervoort, J., van Wijk, M., van Zanten, H., west, P., Wood, S. and Rockström, J. (2021). Articulating the effect of food systems innovation on the Sustainable Development Goals. *The Lancet Planetary Health* 5(1), e50–62. doi.org/10.1016/ S2542-5196(20)30277-1

Hetherington, P. (2021) *Land Renewed: Reworking the Countryside*. Bristol: Bristol University Press.

Hodgson, C. (2021) World likely to be 1.5C warmer by 2040, UN's science panel warns. *Financial Times* 9th August, p. 1. www.ft.com/content/9a11b08c-4fb3-49ec-8939-9d853745bfce (Accessed 3 January 2022).

Hoek, A., Pearson, D., James, S., Lawrence, M. and Friel, S. (2017). Shrinking the food-print: a qualitative study into consumer perceptions, experiences and attitudes towards healthy and environmentally friendly food behaviours. *Appetite* 108, 117–31. doi:10.1016/j.appet.2016.09.030

Holmes, C. (1988) Science and the farmer: the development of the Agricultural Advisory Service in England and Wales, 1900–1939. *Agricultural History Review* 36, 77–86.

Honegger, M. and Reiner, D. (2018) The political economy of negative emissions technologies: consequences for international policy design. *Climate Policy* 18, 306–21. doi:10.1080/14693062.2017.1413322

Hook, L. (2021) Relief and frustration as climate deal is done. *Financial Times* 15 November, p. 2. www.ft.com/content/cdee515a-40d7-4605-a25c-c49401327264 (Accessed 3 January 2022).

House of Commons Agriculture Committee (1990) *Bovine Spongiform Encephalopathy*. London: HMSO.

House of Commons Environment Committee (1987) *Pollution of Rivers and Estuaries*. Fourth Report, Session 1921–22. London: HMSO.

House of Commons Environment, Food and Rural Affairs Committee (2008) *Badgers and Cattle TB: The Final Report of the Independent Scientific Group on Cattle TB*. London: The Stationary Office. https://publications.parliament.uk/pa/cm200708/cmselect/cmenvfru/130/130i.pdf (Accessed 3 January 2022).

House of Commons Environment, Food and Rural Affairs Committee (2021) *Environmental Land Management and the Agricultural Transition*. Second Report, Session 2021–22. London: House of Commons. https://committees.parliament.uk/publications/7663/documents/79987/default/ (Accessed 3 January 2022).

House of Commons Environmental Audit Committee (2022) *Water Quality in Rivers*. Third Report, Session 1986–87. London: The Stationary Office. https://committees.parliament.uk/publications/8460/documents/85659/default/ (Accessed 13 January 2022).

House of Commons Library (2015) *Paris Climate Change Conference*. House of Commons Library Papers CPB 7393. London: House of Commons.

House of Lords Science and Technology Committee (2011) *Behaviour Change*. Session 2010–12. London: Stationary Office. https://publications.parliament.uk/pa/ld201012/ldselect/ldsctech/179/179.pdf (Accessed 3 January 2022).

House of Lords Select Committee on the European Communities (1990) *The Future of Rural Society*. HL Paper 80–I. London: Stationery Office.

Howard, P. (2021) *Concentration and Power in the Food System: Who Controls What We Eat?* Revised Edition. London: Bloomsbury Academic.

Hughes, T. (1983) *Networks of Power: Electrification in Western Society, 1880–1930*. Baltimore, MD: Johns Hopkins University Press.

Hughes, T. (1987) The evolution of large technological systems, pp. 51–82 in W. Bijker, T. Hughes and T. Pinch (eds.) *The Social Construction of Technological Systems: New Directions in the Sociology and History of Technology*. London: MIT Press.

Hughes, T. (1994) Technological momentum, pp. 101–14 in M. Roe Smith and L. Marx (eds.) *Does Technology Drive History? The Dilemma of Technological Determinism*. Cambridge, MA: MIT Press.

Hulme, M. (2009) *Why We Disagree About Climate Change: Understanding Controversy, Inaction and Opportunity*. Cambridge: Cambridge University Press.

Hulme, M. (2010) Cosmopolitan climates: hybridity, foresight and meaning. *Theory, Culture and Society* 27, 267–76. doi:10.1177/0263276409358730

Hulme, M. (2014) *Can Science Fix Climate Change?* Cambridge: Polity Press.

Ilbery, B. and Bowler, I. (1998) From agricultural productivism to post-productivism, pp. 57–84 in B. Ilbery (ed.) *The Geography of Rural Change*. Harlow: Longman.

Independent Commission on International Development Issues (1980) *North-South: A Programme for Survival*. Basingstoke: Macmillan.

Innovation for Agriculture (2022) *Reducing Greenhouse Gas Emissions at Farm Level.* Stoneleigh: Innovation for Agriculture. www.innovationforagriculture.org.uk/news-article/Go-to-guide%20for%20reducing%20on%20farm%20GHG%20emissions

Institute for Government (2020) *Net Zero: How Government Can Meet Its Climate Change Target.* London: Institute for Government. www.instituteforgovernment.org.uk/publications/net-zero (Accessed 3 January 2022).

Intergovernmental Panel on Climate Change (2019) *Special Report on Climate Change and Land.* Geneva: IPCC. www.ipcc.ch/srccl/ (Accessed 3 January 2022).

Intergovernmental Panel on Climate Change (2020) *Climate Change and Land: Summary for Policymakers.* Geneva: IPCC. www.ipcc.ch/srccl/chapter/summary-for-policymakers/ (Accessed 3 January 2022).

Intergovernmental Panel on Climate Change (2021) Summary for policymakers, in V. Masson-Delmotte, P. Zhai, A. Pirani, S. L. Connors, C. Péan, S. Berger, N. Caud, Y. Chen, L. Goldfarb, M. I. Gomis, M. Huang, K. Leitzell, E. Lonnoy, J. B. R. Matthews, T. K. Maycock, T. Waterfield, O. Yelekçi, R. Yu and B. Zhou (eds.) *Climate Change 2021: The Physical Science Basis. Contribution of Working Group I to the Sixth Assessment Report of the Intergovernmental Panel on Climate Change.* Cambridge University Press. www.ipcc.ch/report/sixth-assessment-report-working-group-i/ (Accessed 3 January 2022).

International Panel of Experts on Sustainable Food Systems and ETC Group (2021) *A Long Food Movement: Transforming Food Systems by 2045.* Brussels: IPES-Food. www.ipes-food.org/pages/LongFoodMovement (Accessed 11 January 2022).

Ivers, C. (2022) Bereft without Brexit, the Tories have a new bone to fight over: net zero. *The Sunday Times* 16 January, p. 7. www.thetimes.co.uk/article/bereft-without-brexit-the-tories-have-a-new-bone-to-fight-over-net-zero-j9dv0szq7 (Accessed 19 January 2022).

Jackson, P. and Ward, N. (2008). Connections and responsibilities: the moral geographies of sugar, pp. 235–52 in A. Nützenadel and F. Trentmann (eds.) *Food and Globalisation.* Oxford: Berg.

Jackson, P., Russell, P. and Ward, N. (2007) The appropriation of "alternative" discourses by "mainstream" food retailers, pp. 309–30 in D. Maye, L. Holloway and M. Kneafsey (eds.) *Alternative Food Geographies: Representation and Practice.* Amsterdam: Elsevier.

Jackson, P., Ward, N. and Russell, P. (2009) Moral economies of food and geographies of responsibility. *Transactions of the Institute of British Geographers* 34, 12–24. doi:10.1111/j.1475-5661.2008.00330.x

Jackson, P., Ward, N. and Russell, P. (2010) Manufacturing meaning along the chicken supply chain, pp. 163–87 in D. Goodman, M. Goodman and M. Redclift (eds.) *Consuming Space: Placing Consumption in Perspective.* Aldershot: Ashgate.

Jackson, P., Russell, P. and Ward, N. (2011) Brands in the making: a life history approach, pp. 59–74 in A. Pike (ed.) *Brands and Branding Geographies.* Cheltenham: Edward Elgar.

Jackson, P., Brembeck, H., Everts, J., Fuentes, M., Halker, B., Hertz, F.D., Meah, A., Viehoff, V. and Wenzl, C. (2018) *Reframing Convenience Food.* Cham: Springer & Palgrave Macmillan.

Jayasinghe, K., Jayasinghe, T., Wijethilake, C. and Adhika, P. (2021) Biopolitics and calculative technologies in Covid-19 governance: reflections from England. *International Journal of Health Policy and Management* 10, 1–9. doi:10.34172/IJHPM.2021.134

Johnson, B. (2003) *Lend Me Your Ears: The Essential Boris Johnson.* London: Harper Collins.

Johnson, B. (2021) Prime Minister's speech at the Global Investment Summit, 19th October. www.gov.uk/government/speeches/pm-speech-at-the-global-investment-summit-19-october-2021 (Accessed 3 January 2022).

Jones, R., Pykett, J. and Whitehead, M. (2013) *Changing Behaviours: On the Rise of the Psychological State.* Cheltenham: Edward Elgar.

Kahneman, D. (2011) *Thinking Fast and Slow.* London: Allen Lane.

Kahnerman, D., Slavic, P. and Tversky, A. (eds.) (1982) *Judgement under Uncertainty: Heuristics and Biases*. Cambridge: Cambridge University Press.

Keenor, S., Rodrigues, A., Mao, L., Latawiec, A., Harwood, A. and Reid, B. (2021) Capturing a soil carbon economy. *Royal Society Open Science* 8, 202305. doi:10.1098/rsos.202305

Keller, E. (2015) *Greenhouse Gas Management in Agri-food Supply Chains: A Focus at the Farm Level*. PhD thesis. University of Surrey, Centre for Environmental Strategy.

Keller, E. (2021) Decarbonisation in the food and drink sector – implementing greener processes, supporting innovation in technology, and priorities for investment, presentation to the Westminster Food & Nutrition Forum, *Net-Zero, Climate Change and the Food, Drink and Agriculture Sector* conference, 23 June 2021.

Kenton. M., McCarthy, M., Jevrejeva, S., Matthews, A., Sparks, T. and Garforth, J. (2021) State of the UK climate 2020. *International Journal of Climatology* 41, 1–76. doi:10.1002/joc.7285

Kinnersley, D. (1994) *Coming Clean: The Politics of Water and the Environment*. London: Penguin

Kinney, M., Weston, Z. and Bauman, J. (2019) *Plant-Based Meat Manufacturing by Extrusion*. Washington, DC: The Good Food Institute. https://gfi.org/wp-content/uploads/2021/01/Plant-Based-Meat-Manufacturing-Guide-_GFI.pdf (Accessed 3 January 2022).

Klein. N. (2007) *The Shock Doctrine*. London: Penguin Allen Lane.

Klimaatakkoord (2018), *Proposal for key points of the Climate Agreement*. www.klimaatakkoord.nl/documenten/publicaties/2018/09/19/proposal-for-key-points-ofthe-climate-agreement (Accessed 11 January 2022).

Kmietowicz, E. and Thillainathan, I. (2020) *The Smart Agriculture Inventory: Technical Annex*. London: Climate Change Committee. www.theccc.org.uk/wp-content/uploads/2018/08/PR18-Chapter-6-Annex-The-Smart-Agriculture-Inventory.pdf (Accessed 19 January 2022).

Köhler, J., Geels, F., Kern, F., Markard, J., Onsongo, E., Wieczorek, A., Alkemade, F., Avelino, F., Bergek, A., Boons, F., Fünsfschilling, L., Hess, D., Holtz, G., Hyysalo, S., Jenkins, K., Kivimaa, P., Martiskainene, M., McMeekin, A., Mühlemeier, M., Nykvist, B., Pel, B., Raven, R., Rohracher, H., Sandén, B., Schot, J., Sovacool, B., Turnheim, B., Welsh, D and Wells, P. (2019) An agenda for sustainability transitions research: State of the art and future directions. *Environmental Innovation and Societal Transitions* 31, 1–32. doi:10.1016/j.eist.2019.01.004

Kuhn, T. (1962) *The Structure of Scientific Revolutions*. Chicago: University of Chicago Press (and Third Edition, 1996).

Lahsen, M. (1999) The detection and attribution of conspiracies: the controversy over Chapter 8, pp. 111–36 in G. Marcus (ed.) *Paranoia Within Reason: A Casebook on Conspiracy as Explanation*. Chicago, IL: Chicago University Press.

Lane, S., Odoni, N., Whatmore, S., Landström, C., Ward, N. and Bradley, S. (2011) Doing flood risk science differently: an experiment in radical scientific method. *Transactions of the Institute of British Geographers* 36, 15–36. doi:/10.1111/j.1475-5661.2010.00410.x

Lang, T. (2020) *Feeding Britain: Our Food Problems and How to Fix Them*. London: Pelican.

Latour, B. (1987) *Science in Action: How to Follow Scientists and Engineers Through Society*. Milton Keynes: Open University Press.

Latour, B. (1991) Technology is society made durable, pp. 103–31 in J. Law (ed.) *A Sociology of Monsters: Essays on Power, Technology and Domination*. London: Routledge.

Latour, B. (2018) *Down to Earth: Politics in the New Climate Regime*. Cambridge: Polity Press.

Latour, B. (2021) *After Lockdown: A Metamorphosis*. Cambridge: Polity Press.

Lear, L. (1997) *Rachel Carson: The Life of the Author of Silent Spring*. London: Penguin.

Lee, H. and Sumner, D. (2018), Dependence on policy revenue poses risks for investments in dairy digesters. *California Agriculture* 72, 226–35. doi:10.3733/ca.2018a0037

Le Quéré, C., Andres, R. J., Boden, T., Conway, T., Houghton, R., House, J., Marland, G., Peters, G., van der Werf, G., Ahlström, A., Andrew, R., Bopp, L., Canadell, J., Cias, P., Doney, S., Enright, C., Friedlingstein, P., Huntingford, C., Jain, A., Jourdain, C., Kato, E., Keeling, R., Kelin Goldewijk, K., Levis, S., Levy, P., Lomas, M., Poulter, B., Raupach, M., Schwinger, J., Sitch, S., Stocker, B., Viovy, N., Zaehle, S. and Zeng, N. (2013) The global carbon budget 1959–2011. *Earth Systems Science Data* 5, 165–85. doi:10.5194/essd-5-165-2013

Lobley, M., Winter, M. and Wheeler, R. (2019) *The Changing World of Farming in Brexit UK.* London: Routledge.

Loconto, A., Desquilbet, M., Moreau, T., Couvet, D. and Dorin, B. (2020) The land sparing – land sharing controversy: tracing the politics of knowledge. *Land Use Policy* 96, 103610. doi:10.1016/j.landusepol.2018.09.014

Londakova, K., Park, T., Reynolds, J. and Wodak, S. (2021) *Net Zero: Principles for Successful Behaviour Change Initiatives.* BEIS Research Paper No. 2021/063. London: Department for Business, Energy and Industrial Strategy.

Lóránt, A. and Allen, B. (2019) *Net Zero Agriculture in 2050: How to Get There.* London: Institute for European Environmental Policy. https://ieep.eu/publications/net-zero-agriculture-in-2050-how-to-get-there (Accessed 3 January 2022).

Lord, T. (2021) *Covid-19 and Climate Change: How to Apply the Lessons of the Pandemic to the Climate Emergency.* London: Tony Blair Institute for Global Change, 7 April. https://institute.global/policy/covid-19-and-climate-change-how-apply-lessons-pandemic-climate-emergency (Accessed 3 January 2022).

Lorenzoni, I. and Benson, D. (2014) Radical institutional change in environmental governance: explaining the origins of the UK Climate Change Act 2008 through discursive and streams perspectives. *Global Environmental Change* 29, 10–21. doi:10.1016/j.gloenvcha.2014.07.011

Lövebrand, E. and Stripple, J. (2011) Making climate change governable: accounting for carbon as sinks, credits and personal budgets. *Critical Policy Studies* 5, 187–200.

Low, S. and Boettcher, M. (2020) Delaying decarbonization: climate governmentalities and sociotechnical strategies from Copenhagen to Paris. *Earth Systems Governance* 5, 100073. doi:10.1016/j.esg.2020.100073

Lowe, P. (1992) Industrial agriculture and environmental regulation: a new agenda for rural sociology. *Sociologia Ruralis* 32, 4–10. doi:10.1111/j.1467-9523.1992.tb00915.x

Lowe, P. and Goyder, J. (1983) *Environmental Groups in Politics.* London: George Allen & Unwin.

Lowe, P. and Phillipson J. (2009) Barriers to research collaboration across disciplines: scientific paradigms and institutional practices. *Environment and Planning A* 41, 1171–84 doi:10.1068/a4175

Lowe, P. and Ward, N. (1994) Environmental policy and regulation, pp. 85–9 in M. Whitby and N. Ward (eds.) *The UK Strategy for Sustainable Agriculture: A Critical Analysis.* CRE Report. Newcastle upon Tyne: University of Newcastle.

Lowe, P. and Ward, S. (eds.) (1998) *British Environmental Policy and Europe: Politics and Policy in Transition.* London: Routledge.

Lowe, P., Cox, G., MacEwen, M., O'Riordan, T. and Winter, M. (1986) *Countryside Conflicts: The Politics of Farming, Forestry and Conservation.* Aldershot: Gower.

Lowe, P., Ward, N. and Munton, R. (1992) Social analysis of land use change: the role of the farmer, pp. 42–51 in M. Whitby (ed.) *Land Use Change: Causes and Consequences.* London: HMSO.

Lowe, P., Clark, J., Seymour, S. and Ward, N. (1997) *Moralising the Environment: Countryside Change, Farming and Pollution.* London: Routledge.

Lowe, P., Falconer, K., Hodge, I., Moxey, A., Ward, N. and Whitby, M. (1999) *Integrating the Environment into CAP Reform*. CRE Research Report. Newcastle upon Tyne: Newcastle University.

Lowe, P., Buller, H. and Ward, N. (2002) Setting the next agenda? British and French approaches to the second pillar of the Common Agricultural Policy. *Journal of Rural Studies* 18, 1–17. doi:10.1016/S0743-0167(01)00025-0

MacKenzie, D. and Wajcman, J. (eds.) (1985) *The Social Shaping of Technology*. Milton Keynes: Open University Press.

MacLeod, M. *et al.* (2010) Developing greenhouse gas marginal abatement cost curves for agricultural emissions from crops and soils in the UK. *Agricultural Systems* 103, 198–209. doi:10.1016/j.agsy.2010.01.002

Maddison, D. and Pearce, D. (1995) The UK and global warming policy, pp. 123–43 in T. Gray (ed.) *UK Environmental Policy in the 1990s*. Basingstoke: Macmillan.

Maloney, W. and Richardson, J. (1995) *Managing Policy Change in Britain: The Politics of Water*. Edinburgh: Edinburgh University Press.

Mann, M. (2021) *The New Climate War: The Fight to Take Back Our Planet*. London: Scribe.

Marks, H. and Britton, D. (1989) *A Hundred Years of British Food and Farming – A Statistical Survey*. London: Taylor and Francis.

Marsden, T. and Munton, R. (1991) The farmed landscape and the occupancy change process. *Environment and Planning A* 23, 663–76. doi:10.1068/a230663

Marsden, T., Murdoch, J., Lowe, P., Munton, R. and Flynn, A. (1993) *Constructing the Countryside*. London: University College London Press.

Masika, R. (ed.) (2002) *Gender, Development and Climate Change*. Oxford: Oxfam.

Mazzucato, M. (2021) *Mission Economy: A Moonshot Guide to Changing Capitalism*. London: Allen Lane.

McCann, N. (1989) *The Story of the National Agricultural Advisory Service: A Mainspring of Agricultural Revival, 1946–1971*. Ely: Providence Press.

McClaren, D., Willis, R., Szerszynski, B., Tyfield, D. and Markussen, N. (2021) Attractions of delay: using deliberative engagement to investigate the political and strategic impacts of greenhouse gas removal technologies. *Environment and Planning E: Nature and Space* (Online first). doi:10.1177/25148486211066238

Meadows, D., Meadows, D., Randers, J. and Behrens, W. (1972) *The Limits to Growth. A Report for the Club of Rome's Project on the Predicament of Mankind*. London: Pan Books.

Meat and Livestock Australia (2020) *The Australian Red Meat Industry's Carbon Neutral by 2030 Roadmap*. Sydney: Meat and Livestock Australia. www.mla.com.au/globalassets/mla-corporate/research-and-development/program-areas/livestock-production/mla-cn30-roadmap_031221.pdf (Accessed 13 January 2022).

Mellon, J. (2020) *Moo's Law^{TM}: An Investor's Guide to the New Agrarian Revolution*. Sudbury: Fruitful Publications.

Merk, C., Pönitzsch, G. and Rehdanz, K. (2019). Do climate engineering experts display moral-hazard behaviour? *Climate Policy* 19(2), 231–43. doi:10.1080/14693062.2018.1494534

Met Office (2019) *UKCP18 Science Overview Executive Summary*. Exeter: Met Office. www.metoffice.gov.uk/binaries/content/assets/metofficegovuk/pdf/research/ukcp/ukcp18-overview-summary.pdf (Accessed 3 January 2022).

Millard, R. (2021) City investors planning to turn reforestation into a growth industry. *The Sunday Telegraph*, 17 October, Business Section, p. 8.

Miller, A. (1987) *Timebends: A Life*. London: Bloomsbury.

Miller, P. and Rose, N. (2008) *Governing the Present*. Cambridge: Polity Press.

Ministry of Agriculture, Fisheries and Food (1975) *Food from Our Own Resources*. Cmnd.6020. London: HMSO.

Ministry of Agriculture, Fisheries and Food (1979) *Farming and the Nation.* Cmnd.7458. London: HMSO.

Minx, J., Lamb, W., Callaghan, M., Fuss, S., Hilaire, J., Creutzig, F., Amann, T., Beringer, T., Garcia, W., Hartmann, J., Khanna, T., Lenzi, D., Luderer, G., Nemet, G., Rogelj, J., Smith, P., Vicente, J., Wilcox, J. and Dominguez, M.. (2018) Negative emissions – part 1: research landscape and synthesis. *Environmental Research Letters* 13, 063001. doi:10.1088/1748-9326/aabf9b

Moore, C. (2021) Eating up your greens is not very much to do with saving the planet. *Daily Telegraph*, 17 July, p. 18. www.telegraph.co.uk/news/2021/07/16/eating-greens-not-much-do-saving-planet/ (Accessed 3 January 2022).

Morelli, C. (1998) Constructing a balance between price and non-price competition in British multiple food retailing 1954–64. *Business History* 40 (2), 45–61. doi:10.1080/00076799800000168

Morgan, K. (2010) Local and green, global and fair: the ethical foodscape and the politics of care. *Environment and Planning A* 42, 1852–67. doi:10.1068/a42364

Morgan, K., Marsden, T. and Murdoch, J. (2006) *Worlds of Food: Place, Power, and Provenance in the Food Chain.* Oxford: Oxford University Press.

MORI (1987) *Farmers Attitudes Towards Nature Conservation.* A report on qualitative research prepared for the NCC. London: MORI.

Moser, S. and Kleinhückelkotten, S. (2018). Good intents, but low impacts: diverging importance of motivational and socioeconomic determinants explaining pro-environmental behaviour, energy use, and carbon footprint. *Environment and Behaviour*, 50, 626–56. doi:10.1177/0013916517710685

Moss, R. (2016) We now spend more time watching other people cook than doing it ourselves. *Huffington Post* 22 September. www.huffingtonpost.co.uk/entry/we-spend-more-time-watching-food-shows-than-cookin_uk_57e3d141e4b004d4d86237fd (Accessed 3 January 2022).

Mouton, E. (1872) The end of the world, pp. 1–9 in D. Ford (ed.) *Grave Predictions: Tales of Mankind's Post-apocalyptic, Dystopian and Disastrous Destiny.* New York: Dover Publications.

Munton, R. and Marsden, T. (1991) Occupancy change and the farmed landscape: an analysis of farm-level trends, 1970–85. *Environment and Planning A* 23, 499–510. doi:10.1068/a230499

Murcott, A. (ed.) (1998) *The Nation's Diet: The Social Science of Food Choice.* London: Longman.

Murdoch, J. (2001) Ecologising sociology: actor-network theory, co-construction and the problem of human exemptionalism. *Sociology* 35, 111–33. doi:10.1177/0038038501035001008

Murdoch, J. (2006) *Post-structuralist Geography.* London: Sage.

Murdoch, J. and Ward, N. (1997) Governmentality and territoriality: the statistical manufacture of Britain's "national farm". *Political Geography* 16, 307–24. doi:10.1016/S0962-6298(96)00007-8

Murray, K. (1955) *Agriculture – History of the Second World War Series.* London: HMSO.

National Academy of Sciences, National Academy of Engineering and Institute of Medicine (1992) *Policy Implications of Greenhouse Warming: Mitigation, Adaptation, and the Science Base.* Washington, DC: The National Academies Press. www.nap.edu/catalog/1605/policy-implications-of-greenhouse-warming-mitigation-adaptation-and-the-science (Accessed 3 January 2022).

National Atmospheric and Oceanographic Administration (2021) It's official: July was the Earth's hottest month on record. *News Release*, 13th August. US Department of Commerce, National Atmospheric and Oceanographic Administration. www.noaa.gov/news/its-official-july-2021-was-earths-hottest-month-on-record (Accessed 3 January 2022).

National Farmers' Union (2019a) *Achieving Net Zero: Farming's 2040 Goal*. London: NFU. www.nfuonline.com/archive?treeid=138313 (Accessed 3 January 2022).

National Farmers' Union (2019b) *Memorandum of Evidence to the House of Commons Environment, Food and Rural Affairs Committee Inquiry into Agriculture – Achieving Net Zero Emissions*. https://data.parliament.uk/writtenevidence/committeeevidence.svc/evidencedocument/environment-food-and-rural-affairs-committee/agriculture-achieving-netzero-emissions/written/ (Accessed May 2021).

National Farmers' Union (2021) Australia trade deal: five questions the UK government must answer. *NFU Press Release*, 15 June. www.nfuonline.com/archive?treeid=150844 (Accessed 3 January 2022).

National Food Strategy (2020) *National Food Strategy – Part One*. London: National Food Strategy. www.nationalfoodstrategy.org/ (Accessed 3 January 2022).

National Food Strategy (2021) *National Food Strategy – Independent Review: The Plan*. London: National Food Strategy. www.nationalfoodstrategy.org/ (Accessed 3 January 2022).

National Health Service (2020) *Statistics on Obesity, Physical Activity and Diet, England*. Leeds: NHS Digital. https://digital.nhs.uk/data-and-information/publications/statistical/statistics-on-obesity-physical-activity-and-diet (Accessed 3 January 2022).

National Parks England (2019) *Memorandum of Evidence to the House of Commons Environment, Food and Rural Affairs Committee Inquiry into Agriculture: Achieving Net Zero Emissions*. https://data.parliament.uk/writtenevidence/committeeevidence.svc/evidencedocument/environment-food-and-rural-affairs-committee/agriculture-achieving-netzero-emissions/written/ (Accessed May 2021).

National Rivers Authority (1992) *The Influence of Agriculture on the Quality of Natural Waters in England and Wales*. Bristol: National Rivers Authority.

Natural England (2019) *Memorandum of Evidence to the House of Commons Environment, Food and Rural Affairs Committee Inquiry into Agriculture: Achieving Net Zero Emissions*. https://data.parliament.uk/writtenevidence/committeeevidence.svc/evidencedocument/environment-food-and-rural-affairs-committee/agriculture-achieving-netzero-emissions/written/ (Accessed May 2021).

Nature Conservancy Council (1984) *Nature Conservation in Great Britain*. London: Nature Conservancy Council.

Nelson, R. and Winter, S. (1982) *An Evolutionary Theory of Economic Change*. Cambridge, MA: Harvard University Press.

Nemet, G., Callaghan, M., Creutzig, F., Fuss, S., Hartmann, J., Hilaire, J., Lamb, W., Rogers, S. and Smith, P. (2018) Negative emissions – part 3: innovation and upscaling. *Environmental Research Letters* 13, 063003. doi:10.1088/1748-9326/aabff4

New Zealand Ministry for the Environment (2019) *Climate Change Response (Zero Carbon) Amendment Bill: Summary*. https://environment.govt.nz/publications/proposed-climate-change-bill/ (Accessed 3 January 2022).

Nisbet, E., Manning, R., Dlugokencky, E., Fisher, R. *et al.* (2019) Very strong atmospheric methane growth in the 4 years 2014–2017: implications for the Paris Agreement. *Global Biogeochemical Cycles* 33(3), 318–42. doi:10.1029/2018gb006009.

Norris, P. and Inglehart, R. (2009) *Cosmopolitan Communications: Cultural Diversity in a Globalized World*. New York: Cambridge University Press.

North, R. (2001) *The Death of British Agriculture: The Wanton Destruction of a Key Industry*. London: Duckworth.

OECD (2019) *Enhancing Climate Change Mitigation Through Agriculture*. Paris: OECD. www.oecd.org/publications/enhancing-the-mitigation-of-climate-change-though-agriculture-e9a79226-en.htm (Accessed 3 January 2022).

Oreskes, N. and Conway, E. (2010) *Merchants of Doubt: How a Handful of Scientists Obscured the Truth on Issues from Tobacco Smoke to Global Warming*. New York: Bloomsbury.

Ortiz, M., Baldock, D., Willan, C. and Dalin, C. (2021) *Towards Net Zero in UK Agriculture: Key Information, Perspectives and Practical Guidance*. London: University College London Institute for Sustainable Resources. www.sustainablefinance.hsbc.com/ (Accessed 3 January 2022).

Ortiz-Bobea, A., Ault, T., Carrillo, M, Chambers, R. and Lobell, D. (2021) Anthropogenic climate change has slowed agricultural productivity growth. *Nature Climate Change* 11, 306–12 doi:10.1038/s41558-021-01000-1

Ouma, S. (2020) *Farming as a Financial Asset: Global Finance and the Making of Institutional Landscapes*. Newcastle upon Tyne: Agenda Publishing.

Overton, M. (1996) *Agricultural Revolution in England: The Transformation of the Agrarian Economy 1500–1850*. Cambridge: Cambridge University Press.

Packer, R. (2006) *The Politics of BSE*. Basingstoke: Palgrave Macmillan.

Parry, M., Arnell, N., Hulme, M., Nicholls, R. and Livermore, M. (1998) Buenos Aires and Kyoto targets do little to reduce climate change impacts. *Global Environmental Change* 8, 285–9. doi:10.1016/S0959-3780(98)00019-3

Pearce, D., Markandya, A. and Barbier, E. (1989) *Blueprint for a Green Economy*. London: Earthscan.

Pearce, F. (2010) *The Climate Files: The Battle for the Truth About Global Warming*. London: Guardian Books.

Percival, R. (2022) *The Meat Paradox: Eating, Empathy and the Future of Meat*. London: Little Brown.

Piketty, T. (2014) *Capital in the Twenty-First Century*. Cambridge, MA: Harvard University Press.

van der Ploeg, J. D. (2018) *The New Peasantries: Rural Development in Times of Globalisation*. London: Earthscan.

Policy Commission on the Future of Food and Farming (2002) *Farming and Food: A Sustainable Future*. London: Cabinet Office.

Poore, J. and Nemecek, T. (2018) Reducing food's environmental impacts through producers and consumers. *Science* 360, 987–92. doi:10.1126/science.aaq0216

Poruschi, L., Dhakal, S. and Canadell, J. (2010) *Ten Years of Advancing Knowledge on the Global Carbon Cycle and Its Management*. Tsukuba: Global Carbon Project. www.globalcarbonproject.org/global/pdf/GCP_10years_med_res.pdf (Accessed 3 January 2022).

Potter, C. (1986) Investment styles and countryside change in lowland England, pp.146–59 in G. Cox, P. Lowe and M. Winter (eds.) *Agriculture, People and Policies*. London: Allen & Unwin.

Poux, X., Schiavo, M. and Aubert, P.M. (2021). *Modelling an Agroecological UK in 2050*. Paris: IDDRI, Sciences Po. https://euagenda.eu/publications/modelling-an-agroecological-uk-in-2050 (Accessed 3 January 2022).

Pretty, J. and Bharucha, Z.P. (2018) *Sustainable Intensification of Agriculture: Greening the World's Food Economy*. London: Earthscan.

Pretty, J., Benton, T., Bharucha, Z., Dicks, L, Flora, C., Godfray, C., Goulson, D., Hartley, S., Lampkin, N., Moris, C., Pierzynski, G., Prasad, P., Reganold, J., Rockström, J., Smith, P., Thorne, P. and Wratten, S. (2018). Global assessment of agricultural system redesign for sustainable intensification. *Nature Sustainability* 1(8), 441–6. doi.org/10.1038/s41893-018-0114-0

Price, A. (2021) *Dairy and Non-Dairy Drinks, Milk and Cream – UK – 2021*. London: Mintel, 9 November (Accessed Business and IP Centre, British Library).

Prime Minister's Office (2021) Over 100 leaders make landmark pledge to end deforestation at COP26. *10 Downing Street Press Release*, 2 November. www.gov.uk/government/news/over-100-leaders-make-landmark-pledge-to-end-deforestation-at-cop26 (Accessed 3 January 2022).

Purnell, S. (2012) *Just Boris: A Tale of Blond Ambition*. London: Aurum Press.

Pye-Smith, C. and North, R. (1984) *Working the Land*. London: Maurice Temple Smith.

Reynolds, C. (2021). *Food waste, sustainable diets and climate change: Coherent solutions in the long view*. Paper presented at the Food Values Research Group, The University of Adelaide, June 2021 seminar, 28 June, Virtual. https://openaccess.city.ac.uk/id/eprint/26389/ (Accessed 3 January 2022).

Ritchie, H., Reay, D. and Higgins, P. (2018) The impact of global dietary guidelines on climate change. *Global Environmental Change* 49, 46–55. doi:10.1016/j.gloenvcha.2018.02.005

Robbins, B. and Horta, P. L. (2017) *Cosmopolitanisms*. New York: New York University Press.

Robinson, D. (1980) The impact of herbicides on crop production, pp.297–312 in R. Hurd, P. Biscoe and C. Dennis (eds.) *Opportunities for Increasing Crop Yields*. London: Pitman.

Rogers, A. (1999) *The Most Revolutionary Measure: A History of the Rural Development Commission 1909–1999*. Salisbury: Rural Development Commission.

Rose, C. (1990) *The Dirty Man of Europe: The Great British Pollution Scandal*. London: Simon and Schuster.

Rose, N. (1993) Government, authority and expertise in advanced liberalism. *Economy and Society* 22, 283–99. doi:10.1080/03085149300000019

Rose, N. (1996) Governing "advanced" liberal democracies, pp. 37–64 in A. Barry., T. Osbourne and N. Rose (eds.) *Foucault and Political Reason: Liberalism, Neo-liberalism and Rationalities of Government*. London: UCL Press.

Royal Academy of Engineering and Royal Society (2018) *Greenhouse Gas Removal*. London: Royal Society and Royal Academy of Engineering. https://royalsociety.org/topics-policy/projects/greenhouse-gas-removal/ (Accessed 3 January 2022).

Royal Commission on Environmental Pollution (1979) *Agriculture and Pollution*. Seventh Report. London: HMSO.

Royal Commission on Environmental Pollution (1992) *Freshwater Quality*. Sixteenth Report. London: HMSO.

Royal Society (2021) *Nourishing Ten Billion Sustainably: Resilient Food Production in a Time of Climate Change*. Climate Change: Science and Solutions Briefing 10. London: Royal Society. https://royalsociety.org/-/media/policy/projects/climate-change-science-solutions/climate-science-solutions-food.pdf (Accessed 3 January 2022).

Royal Society for the Protection of Birds (2019) *Evidence to the House of Commons Environment, Food and Rural Affairs Committee Inquiry into Agriculture: Achieving Net Zero Emissions*. https://data.parliament.uk/writtenevidence/committeeevidence.svc/evidencedocument/environment-food-and-rural-affairs-committee/agriculture-achieving-netzero-emissions/written/ (Accessed May 2021).

Rutter, J. (2021) *Evidence to the House of Common Business, Energy and Industrial Strategy Committee inquiry into Net Zero Governance*. 21st September. https://committees.parliament.uk/event/5418/formal-meeting-oral-evidence-session/ (Accessed 3 January 2022).

Sainsbury's (2019) *Future of Food Report*. London: Sainsbury's. www.about.sainsburys.co.uk/~/media/Files/S/Sainsburys/pdf-downloads/futureoffood-10c.pdf (Accessed 3 January 2022).

Savage, M. (2021) *The Return of Inequality: Social Change and the Weight of the Past*. Cambridge, MA: Harvard University Press.

Scarborough, P., Appleby, P., Mizdrak, A., Briggs, A., Travis, R., Bradbury, K. and Key, T. (2014) Dietary greenhouse gas emissions of meat-eaters, fish-eaters, vegetarians and vegans in the UK. *Climatic Change* 125 (2), 179–92. doi:10.1007/s10584-014-1169-1

Searchinger, T., Malins, C., Dumas, P., Baldock, D., Glauber, J., Jayne, T., Huang, J. and Marenya, P. (2020) *Revising Public Agricultural Support to Mitigate Climate Change*. Development Knowledge and Learning. Washington, DC: World Bank. https://documents1.worldb ank.org/curated/en/773701588657353273/pdf/Development-Knowledge-and-Learn ing-Revising-Public-Agricultural-Support-to-Mitigate-Climate-Change.pdf (Accessed 3 January 2022).

Self, P. and Storing, H. (1962) *The State and the Farmer*. London: George Allen & Unwin.

Sen, A. and Darbi, N. (2021) *Tightening the Net: Net Zero Climate Targets – Implications for Land and Food Quality*. Oxford: Oxfam International. www.oxfam.org/en/research/ tightening-net-implications-net-zero-climate-targets-land-and-food-equity (Accessed 11 January 2022).

Sexton, A., Garnett, T. and Lorimer, J. (2019) Framing the future of food: the contested promises of alternative proteins. *Environment and Planning E: Nature and Space* 2, 47–72. doi:10.1177/2514848619827009

Sharman, A. (2014) Mapping the climate sceptical blogosphere. *Global Environmental Change* 26, 159–70. doi:10.1016/j.gloenvcha.2014.03.003

Shoard, M. (1980) *The Theft of the Countryside*. London: Temple Smith.

Short, B. (2014) *The Battle of the Fields: Rural Community and Authority in Britain During the Second World War*. Woodbridge: Boydell Press.

Short, B., Watkins, C., Foot, W. and Kinsman, P. (2000) *The National Farm Survey 1941– 1943: State Surveillance and the Countryside in England and Wales in the Second World War*. Wallingford: CAB International.

Shove, E. (2010) Beyond the ABC: climate change policy and theories of social change. *Environment and Planning A* 42, 1273–85. doi.org/10.1068/a42282

Siriwardena, G., Baillie, S., Buckland, S., Fewster, R., Marchant, J. and Wilson, J. (1998) Trends in the abundance of farmland birds: a quantitative comparison of smoothed common birds census indices. *Journal of Applied Ecology* 35, 24–43. doi:10.1046/ j.1365-2664.1998.00275.x

Smith, D., Diack, H., Pennington, H. and Russell, E. (2005) *Food Poisoning, Policy and Politics: Corned Beef and Typhoid in Britain in 1960s*. Woodbridge: Boydell Press.

Smith, M. (1990) *The Politics of Agricultural Support in Britain*. Aldershot: Dartmouth.

Smith, M. (1991) From policy community to issue network: Salmonella in eggs and the new politics of food. *Public Administration* 69, 235–55. doi:10.1111/j.1467-9299.1991.tb00792.x

Smith, P. (2016), Soil carbon sequestration and biochar as negative emission technologies. *Global Change Biology* 22, 1315–24. doi:10.1111/gcb.13178

Smith, P., Haszeldine, R. and Smith, S. (2016). Preliminary assessment of the potential for, and limitations to, terrestrial negative emission technologies in the UK. *Environmental Science: Processes & Impacts* 18, 1400–5. doi:10.1039/C6EM00386A

Soil Association (2021) *The Roadmap to a Soil Carbon Marketplace*. Bristol: Soil Association. www.soilassociation.org/farmers-growers/farming-news/2021/july/23/landscape-to-carbonscape-event/ (Accessed 13 January 2022).

Southcombe, E. (1980) Developments in herbicide application, pp. 232–333 in R. Hurd, P. Biscoe and C. Dennis (eds.) *Opportunities for Increasing Crop Yields*. London: Pitman.

Springman, M., Godfray, H., Rayner, M. and Scarborough, P. (2016) Analysis and valuation of the health and climate change co-benefits of dietary change. *Proceedings of the National Academy of Sciences USA* 113 (15), 4146–51. doi:10.1073/pnas.1523119113

Springman, M., Clark, M., Mason-D'Croz, D., Wiebe, K., Bodirsky, B., Lassaletta, L., de Vries, W., Vermeulen, S., Herrero, M., Carlson, K., Jonell, M., Troell, M., deClerck, F., Gordon, L., Zurayk, R., Scatborough, P., Rayner, M., Loken, B., Fanzo, J., Godfray, H., Tilman, D., Rockström, J. and Willett, W. (2018) Options for keeping the food system within environmental limits. *Nature* 562, 519–25. doi:10.1038/s41586-018-0594-0

Steel, C. (2021) *Sitopia: How Food Can Save the World*. London: Penguin.

Steffen, W., Richardson, K., Rockström, J., Schellnhuber, H., Dube, O., Dutreuil, S., Lenton, T. and Lubchenco, J. (2020) The emergence and evolution of Earth System Science. *Nature Reviews Earth and Environment* 1, 54–63. doi:10.1038/s43017-019-0005-6

Steil, B. (2018) *The Marshall Plan: Dawn of the Cold War*. Oxford: Oxford University Press.

Stengers, I. (2010) *Cosmopolitics I*. Minneapolis: University of Minnesota Press.

Stengers, I. (2011) *Cosmopolitics II*. Minneapolis: University of Minnesota Press.

Stengers, I. (2015) *In Catastrophic Times: Resisting the Coming Barbarism*. London: Open Humanities Press.

Stengers, I. (2017) *Another Science is Possible*. Cambridge: Polity.

Stern, N. (2007) *The Economics of Climate Change: The Stern Review*. Cambridge University Press. www.lse.ac.uk/granthaminstitute/publication/the-economics-of-climate-change-the-stern-review/ (Accessed 3 January 2022).

Stern, N. (2009) *A Blueprint for a Safer Planet: How to Manage Climate Change and Create a New Era of Progress and Prosperity*. London: Bodley Head.

Stoll-Kleemann, S. and Schmidt, U. (2017). Reducing meat consumption in developed and transition countries to counter climate change and biodiversity loss: a review of influence factors. *Regional Environmental Change* 17, 1261–77. doi:10.1007/s10113-016-1057-5

Symons, J. (2019) *Ecomodernism: Technology, Politics and the Climate Crisis*. Cambridge: Polity Press.

Szerszynski, B. and Urry, J. (2002) Cultures of cosmopolitanism. *The Sociological Review* 50, 461–81. doi:10.1177/003802610205000401

Tait, E. J. (1981) The flow of pesticides: industrial and farming perspectives, pp. 219–50 in T. O'Riordan and R. K. Turner (eds.) *Progress in Resource Management and Environmental Planning*, Volume 3. London: John Wiley.

Tansey, G. (2008) Food, farming and global rules, pp. 3–4 in G. Tansey and T. Rajotte (eds.) *The Future Control of Food: A Guide to International Negotiations and Rules on Intellectual Property, Biodiversity and Food Security*. London: Earthscan.

Tansey, G. and Rajotte, T. (2008) (eds.) *The Future Control of Food: A Guide to International Negotiations and Rules on Intellectual Property, Biodiversity and Food Security*. London: Earthscan.

Tansey, G. and Worsley, T. (1995) *The Food System: A Guide*. London: Earthscan.

Tenant Farmers Association (2019) *Memorandum of Evidence to the House of Commons Environment, Food and Rural Affairs Committee Inquiry into Agriculture: Achieving Net Zero Emissions*. https://data.parliament.uk/writtenevidence/committeeevidence.svc/evidencedocument/environment-food-and-rural-affairs-committee/agriculture-achieving-netzero-emissions/written/ (Accessed May 2021).

Terazono. E. and Hodgson, C. (2021) Raising climate friendly cows. *Financial Times* 11 October, p. 23. www.ft.com/content/73e5f1fc-76ac-48b0-871a-7fa4e8bda69b (Accessed 3 January 2022).

Thaler, R. and Sunstein, R. (2008) *Nudge: Improving Decisions about Health, Wealth and Happiness*. London: Yale University Press.

The Economist (2021) A new reality. *The Economist* 14 August, pp. 65–7.

The Economist (2022) The new interventionism, special report – business and the state. *The Economist* 15 January, pp. 3–12.

The Observer (1989) Poison on tap: the first region by region guide to your drinking water. *The Observer Magazine* 6 August.

Thomas, G., Pidgeon, N. and Roberts, E. (2018) Ambivalence, naturalness and normality in public perceptions of carbon capture and storage in biomass, fossil energy, and industrial applications in the United Kingdom. *Energy Research and Social Science* 46, 1–9. doi:10.1016/j.erss.2018.06.007

Tilman, D. and Clark, M. (2014) Global diets link environmental sustainability and human health. *Nature* 515 (7528), 518–22. doi:10.1038/nature13959

Tobler, C., Visschers, V. and Siegrist, M. (2011) Eating green. Consumers' willingness to adopt ecological food consumption behaviours. *Appetite* 57, 674–82 doi:10.1016/j.appet.2011.08.010

Tooze, A. (2021) *Shutdown: How Covid Shook the World's Economy*. London: Allen Lane.

Tracy, M. (1989) *Government and Agriculture in Western Europe, 1880–1988*. Hemel Hempstead: Harvester Wheatsheaf.

Tubb, C. and Seba, T. (2019) *Rethinking Food and Agriculture 2020–2030: The Second Domestication of Plants and Animals, the Disruption of the Cow, and the Collapse of Industrial Livestock Farming*. RethinkX Disruption Report. www.rethinkx.com/food-and-agriculture (Accessed 3 January 2022).

Tubiana, L. (1989) World trade in agricultural products: from global regulation to market fragmentation, pp. 23–45 in D. Goodman and M. Redclift (eds.) *The International Farm Crisis*. Basingstoke: MacMillan.

Tubiello, F. N., Rosenzweig, C., Conchedda, G., Karl, K., Gütschow, J., Pan, X., Obli-Laryea, G., Wanner, N., Yue Qiu, S., De Barros, J., Flammini, A., Mencos-Contreras, E., Souza, L., Quadrelli, R., Heiðarsdóttir, H., Benoit, P., Hayek, M. and Sandalow, D. (2021a) Greenhouse gas emissions from food systems: building the evidence base. *Environmental Research Letters* 16(6). doi:10.1088/1748-9326/ac018e

Tubiello, F. N., Flammini, A., Karl, K., Obli-Laryea, G., Qiu, S. Y., Heiðarsdóttir, H., Pan, X. and Conchedda, G. (2021b) *Methods for Estimating Greenhouse Gas Emissions from Food Systems, Part III: Energy Use in Fertilizer Manufacturing, Food Processing, Packaging, Retail and Household Consumption*. FAO Statistics Working Papers Series, 21–9. www.fao.org/documents/card/en/c/cb7473en/ (Accessed 3 January 2022).

Turnheim, B. and Geels, F. (2013) The destabilisation of existing regimes: Confronting a multi-dimensional framework with a case study of the British coal industry (1913–1967). *Research Policy* 42, 1749–67. doi:10.1016/j.respol.2013.04.009

UK Government (1994) *Sustainable Development: The UK Strategy*. Cm 2426. London: HMSO.

UK Government (2021) *Net Zero Strategy: Build Back Greener*. London: Stationary Office. www.gov.uk/government/publications/net-zero-strategy (Accessed 3 January 2022).

Urry, J. (2011) *Climate Change and Society*. Cambridge: Polity Press.

Urry, J. (2016) *What is the Future?* Cambridge: Polity Press.

Vaughan, A. (2021) COP26: 105 countries pledge to cut methane emissions by 30 per cent. *New Scientist* 2 November. www.newscientist.com/article/2295810-cop26-105-countries-pledge-to-cut-methane-emissions-by-30-per-cent/ (Accessed 3 January 2022).

Vaughan, N. and Gough, C. (2016). Expert assessment concludes negative emissions scenarios may not deliver. *Environmental Research Letters* 11(9), 095003. doi:10.1088/1748-9326/11/9/095003

Vaughan, N., Gough, C., Mander, S., Littleton, E., Welfle, A., Gernaat, D. and van Vuuren, D (2018) Evaluating the use of biomass energy with carbon capture and storage in low emission scenarios. *Environmental Research Letters* 13, 044014. doi:10.1088/1748-9326/aaaa02

Vermeulen, S., Park, T., Khoury, C. and Béné, C. (2020) Changing diets and the transformation of the global food system. *Annals of the New York Academy of Sciences* 1478, 1–15. doi:10.1111/nyas.14446

Wallace Brown, G. and Held, D. (2010) *The Cosmopolitanism Reader*. Cambridge: Polity Press.

Waller, L., Rayner, T., Chilvers, J., Gough, C. A., Lorenzoni, I., Jordan, A. and Vaughan, N., (2020) Contested framings of greenhouse gas removal and its feasibility: social and political dimensions. *Wiley Interdisciplinary Reviews: Climate Change* 11, e649. doi:10.1002/wcc.649

Ward, N. (1990) A preliminary analysis of the UK food chain. *Food Policy* 15, 439–41. doi:10.1016/0306-9192(90)90060-D

Ward, N. (1993) The agricultural treadmill and the rural environment in the post-productivist era. *Sociologia Ruralis* 33, 348–64. doi:10.1111/j.1467-9523.1993.tb00969.x

Ward, N. (1995) Technological change and the regulation of pollution from agricultural pesticides. *Geoforum* 26, 19–33. doi:10.1016/0016-7185(94)00019-4

Ward, N. and Lowe, P. (2002) Devolution and the governance of rural affairs in the UK, pp. 117–39 in J. Adams and P. Robinson (eds.) *Devolution in Practice: Public Policy Differences within the UK.* London: IPPR.

Ward, N., Marsden, T. and Munton, R. (1990) Farm landscape change: trends in upland and lowland England. *Land Use Policy* 7, 291–302. doi:10.1016/0264-8377(90)90019-U

Ward, N., Lowe, P., Seymour, S. and Clark, J. (1995) Rural restructuring and the regulation of farm pollution. *Environment and Planning A* 27, 1193–211. doi:10.1068/a271193

Ward, N., Clark, J., Lowe, P. and Seymour, S. (1998) Keeping matter in its place: pollution regulation and the reconfiguring of farmers and farming. *Environment and Planning A* 30, 1165–78. doi:10.1068/a301165

Ward, N., Donaldson, A. and Lowe, P. (2004) Policy framing and learning the lessons from the UK's foot and mouth disease crisis. *Environment and Planning C: Government and Policy* 22, 291–306. doi:10.1068/c0209s

Weart, S. (2003) *The Discovery of Global Warming.* Cambridge, MA: Harvard University Press.

Webb, D. (2021) *UK-Australia Free Trade Agreement.* House of Commons Library Paper 9204. London: House of Commons Library. https://researchbriefings.files.parliament.uk/documents/CBP-9204/CBP-9204.pdf (Accessed 3 January 2022).

Wellesley, L., Happer, C. and Froggatt, A. (2015) *Changing Climate, Changing Diets: Pathways to Lower Meat Consumption.* Chatham House. www.chathamhouse.org/2015/11/changing-climate-changing-diets-pathways-lower-meat-consumption (Accessed 3 January 2022).

Welsh Government (2021) *Net Zero Wales Carbon Budget 2021–25.* WG42949. Cardiff: Welsh Government. https://gov.wales/sites/default/files/publications/2021-10/net-zero-wales-carbon-budget-2-2021-25.pdf (Accessed 18 January 2022).

Werksman, J. (1995) The United Nations Framework Convention on Climate Change: The first conference of the parties opening in Berlin. *Global Environmental Change* 4, 339–40. doi:10.1016/0959-3780(94)90034-5

Westmacott, R. and Worthington, T. (1974) *New Agricultural Landscapes.* Cheltenham: Countryside Commission.

Westmacott, R. and Worthington, T. (1984) *Agricultural Landscapes: A Second Look.* CCP168. Cheltenham: Countryside Commission.

Whatmore, S. (2002) *Hybrid Geographies: Natures, Cultures, Spaces.* London: Sage.

Whatmore, S. (2009) Mapping knowledge controversies: science, democracy and the redistribution of expertise. *Progress in Human Geography* 33 587–98. doi:10.1177/0309132509339841

Whetham, E. (1974) The Agriculture Act 1920 and its repeal – the "Great Betrayal". *Agriculture History Review* 22, 36–49.

Whetham, E. (1978) *The Agrarian History of England and Wales Volume VIII 1914–1939.* Cambridge: Cambridge University Press.

Whitby, M. and Ward, N. (1994) *The UK Strategy for Sustainable Agriculture: A Critical Analysis.* Centre for Rural Economy Research Report, Newcastle upon Tyne: University of Newcastle upon Tyne.

White House Office of Domestic Climate Policy (2021) *US Methane Emissions Reduction Action Plan: Critical and Commonsense Steps to Cut Pollution and Consumer Costs, While Boosting Good-Paying Jobs and American Competitiveness.* file:///E:/AAA%20-%20A%20-%20Net%20

Zero/Achieiving%20net%20zero/Methane/2021%20-%20US-Methane-Emissions-Reduction-Action-Plan-1%20November%202021.pdf (Accessed 3 January 2022).

Whitmarsh, L., Poortinga, W. and Capstick, S. (2021) Behaviour change to address climate change. *Current Opinion in Psychology* 42, 76–81. doi:10.1016/j.copsyc.2021.04.002

Wildlife and Countryside Link (2019) *Memorandum of Evidence to House of Commons Environment, Food and Rural Affairs Committee Inquiry into Agriculture: Achieving Net Zero Emissions.* https://data.parliament.uk/writtenevidence/committeeevidence.svc/evidencedocument/environment-food-and-rural-affairs-committee/agriculture-achieving-netzero-emissions/written/ (Accessed May 2021).

Winter, M. (1985) Administering land-use policies for agriculture: a possible role for County Agriculture and Conservation Committees. *Agricultural Administration* 18, 235–49.

Winter, M. (1996) *Rural Politics: Policies for Agriculture, Forestry and the Environment.* London: Routledge.

Woods, A. (2004) *A Manufactured Plague: The History of Foot and Mouth Disease in Britain.* London: Routledge.

Woods, A. (2011) A historical synopsis of farm animal disease and public policy in twentieth century Britain. *Philosophical Transactions of the Royal Society* 366, 1943–54. doi:10.1098/rstb.2010.0388

Woods, A. (2012) Rethinking the history of modern agriculture: British pig production, c.1910–65. *Twentieth Century British History* 23, 165–91. doi:10.1093/tcbh/hwr010

World Business Council for Sustainable Development (2018) *The Future of Food: A Lighthouse for Future Living, Today,* 23 October. www.wbcsd.org/Programs/People/Sustainable-Lifestyles/Resources/A-lighthouse-for-future-living-today (Accessed 3 January 2022).

World Commission on Environment and Development (1987) *Our Common Future.* Oxford: Oxford University Press.

World Health Organisation (2015) *Healthy Diet Fact Sheet No, 394.* Geneva: WHO. www.who.int/publications/m/item/healthy-diet-factsheet394 (Accessed 3 January 2022).

World Resources Institute (2018) *Creating a Sustainable Food Future: A Menu of Solutions to Feed Nearly 10 Billion People by 2050.* Synthesis Report. Washington, DC: World Resources Institute. www.wri.org/research/creating-sustainable-food-future (Accessed 3 January 2022).

World Resources Institute (2019) *Creating a Sustainable Food Future: A Menu of Solutions to Feed Nearly 10 Billion People by 2050.* Full Report. Washington, DC: World Resources Institute.

WRAP (2021) *Food Surplus and Waste in the UK – Key Facts.* https://wrap.org.uk/resources/report/food-surplus-and-waste-uk-key-facts (Accessed 3 January 2022).

Wrigley, N. (1998) How British retailers have shaped food choice, pp. 112–28 in A. Murcott (ed.) *The Nation's Diet: The Social Science of Food Choice.* London: Longman.

Wrigley, N., Wood, S. M., Lambiri, D. and Lowe, M. (2019). Corporate convenience store development effects in small towns: Convenience culture during economic and digital storms. *Environment and Planning A* 51(1), 112–32. doi:10.1177/0308518X18796507

Wyker B. and Davison K. (2010) Behavioral change theories can inform the prediction of young adults' adoption of a plant-based diet. *Journal of Nutrition Education and Behaviour* 42, 168–77. doi:10.1016/j.jneb.2009.03.124

Zedler J. and Kercher S. (2005) Wetland resources: status, trends, ecosystem services, and restorability. *Annual Review of Environment and Resources* 30(1), 39– 74. doi:10.1146/annurev.energy.30.050504.144248

van Zwanenberg, P. and Millstone, E. (2005) *BSE: Risk, Science and Governance.* Oxford: Oxford University Press.

INDEX

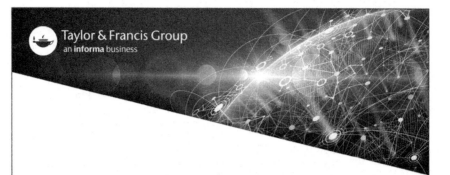

Printed in the United States
by Baker & Taylor Publisher Services